Corporate
Media
Production

Corporate Media Production

Ray DiZazzo

ELSEVIER

Focal Press

An Imprint of Elsevier

Amsterdam   Boston   Heidelberg   London   New York   Oxford   Paris   San Diego
San Francisco   Singapore   Sydney   Tokyo

Focal Press
An Imprint of Elsevier
Copyright © 2004 Elsevier. All rights reserved.

∞ Recognizing the importance of preserving what has been written, Elsevier prints its books on acid-free paper whenever possible.

Library of Congress Cataloging-in-Publication Data
DiZazzo, Raymond.
    Corporate media production / by Ray DiZazzo.
        p. cm.
    Includes bibliographical references and index.
    ISBN-13: 978-0-240-80514-6 ISBN-10: 0-240-80514-3 (alk. paper)
    1. Video recordings–Production and direction. 2. Industrial television. 3. Industrial television–Authorship. I. Title.
    PN1992.94.D57 2003
    384.55'8–dc21
    ISBN-13: 978-0-240-80514-6   2003051422
    ISBN-10: 0-240-80514-3

British Library Cataloguing-in-Publication Data
A catalogue record for this book is available from the British Library.

The publisher offers special discounts on bulk orders of this book.
For information, please contact:
Manager of Special Sales
Elsevier
200 Wheeler Road
Burlington, MA 01803
Tel: 781-313-4700
Fax: 781-313-4882

For information on all Focal Press publications available, contact our World Wide Web home page at: http://www.focalpress.com

Transferred to Digital Printing 2011.

To Neal Spruce, Alan Curtis, and Richard Stewart—three of the best.

Contents

Preface and Acknowledgments xiii

I The Corporate Media Evolution 1

1 The Changing Role of Corporate Media 3
USES OF MEDIA IN THE
    CORPORATE WORLD 4
DISTRIBUTION AND DELIVERY
    SYSTEMS 4
    Videocassettes 4
    Corporate Broadcasts 4
    Distance Learning 5
    CD-ROM, DVD, Streaming
      Video/Audio 5
    Interactivity—A Key 5
    The World Wide Web 5
    Local Area Networks and Intranets 6
CREATIVE CHANGES? 6

2 The Key Players 7
THE CORPORATE MEDIA
    PRODUCER 7
    Staff and Freelance Producers 7
    Producer "Musts" 7
    The Reward 8
THE DIRECTOR 8
    A Definition 8
    The Director as an Artist 9
    Not for the Fainthearted 10
    The Reward 10
THE SCRIPTWRITER 10
    The Real Differences 10
    The Working Environment 10

The Research Factor 11
Staff and Freelance Writers 11
CLIENTS 12
    Client Profiles 12
    A Dynamic Relationship 13

3 Media Groups in the Corporate World 14
LARGE IN-HOUSE MEDIA GROUPS 14
    Advantages and Disadvantages 14
SMALL IN-HOUSE MEDIA GROUPS 15
    Advantages and Disadvantages 15
OUTSIDE PRODUCTION
    COMPANIES 15
    Advantages and Disadvantages 15
PROSUMERS 15
    Advantages and Disadvantages 15
FREELANCERS 16
    Advantages and Disadvantages 16

4 A Production Overview 17
WRITING 17
    Program Design 17
    Scriptwriting 17
PREPRODUCTION 18
    Budgeting 18
    Talent Auditions and Bookings 18
    Crew Bookings 18
    Equipment Reservations or Rentals 18
    Location and Set Arrangements 18
    Blocking, Storyboards, and
      Diagrams 18
    Rehearsals and Meetings 18
    Production Scheduling 19

PRODUCTION 19
   Location Production 19
   Studio Production 19
   Graphic Arts Production 20
   Audio Production 20
POSTPRODUCTION 20
   The Traditional Offline Edit 20
   The Traditional Online Edit 20
   Nonlinear Editing 21
   Audio "Sweetening" 21
   The Traditional Laydown and
     Layback 21
   Nonlinear Audio Sweetening 21
   Duplication/Distribution 21

5 Production People **22**
THE LINE PRODUCER 22
THE PRODUCTION MANAGER 22
THE ASSISTANT DIRECTOR (AD) 22
THE PRODUCTION ASSISTANT (PA) 22
THE DIRECTOR OF PHOTOGRAPHY
   (DP) OR VIDEOGRAPHER 23
THE CAMERA OPERATOR 23
THE GAFFER 23
THE GRIP 23
THE SOUND RECORDIST/MIXER 23
THE AUDIO BOOM OPERATOR 23
THE FLOOR MANAGER OR STAGE
   MANAGER 23
TECHNICAL DIRECTOR (TD) 23
VIDEOTAPE RECORDER OPERATOR
   (TAPE OP) 24
VIDEO CONTROL ENGINEER (VC) 24
ENGINEER IN CHARGE (EIC) 24
TELEPROMPTER OPERATOR 24
THE MAKEUP ARTIST 24
GRAPHIC ARTIST 24
THE OFFLINE EDITOR 24
THE ONLINE EDITOR 24
THE AUDIO SWEETENING ENGINEER . . .25
PART ONE SUMMARY 25

II The Script **27**

6 The Program Needs Analysis **29**
THE SCENARIO OF THE UNNEEDED
   MEDIA PROGRAM 29
PROGRAM DESIGN 29
THE PROBLEM OR NEED 30

OBJECTIVES 30
   Instructional Objectives 30
   Motivational Objectives 31
   Mixing Objectives 31
AUDIENCE ANALYSIS 31
   Multiple Audiences 32
UTILIZATION 32
INTERACTIVE DESIGN 33
DESIGN SUMMARY 34
A COMPLETE PROGRAM NEEDS
   ANALYSIS 34
COMMENTARY 36
THE DECISION 37

7 The Content Outline **39**
ACQUIRING CONTENT
   INFORMATION .39
INTERVIEW TECHNIQUES AND
   RESEARCH SOURCES 40
   Use a Tape Recorder if Possible 40
   Use Open-Ended Questions 40
   Guide the Discussion 41
   Keep it Simple 41
   Listen 41
   Other Sources 41
ORGANIZING CONTENT
   INFORMATION .42
CONTENT OUTLINE FORMATS 42
   Informal 42
   Formal 42
   Other Structures 43
A FORMAL CONTENT OUTLINE 44
COMMENTARY 46

8 The Creative Concept **47**
PRINT VERSUS VISUAL (SHOWING
   VERSUS TELLING) 47
   Telling (Print-Oriented Writing) 47
   Showing (Visual Writing) 47
THE CREATIVE VISUAL CONCEPT 48
TYPES OF CONCEPTS 48
CONCEPT THINKING 48
CONCEPT EXAMPLES 49
   Host on Camera with Stills
     Transferred to Tape 49
   Music Video 50
   Documentary 50
   Children Interviewed on Clean Air 50
CONCEPT SUMMARY 51

9 The Treatment 52
A DEFINITION 52
TREATMENT SUMMARY 53
A COMPLETE PROGRAM
   TREATMENT 53
COMMENTARY 55

10 The Script 56
FORMATS 56
  The Two-Column Format 57
  The Screenplay Format 58
  Interactive Scripts 58
  Storyboard 59
  Narration Script 59

11 Script Terminology 62
EDITING TERMS 62
  Fade In/Fade Out 62
  Dissolve 62
  Cut 62
  Wipe 63
  Digital Video Effect (DVE) 63
CAMERA TERMS 63
  Wide Shot (WS) 63
  Establishing Shot 63
  Long Shot 63
  Medium Shot (MS) 64
  Medium Close-up (MCU) 64
  Close-up (CU) 64
  Extreme Close-up (ECU) 64
  Two Shot 64
  Over the Shoulder (OTS) 64
  Point of View (POV) 64
  Reverse Angle 65
  Rack Focus 65
  f.g./b.g. 65
  Low Angle 65
  High Angle 65
  Pan/Tilt 65
  Dolly/Truck 65
SCENE HEADING TERMS 65
  Int./Ext./Day/Night 65
SOUND TERMS 66
  Sound Effects (SFX) 66
  Music Up/Under/In/Out/Sting 66
  Sound Terms 66
MASTER SCENES VERSUS DETAILED
  DESCRIPTIONS 66

12 Dialogue and Narration 68
DIALOGUE CREDIBILITY 68
  Natural Speech Patterns 70
  Believable Character Motivation 70
  Use of Contractions and
    Colloquialisms 71
THE DIALOGUE TEST 71
NARRATION 71
  Effective Narration Qualities 71

13 Structure and Transitions 74
TYPES OF STRUCTURES 74
STRUCTURE VERSUS STORYLINE 75
CORPORATE STRUCTURES 75
  The Tell 'em Structure 75
  Benefits Bookends 77
  Contrasting Actions 78
  Creative Use of Structure 78

14 A Screenplay Format Script 79
COMMENTARY 85
PART TWO SUMMARY 85

**III Preproduction: The Plan
   for Success** 87

15 Preproduction 89
DETAIL–THE KEY 89
THE PLAYERS 89
  The Client 90
  The Producer 90
  The Director 90
  The Assistant Director 90
  The Production Assistant 90
CREW COSTS 90
RUN 'N' GUN SHOOTS 90
PREPRODUCTION TASKS 91
  Budgeting 91
  Creating the Master File 92
  Reviewing and Breaking Down
    the Script 99
  Obtaining Props and Wardrobe 102
  Scouting and Confirming Locations and
    Obtaining Permits and Releases 102
  Auditioning and Selecting Talent,
    Professional and Otherwise 102
  Developing and Writing the Shooting
    Schedule 102

Hiring the Crew 103
Designing Sets 103
Renting or Reserving Production
  Equipment and Vehicles 103
Designing and Creating Artwork,
  Animation, and Character-Generated
  Titles 104
Reviewing and Selecting Stock
  Footage 104
Reviewing and Selecting Music 104
Blocking the Script 105
Rehearsals 105
Conducting Preproduction Meetings ...105
Preparing Equipment for the Shoot ...105
PART THREE SUMMARY 107

IV Production **109**

**16 Production Formats, Equipment,
  and Shooting Styles** **111**
GLAMOUR OR GRIND? 111
THE VIDEOTAPE, DIGITAL VIDEO,
  AND FILM RECORDING
  PROCESSES 111
  Film Recording 111
  Analog and Digital Video Recording 112
FORMATS 112
  One-Inch Reel-to-Reel 112
  Three-Quarter-Inch U-Matic 112
  Half-Inch Camcorders 113
  D (Digital) Formats 114
  Mini DV (Digital Video) 114
  Custom Mini DV Formats 114
  High Definition 114
EQUIPMENT 115
  Cameras 115
  Video Streaming 116
  Videotape Recorders (VTRs) 116
  Microphones 117
  Mixers 118
  Monitors 118
  Lights 119
  Lighting Accessories 120
  Other Equipment 120
PRODUCTION STYLES 121
  Location Shooting 121
  Studio Shooting 121
  "Virtual" Production 122
  Compositing Systems 123
  Modern Authoring Programs 123

**17 A Day on Location and a Day in
  the Studio** **125**
LOCATION PRODUCTION 125
  Set-up 125
  Rehearsal 127
  Take One 127
  The Strike 127
SMALL LOCATION SHOOTS 130
STUDIO PRODUCTION 130
  Rehearsal 131
  Switching Live-on-Tape 131
NONDRAMATIC STUDIO
  SHOOTS 132
SMALLER STUDIO SHOOTS 132

18 Audio Production **134**
AUDIO RECORDING IN THE
  STUDIO 134
THE PRODUCTION AUDIO
  ROOM 134
THE RECORDING SESSION 134
THE AUDIO SCRIPT 135
TRANSFER TO VIDEOTAPE 136
AUDIO RECORDING ON LOCATION ..136
FIELD OR STUDIO? 136
THE IMPORTANCE OF SOUND 136
PART FOUR SUMMARY 136

V The Director **139**

19 The Director's Role **141**
ILLUSIONISM: THE DIRECTOR'S
  ART 141
SCRIPT AESTHETICS 141
  Informational Clarity 142
  Character Profiles 143
  Plot 144
  Structure and Transitions 145
  Tone and Pace 146
SUMMARY 146

20 Human Aesthetics **147**
IMAGE AND PERFORMANCE–
  THE CRITICAL INGREDIENTS 147
CASTING 147
AUDITIONS 147
  Appearance ("Look") 148
  Performance Capability 148

Ability to Take Direction 149
Personality .149
Audition Review 149
REHEARSAL 150
Before the Shoot 150
Rehearsal on the Set 151
EXECUTION 152
Distractions 152
Directing Nonprofessional
Talent 153

21 Audiovisual Aesthetics 156
PICTURES AND SOUND 156
SCRIPT ANALYSIS AND
VISUALIZATION 156
VISUAL ELEMENTS 157
CAMERA PLACEMENT AND
MOVEMENT 157
STANDARD COVERAGE 157
EDITING COVERAGE 159
NONSTANDARD CAMERA
PLACEMENT AND MOVEMENT 160
MOVEMENT 161
FRAME SIZE 162
Short Focal Lengths 162
Mid-Range Focal Lengths 162
Long Focal Lengths 162
PRIME LENSES 162
ZOOM LENSES 163
SHOT DESCRIPTIONS 163
Wide Shot (WS) 163
Medium Shot (MS) 163
Medium Close-up (MCU) 163
Close-up (CU) 166
Extreme Close-up (ECU) 166
Insert 166
AVOIDING "JUMP CUTS" 166
Change Focal Lengths 167
Change Camera Positions 167
Plan Edits Carefully 168
FRAME COMPOSITION 168
Balance 168
Depth 171
Lighting 173
SOUND 177
Sound Quality 177
Microphone Choices 177
Types of Sounds 177
SUMMARY 178

22 Technical Aesthetics 179
AVOIDING TECHNICAL
INACCURACIES 179
Props 179
Makeup 180
Wardrobe 180
CONTINUITY PROBLEMS 181
Physical Continuity 181
Performance Continuity 182
SCREEN DIRECTION 183
"Sneaking" Across the Line 189
SUMMARY 192

23 General Aesthetics 193
A DEFINITION 193
TONE 193
Corporate Tone Considerations 194
PACE 194
Shot Content 194
Shot Length 195
Editing for Pace 195
TRANSITIONS 196
Use of the Cut 196
Use of Dissolves 196
Use of Wipes 197
Use of Digital Video Effects (DVE) 197
SUMMARY 197

24 People Skills 198
THE DIRECTOR AS CONSULTANT 198
THE DIRECTOR AS MANAGER 199
Planning 199
Organizing .199
Confirming .199
Preproduction Meetings 200
THE DIRECTOR AS SUPERVISOR 201
Communicate 201
Be Accessible 201
Be Decisive 201
Be Reasonable 201
Recognize Good Work 202
Have Fun 202
Say Thanks .202
THE DIRECTOR AS COACH 202
Communicating with Actors 202
Articulating 202
Allowing Flexibility 203
Clarifying Motivation 204
Recognizing the "Real World" 204

Encouraging Actors 204
Demanding Excellence 205
Recognizing Effort 205
Knowing When to Let Up 205
Gaining Respect 206
Coaching Employee Talent 206
SUMMARY 207

25 Judgment Skills **208**
SENSITIVITY TO THE PEOPLE AND
    THE WORLD AROUND US 208
SENSITIVITY TO AUDIENCE TASTES . . .209
SENSITIVITY TO THE CLIENT'S AND
    PRODUCER'S TASTES 209
OTHER JUDGMENT CALLS 210
JUDGMENT UNDER PRESSURE 210
VISUAL VERSUS CONTENT 210
CONTENT VERSUS VISUAL 211
SUMMARY 212
PART FIVE SUMMARY 212

VI Postproduction **213**

26 A Postproduction Overview **215**
TRADITIONAL VERSUS NONLINEAR . . .215
TRADITIONAL EDITING OVERVIEW . . .215
Duplication 215
The Master Script Package 216
The Editing Process and Time Code 216
Time Code and Control Track 216

**27 The Traditional Offline and Online
    Edit** **219**
THE OFFLINE EDIT 219
The Editor 219
The Offline 219
The Editing Process 220
THE TRADITIONAL ROUGH-CUT
    SCREENING 221
ADDITIONAL NOTES 221
THE ONLINE EDIT 222
AUTO ASSEMBLE 223
SPECIAL EFFECTS 223

28 Nonlinear Editing **224**
A NONLINEAR ANALOGY 224
THE NONLINEAR EDITING PROCESS . . .227
Logging and Digitization 227
Editing 228

Titles and Artwork 229
Client and Producer Review 230
Rendering Effects 230
Output 230
THE FUTURE OF NONLINEAR
    EDITING 230
SUMMARY 230

29 Audio Sweetening **232**
THE SWEETENING ROOM–
    TRADITIONAL AUDIO
    SWEETENING 232
THE LAYDOWN, MIX, AND LAYBACK . .232
NONLINEAR AUDIO SWEETENING 234
PART SIX SUMMARY 235

30 Why Evaluate? **236**
THE EVALUATION PAYBACK 236
FEEDBACK AND THE NEED TO
    IMPROVE 236
DOCUMENTATION: AMMUNITION
    AGAINST EXECUTIVE ATTACK 237
WHICH EVALUATION? 237
ADMINISTERING THE EVALUATION . . .238
WHAT NEXT? 238
INDICES EVALUATIONS 240
CONSIDERATIONS 240
A FEW FINAL NOTES ON
    EVALUATIONS 240

**31 The Future of Corporate
    Media** **241**
NETWORK MEDIA DELIVERY 241
INTERACTIVITY 241
GOING GLOBAL–AND WIRELESS! 241
DISTANCE LEARNING 242
SALES AND INFORMATION
    PROGRAMMING ON THE NETS 242
A CHALLENGING TOMORROW 242

Glossary **243**
Bibliography **253**
Index **255**

Preface and Acknowledgments

In 1998 and 1999, when the first edition of *Corporate Media Production* was being written, the corporate video field was in the midst of a major transition. Processes and equipment that had been used for nearly a half century were quickly becoming outdated. Video switchers, audio mixers, cameras, videotape formats, and most of all, editing and delivery systems were all taking on new forms. The growing buzzword was "digital."

Because of this transition, I felt *Corporate Media Production* should reflect both sides of the technology continuum. It seemed appropriate to prepare students for both the analog and digital worlds of video production. This meant explaining, for example, both the traditional video editing processes as well as the new, nonlinear processes. The same rationale prompted me to cover traditional videotape recording formats, including ¾-inch U-Matic, along with the newer Mini-DV formats.

Today, although the transition continues, I believe we have come far enough into the new digital age to feel confident that very few students will encounter the traditional video processes and equipment. Most will begin their production careers in the new, digital world, in particular utilizing the new Mini-DV recording systems and nonlinear editing systems. For this reason, when the editors at Focal Press and I began discussing the possibility of a 2nd edition, the timing seemed perfect.

The book now reflects the most current media production, editing, delivery formats, and processes. Most of the traditional processes and pieces of equipment are still included, for three reasons. First, I believe it is important for students to understand how the electronic motion picture recording process has evolved. Second, those parts of the book can serve as references or examples illustrating some point or contrast with

today's digital world. And finally, many traditional recording and editing systems are still in use today.

The writing, preproduction, and directing processes covered in the book required only minor revisions since these activities remain, in many ways, timeless. The majority of changes have been made in the production equipment and postproduction sections. These include new types of production and editing equipment as well as contemporary processes and techniques.

As with the first edition, *Corporate Media Production* is not intended as a complete resource. Although it does go into considerable depth in most areas, others (primarily those involving technical skills) are covered as a primer which will hopefully motivate the interested student to dig deeper.

As with all of my previous works on the subject of corporate media, my intent with this book is to be as direct and simple as possible, leaving the student with a clear and comfortable understanding of a subject that can seem anything but clear and comfortable to the newcomer.

A few additional notes. I have also updated relevant bibliography material following each appropriate section of this book and the Glossary. I also updated the Glossary itself and a listing of relevant Internet sites. Any student whose goal is to dig deeper into one particular discipline would be wise to explore these and other available resources. The Internet has become a versatile and easily accessible source of valuable information on countless topics—including corporate media production.

Finally, I would like to thank Larry Chong and his company, Westcoast Video Productions, Inc. (www.wvpinc.com), for his generous assistance. I would also like to thank Jose Altonaga, a good friend and fellow corporate producer, and Videomaker Magazine for their help and support with this project.

part one

The Corporate Media Evolution

1

The Changing Role of Corporate Media

Remember them? Those corny slices of picture-perfect American life known as training films? They helped teach a postwar generation of young people about topics such as personal hygiene, moral values, history, geography, and even why we pledge allegiance to the flag.

In the 1940s and 1950s, training films helped educate our armed forces—and they still do today. In the 1950s and 1960s, they became part of our classroom experience. Ever heard of the title "audiovisual specialist?" This person rolled the 16-millimeter projector into the classroom, threaded the reels, set up the screen, and ran the show for the teacher.

It wasn't long after this era that America's business managers began to consider an interesting question: If the medium was good enough for our soldiers and our kids, why not for employees as well?

The original production medium for these industrial training films, or "industrials" as they came to be known, was 16-millimeter film. Then in the 1970s, a new, much simpler, and more economical medium (one that was becoming more and more common on broadcast television) became viable—videotape.

Why was videotape simpler and more economical? Because this new medium was electronic. That meant it was both immediate and much less laborious as a means of recording and playing back pictures and sound. With videotape, there was no need to thread cameras, load magazines in changing bags, record sound separately on special audio recorders, or send the exposed film and audiotape off to the lab for the multistage process of development and printing.

With video, pictures and sounds were recorded on the same piece of tape, and new, "high-tech," innovations such as ¾-inch U-Matic cassettes made handling it a snap. No threading, no darkrooms, and no threat of exposure were necessary. Not only that, but you could set up a TV monitor, actually watch your scene being recorded, and play it back on the spot! *Amazing!*

Ah, yes. Technology.

We've come a long way since the first days of those early recording systems. The ¾-inch, 2-inch, and even 1-inch reel-to-reel formats have all but disappeared with the emergence of high-quality smaller formats such as ½-inch Beta SP, Digital Beta and ¾-inch D-2. Even smaller, more economical formats, such as 6-millimeter mini digital video (Mini DV), have come on the scene. The often cumbersome to transfer and manipulate analog signals that were the mainstay of early video recording and playback systems have been almost exclusively replaced by digital signals—a change that has resulted in higher image and sound quality and much greater ease in duplication and editing.

Speaking of editing, how about the early, cut-only edit bays? The rooms were stacked with piles of "window dub" videocassettes and reams of scribbled notes, and editors pulled out their hair as they rambled on about "dirty" edit decision lists and generation loss.

The digital era has catapulted the dark, frustrating world of the traditional video edit bay into the future as well. Most of the controllers and ¾-inch videocassette recorders (VCRs) have been replaced by computer monitors, keyboards, and hard drives. These new nonlinear systems such as AVID, Final Cut Pro, Adobe Premier, and others are capable of digitizing, compressing, storing, and editing pictures and sound—without the use of videotape!

This advance is possible because picture and sound information has become streams of ones and zeros, just like any other file in your PC. Want to move a shot? No problem, just drag and drop it as you would cut and paste a piece of text in a word processing document. Don't like it there? Want it back where it was? No problem, just lift it out and drop it back in wherever you like. No generation loss, no dirty lists, no confusion, no problem! It's digital!

There's no question about it—an evolution is underway. The industrial film evolved into the **corporate video,** which is continuing to evolve into a new digital medium that we often refer to as **multimedia.** This medium encompasses multiple types of images and sounds processed and delivered not on film or videotape, but rather as digital files on computerized systems such as **compact disc (CD-ROM), digital video disc (DVD),** and the **World Wide Web.**

But how about the content of **corporate media** programs? Has it evolved as well? Absolutely. The corny, picture-perfect characters posed in front of the camera in their ideal settings have vanished. The slices of industrial American pie have "grown up" into serious, broadcast-quality programs—often news magazine and documentary-style explorations of issues critically important to modern business and its employees.

USES OF MEDIA IN THE CORPORATE WORLD

Those "critical issues" fall into the following four general categories: training, motivating, and informing employees, as well as informing or motivating the public.

Training Programs can teach employees specific ways to sell a product, follow a procedure, or deal professionally with customers on the phone or in person.

Motivational Programs can emphasize how high a company's productivity was for the previous quarter and rally employees to achieve even better results in the next quarter.

Informational Programs can keep employees abreast of changes within the company, thus helping to maintain good morale, open communications, and high productivity.

Public Programs can help market a company's products or perhaps inform the public about its latest goodwill efforts or promotional events.

And what changes have taken place in how these programs reach employees or public viewers?

DISTRIBUTION AND DELIVERY SYSTEMS

Videocassettes

As we all know, the audiovisual specialist with his or her projector on wheels and precarious screen on a three-legged stand is now virtually an extinct breed. The "silver screen" has been replaced by the television and VCR. Today, corporate programs are most often duplicated to VHS videotape and distributed on videocassettes to employee work locations. Employees gather around VCRs and TV sets in break and conference rooms. They watch these videos, perhaps receive accompanying handouts, and often take part in subsequent discussions on issues ranging from safety to job burnout. VHS videocassette is the most common distribution system currently in use in corporate America.

Corporate Broadcasts

During the 1980s, satellite technology also became a widely used medium for disseminating information in the corporate world. Key executives and product technicians discovered they could go "on the air" in a **corporate television** studio and have their message aired live via satellite. Though not cheap by any means, this direct broadcast satellite (DBS) proved to be a cost-effective way to distribute a consistent message to large numbers of employees in a short, critical period. DBS has also been used extensively to "roll out" new products to employees at different geographic locations without the use of expensive traveling demonstrations. Corporate broadcasts have another distinct advantage over prerecorded video programs—they can be interactive! Employees at distant locations are able to call in to submit questions or make comments, and in some cases they can talk live to key executives or technical experts on the air.

Distance Learning

Speaking of interactive programming and distant locations, the term *corporate broadcast* also encompasses distance learning programs in the business world. These are satellite broadcasts in which an instructor or **subject matter expert (SME)** teaches a subject before one or more cameras. Employees at distant locations are able to not only view but also interact with the instructor via signaling devices and telephone lines. Distance learning has also found a home in our educational systems, becoming a commonly used method of teaching college courses.

CD-ROM, DVD, Streaming Video/Audio

But the digital era has brought even more profound changes to this "interactive" part of the media story. These days, delivery systems such as CD-ROM (Figures 1.1 and 1.2), DVD, and streaming video are also becoming viable means of delivering corporate information.

Interactivity—A Key

Because these new delivery systems are computer based, they also add a new, higher level of interaction to corporate media. Employees are able to not only sit and watch a program, but interact with it in ways that tremendously enhance the learning process.

Have you seen or experienced the latest video arcade games? They are examples of digital sound and

Figure 1.2 Marketing CD-ROMs the size of business cards are often given away at trade shows or sales gatherings. They allow the user to sit at his or her computer and view products and services through the use of an interactive multimedia program.

image technology combined with computer programming (authoring) to create an intensely interactive experience for the user. In the case of the typical race car or warrior battle game, the experience is primarily designed to entertain (although you do tend to learn quite a bit about how to defeat that warrior after a few tries, right?). In the case of business programs, however, such as flight and job simulators, media experiences very similar to videogames are designed to teach employees critical skills, such as how to operate electronic and other work-related pieces of equipment.

The World Wide Web

And how about cyberspace? With the advent of streaming video technology, which allows a digital stream of live or recorded sound and images to play on a PC, the use of digital corporate media has taken another tremendous step forward. Prior to streaming technology, an employee wanting to obtain motion pictures from an online connection had to first download that information onto a hard drive. But as you may know, colored moving pictures consist of very large amounts of digital information—too much for the average PC hard drive. Streaming technology, however, eliminates the need to download. It simply streams the sound and pictures through a software "player," which captures, displays, and drops out the viewed information, with no permanent hard drive storage required. This streaming technology is now being used as a much less expensive alternative to the traditional corporate broadcast. Instead of requiring a fully equipped television studio,

Figure 1.1 A CD-ROM inserted in a personal computer. The user is able to view and interact with content using a standard desktop PC.

a satellite uplink, and multiple downlinks, streaming video allows an executive or instructor to simply sit in front of his or her computer and stream a presentation out to employee PC locations on the World Wide Web (Figure 1.3).

Local Area Networks and Intranets

Local area networks (LANs) utilize this type of technology on dispersed groups of computer stations, perhaps in one large building or through an internal computer system spread over offices in different areas. Intranets

Figure 1.3 A typical World Wide Web page. From "virtual" locations such as this one, users can interact with information and training programs or run streaming audio and video applications.

provide this same type of service to private online networks, either locally or over wide geographic areas.

CREATIVE CHANGES?

The massive technological changes taking place in corporate media prompt an interesting question: How about the creative aspects of the medium? Have the jobs of the writer, director, and producer changed as well?

The answer is yes, but not to the extent the technology of recording and delivery systems has changed. A script must still be written, and although interactive programs often involve complex branching sequences, a typical scene must have the same qualities on CD-ROM or videotape. A scene involving actors must still be blocked by a director and recorded, whether it's going on film, tape, or a computer hard drive. A budget must still be developed. Equipment and studio time or locations must be arranged. Actors and perhaps employees must be booked to appear in the program. Artwork must be developed. Music must be picked. A crew of professionals must be hired, or a multiskilled producer must be prepared to accomplish a variety of technical and creative roles by him or herself.

All of which brings us to what this book is about: *how* corporate media programs are made, *who* makes them, and the direction their evolution may take in the future. The subject of "who" is probably as good a place as any to start.

2 The Key Players

Many professionals are typically involved in the making of a corporate media program. All play critical roles, which we will examine shortly. First, however, let's look at the following four key players who share a dynamic working relationship in actually "driving" the world of corporate media:

Producers

Writers

Directors

Clients

THE CORPORATE MEDIA PRODUCER

The corporate media **producer** is any person who manages and guides both the creative and business aspects of producing media programs used in the business world.

Staff and Freelance Producers

The on-staff corporate producer's job is typically a mid-level management position. In most cases, it involves supervising support employees, such as staff associate producers, secretaries, or production assistants. In many cases, this job involves hiring and supervising freelancers, such as writers, directors, camera operators, and editors.

But not all producers are on staff. A corporate producer may also be a freelancer, working for an assortment of companies on an independent, per-project basis. Some freelancers work in both the entertainment and the corporate world at different times, depending on where they can find work.

This is possible for the producer and other key players in the corporate world because of the relationship between corporate media productions or "industrials" as they are often called and broadcast television. Industrials are generally considered scaled down versions of their commercial counterparts—news and entertainment programs. It's interesting to note that although corporate production is thought of as the "little brother" in the world of media, it often pays more money, provides better working conditions, and offers more overall job opportunities than its "big brother." The reasons are simple. Far fewer commercial media jobs exist, most are located in a handful of metropolitan areas, and because of the "glamour" factor, many more people compete for those jobs.

Producer "Musts"

Whether the producer is a staffer or "playing the field" makes little difference when it comes to the business of producing programs. In either case, the corporate producer must be a jack-of-all-media-trades. His or her primary skills must lie in the areas of project and people management. The producer must be able to closely guide the many elements of the production process and supervise the creative people who conceive and carry out those elements.

This is not to say that the producer is not creative, as well. Not only must this person be extremely creative in the expected areas—writing, directing, and editing—but he or she must also creatively use the company's time, money, and human resources.

In order to effectively guide and supervise media productions, the producer must have a working knowledge of all the functions involved in that process. He or she must know what it is like to sit in front of a word processor staring at the blank screen, under pressure to have a shooting script by the next morning. He or she must know all the labors of actually getting that script written, revised, approved, and placed in the hands of a capable director. He or she must also be well aware of and able to use the human skills involved in questioning a difficult executive or client.

The producer must also know the director's job intimately. He or she must stay closely in touch with the aesthetic process of motion picture videography, the needs and temperaments of actors, and the wants and needs of the crew that helps bring the pages of the script to life on the television screen. He or she must know how to tactfully convince clients that their opinions are wrong, how to tell the company president to straighten up for the camera, and how to make valid creative decisions under extreme pressure. The corporate producer must be able to break down a script, write a shooting schedule, set a key light, create a budget, and develop a shot list.

But the producer's "musts" don't stop there. He or she must also know the postproduction process—how it feels to sit in a dimly lit room staring at television monitors and trying to make a coherent scene out of footage that was shot with no thought given to screen direction, proper focal lengths, or continuity.

As if these demands aren't enough, the corporate producer must also be a politician able to defend the corporate media department to executives who know little and care less about the television production process. He or she must be an accountant able to effectively manage large sums of money, and often a psychologist as well.

Not only must the producer understand all these things, but in many cases this person must also be able to do them. This requirement exists because the corporate producer is often a one-person crew, without the luxury of being able to bring in people to staff various crew positions.

Above all, the successful producer must have a sense of what works. And although this "must" may sound like the easy part, it is probably the most difficult. The ability to know what works on the screen and the confidence to fight for it do not come overnight.

They are the product of time, experience, success, failure, and plenty of old-fashioned hard work.

The Reward

And what is the payoff for all these "musts?" On one level, of course, there is the paycheck, which can be quite comfortable if the producer is good at what he or she does—$60,000 to $70,000 a year is fairly common, and some producers make much more. On another perhaps more important level, there is the self-satisfaction that comes when the producer sits in a screening room and watches the final program.

In this case, the payoff is a series of shots that cut with seamless precision, actors who bring their roles to life with unquestionable sincerity, a script that flows with simple eloquence from one scene to the next, a sparkle of excitement in the client's eye, the knowledge that hundreds or even thousands of employees will be helped, and most of all, the self-satisfaction that comes from having supervised, nurtured, guided, and helped make every element playing on the television screen a reality.

THE DIRECTOR

What exactly does a director do? At first that sounds like a simple question. The average person would probably answer, "A director sits on the set in a chair that has his or her name on it. When everything is ready, he or she says 'Action' and the camera rolls. He or she watches as the actors do the scene. When the scene is over, he or she says 'Cut,' and the camera stops. The director gets up, walks onto the set, and talks to the actors about what they should do differently, then sits down and calls 'Action' again."

True. A director decides when the camera rolls and stops, and he or she works with the actors to shape their performances. The problem with this brief description is that those few critical moments on a set or location reflect only a fraction of the director's responsibilities. The true scope of his or her work is vastly broader and more complex.

A Definition

Before we go further, let's closely examine that phrase "vastly broader and more complex." To do so, let's start with a definition of what a **director** is.

The person responsible to the producer for carefully guiding and shaping a complex series of human and technical elements during the preparation and recording of film, videotape, audiotape, or digital segments that must later edit together into an effective audiovisual entity.

Let's examine each part of this statement more closely.

"The person responsible to the producer..." means exactly that. In a large sense, the director's chair is where the buck stops with regard to the pre-production and production phases of a program's development.

If his or her program turns up a series of poor sound recordings, the director cannot blame it on the sound recordist or boom operator. If the video or digital images do not meet the technical standards required by the producer, the director cannot blame it on the camera operator or graphic artist. If the performances of the actors are weak, the director cannot blame the casting agency. If the shoot goes over budget, the director cannot blame the assistant director or production assistant who helped with the scheduling. In each of these cases, although a subordinate to the director may have goofed, the director must bear the responsibility for that person's actions.

"Carefully guiding and shaping . . ." are the director's primary jobs. He or she continually guides and shapes all of the elements at his or her disposal toward an end result that reflects the interpretation of the script he or she has been charged with recording. "A complex series of human and technical elements . . ." are what the director guides and shapes. Let's touch on both.

The *human* elements are the performances of actors, the comfort level of the client, the satisfaction of the producer, and the chemistry between the director and the crew. The *technical* elements are focal lengths, the choice of lenses or filters, the composition of a shot, lighting decisions, and the choice of when, where, and *if* the camera moves.

"During the preparation and recording of videotape, audiotape, or digital segments that must later edit together into an effective audiovisual entity" takes into account the medium in which the director is working and the edit sessions that follow production. Edit sessions are the "proof of the pudding," in a sense, because the director ultimately finds out in the editing suite if everything he or she shaped and guided according to an aesthetic vision now blends seamlessly into a successful overall piece of audiovisual work.

The Director as an Artist

The director is also an artist in a very real and exciting sense. The excitement comes from both the process and the raw materials used in creating the work.

The painter creates with a canvas and brushes. His or her work is made of colors, textures, lines, strokes, and shapes. The musician creates with an instrument. The manifestation of his or her work is sound—notes, melodies, rhythms, volumes, paces, and intensities. The writer creates with the printed word creating exciting images that play out in the minds of readers.

The director, however, creates with all the elements of our world. His or her materials are people, houses, cars, props, wardrobe, locations, emotions, and character traits. The director's creations are precisely choreographed illusions of reality—pieces of pre-visualized life that unfold not on a canvas, through a speaker, or on a sheet of paper, but as live events before the eyes of a viewer.

The word "live" and the numerous subtleties inherent in the concept add tremendous scope, complexity, and excitement to the director's work.

To change his or her work, the director does not replay a note, remake a brush stroke, or rewrite a passage. The director must change the way people think about and perceive human interactions. If a performance is too static, he or she must work with the actors to find true motivation for movement. This process means exploring what drives the scene, how the actors feel about those things, and how those feelings should be manifested on the screen—with a glance? A movement? A word? Or a combination of these things?

If the director believes that a piece of dialogue breaks the sense of reality, he or she must examine what words are wrong and why—are they unmotivated? Insincere? Erroneous? Corny? Then he or she must change how the scene plays out to create and support the right dialogue.

If the framing or composition of a shot is disturbing or uncomfortable, the director must question what subtlety is out of balance—the positions of the actors? The movement of the camera? The focal length? The lighting? The background or foreground? He or she must then determine what pieces of the scene need to be changed to make the shot aesthetically proper for the work's tone.

Not for the Fainthearted

When these or any of numerous other elements are not all working together to support the desired illusion, the director is placed under intense pressure. His or her job is to make everything work in perfect sync and with complete believability in front of the camera. Thousands of dollars and a tremendous amount of effort are at stake. Crew, cast, and equipment have been paid for. Props have been ordered, created, painted, and positioned and sets have been designed and built. Wardrobe has been selected and locations have been scouted, reserved, and rented.

Each of these elements has been acquired largely based on the director's wishes. The director is well aware that clients and producers—the persons paying for the creation of his or her vision—are waiting in the wings for the result.

For the director, it has to work.

The Reward

And the reward comes when it does work.

When everything happens exactly as it was envisioned, the director is fulfilled. When the composition has the proper depth, color, and balance; the actor's lines, movements, and inflections are delivered with complete sincerity; and the camera dollies in to the proper focal length and angle at the right moment, the sense of satisfaction is incredible. It can only be matched later in the editing suite when every scene recorded, containing those same perfect elements, is assembled into a larger whole—the program itself.

At this point, the creation is complete, and if everything was directed properly, the illusion is perfect. The viewer sits and watches, and it never occurs to him or her that a camera was present, that the people moving on the screen are actors, or that virtually every element in the frame was painstakingly positioned according largely to one person's wishes. As the scene plays out, all the subtleties of the director's work—all his or her "shaping and guiding"—become invisible. They simply dissolve into the fabric of "reality" created on the screen.

Directors are driven people, and these creative elements drive them—the intense rewards and the agonizing risks of creating art as a live illusion.

THE SCRIPTWRITER

Like all participants in the world of corporate media, writers work for a paycheck. But money is only part of the writer's reward. Probably more important to most scriptwriters is the fact that, similar to television or feature film writing, corporate scriptwriting is a creative and exciting way to earn a living. Someone who has not written for the corporate market might dispute this claim, but those who write corporate scripts are keenly aware of its truth. If corporate projects didn't require high levels of skill and creativity, most writers wouldn't continue to focus their energies on the corporate market once they've worked in it. Once writers become aware that they can earn good money, flex their creative muscles, and see their work produced intact, they quickly become corporate believers.

The Real Differences

In the final analysis, two meaningful differences separate entertainment and corporate scriptwriting: the working environment and the research factor.

The Working Environment

To someone not familiar with the business world, the inner workings of corporations can appear intimidating. Large companies often seem to have an underlying tension and robotic orderliness about them. In reality, the three words that probably best describe a typical corporate environment are bureaucratic, political, and conservative.

Corporations are *bureaucratic* because they are structured like pyramids. Descending, broadening layers of departments usually function according to very specific rules and regulations. Corporations are also *political* because regardless of the volumes of regulations, policies, and procedures in any company, who you know and how you operate make a big difference. Corporations are *conservative* as well because they require their employees to look professional, act professional, and function as team players who are supportive of the policies and **corporate culture** of that company.

What does all this mean to a potential corporate scriptwriter? To be successful, the writer must gain a healthy respect for the corporate world and learn to function in the business environment with ease and comfort.

The Research Factor

Corporate scripts, unlike many of those written for entertainment, require that the writer learn something about the corporation's people, policies, objectives, or work. This background is important because most corporate programs are informational, instructional, motivational, or a combination of these elements. The majority are produced to help viewers function better as employees and, as a result, keep the company's bottom line in the black.

These elements of information, instruction, and motivation may at first turn off some writers. After all, who would want to write a script about something like the probing techniques used by salespeople to learn about their customers? One West Coast writer did, and he decided it didn't have to be a boring program. A portion of the story outline follows:

PROBING: A STORY OUTLINE

We open on a close up of a door marked "Interrogation Room." Off camera a conversation is taking place between two detectives, Doris McIntire and Gordon "Gordi" Hansen.

Gordi is saying, "Why all the intellectual stuff! Just give me five minutes with this pigeon and I'll have 'im singin' like a canary!"

"How do I make you understand?" Doris replies. "These are not the old days! There happen to be much more effective ways of getting people to give you information."

As the conversation continues camera pans and widens to reveal Doris and Gordi. We see them standing at a coffeepot in a police office. Gordi is a large man in his fifties. His grey hair and hardened features tell us he's a veteran cop with considerably more brawn than brains. His sleeves are rolled up, and a shoulder holster and gun hang at his side. Doris, on the other hand, is an attractive, intelligent-looking woman in her late twenties. She is neatly dressed and wearing no gun.

Although it's obvious Gordi isn't going to be convinced, Doris continues to explain. "It's called probing," she says. "And not only is it ideal in our line of work, it's also a good management tool. Bosses can use probing techniques for

effective communications with their people. It's even great for everyday person-to-person communications!"

"Yeah?" Gordi says, pulling a pair of brass knuckles from his pocket. "Well, I ain't no mumbo-jumbo expert, but I got my own person-to-person technique. And my way's only got one management tool . . . pain!"

Doris isn't giving up. She tells Gordi that his method may be the old way, but today's experts use six simple techniques to probe effectively: (1) Tell why, (2) Mention benefits, (3) Be specific, (4) Ask open-ended questions, (5) Listen actively, and (6) Question clues.

"You got any 'clues' about the guy you're dealin' with in there?" Gordi asks, pointing at the Interrogation Room. "This guy's a three-time graduate of the Big House! He ain't gonna hear a word you're sayin'!"

"Come on," Doris says, heading for the Interrogation Room. "We'll just see about that." As she and Gordi reach the door, Gordi flips a light switch, and Doris reaches for the knob.

We cut to a blinding light clicking on, filling the frame. A reverse-angle shot reveals a close up of Vincent "Vini" Legatta, his hands thrown up in front of his face. Vini is a small, greasy New York type, chewing bubble gum.

Doris and Gordi enter as silhouettes and take seats across the table from Vini. As Vini's eyes adjust to the light, Doris leans forward revealing her attractive face. Vini is obviously pleased. "Well, well," he says, "beauty. . . (squinting, trying to make out Gordi) . . . and the beast."

I'd call that a pretty creative way to handle a "boring" subject. Granted, many corporate scripts are less elaborate. Do corporate scriptwriters mind this? Rarely. In fact, most writers seem to find that just the process of learning some supposedly boring subject often turns out to be extremely interesting. Then, finding a creative way to communicate what they've learned to the employees in a company becomes an even more challenging and rewarding process.

Staff and Freelance Writers

A staff scriptwriter in a large company earns approximately $50,000 per year with a solid benefits package. After a few years of gaining depth and experience, he or she may be able to progress into producing or directing.

Many companies, however, hire out their scriptwriting work to freelancers. A writer who takes this path writes for different companies on an independent, per-project basis. Rates typically run from approximately $1,500 to $2,500 for a 10- to 15-minute corporate script. The freelancer may eventually move into producing and directing as well, or expand into other types of writing, such as screenplays and teleplays for the entertainment industry, or perhaps books or print work for general publication.

CLIENTS

Clients are the middle- and upper-level managers for whom producers, writers, and directors work. A corporate client might be the safety manager, the human resources director, or the vice president of marketing. All corporate clients share the following two characteristics: (1) they are business people and (2) they come to the media department with a communication problem they hope to get solved through the use of a video or some other type of media program.

Client Profiles

Clients come in various personality types. Most are helpful, cooperative, and grateful to have media resources available to them. Clients can also be quite demanding, however, especially in chargeback situations requiring that they pay either part or all of what can be an expensive media bill. The following are several typical client profiles:

> Busybodies
>
> Instant decision makers
>
> Yessirees
>
> Committee heads
>
> Plain old perfect clients

Busybodies

These are overworked managers who often seem to want a program pulled out of a hat. They have half an hour to sit in on an initial meeting, but after that they'll be in Chicago next week, up to their ears in reports the following week, doing sales seminars on the road for the next two weeks, in training, revising the budget, and writing performance reviews. As luck would have it, they happen to be able to squeeze in 30 more minutes with you in 2 weeks—to approve the final program!

What busybodies sometimes don't realize is that developing media programs takes more than a creative team. It also takes client input, support, and approvals at many places along the way. It also requires that content experts provide information or at least the proper guidance and contacts to get that information. Developing a successful media program also frequently requires someone to open doors to other departments and to act as a liaison to possible interviewees, executives, and other sources.

Instant Decision Makers

These managers may make on-the-spot or "instant" decisions about program development with little or no thought about whether it will really work.

For example, I was once describing to an instant decision maker how a series of interviews might work into a script concept I was considering. I said, "We could do them as scripted pieces with each interviewee looking directly into the camera, or—"

He stopped me there. "Yes!" he exclaimed, leaning forward in his chair. "That's exactly what I want. Looking directly into the camera. Eye contact. Perfect!"

As it turned out, the interviews were eventually written and shot in a totally unscripted fashion with the interviewees looking slightly away from the camera at an interviewer. Had they been done with "eye contact," they wouldn't have worked nearly as well. A productive tact when working with instant decision makers is to tentatively agree with their decisions for the moment, but take those ideas with a grain of salt.

Yessirees

These clients seem too good to be true. Everything a producer says sounds perfect to them. Tell them you're considering a role-play scenario, and they'll tell you what a wonderful idea that is. Five minutes later, say you're considering a documentary approach, and they'll follow right along, saying that does actually seem like a much better way to go. Later, pitch a music video, and watch them start picking song titles.

These clients usually have no idea what they really want, which means their decisions can be dangerous. It also means that it's up to the production team to lead them down the right path. The important thing to remember with the yessirees is not to base decisions on what they think they want. Instead, those decisions should be based on the type of solid design and content research we'll be discussing shortly.

Committee Heads

The people who speak for committees are often the opposite of instant decision makers. This is because they represent a group of people who all have a vested interest in the project and who all want a say in the decision-making process. As a result, committee heads want to bring 5, 7, possibly even 15 people to development meetings and have roundtable discussions about many aspects of the production.

This situation is highly problematic, although sometimes unavoidable. Why? Because one person feels humor is right, and the other despises laughs. Another person wants every detail on the subject included in the script, and still another feels only an overview is needed. One committee member wants actors, and another wants employees to play the roles, and so forth.

Most writers, producers, and directors attempt to avoid approval by committee at all costs. They do this by stressing to the committee head that although various people may need input into the process, following one simple rule will help the project along much more quickly and lead to a better end product. The client or a person he or she delegates should be the single point of contact for the writer, director, or producer. This stipulation means that all input from others with a stake in the project should be filtered through this contact person in private committee meetings. In this way, some redundancy and unacceptable changes can be weeded out before clients ever get to production meetings.

Plain Old Perfect Clients

As mentioned previously, the kind of people producers work with more than any other are plain old perfect clients. They are enthusiastic about the project, and they are more than willing to dig in and provide whatever help may be requested. They have content experts available, audience members to interview, job locations to visit, telephone numbers, names, good ideas, and as much time and energy as a producer may need from them. They're capable of making good, solid decisions, but they also have a keen sense of when more scrutiny or higher approval is needed.

Perhaps the best thing about plain old perfect clients is that they regard the key players on the production team as experts in their field. They trust creative decisions and, in most cases, recognize when they are starting to overstep their boundaries as clients.

The result is plenty of creative fuel in the form of support, approvals, and input, but a producer who always remains in the driver's seat. The only real problem with plain old perfect clients is fighting off the urge to adopt them as permanent clients on every project you produce!

A Dynamic Relationship

As you've no doubt gathered, these four key players have various motivations in the production of a media program. Producers want the project handled as simply and cost-effectively as possible. Writers want to deliver their best writing; they view scriptwriting as the most critical activity in the entire production process. Directors would no doubt agree that a good script is critical, but many would argue that translating that script into a credible on-screen performance is the most important part of the process. Clients, on the other hand, are interested in low-cost, high-quality deliverables. They have an objective to meet, a problem to be solved, a boss to satisfy, and typically not much money to spend. They are hoping for a program that takes care of all these issues, doesn't require too much of their time or money, and makes them into a hero to boot.

How do these dynamics affect the process of producing programs? They make it an intense, often delicate, and highly charged evolution of technical and creative events—a creative and business effort that, if executed properly, results in significant rewards for all parties, including the viewers for whom the work was done in the first place.

3 Media Groups in the Corporate World

The key players discussed in the previous chapter all exercise some form of control over the process of corporate media production. The type and amount of that control and their interaction as collaborators in the process of media production can depend on how the media department is staffed and positioned in the corporate environment.

For the most part, corporate media professionals work in groups of five general shapes and sizes, as follows:

Large in-house media groups

Small in-house media groups

Outside production companies

Prosumers

Freelancers

LARGE IN-HOUSE MEDIA GROUPS

Some large companies are so committed to motion pictures as a communication medium that they invest significant amounts of money in developing and maintaining studio and editing facilities. These facilities are often equipped with modern broadcast-quality production equipment and cutting-edge graphic and editing systems.

Large in-house units may house a staff of producers, editors, directors, and even videographers, artists, and support people. In some cases, these production groups are funded solely by the company, but many work as internal profit centers. That means they produce programs for their internal clients, who in turn pay for the productions out of their operating budgets. In this way, the media group maintains its place in the company as a profit or "break-even" center. If the internal company business does not produce sufficient income, the large in-house media group may do work for external clients or even rent its facility to outside producers.

Some large in-house groups boast an impressive facility but maintain a small, core staff of producers. These groups hire freelance writers, directors, and crew people on a per-project basis.

Advantages and Disadvantages

The advantage of the large in-house media group lies in the quality, custom work it produces for the departments that utilize its services. Large facilities and cutting-edge equipment usually mean programs that look and sound like broadcast shows. The disadvantage of the large in-house media group, of course, is its cost. Maintaining a full television production unit is at minimum a six-figure budgetary consideration. If many departments in the company are offsetting this cost by paying for productions out of their own budgets, all remains well. If internal production work slows down, however, the large in-house unit can quickly become a drain, and thus an expendable box on the organizational chart.

SMALL IN-HOUSE MEDIA GROUPS

Smaller in-house units are more likely to function on the "one-man band" premise of media production. These units might consist of one or a small group of producers with perhaps very limited facilities and in some cases "Prosumer-grade" equipment, such as S-VHS, Hi-8, or mini DV format camcorders, a few light kits and microphones, and minimal graphic and editing gear. In some cases, smaller groups maintain broadcast-quality cameras and editing systems and draw their savings from the small employee count and the absence of a large studio.

In small groups, the core employees often work together as writers, producers, and directors, crewing for each other or providing some type of support function. As you might guess, in these units, having multiple skills is an absolute necessity.

Small in-house units might shoot in converted offices instead of in a studio. Instead of professional actors, they often utilize employees. The producer often writes and directs with only minimal support and may edit the program as well. The broadcast-quality images and high production values considered standard by their larger counterparts are sometimes sacrificed in smaller units, based on the idea that such image quality may not be necessary for corporate programs.

Advantages and Disadvantages

Although programs produced by small in-house groups may not always look and sound as sophisticated as those produced by the larger groups, the smaller groups are much less expensive to maintain and typically quicker to respond to client needs. The lack of studio space and expensive equipment makes their overhead a fraction of what the large in-house units must cover. This savings translates into lower costs for clients and lower operating costs for the company.

OUTSIDE PRODUCTION COMPANIES

Many companies maintain no media group. They operate on the premise that media productions are specialized products that should be purchased from outside production companies that deal only in this type of work.

These outside production companies can range from quite large to one-person operations working out of a home office. Most times, their job is to come in on a project at the outset and handle all aspects of the production in a turnkey manner. They spare their clients—usually company employees with little or no knowledge of the production process—the details of script development, production headaches, and editing. Outside production companies simply deliver a completed program of an agreed-upon length and quality level for an agreed-upon price. Similar to any other large, multistage project, their clients are given points of approval along the way.

Advantages and Disadvantages

The advantages of using outside production companies are primarily monetary. When projects are not being produced, no staff, facility, or equipment is being paid for. Because competition for large corporate contracts is often intense, companies can demand high-quality productions while continually applying pressure to lower the prices they must pay. On the other hand, large production companies are completely detached from the departments for which they work, and thus have very little internal company knowledge and no company loyalty whatsoever. This relationship means they are more likely to find reasons to increase prices if they can. Also, because they are strictly in the business of making money, they may even attempt to "sell" a company on programs that may not be necessary.

PROSUMERS

The word prosumer is a cross between the words professional and consumer. In the corporate media world, the prosumer could be considered a very small outside production company. He or she typically owns consumer or mid-range equipment—Hi 8, S-VHS, or mini DV—and comparatively inexpensive art and editing systems.

Advantages and Disadvantages

A prosumer with good business and creative skills can produce very acceptable programs for a fraction of the cost of his or her corporate counterparts. With equipment prices continually dropping and prosumer-quality levels moving closer to broadcast, some prosumers make a good living producing for small and mid-sized companies that don't have substantial money to spend on media production. The disadvantage is that some prosumers may not have the creative and technical skills or the equipment to produce programs up to the quality level of their larger counterparts.

FREELANCERS

Freelancers often play an important part in corporate media. They supplement both large and small in-house units as well as outside production companies. Freelancers work for anyone who will pay for their services, and they are typically brought in on a per-project basis. That arrangement means they may be hired to write, produce, or direct a single program, but when the project is completed, they're back on the street looking for more work.

Advantages and Disadvantages

To the in-house producer, the use of freelancers is typically a matter of saving time and money. Freelancers come on the job for a project and then leave. They require no desks, benefits, equipment, or other staff employee necessities.

To the freelancer, the freelance world has its advantages and disadvantages. Freelancers are their own bosses, and they are never stuck in the day-to-day labors of mundane paperwork and politics that in-house producers must deal with continually. By contrast, where an in-house producer might be paid $60,000 a year and a comfortable benefits package, the freelancer is paid an agreed-upon daily rate, and when the job is done, that's it. They receive no vacation pay, no 401K plan, no medical or dental benefits, and so forth. Obviously, the price of freedom can be steep. On the other hand, if freelancers are good at what they do and happen to be working in an active market, they can make a good living. This situation results because hourly or daily freelance rates are typically higher than salaries of equivalent in-house employees.

In addition, freelancers in areas such as Los Angeles and New York often cross the line into news, news magazine, or entertainment work when pickings are slim in the corporate world. This cross-over is especially true of camera and crew people. Why is this possible? Partly because the production process—which we are now about to explore—is basically the same in all worlds.

4

A Production Overview

Whether the production unit is large or small, freelance or staff, visual media production most often takes place in the following four distinct phases:

Writing

Preproduction

Production

Postproduction

Considerable time and on-the-job experience are required to become completely knowledgeable in all of these areas. The purpose of this book is to explore each phase in considerable detail, but let's create a foundation by starting with an overview of the process.

WRITING

When a client comes to the corporate producer with a communication problem, a corporate media project is in its inception.

Program Design

The producer often begins a project by writing a **program needs analysis (PNA).** This brief document explores the facts that determine whether the project represents an appropriate use of the corporation's money. It also examines the design factors that guide the entire project development.

Scriptwriting

Following this initial assessment and design period, a writer is brought in on the project, unless the producer writes the **script.** The writer does the appropriate research, meets with clients, **content experts,** and audience members and, from this input, first develops a content outline, one or more creative concepts, and a treatment.

The Content Outline is typically used on complex and heavily instructional projects. It is a carefully structured arrangement of all the facts required to successfully present the program.

Creative Concepts are visual ideas drawn from both the design and content information. They provide the means of most effectively communicating the message in visual terms.

The Treatment is a scene-by-scene narrative description of the program that elaborates on the visual concept. It explains the basic visualization to both the client and the producer.

After approval of the **program needs analysis, content outline,** and/or **concept** and **treatment,** the script is written. This process is usually accomplished in three drafts, with each draft presented to the client and producer for their input and approval. The writing phase ends with the writer's delivery of a **shooting script** that is approved by the client and the producer.

PREPRODUCTION

Preproduction or **"prep"** is the process of gathering, organizing, confirming, and scheduling all elements required to complete a successful production. Although a great many small tasks take place during a typical preproduction period, the following are the major tasks.

Budgeting

The producer typically budgets a project based on the client's dictate or a **breakdown** of the shooting script. The breakdown takes into account such items as the number of actors needed and their fees, the number of shooting days required, the crew size required and each of their fees, equipment and facility rentals, and the editing time and personnel required.

Talent Auditions and Bookings

Normally, the director and an assistant—usually a **production assistant (PA)** or **assistant director (AD)**—arrange for actor **auditions,** selections, callbacks, and bookings. Clients and producers frequently become a part of the **talent** selection process, either approving the director's choices or actually making choices themselves. In some cases, company employees become the talent, alleviating the need for a formal audition and casting process.

Crew Bookings

Crews are usually hired by the PA or AD based on the producer's or director's request. Typically, the director is most concerned with the **director of photography (DP)** or **videographer** because this person executes the lighting and major camera work. In smaller unit situations, the crew may consist of the producer, a sound and/or cameraperson, and an assistant.

Equipment Reservations or Rentals

The producer, AD, or PA books the camera, lights, mics, and other equipment either by reserving in-house equipment or calling equipment rental houses. In the case of rental houses, the arrangements are often made to have the equipment delivered the day before the production and picked up the day after. Studio and editing facilities are reserved or rented in much the same way.

Location and Set Arrangements

On feature films and network television programs, professional set designers and builders create sets under the supervision of an art director, who in turn reports to the director. In corporate program production, the producer or director often designs a much less elaborate set and supervises having it built and lit. The DP and one to three crew members, perhaps the **gaffer** and a **grip,** may be brought in one or two days before the production to accomplish this task.

On a feature film, initial **location** scouting is usually handled by a location manager and his or her staff or a location service. However, in the corporate world, the producer typically can't afford this luxury. He or she must find locations that meet the production's needs and, working through the AD or PA, arrange to reserve, pay for, and schedule their use.

In corporate program production, locations often consist of company office areas and crew members' or clients' homes. When securing public locations, however, the AD or PA must apply for permits and insurance and pay the appropriate fees charged by cities, businesses, or local government agencies.

Blocking, Storyboards, and Diagrams

Having decided on locations and carefully visualized the script, the director decides where the basic camera positions will be, the desired look, and how the actors will move in and out of each scene.

This movement of actors in relation to the camera is called **blocking.** If the scene involves a **host** on camera, the blocking may be as simple as an **entrance** and an **exit.** If the scene involves characters in a dramatic or humorous situation, blocking becomes more complicated and is usually finalized either in rehearsal or on location when actually working with the actors. Directors often draw simple storyboards and blocking diagrams.

Rehearsals and Meetings

Talent rehearsals are the exception rather than the rule in corporate television for two reasons. First, corporate budgets often will not allow for the extra expense. Second, most corporate scripts are considerably less involved than those for feature films or network television programs. In the case of corporate broadcasts and distance learning programs, involving on-air, multicamera production, rehearsals for crew, executives, and subject matter experts (SMEs) is essential.

Technical rehearsals are held more often in high-end studio productions. A *tech*, as it's called, is usually scheduled when a set has been built and multiple cameras will be used. In a tech, all crew members attend and assume their positions, and a stand-in actor may walk through the various angles, ensuring that the lighting and sound setups will work error-free on the following production day.

Crew meetings are sometimes held during preproduction, especially when the shoot is a complicated one requiring updates by the various crew members. In most cases, however, the director and the AD have most preproduction meetings, along with a brief meeting for the entire cast and crew, on the first day of production.

Production Scheduling

Finally, a schedule must be created to ensure that the various scenes are recorded in the most economical order, considering factors such as actors' daily fees, location fees and availability, travel times, equipment rental fees, and studio fees and availability. The producer or director usually creates the **shooting schedule** after the director has made all location, talent, and basic blocking decisions. After these elements are decided, the director can accurately gauge personnel and logistic considerations, thus how much *time* and resources each shot will take.

PRODUCTION

Production is the shoot itself. It might take place in a company cafeteria, on a prebuilt set, in an audio recording booth, or at a combination of these locations. Wherever it takes place, production is the short, critical period when everything must work right.

Complicated human and technical elements are brought together during production to create an illusion of reality. If everything has been prepared properly, that illusion can be successfully created in the time allotted for each scene to be shot. If preparations have not been adequate, however, production can turn into a frantic catch-up game involving long, grueling days and continual compromises on picture, sound, and performance quality.

Location Production

Location production is usually carried out with a single camera. The crew drives to the scheduled location, and the lights, camera, and all accessory equipment are set up. Some **setups** are simple, involving only a camera and no lights. Other setups are complex, involving extensive lighting, camera movement on a **crane** or a **dolly,** and complicated blocking.

The scene is rehearsed until the director feels it is ready to be recorded. At this point, a first master scene is shot. Typically, anywhere from two to ten takes of this scene are required to get what the director terms a **"buy"**—the actual take to be used in the program. Once the director declares the scene a buy, the AD indicates **circled takes** in the notes on the **master script** and tape log for later reference by the editor.

Additional **"coverage"** of the same scene—or parts of it—is then recorded. This is accomplished by moving the camera to new positions, changing focal lengths, and recording the same action and dialogue or portions of it. Just as with the master scene, multiple takes are usually required at each position to finally record the buys.

During this entire time, the client or a **technical adviser** may be present on the set, giving input on the technical accuracy of each shot. The producer may also be present, sharing an additional aesthetic perspective.

When the director is satisfied that the best performances and adequate coverage of the scene have been obtained, he or she calls **"strike"** and the setup is dismantled. The crew, cast, and clients then move to a new location to repeat the process.

Studio Production

Studio production often involves a **multicamera** setup. In this case, a set is built and "dressed" in the days before production, and all lighting and sound setups are also completed in advance.

As the shoot gets under way, the actors rehearse with the director and walk through blocking. At the same time, camera operators rehearse their focal lengths, moves, and positions based on the director's previous instructions or a shot list he or she has provided.

When the director is satisfied that the actors' performances are polished enough to record and the camera operators are fully rehearsed, he or she typically retires to a master control room. This "booth," as it's often called, provides the director with images displayed on a wall of monitors, from the cameras on the floor and other sources.

As the director gives the action cue and the scene plays out, he or she instructs the camera operators to line up the proper shots on the fly. At the same time, he or she calls out to a **technical director (TD)** to switch signals at the proper times. In this way, the selected images are recorded in sequence and the director can record all coverage of the scene—the **master shot, medium shots (MS),** and **close ups (CU)**—in a single good pass. When this process has been accomplished, the next scene is rehearsed, and so on.

Graphic Arts Production

As corporate media becomes more **interactive** and the digital world expands, graphic arts sequences are playing more significant roles in media productions. Sophisticated animation and compositing systems create polished, 2-D and 3-D artwork that can provide animated sequences, dynamic text and logo sequences, mixtures of live action and animation, and instructional sequences that might otherwise be impossible to convey.

Graphic arts production typically requires that the producer or director conceptualize and carefully map out a storyboard of a graphic sequence, then sit down with an artist to actually create it.

Audio Production

Audio production can take place either on location or in a studio. In a studio, an audio control room and soundproof booth arrangement is maintained for this purpose. Typically, an audio engineer, the director and perhaps the AD sit in the control booth. They utilize a sound mixing board and instruct the actors via microphone and headsets through a soundproof glass window. Multiple takes are rehearsed and recorded similar to the video portion of the program.

On location, audio recording is often accomplished in a quiet room or area. Sound is recorded onto videotape by using the camera as the recording system but disregarding the visual element. For instance, the

camera might be pointed at a **slate** for that scene and put into "record." It is left in this position as the actor reads his or her lines. During editing, only the audio portion of the recording is usable.

POSTPRODUCTION

When all sound and picture elements of the script are recorded, production is "wrapped." The project then moves into postproduction or **editing.** Traditionally, corporate programs have required two editing processes: a **rough cut,** or **offline edit,** and a **fine cut,** or **online edit.** With today's nonlinear editing systems, however, these two phases are merging.

The Traditional Offline Edit

Traditionally, offline editing is carried out on a comparatively simple editing system that has two purposes. The first purpose is to create a rough cut of the program. This is accomplished by editing duplicate, work print copies of the buy takes into a rough but accurate version of the show. A viewing of the rough cut is arranged, and the client and producer then approve it or suggest changes if appropriate.

The second purpose of the offline edit is to create an **edit decisions list (EDL).** The EDL is a list of time code numbers that reflect the exact edit points chosen by the offline editor. Every segment of video or audio in the rough cut has a unique time code "address" that corresponds exactly to the identical segments on the high-quality **original footage.**

Once client and producer changes have been made, the EDL is revised and "cleaned" to reflect the exact "in" and "out" address points of every edit. This list of final addresses can then be used as the backbone of the online editing process.

The Traditional Online Edit

The online is the final edit. It involves using the time code EDL created in the offline to edit the original, high-quality segments of that same footage into what is called an **edit master.**

The online is accomplished by loading the cleaned EDL into a much more sophisticated editing system. Typically, the EDL is inputted via floppy disk and used as a control tool to cue the operation of videotape recorders (VTRs) containing the original footage reels.

Because the online system cues VTRs according to the EDL and has the ability to control multiple VTRs as well as "outboard" or periphery equipment, much of an online edit can often be carried out very rapidly in an "auto assemble" mode.

A video **switcher** is also used in the online edit. The switcher is a powerful tool that combines sources, adds visual effects, such as **dissolves** and **wipes,** and provides many other functions. **Digital video effects (DVE)** "moves" are also included at this point with special-effects. Titles are also added, using a character generator, and music is typically inserted at this point as well.

Nonlinear Editing

As previously mentioned, nonlinear editing systems are quickly making traditional systems obsolete. In the nonlinear world, recorded footage is digitized and input into a computer system such as the Avid Express, Adobe Premiere, or Final Cut Pro. Once entered, the images and sound become digital information capable of being cut, pasted, moved, slowed down, sped up, textured, or any number of other special effects virtually at the click of a mouse. Sound is also handled digitally in nonlinear editing. Graphics can be easily digitized and input, and titles can be created.

All of this technological advancement means that, with today's high-quality systems, online and offline editing can be carried out in a nonlinear fashion as one event. When completed, the program is simply output to the predetermined master format, from which the distribution copies will be struck.

Nonlinear editing has revolutionized the world of media editing, and its impact is continually becoming more profound.

Audio "Sweetening"

In some programs, more than just simple music insertions are required. In some cases, the audio recordings must be enhanced or changed, which is called **audio sweetening. Sound effects** may also be required, as may

tonal adjustments to certain audio recordings. This would be the case, for instance, when one part of a scene includes **voiceover (VO)** dialogue that is supposed to be the distant end of a telephone conversation. To make this conversation sound real, the "distant" voice, which was recorded in the field similar to all other sound segments, is equalized or "EQ'd" to give it the distinct, hollow tone of someone speaking on a telephone.

The Traditional Laydown and Layback

When such sweetening is required, the audio tracks from the edited master of the program created in the online edit must be "laid down" onto a special multitrack audiotape, using an audio recorder. All recorded sounds are then enhanced using multiple channels and an assortment of sound manipulation gear, including a multitrack audio board. Finally, the various enhanced recordings are "mixed down," typically to two tracks—one with narration and dialogue and the other with music and effects.

Once this sweetening is accomplished, the mixed-down audio tracks are "laid back" onto the original edited master of the program in sync with the pictures. At this point, the show is nearly complete.

Nonlinear Audio Sweetening

As with visual image editing, nonlinear audio sweetening systems are also revolutionizing the production process. In the nonlinear world, sound files can simply be sent from computer to computer, changed, adjusted, mixed, and sent back to the original nonlinear system. They can also be cut and pasted easily, eliminating the need for the laydown and layback process.

Duplication/Distribution

As a final step, a duplication master or **"dupe master"** is created, on which audio tracks are mixed a final time or "summed" to one or two channels. This dupe master is then used to make the distribution copies that are handed to the client for employee showings.

5 Production People

As you've no doubt gathered, the television production process is not a simple one. On the contrary, it is a highly complicated and exacting profession that requires skilled creative and technical craftspeople.

The following pages contain a listing of the professionals who are involved in this process and a brief description of the role each plays. Since we have already discussed the four key creative "drivers" of the process—writers, producers, directors, and clients—we will now focus on those people who work in support functions.

THE LINE PRODUCER

A line producer might also be described as a producer's representative. He or she typically manages all aspects of a shoot, its preparation, and sometimes even postproduction when the producer is too busy to be involved in a hands-on manner. Line producers are rare in corporate media, but they are required on occasion, especially on shoots that are very large, geographically dispersed, or that continue for an extended period.

THE PRODUCTION MANAGER

Similar to a line producer, a production manager oversees one or a number of shoots. The production manager differs from the line producer in that he or she is typically responsible for scheduling resources, such as equipment, locations, crew, and props, with less emphasis on the creative/executive aspect, or what is sometimes called the "above the line" side of the production. Also, production managers leave the project after production and have no involvement in postproduction.

THE ASSISTANT DIRECTOR (AD)

The AD is the director's right-hand person. He or she helps arrange all aspects of preproduction and coordinates client, crew, and talent on location or in the studio. In corporate productions, the AD usually also takes script notes and makes video shot logs. In preproduction, the AD relieves the director of many tasks, allowing him or her to focus on script interpretation, talent selection and rehearsal, location selection, scheduling, and handling of client and producer relationships.

THE PRODUCTION ASSISTANT (PA)

The PA works for the AD, line producer, production manager, or director. The PA handles telephone calls, equipment rentals, prop deliveries, mail, facsimiles, personal pickups and deliveries, and many other important production details. The PA may also work for the producer at times, doing filing or runner-type activities.

THE DIRECTOR OF PHOTOGRAPHY (DP) OR VIDEOGRAPHER

The DP is responsible to the producer or director for the entire visual look of the program, including all camera work and lighting. The DP is the director's closest aesthetic ally because he or she understands what the director is attempting to achieve visually and uses photographic or videographic skills to help achieve this end. On simple programs consisting of interviews and documentation-type footage, the producer or director often operates the camera and no DP is required.

THE CAMERA OPERATOR

The camera operator operates a camera but is not responsible for lighting. On corporate location shoots, the DP usually also operates the single camera. On multicamera studio shoots, the DP works one camera and camera operators work the others.

THE GAFFER

The gaffer is an electrician. He or she is the DP's main assistant. The gaffer sets up lights, checks amperage loads, verifies fuses and breakers, connects generator cables, and basically provides constant lighting and electrical expertise. On corporate shoots, gaffers also frequently act as camera assistants, "pulling focus" when necessary, changing batteries, setting up tripods, and attaching other accessories.

THE GRIP

The grip is a general but skilled labor assistant. He or she works mainly for the gaffer by carrying cables and setting up **"C" stands, flags, silks,** and **nets.** The grip also loads and unloads tools and equipment during setups and strikes. A dolly grip pushes or pulls the dolly on which the DP and sometimes an assistant ride.

THE SOUND RECORDIST/MIXER

This person is responsible to the director for all sound recordings made on the program. The sound recordist, or audio person, suggests the proper mics and placement and ensures that the recorded pieces are of the best quality and consistency under the circumstances. He or she also operates a mixer to ensure that sound levels are consistent in terms of tone and volume.

THE AUDIO BOOM OPERATOR

The audio boom operator is the sound recordist's assistant. He or she attaches the mics or holds them on a boom in position during recordings. He or she may also operate a mixer and maintains mics and batteries to ensure that they are in good working order when needed.

THE FLOOR MANAGER OR STAGE MANAGER

On studio shoots, when several cameras and a number of actors and crew members are working in unison, a coordinator is needed to act as the director's voice on the studio floor. The floor manager carries out this responsibility. At the director's request, he or she cues talent, gives start and stop signals, and handles any general questions or problems that may arise during production.

TECHNICAL DIRECTOR (TD)

Multicamera shoots require a video switcher to instantly change the various sources being fed to the production recorder and to the air, in the case of live broadcasts. The TD typically sits at the director's side in the control room to carry out this function. Using the switcher, the TD can cut or dissolve between sources at the director's command. He or she can also "switch in" special effects such as graphic elements and layered insets over the primary source.

VIDEOTAPE RECORDER OPERATOR (TAPE OP)

Multiple VTRs are often required on live or live-to-tape shoots. When this is the case, a **tape op** manages these VTRs and the material loaded and unloaded from them. As an example, a shoot may call for playback of a roll-in tape at a certain point. The tape op loads that tape in advance and cues it up to the spot where the director can "take it" to the air. The tape op also manages the single or multiple VTRs on which the program is being recorded.

VIDEO CONTROL ENGINEER (VC)

The video control engineer monitors the color and luminance qualities of various sources before they are "taken" by the director. This is sometimes called "shading." As an example, a camera about to be taken to the air may have a different "look" than the one currently on the air. The VC color corrects the new signal so the images match, creating a seamless transition. The same type of correction is sometimes required for incoming signals from roll-in VTRs.

ENGINEER IN CHARGE (EIC)

The **engineer in charge (EIC)** provides technical support on location shoots. He or she typically operates waveform and video monitors, plugs in video and audio cables, operates non-camcorder VTRs if they are required, and generally ensures that all electronic elements of the production are handled properly. With the advent of camcorders and digital video, the EIC position is becoming much less prevalent.

TELEPROMPTER OPERATOR

A **teleprompter** is a word processing unit that projects a host's narration onto a translucent pane of glass mounted over the camera's lens. The host can thus appear to be speaking from memory as he or she looks directly into the camera and reads the lines. The teleprompter operator usually inputs the script text and controls its scrolling action in production, thus ensuring that the words the host is reading move along at the proper pace.

THE MAKEUP ARTIST

Makeup artists are not used on many corporate shoots. They are hired from time to time, however, especially when the production involves a number of actors, celebrities, or key executives such as the company president. In corporate programs, makeup is often handled by the actors themselves, and minor touchups are taken care of by the floor manager, AD, or PA.

GRAPHIC ARTIST

Computer animation and still graphic images are developed by the graphic artist. These images are most often developed in preproduction or postproduction, but a graphic artist is sometimes required in live productions as well when the images created need quick revision or updating before going on the air.

THE OFFLINE EDITOR

The offline editor works closely with the director immediately following production. He or she uses workprints of the footage to create a rough cut of the program. The director may sit in on these edit sessions to verify that the scenes are playing out as he or she had envisioned. In some corporate situations, the director and producer may sit with the offline editor at the outset of the edit session, providing specific instructions and then allowing him or her to independently edit portions of the show. The offline editor's work is periodically reviewed, and changes are made as needed. As mentioned earlier, with the emergence of digital, nonlinear editing systems, the term "offline" is quickly becoming obsolete. This means the job of the offline editor is being combined with that of the online editor.

THE ONLINE EDITOR

The online editor performs the final edit. When he or she begins work on a project, most of the aesthetic decisions relating to composition, pace, and visual continuity have been made. The online editor, however, adds the final touches, which often enhance the show greatly. These touches include dissolves, wipes, fades, sound effects, music, titles, and digital video effects (DVE).

THE AUDIO SWEETENING ENGINEER

The audio sweetening engineer or postaudio engineer is skilled at incorporating and manipulating multiple sound elements into an existing soundtrack. He or she is also skilled at mixing down work onto only one or two audio channels. This position adds music, sound effects, and various enhancements to the existing recorded sound to enrich the program's final soundtrack.

So, we've met the people who make media productions possible, and briefly explored their professional skills. Before we look in much greater detail at something mentioned earlier—how all these people come together in the making of a corporate media program—let's briefly summarize.

PART ONE SUMMARY

Corporate media production has evolved from the old days of film and projectors to television screens and computer monitors. That evolution continues. The key players are writers, producers, directors, and clients. The media groups they operate in range from large studio facilities to small one-person shops. In many instances, one individual wears several hats in the corporate media world. Regardless of the number of jobs they must perform, each time they change hats, they must display the skills required to do an effective job in that particular discipline.

As someone who is perhaps just entering the field of corporate media, or hoping to change your place in it, it might be wise to ask yourself where you would fit best. In other words, what "hats" do you prefer to wear and what are your ultimate career aspirations? And how would you most prefer to operate—as a jack-of-all-trades in a small shop or as a person with one primary set of skills in a larger arena? Or, do jobs such as Assistant Director, Audio Recordist, or Videographer sound most attractive to you? As you continue to read and study, this type of self-analysis will help you focus on the skills that you will need most to succeed.

The following Web sites may offer you additional assistance:

www.filmworkshops.com

www.videouniversity.com

www.Videomaker.com

directory.google.com/Top/Arts/Video/Training/

www.TheWorkshops.com

www.AFI.com

www.Creativecow.net

Sony training Institute: (http:gsscsel.sony.com/professional/training/index)

www.ITVA.org (International Television Association/mci-a)

www.BHUSA.com

www.Digitalmedianet.com (has streamline newsletter) also, www.dmforums. com

http://www.dmnnewsletter.com/cgi-bin/sub_news_main.cgi

www.411publilshing.com

www.sag.com

www.aftra.com

part two

The Script

6

The Program Needs Analysis

"This is Ellen Prescott in Safety. We've got a real problem that we need some help on—back injuries. How bad a problem? During the past year we figure the company has lost over $90,000 in direct medical expenses due to back problems—and that doesn't count the productivity loss. We need to get a video out to these people to educate them on how to lift the right way and maybe some steps on how to take care of their backs."

The request is a typical one. In this case, it takes the form of a phone call from a prospective client. The request could just as easily be a letter, a memo, or a note to call someone in the training or public affairs department. The request can come in any number of ways; the point is that it usually comes from someone who needs help communicating a message and sees videotape or some other form of visual media as the perfect solution.

In many cases, a media program does indeed turn out to be the best tool for the job. For the moment, however, let's assume it's not, but the program is made anyway.

THE SCENARIO OF THE UNNEEDED MEDIA PROGRAM

The scenario of the unneeded program usually goes something like this. A tape or CD is produced at a cost of hundreds or even thousands of times the cost of solving the problem in some simpler form. The production doesn't do what it was really intended to do because it wasn't the right tool for the job in the first

place. It may be used a little at first, but then it is shelved forever. The client's objective is met in one sense because he or she took some action to try to solve the problem, but the trouble persists.

And what about the corporate media department that produced it? It won't be long before key executives begin to ask a very good question: What are numerous programs doing sitting on shelves, costing significant money to produce, when many of the communication problems in the company are going unsolved?

How does a producer avoid this pitfall and, at the same time, obtain the information needed to design a successfully targeted program? By taking the first logical step in producing a corporate program: developing a simple front-end analysis—a brief, highly focused look at the basics of what the client wants to accomplish, who the audience is, how the program will be used, and whether it will really benefit the department and the company as a whole.

In other words, the producer sets up an initial client meeting and, from the facts gathered in that meeting, develops a document called a program needs analysis (PNA).

PROGRAM DESIGN

In order to write the PNA and use it effectively, a producer must first understand how design information helps guide program development. Program design information has very little relationship to content, and it is not conceptual or visual in nature. It is the raw material from which the design of a program is molded, such as the following:

- The basic *problem* or need behind the program
- The program *objectives*
- An *audience analysis*
- Proposed *utilization* of the program

THE PROBLEM OR NEED

This is the justification for making the program. It also acts as a basic conflict that the program objectives (we'll discuss these in a moment) are meant to resolve. A typical problem statement for a new program dealing with vehicle-backing procedures, for instance, might be written in a needs analysis.

Problem

Employees who drive company vehicles do not understand safe backing procedures. As a result, $120,000 was lost last year in accident claims.

This problem is a major one for the organization, and it brings to light a basic *need:* the requirement to teach employees how to back their vehicles safely.

This problem (sometimes referred to as the *purpose*) should be one of the first topics of discussion between the client and the producer. If, in these initial discussions, a producer begins to sense that a real problem or need does *not* exist, there's a good chance he or she shouldn't be making a videotape or film in the first place.

OBJECTIVES

These are a series of statements that, if accomplished, will help solve the established problem and thus meet the client's need. There are several types of objectives. The two most common are instructional objectives and motivational objectives.

Instructional Objectives

Instructional objectives establish benchmarks for how well a media program *teaches* employees something. This might be a skill, such as customer handling or a procedure such as how to properly process service orders. To be most effective, instructional objectives should be stated so that the viewer of the program could actually be *tested* on how well they were met. For instance,

Objective

Having viewed the proposed videotape program, audience members will be able to state the three company-approved backing rules, as follows:

1. Do not back up unless absolutely necessary.
2. Exit the vehicle and physically check the rear before backing.
3. Honk before backing the vehicle.

These objectives state very specific results the client hopes to elicit from its audience. They are sometimes called *behavioral* objectives because they set up a predictable behavior an audience member should be able to carry out, having seen the program. The key behavioral phrase in this objective is "be able to *state*." Objectives such as this one make the effectiveness of a film or videotape program very measurable. If this objective is agreed upon and 90% of the people who view this program can actually state the three points, then the program is a success.

By contrast, our objective might have read

Objective

Having viewed this program, audience members will have greatly improved their backing ability.

This objective is very vague because of the phrase "will have *improved*." How would we know if the film or videotape actually accomplished this objective? What exactly is an improvement? Could we give a backing test to every employee in the company? At a great deal of expense, we probably could. Even if we did, however, and they all backed their vehicles wonderfully, how could we be sure that the *program* actually improved their skills?

Although this type of semantic scrutiny may seem like splitting hairs, a producer learns very quickly that when it comes to instructional objectives, specific agreement on what the program will accomplish is extremely important. This agreement should be made between the producer, the client, and any other key decision makers involved in the production. Similar to the problem information, instructional objectives should be discussed early in the research process.

Motivational Objectives

Motivational objectives can be stated less specifically because they do not require a measurable behavioral response from the audience. For example,

Objective
Having viewed the proposed program, audience members will feel very positive about the company's new product line.

Creating a positive feeling may be a very important objective of your program. If employees "feel very positive," however, we could not really test them in terms of any specific behavior. Feeling positive is a much more personal and general state that the employer hopes will manifest itself in future attitudes and the sales figures of the new product line.

Mixing Objectives

Media programs often have both kinds of objectives. Perhaps a client is attempting to accomplish the following:

Objective
Having viewed the proposed program, audience members will be able to

Primary
Demonstrate the three sales techniques used to inform customers about the new Futura II, as follows:

1. Inquire with tact.
2. Overcome objections.
3. Confirm a sales call.

Secondary
4. Feel positive about meeting this quarter's sales quota for the Futura II.

In this case, the instructional (primary) objective requires that audience members be able to *demonstrate* a behavior sequence. The motivational (secondary) objective requires that they *feel positive* about the prospect of selling the product. If both objectives are accomplished, the audience will be well equipped to kick off a very successful sales campaign on this product.

AUDIENCE ANALYSIS

This may well be the most critical factor in the success of a script. To write an effective program, a writer must know exactly who will be expected to perform those objectives just established. He or she must also know a good deal about this audience. Audience analysis often falls into the following five general categories:

1. Size/discipline
2. Demographics
3. Attitudes
4. Needs/interest
5. Knowledge level

Here are a few examples of how an audience analysis might be written in a PNA. As you read through them, ask yourself how they could influence the type of script a writer might develop.

Audience Size/Discipline
This audience is made up of approximately 900 company truck drivers.

Audience Demographics
Audience members are roughly 95% male. Most are between 30 and 50 years of age and have considerable seniority with the company. Approximately 5% of audience members have college degrees; 90% have high school diplomas or equivalent. Most audience members are from the lower end of the middle-income bracket.

Audience Attitudes
Company truck drivers have overall positive attitudes toward the company, but they also feel they are experts in their craft, and thus are generally above any instruction on how to drive properly. Their initial attitudes toward a program on backing procedures will probably be somewhat negative or at best viewed as a waste of their time. In addition, most drivers will probably feel that following the company's new parking rules, which include exiting the truck to check the rear, will be time-consuming and unnecessary.

Audience Needs/Interest
Initially, audience members will see little need for this program; nor will they have much interest in it. They would argue that the real need is to educate warehouse employees on how to park their carts and place their containers so that they do not become unseen obstacles in large truck-parking ramp areas. In fact, when really nailed down, many audience members say that warehouse employees should simply not be allowed to park or leave containers anywhere near trucking areas.

Audience Knowledge Level
Audience members are very knowledgeable about driving and parking trucks. Most have been at their jobs

for a minimum of 5 years. What they will *not* be aware of is the newest data, which indicate that 99% of backing accidents could be avoided simply by exiting the vehicle and checking to the rear. They will also be unaware of the recent monetary impact backing accidents have had on the company and the equation that suggests that the time spent by drivers following the new rules will equate to far less than the current accident costs.

Many facts here would affect the design of a script. For instance, if the audience is made up of middle-aged truck drivers who are 95% male, we probably would *not* want a female narrator or hostess in this case.

If the drivers' attitude toward exiting the trucks is a main negative point, this part of the script deserves special consideration. It would probably not be a good idea to show a role-play of this topic because actors agreeably going through the motions of doing the job according to an unpopular company rule would probably get a healthy round of chuckles and jeers. The example would have little if any credibility with this audience. What might have credibility, however, is attention to two other factors: (1) their lack of knowledge about how much backing accidents have cost and (2) the equation that says checking is cheaper than paying the damages. These may not be popular ideas, but they're credible and they make sense.

Other factors in this audience analysis that would affect script design are the audience's

> Education: Would audience members best identify with an executive or blue-collar approach? A blue-collar slant would probably work better.
>
> Age: Would very young actors or interviewees be as effective as those in the more mature age range of the audience? It's doubtful.
>
> Social status: Would a story or setting in a rich, upper-class neighborhood work in this situation as well as one set in a middle-class blue collar neighborhood? Probably not.

The truck drivers' seniority, job knowledge, and animosity toward warehouse employees are among the additional factors the scriptwriter should seriously consider.

Multiple Audiences

It is generally not a good idea to produce one program for two or more totally different types of audiences. For instance, you would not design a program on cost-control methods in the same way for both assembly-line

technicians and senior executives. These two audiences view cost controls from very different perspectives.

A program will, however, occasionally be aimed at two similar types of audiences. For example, you might produce a single program on cost-control methods for technicians and their supervisors because both probably view the subject from very similar perspectives. When this happens, it is often a good idea to designate one audience as primary and one as secondary. Both audiences then require a complete audience analysis.

In the case just stated, the audience analysis might start out with the audience size and discipline as follows:

Primary
This audience consists of 750 auto assembly-line technicians.

Secondary
This audience consists of the 57 assembly supervisors who oversee the primary audience.

Each of the other audience categories would also be divided in this way. Objectives are also established individually for multiple audiences. Thus, the client would still be able to accurately predict what the two different types of employees would gain from the program. For instance,

Objectives
Having viewed the proposed program, audience members will be able to

Primary audience
State two ways they can control costs.

1. by following attendance policies
2. by following assembly-line efficiency procedures

Secondary audience
State why attendance policies and efficiency procedures are critical cost savers, as follows.

1. Because when adhered to, these policies have been shown to increase productivity to maximum levels.

UTILIZATION

Utilization of the program—that is, how it will be shown—also influences the way the script should be written. Consider the following two utilization statements and their impact on your script.

Utilization
This program will be utilized as a specific segment of a company course on safe driving. A company instructor

will administer the course and will provide the introduction to the program, as well as discussion before and after the program on the subject of backing. Students will also receive a course workbook that includes descriptive artwork showing the new backing procedures.

Utilization

Drivers will utilize this program on a stand-alone basis in the field. The program will be viewed in yard coffee rooms following the employee's shift. Each employee will be required to view the program and then pass the videotape on to another employee.

Would a program shown as part of a formal training course, with considerable support in terms of an instructor and workbooks, be written in the same manner as one to be viewed by truckers at the end of their shifts on an honor basis? Absolutely not.

The first type of utilization would call for a program with a minimal number of facts because an instructor and the workbook would also be there to provide information. In fact, this program might not even need an introduction, title, open, close, and so on. It might simply be a series of **vignettes** or interviews with authorities in the field expounding on the amount of insurance and material loss businesses must absorb because drivers don't exit their trucks before they back up. In this case, the instructor would provide the opening, the closing, and the discussion; written material and artwork would provide additional facts.

With the second type of utilization, the program had better include an open, and it had better be a catchy one. If drivers who don't really like the idea of the program in the first place are expected to watch and learn from it after a full day's work when they're hungry, tired, and eager to get home, something on the screen had better catch their attention quickly. Also, because no other type of support material will be provided, this version of the program must include a good deal more information.

INTERACTIVE DESIGN

Program design is intended to assure that the media presentation ultimately produced will meet the needs of its audience and accomplish a predetermined set of objectives. But an additional design step must be undertaken when the program will be interactive, for instance in the case of an interactive CD-ROM or on-line, streaming media training program.

Interactivity means audience members have the ability to interact with, and alter the presentation of the program, based on any number of factors. If an employee viewing an interactive CD-ROM on the topic of sales skills, for instance, would like more information in a certain content area, he or she may be able to stop the presentation at any time and temporarily "branch" away from the main program. On-line programs may offer the same option. Perhaps the employee is interested in a definition of the phrase "consultative selling skills." Many CD-ROM programs contain a glossary for just this type of need. So, in order to make the branch, the employee might click on a "Stop" icon and then on an icon labeled "Glossary." Once in the glossary, he or she might be required to make additional branches to get to the desired definition. Having found and reviewed the definition, the employee would then branch back into the main program and continue.

In another instance, having completed viewing a specific on-line module, the employee might be automatically branched to a competency test. If he or she inputs the required number of correct answers, the result would be an automatic branch to the next program module to continue training. If the employee fails the test, however, he or she may be automatically branched back to the previous module to view it a second time and repeat the test.

The ability to "navigate" to and from these various activities requires an *interactive design* that integrates the script with a custom set of computer commands. Interactive design uses software "authoring tools" to integrate these commands in concert with the types of *program design* topics we have covered.

For example, if one main objective in a program design requires that an employee be able to state the three steps involved in successfully greeting a customer, an interactive program would no doubt contain a test to verify that the employee can, in fact, accomplish this task. Thus, having completed an interactive design as well as a program design, the producers would know at an early stage that a branching sequence would be required at this point in the program.

With this knowledge, the producers could then design or author the software portion of the program to work seamlessly with the content. The authoring process might be an in-house activity carried out by an employee assigned to this type of interactive design work, or it might be assigned to an outside firm whose specialty is interfacing with corporate media departments in this area. In either case, the interactive designer would work closely with the writer throughout the design and scriptwriting process.

DESIGN SUMMARY

Design research allows the producer to obtain valuable program, and in some cases, interactive information. These basic "noncontent" facts, when combined with certain other factors we will discuss shortly, act as a solid program foundation that allows a producer and a writer to customize the most effective script for the audience being addressed. As previously mentioned, this information should be obtained early in the script development process, beginning with the first client meeting.

A COMPLETE PROGRAM NEEDS ANALYSIS

The following PNA is one final form design research can take. In different companies, it may take different forms. It may be more or less extensive, getting into areas such as in-depth cost analysis, visualization, or long- and short-term company goals.

Whatever the situation, design research is an essential part of the scriptwriting process, and it should be carried out on every script developed by the media department.

PROGRAM NEEDS ANALYSIS

PRODUCTION NUMBER   PP-8910

DATE NOVEMBER 27, 2001

WORKING TITLE   WIN THE CONNECTION

SUBJECT   EMPLOYEE SALES REFERRAL PROGRAM

*CLIENT   RITA WALLACE, SALES SUPPORT MGR., 117 6TH, LOS ANGELES, CA
        91301 2908/500, 213/555-1456, rwall@nocio.com*

*OTHER APPROVALS   JILLY VERNA, KLEIN & ASSOC., FOUR BOSTON FORUM,
                BOSTON, MASSACHUSETTS 06904, 203/555-3872,
                IVERA.BA.COM*

*   TIM ANDERS, PUB. AFFAIRS DIR., 117 6TH,
                LOS ANGELES, CA 91301 3110/500, 805/555-7150,
                atimill@nocio.com*

*CONTENT EXPERTS   JOHN JENNINGS, SALES SUPPORT MGR., 117 6TH,
                LOS ANGELES, CA 91301 2908B/500, 555-6145,
                john@nocio.com*

FYI COPIES   N/A

DEADLINE   February 4, 1999

COST/BENEFITS/IMPACT

The program outlined in this PNA will cost approximately $42,000 to produce. When completed, it will be used as a motivational session starter for kickoff presentations of the Win the Connection Program at NuComm, Inc.

Win the Connection has the potential to help produce millions of dollars in revenue for NuComm. Because the videotape described in this proposal will in essence "set the stage" for Win the Connection, it will be a critical factor in determining how employees view the program and how profitable it may become.

PROBLEM

Employees in NuComm are not aware of the Win the Connection program or the exciting benefits it has to offer.

BACKGROUND

Win the Connection was previously implemented at NuComm as a referral program called Sell One Service. As most employees will remember, Sell One Service was canceled in California approximately two years ago. The concept was continued, however, in several other NuComm companies, and it is with the benefit of those experiences that Win the Connection is now being piloted in California.

RELATIONSHIP TO COMPANY GOALS

Because Win the Connection is a companywide program, providing a videotape to support it is in keeping with the company's goals. In addition, company goal #4 specifically calls for NuComm to "explore new methods of generating revenue." Win the Connection certainly fits this definition.

AUDIENCE

Primary: All NuComm craft employees
Size/Discipline: Approximately 12,000

AUDIENCE DEMOGRAPHICS

Most audience members are experienced NuComm employees. All have high school educations and roughly 25% have college degrees. The male-to-female split is approximately 50-50 and the ethnic mix is typical for Southern California, mostly Caucasian, African-American, Hispanic, and Asian-Pacific employees.

AUDIENCE INTEREST/NEED

Employees interested in exciting prizes and luxury vacations will see a personal need for the Win the Connection program. Other audience members will at least have an initial interest in Win the Connection. Whether or not that interest turns into open support will probably depend on the following two factors: (1) whether employees view the program as viable and (2) whether they feel there is definite reward in it for them. This videotape program will attempt to capitalize on these two factors to excite and motivate employees.

AUDIENCE KNOWLEDGE/EXPERIENCE

Many audience members will have had brief contact with the Sell One Service program, and thus will be familiar with its general workings. Details of Win the Connection will be very similar and will be provided by the live presenter. The videotape, however, may provide a basic overview.

AUDIENCE ATTITUDES

Audience attitude is a key factor in the success of Win the Connection. Sales referral programs similar to this one have sometimes carried a negative image because selling seems to be uncomfortable for many employees. In addition, the return for effort in some programs has been perceived as minimal. For these reasons, the first impression employees get of Win the Connection should be positive, fun, and exciting. In addition, acknowledging the fact that Sell One Service was not successful but that we have learned from that experience should help establish credibility. The substantial prizes available through Win the Connection should also have a positive influence on audience attitudes, as should the simplicity and ease of the referral process.

OBJECTIVES

Having viewed the proposed program, audience members will

(Continued)

- Be able to define Win the Connection as an employee sales referral program using an 800 telephone number system.
- Be able to state that the potential for big winnings exists with Win the Connection.
- Be motivated to hear more about the details of Win the Connection from the live presenter.

NOTE: In addition to the stated objectives, top executive support for Win the Connection must also be demonstrated in this program.

DISTRIBUTION

The distribution format and number of copies will be discussed as production moves forward on this project.

UTILIZATION

All copies of this program will be utilized by local managers trained as live presenters. The presenters will follow tape viewings with detailed handout information on the workings of Win the Connection and the paperwork and phone numbers needed to actually start making referrals.

EVALUATION

This program will be evaluated with the use of a brief questionnaire handed out by the live presenter.

COMMENTARY

The initial information contained in this company's PNA format is a series of basic facts about the project, such as dates, project number, clients, and approvals. This information is part of the document because the PNA is one of the handiest places to record this information for easy future reference.

The cost/benefits/impact is another important area taken into account on every media project produced in this company. The producers are always required to state an initial budget figure and a projection of what that investment will "buy back" for the company.

In this case, the budget figure was provided by the client and the buy back is stated in very general terms that do not project a specific monetary return as a result of the tape. Instead, it mentions that the tape will be the first exposure employees will have to Win the Connection, and therefore a critical factor in how much of those "millions of dollars in revenues" will result from their participation.

In some cases, a producer might require that a very specific cost/benefits/impact section be included. If so, an analysis must be done of how much it would cost employees to get the same information they will gain

from the videotape in other ways, such as print material, live presenters, or audiotapes. A total cost is then compared against the cost of the videotape along with a judgment of each other method's effectiveness.

As an example, the management personnel running the Win the Connection program might have determined that another way to achieve the excitement they were after would have been through the use of a live performance of some sort. The cost of this performance would have included the cost of the performers' time and their meals, travel, hotel, and so on as they made their way around the company.

In addition to cost, other elements to be considered would have been time and effectiveness. With the videotape, for example, copies could be distributed to every work location, and, using locally drafted presenters, everyone could get the same message in a very short period. In the case of traveling performances, the "roll-out" or startup of the project would require more time (probably weeks) for the performers to visit each operation.

Whatever the math and other considerations, the reason for this part of the analysis is to be sure that the cost of the videotape program is worth the investment and that the same result cannot be achieved through another method.

The problem statement in this PNA is a single sentence stating the overall purpose of the program. As we've discussed, this problem-oriented way of stating the purpose establishes the need for the videotape to provide a solution to the problem.

An interesting political factor emerged in developing the background section of this PNA. The program had been previously tried in the company two years earlier under another name, Sell One Service. This first attempt had failed and left a bitter taste in employees' mouths. This type of information would be important in the development of any program because it could have an effect on audience perceptions. As it turned out, the client wanted the previous failure included in the PNA, but she made it clear that she *didn't* want it as a point of focus. Instead, she wanted to simply acknowledge the old program briefly and then get to the positive business of kicking off the new program. "Acknowledge the negative but *don't* dwell on it" is a common way many corporate programs deal with politically uncomfortable or controversial issues.

As it turns out, although it was important information, this project took a direction that didn't even need to acknowledge Sell One Service.

The audience size for this program was large. This factor is often considered in determining the amount of money that should be invested in a project. Had the total audience size been 100 instead of 12,000, the potential revenues generated by Win the Connection would have been well below the "millions" mark. In that case, I doubt we would have gotten the budget to do the show as it was eventually written.

Audience demographics, interest, and attitudes explore some of the critical human issues that eventually helped dictate this program's direction. In working through this information and the objectives, we realized at the outset that simply making the new Win the Connection program appear to be fun, exciting, and profitable could get it off to a successful start.

The objectives in this PNA were each developed for important reasons. First, the client felt that we didn't have to impart a great deal of information (that would be done by a presenter and written material), but that the viewers should at least know what type of sales program we were presenting, generally how it worked, and the basis for calling in referrals.

The second objective focuses on the "what's-in-it-for-me" aspect of the program. This element was important because, in this case, the prizes were a primary motivator.

Finally came the least specific but what developed into the most important objective of all. We all felt that if the tape accomplished nothing except stimulating genuine employee interest in and excitement for the Win the Connection program, it would be successful.

The first of these objectives is instructional. It is stated in terms of a specific viewer behavior: being able to define the Win the Connection program. The second objective is also specific and the third is very general or motivational. Although the expected viewer behavior is stated in a less specific way—"be motivated"—the motivation element was the key to the project's success.

Of the final sections in this analysis, the utilization is the most important. The fact that a live presenter was to accompany each showing and provide detailed written information coincided perfectly with the objectives and audience analysis. It meant we could keep the program short and write the script primarily as a motivational piece that included very little "hard" content. Our project could be fun and exciting, and we could leave the boring stuff for the presenter and the written handouts.

THE DECISION

Once the producer has developed the PNA, a decision must be made. Should a program be produced on the subject or not? Do the need and the characteristics of the project justify the time and expense required to produce a program? The answers to these questions depend on a number of factors. Following are a few questions the PNA should help answer:

Question Is the problem best solved with the help of a visual aid or could it be just as well done on paper?

Example Instruction on the numerous dial positions of a circuit analyzer would be just as well presented on paper because very little movement is involved that would require motion pictures, and the information is probably too detailed to retain after one viewing.

Question Is what the client wants achievable in visual media format or is it too detailed or complicated?

Example Instruction on a company expense policy with many facets or alternative actions would probably be too detailed and boring to present in a video program. It might work as an interactive CD-ROM in which the employee actually worked with the numbers, or it might be handled much cheaper as a print handout.

Question Is the time frame achievable? (The typical, fully designed and scripted corporate television program takes about two to three months to produce from start to finish.)

Example A fully designed and scripted program on customer relations is typically not a two-week project. An interview video or broadcast featuring the company president, however, could be done virtually overnight.

Question Is the subject matter changing or dated? Or will it remain "as is" long enough to justify the expense of the program?

Example If a program is to be produced on the rationale behind the development of a new work uniform, the uniform should be *finalized* in terms of colors, patches, ordering, and all other aspects *before* the message is committed to production. In addition, if the uniform design is experimental and may be phased out in a few months, the choice of a videotape or CD may be a mistake.

Question Generally speaking, does the importance of the subject and/or the audience size justify the expense of the production?

Example A program for 30 people on the subject of clocking in and out for coffee breaks would be a waste of money. On the other hand, if the work force is 10,000 people and the loss of productivity is costing the company *$800,000* per year, such a program would definitely be a good investment.

The answers to questions such as these can either confirm the need for your program or bring to light the reasons another method might be a better choice. Provided the answer is to move ahead with program development, the next step in the writing process is to consider the *facts* the program will based on. In other words, the content.

7

The Content Outline

Content information, similar to design information, is critical to the success of any media project. A writer cannot hope to write an effective script if he or she does not thoroughly understand the subject.

What's more likely to happen to the writer who does not do adequate content research is a very embarrassing script review meeting in which the client will begin to ask questions such as the following, for which the writer won't have answers:

"Why was the first part of the procedure included and not the second?"

"You did realize that next year the implementation changes, right?"

"I'm curious why none of the statistics we provided are in this section where they really count?"

"This part is a little too general, isn't it?"

Another, even worse, possibility is that these inaccuracies will get by the client, producer, and content experts and actually be recorded. When discovered after the fact, content errors can cost thousands of dollars to correct.

The single most important aspect of content research, then, is simply for the writer to be positive that he or she has a thorough understanding of the subject before trying to write about it. The writer achieves this important objective by acquiring the proper information and organizing it into a logical, easily understood structure.

ACQUIRING CONTENT INFORMATION

The writer will get most content information from clients, content experts, and written resources. The exchange of this information usually happens in meetings. In each of these meetings, the writer should explore several key questions that are the basis for all factual writing.

Who?

What?

When?

Where?

Why?

How?

Benefits/Drawbacks?

Although the subject matter and situation will dictate the actual questions, let's briefly run through some of the typical types of questions a writer might ask in each of these areas.

Who?

Who is implementing the project? Who is affected by it? Who will administer it? Who developed it? Who will be available to the audience to answer questions about it after the program is seen? Are these people experts on the subject? Are they qualified in the eyes of the audience? Are they popular or unpopular in the eyes of the audience? Where are they located?

What are their phone numbers? Should their input be absolute or subject to verification? How available are they?

What?

What exactly is your subject? How many parts or steps does it have? Is it complicated or simple? Can it be explained or demonstrated in one sitting, or must you go to a number of people and places to fit it all together? Is written, graphic, or other source material available on it? Where and when can you acquire it? Does it lend itself to visual presentation?

When?

When will it take place? Once it takes place, will it be permanent or temporary? Will it take place at the same time for all audience members? If not, what is the implementation schedule? How many phases are involved? Is the schedule final or subject to change? How might it be changed? When might it be changed? Will audience members have advance notice of change?

Where?

Where will (or does) it happen? Will it happen in the same place for all audience members? If there is more than one location, how many are there? If there is an implementation schedule, what is the order of the locations?

Why?

Why is it being done? Are the reasons documented? Are the reasons economical? Are the reasons critical to the company? Are the reasons popular or unpopular with the audience? Is the reasoning long or short term?

How?

How, exactly, does it work or happen? Are a number of steps involved? Can it be demonstrated? Is it complicated or simple? Is it done the same way by all employees? If not, how do the steps differ?

Benefits/Drawbacks?

What positive things will it do for audience members? What negative things will it do? Will audience members recognize the benefits or drawbacks? Are they short or long term? Are the benefits or drawbacks of major or minor importance to the audience? Are they of major or minor concern to the company?

INTERVIEW TECHNIQUES AND RESEARCH SOURCES

As we've established, interviews are often the primary means of acquiring both content and design information. The techniques used to conduct those interviews may vary, but several general techniques are helpful in most situations.

Use a Tape Recorder if Possible

Handwriting notes can be laborious and sketchy. Not only is the writer likely to miss facts, but he or she may also have a difficult time later piecing together the fragments of content that did manage to get written down. Using a portable tape recorder solves this problem. This device frees the writer to think about what is being said and to converse with the client, content expert, or producer. It also allows much more eye contact and interaction, which usually results in a warmer, more personal relationship. Later, the writer is free to absorb parts of it or the entire meeting, including many "tonal" qualities he or she might have missed in written notes.

The only time tape recorders should not be used is when they make the client uncomfortable. This happens occasionally when the subject that is being discussed or the frankness you've elicited from your client runs contrary to corporate policies or loyalties. As an example, if asked why he feels his department's safety statistics are lower than some other department's, a client's truthful answer may be, "Because my boss won't let me provide any safety training." He might be wary of saying this, however, with a tape recorder sitting in front of him.

The solution is to ask all clients at the beginning of a meeting if they have any objections to a tape recording strictly for content use. The writer might also mention that if they come to any part of the conversation the client would rather not have taped, the client need only gesture and the writer will be glad to simply turn it off. Follow this up by reiterating that the tape is strictly for your private, personal use as an alternative to taking notes.

Use Open-Ended Questions

Open-ended questions cannot be answered with a simple yes or no. An *open-ended* question forces a client or content expert to think about what he or she is saying. It also elicits an in-depth answer that often leads to other subjects or areas that may need exploration.

Some examples of open-ended questions, using our earlier example of the truck driver's parking program, might be the following:

"Tell me about how employees park now."

"I'm curious to hear more about how the $120,000 was actually lost."

"What are employees' feelings about getting out of their trucks to check to the rear?"

"What are employees' feelings about the company in general?"

Those same questions, posed in a *closed* manner, would look like this.

"Do employees park according to the current rules?"

"The $120,000 was lost in backing accidents, right?"

"I take it employees hate getting out of their trucks to check the rear?"

"Do employees like working here in general?"

The former series of questions would result in much meatier answers. They would also lead to diversions that might be helpful to the writer. For instance, when the client is responding to the open-ended version of the question on what employees think about getting out of their trucks, she might say something like the following:

Well, I think they feel it's basically a waste of their time. They all try to do a good job, and we're always emphasizing doing the job as quickly as possible, so they're usually in a hurry. They also happen to have very heavy routes at this time of year, so I guess their feelings are understandable.

As the client was saying this, the writer might have quickly noted two things: "in a hurry" and "heavy routes." Both seem to be legitimate reasons why the truck drivers would be against the new rule. As such, these points require more discussion later.

Guide the Discussion

A writer who has prepared in advance for a content meeting should have a good feel for what kind of infor-mation he or she wants and even the order in which he or she would like to get it. The writer could save some time, then, by guiding the discussion toward these areas. Again, he or she would do this by first taking brief notes as the client mentions those items and then by posing other open-ended questions such as: "I'm not sure if I understand . . ." or "Tell me more about . . ."

The only danger in guiding a discussion in this manner is that a writer could focus it too closely on what he or she is after and restrict the client from bringing up some important issue. To alleviate this problem, at various times during the meeting the client may be asked if he or she would like to add anything else.

Keep it Simple

Most clients and content experts know their subjects intimately. A company freelance writer may be hearing them for the first time. This situation can lead to confusion or an inadequate understanding of the subject in the writer's mind. If the writer doesn't understand something, he or she should be sure to say something like the following:

Excuse me. I'm sorry, but you just lost me completely. Let's go back through that slowly and very simply. I want you to take me through each step.

The result is usually a slower, simpler, much more understandable version of the topic.

Listen

This may seem obvious, but not listening is often the reason writers and other people walk away from conversations knowing only generalities about what they've just discussed. This may be all right for informal conversations but not for design or content research meetings.

The writer must focus on what is being said. He or she should also encourage the speaker to continue talking by nodding frequently and saying "aha," "I see," or "right, go on." Above all, try not to interrupt the client's train of thought. Effective listening is a skill that all good corporate writers work at continually.

Other Sources

Content research will often take a writer out of the conference room and into the field. He or she may need to accomplish some or all of the following: (1) interview employees to get their feelings about controversial subjects; (2) meet and talk to engineers who can describe why and how something is done; (3) attend training courses in which the program will be used or on which it is being based; (4) read company booklets, policies, or practices; (5) make calls, watch other films or videotapes, see demonstrations, take pictures, or make sketches; (6) hop on a plane for a different state to do any of these activities.

ORGANIZING CONTENT INFORMATION

The end result of all this factual acquisition is often a jumble of notes, tape recordings, copied pages, pictures, diagrams, tear sheets, and manuals. The next step is to organize this content information into a logical order. In other words, develop a content outline.

CONTENT OUTLINE FORMATS

Content outlines take different forms. For some projects, a simple series of bulleted statements briefly outlining the facts will do. For others, a formally researched and written document is required. The type of outline developed is based on the amount and complexity of information involved in the project and, most likely, the client's or producer's preference.

In many cases, the client or producer may not even require a content outline. Whether it is required of them or not, however, most writers find that developing some sort of outline makes the writing process smoother, faster, and more enjoyable. An outline provides a solid structure for what, up until then, has been a conglomerate of random information. This structure then becomes a road map for development of the treatment and script.

Informal

The informal outline may be a logically structured series of sentence fragments such as the following:

Sales decline—the basic problem

Sales are down since first quarter due to the following:

- Inactivity of sales force
- Product lag time
- Competitive insurance

Objective: Return sales to 1 million annually by attacking the following three problems in first quarter:

1. Fire up sales force with incentives.
2. Speed up product delivery.
3. Overpower competition with new promotional campaign.

Sales force incentive program will include the following:

- 35 trips to Hawaii
- $25,000 in bonuses
- Executive dinners
- Recognition plaques

Whether handwritten, typed on a computer, or spoken into a tape recorder, a script or treatment could be developed by following this outline point by point. The key is the logical arrangement of information; that is, placement of that information in an easy-to-follow structure. During script development, the writer would use these statements as thought-joggers. They would refer him or her to documents or other content sources for further elaboration.

Formal

Most formal outlines follow a similar structure, but they provide a good deal more meat. After writing a formal outline, a writer might not need to refer to anything but that document to further develop the project. Most formal outlines have the following three major parts:

The Introduction   is information used to gain audience interest and present an overview of the primary facts or general ideas. Often used as a hook or tease.

The Body   is an in-depth exploration of the facts and ideas first brought to light in the introduction.

The Conclusion   is one or a series of concluding ideas drawn from the exploration of the facts in the body.

These three different parts are linked together by a subtle repetition of the content information. The *introduction* gains audience interest and briefly presents the main facts. The *body* expands on the specific details of the main facts, and the *conclusion* makes certain deductions about the main facts. This method of organization—the order of presentation and the subtle repetition—makes the formal content outline an effective research tool. Information organized in this manner is easily absorbed and retained by an audience. In essence, audience members are told what they will learn (the introduction); the learning process then takes place (the body); finally, they are reminded what has just been covered (the conclusion).

If you haven't already, you may eventually hear this reinforcement-based learning process referred to in the following well-worn training phrase:

Tell 'em you're gonna tell 'em.

Tell 'em.

Tell 'em you told 'em.

Let's briefly look at three parts from what might be included in a typical formal content outline. We will assume the topic is still our truck drivers' backing program. Part of a content outline introduction on this topic might read something like this.

Because the accident costs are considerably more than those required to perform safe backing procedures, all company truck drivers should be trained on the backing procedures and be required to use them on a continuing basis.

The three steps involved in a safe backing procedure are as follows:

1. Not backing the vehicle unless it is absolutely necessary.
2. When backing is required, exiting the vehicle first and visibly checking to the rear.
3. After reentering the truck, briefly honking before actually backing up.

Studies have shown that performing this procedure takes only 22 seconds on average.

Later, the body of the same content outline would cover each of these three steps, as well as any other pertinent information, in much greater detail. The part of the body covering only the third step, for instance, might read like the following:

After reentering the truck, the driver should briefly honk before actually backing up. This step is required

as a final caution to assure that no one has stepped behind or parked behind the truck after the driver has checked the rear. The step involves the following:

1. Visually confirming that the truck is in neutral.
2. Executing a brief, half-second blast of the horn.
3. Waiting 2 to 3 more seconds while checking all rearview mirrors for any movement.

Step three is important on all occasions, but it becomes most important when time elapses between when the driver first checked to the rear and the actual back up. This lapse of time often occurs when a radio communication interrupts the three-step backing process.

The conclusion of this same content outline might then refer to this same step like the following:

Finally, step three becomes a measure of insurance. It guarantees that the backing path is still clear, even if the driver has taken the time to answer a radio request or has had some other distraction following the check to the rear.

If all content information were organized in this way, it would become a very clear, thorough, and logical means of presentation.

Other Structures

In addition the to the "tell 'em" outline structure, two others are commonly used in corporate programs. The "benefits bookends" structure focuses more on audience benefits in the open and close, thus "book ending" the subject. This method provides a more attractive tease to draw audience members into the program content and leave them on a memorable note. This type of structure might be used when a new company program is being launched in which the audience members may gain significant personal rewards. The "chronological order" structure simply lays the facts out in a logical, easily understood order, with no particular emphasis on either the open or the close. This type of structure is often used in how-to programs that explore a series of steps—for instance, how to safely operate a piece of equipment.

As with most other documents in this book, the content outline does not have to follow an exact format. What's more important is that it be simply and logically structured so that the average reader can follow it effortlessly.

If a well-organized content outline is then presented to the client and producer, it also provides an assurance that the writer has taken the time to fully explore the facts, gained a clear understanding of those facts, and was able to organize them in a way that will make them easily absorbed by the audience.

A FORMAL CONTENT OUTLINE

Writers generate different kinds of content outlines based on their own writing styles and the requirements of each project. A formal outline is more likely to be required on technical projects requiring in-depth research. This development is necessary because technical scripts also tend to require more organization and structure—the very things a content outline provides. There are exceptions, however, to this unspoken rule, and the Win the Connection project turned out to be one such case.

The following content outline was requested by the client, although such a project typically would not require one. Even in its early stages, this project was emerging as more of a motivational program than a content-based project. With development moving in this direction, an informal outline, briefly highlighting the content and establishing a solid structure, would probably have been sufficient. In this case, however, the client wanted to see a content outline as part of her development package for several valid reasons.

First, she really didn't know at this point (nor did I and the producer) exactly what direction the program would take. Second, this project was very important for this particular client. She had been given the job of re-inspiring a sales program that had previously failed. She was determined to make it work, and she wanted every base covered as thoroughly as possible as she implemented her plans, including being sure that the content of the videotape was accurate and well organized. Finally, the client's personality was detailed and orderly. She probably would have wanted a content outline written whether the project was critical or not and regardless of the type of show it was to become, just because she was that type of manager.

As content outlines go, this one is not extensively detailed. In places, for instance, it refers to other documents such as company bulletins for additional details. What it does contain, however, was more than enough information for this particular project.

As you read over this content outline, try to recall our discussions on content research and be aware of the way the information is structured. Also consider which of the facts were considered unimportant enough to have been left to other documents and which were considered necessary for inclusion here.

WIN THE CONNECTION
A Videotape Program Content Outline

I. INTRODUCTION
Win the Connection is an exciting employee sales referral program now being piloted in NuComm, Inc. The program includes an impressive list of valuable prizes, including jewelry, home electronics, tools, furniture, clothing, luxury vacations, and five 10-minute shopping sprees in a San Francisco warehouse packed with nearly *$9 million in prizes!*

II. HOW IT WORKS
"Sales by employee referral" is the key phrase in describing Win the Connection.

Employees of NuComm, Inc., have an immense network of friends, neighbors, and on-the-job contacts. Many times, although an employee may not realize it, one or more of these contacts has a communication problem that might be solved by a NuComm product or service.

Employees involved in the Win the Connection program help solve these problems and win exciting prizes at the same time. This goal is accomplished by mentioning the products and services NuComm offers to the many members of an employee's network of acquaintances. If the acquaintance would like to hear more about the product or service, the employee makes a simple referral to the Win the Connection headquarters by means of a toll-free telephone number.

When a Win the Connection referral results in a sale, the employee who made the referral is awarded points. Total points acquired then give the employee a number of possible ways to win valuable prizes.

The Win the Connection program will be conducted in ongoing 6-month phases. Phase One begins on March 1, 2002, and ends on September 1, 2002.

III. WAYS TO WIN

An employee can win standard prizes through Win the Connection in the following three ways: first three employees to 25,000 points, monthly drawings, and total acquired points.

1. First Three Employees to 25,000 Points

The first three employees to reach a 25,000-point total each month will be automatic two-way winners. Each of the three employees will:

A. Win any 25,000-point prize shown in the Win the Connection catalog.

B. Be included in ongoing monthly "First to 25,000" drawings. Drawings will begin when this milestone is reached by the first 10 employees.

2. Monthly Drawings

Monthly drawings will take place on an ongoing basis throughout the Win the Connection program. All employees with any sales during that month will be included in these drawings. Point totals have no bearing on the monthly drawings.

3. Total Points Acquired

Employees will be eligible to receive prizes of their choice based on total points acquired. Prize point values have been calculated based on list prices and are shown in the Win the Connection catalog. Prize value categories are based on an ascending 1000-point-per-segment structure. There are 100 segments in all, making the top prizes worth 100,000 points.

IV. WHO IS ELIGIBLE

All employees of NuComm, Inc., may participate in the Win the Connection program.

V. POINT VALUES

An earned point value system has been developed for Win the Connection. The earned point value means the amount of points acquired by the employee for the sale of a particular NuComm product or service. Earned point values have been based on two factors:

A. Total retail value of the product sold. This includes products that are direct sale items and produce no monthly revenues.

B. Retail value plus monthly 6-month revenue. This includes both products and services that have an initial retail value and earn a monthly revenue.

Note: Exact point values for each NuComm product are shown in the Win the Connection catalog and Division/Staff Bulletin #S-348.

VI. PRIZES/AWARDS

All prizes available in the Win the Connection program are shown in the Win the Connection catalog and Division/Staff Bulletin #S-348. The general prize categories are as follows:

home electronics
tools
furniture
family fashions
jewelry
hardware

Additional prize categories include luxury vacations.

the Caribbean
the Orient
Alaska
the Mediterranean

The grand prizes are five 10-minute warehouse run-throughs.

Note: A warehouse run-through is a 10-minute free run through the Klein & Associates awards warehouse in San Francisco, California. The five grand prize winners will receive a 2 × 5 × 3-foot loading cart and an assistant to help load items. Details are contained in Division/Staff Bulletin #S-348. Employees will receive company-paid transportation to and from the warehouse and all expenses for themselves and their spouses.

(Continued)

VII. SUMMARY

The Win the Connection employee sales referral program is an exciting and profitable way for employees to help NuComm, Inc., retain its dominance in the telecommunications marketplace.

Employees need only mention NuComm products and services to friends, acquaintances, and customers. A simple 800-number referral process then follows. Resulting sales have the potential to earn employees prizes such as home furnishings, entire wardrobes, or exotic vacations. Grand prize winners will be treated to an all-expenses-paid 10-minute shopping spree in the Klein & Associates warehouse in San Francisco, California.

COMMENTARY

The basic structure chosen for this content outline was a motivational version of the benefits bookends. It begins with an introduction that is actually a "hook" overview of the Win the Connection program. This information establishes the prize categories in the reader's mind and provides motivation to learn more.

Following the introduction comes the body of the outline, five sections centered around a series of key content points. Finally, the piece is wrapped up with a summary that makes a last pitch for the benefits of becoming involved in the Win the Connection program.

I decided that the body of the outline should present the factual aspects of Win the Connection in an order based on what key audience questions or reservations might be about the program: How Win the Connection worked, ways to win, who could be involved, how the point system was set up, and, the old standard, "what's in it for me." These key audience questions were acquired through audience and client interviews during the content research phase of the project. I was comfortable with this type of presentation because I felt that if the program did become an informational one, the type and order of the information could then be lifted almost straight out of the content outline for inclusion in the treatment and script.

As it turns out, the possibility of an informational program was wasted anxiety on my part. The outline was quickly approved by the producer and client, and I then moved ahead into what became a very non-informational program.

8

The Creative Concept

Once the design and content information are clearly focused in the writer's mind, a creative thought process can take place. Like a catalyst, this process will begin to combine the two types of information into something new: a creative visual concept.

PRINT VERSUS VISUAL (SHOWING VERSUS TELLING)

Before getting into the process of actually developing concepts, we should touch on the basic differences between writing for visual and print media. This distinction is important because the medium for which a writer conceptualizes may determine how he or she approaches a subject. In other words, concepts developed for books or magazine articles will often be expressed differently than those for scripts. Writing for print media differs from writing for visual media in much the same way that telling differs from showing.

Telling (Print-Oriented Writing)

When you tell a listener something, you explain the subject with words. Based solely on those word choices, you attempt to coax the listener into imagining what you are trying to communicate. If you tell in verbal form, you are talking. If you tell in written form, you are writing for print. In this case, the words themselves are both the means and the end. They are the critical factor because the recipient (the reader) will use only these elements to understand the information. Telling-oriented concepts, then, are based on precise word choices meant to stimulate a reader's imagination.

Showing (Visual Writing)

When expressing ideas in visual form, the writer does not concentrate so much on telling as on *showing*. Although the words remain important, aside from narration or dialogue, much of their importance is technical rather than artistic. Granted, they must communicate to the producer, director, and the client, but they will not be the final communication elements that spark a reader's imagination. Instead, the words in a script are simply a means to an end. They describe a series of sounds and motion pictures that will ultimately communicate the message, not to a reader, but to a *viewer*.

The critical issue for the scriptwriter becomes not, "What words can I write on the page?" but rather, "What pictures can I create on the screen?"

The ability to see a communication problem in these visual terms is a key trait of all successful scriptwriters. They first use this ability when conceptualizing and then on a much more detailed level when visualizing or "shaping" those concepts into actual script scenes.

THE CREATIVE VISUAL CONCEPT

Keeping this basic "show" instead of "tell" principle in mind as we cover the next few chapters, we can now move forward into the processes of concept thinking and visualization. As a first step, we could describe the creative script concept as:

> A creative visual idea based on all researched information that becomes the foundation for storyline, structure, and visualization.

Does this sound easy? Actually, it is a very simple process. Anyone can glance at a collection of facts and come up with numerous concepts. The tough part is coming up with effective concepts: visual ideas that will communicate the proper content in a way that will help meet the objectives established to solve the communication problem that created the need for a program in the first place.

TYPES OF CONCEPTS

The two basic types of concepts are program and segment. *Program concepts* are general in nature. They are usually single unifying ideas that provide an overall visual method of presenting a program. Some program concepts are:

Humorous Role-Play   A cab driver and his fare comically demonstrate the value of safe driving techniques on a whirlwind ride through the city.

Voiceover Narrator with Graphics   A voiceover narrator takes us through the year-end indices as we see animated graphic trend lines and artwork.

Host on Camera with Vignette Segments   A host discusses substance abuse in an addiction recovery center as we see brief vignettes depicting employees becoming drug dependent.

Segment concepts are the same types of visual ideas, but they focus on individual program parts. Some segment concepts (all of which might be used in the same program) are:

Graphics Animation   "Graphic animated sequences" are used to create moving bar chart visuals for the opening segment.

Split Screen   The old and new products are seen side by side in a series of split screens to provide visual contrast.

Stills with Character-Generated Titles   Still images of the display are combined with instructional, on-screen titles for "Part 1: The Visual Display—An Overview."

CONCEPT THINKING

Both program and segment concepts are arrived at by means of a brainstorming and elimination process called *concept thinking*. It's worth our time to touch on a step-by-step analysis of how concept thinking takes place.

Remember as you read the following steps, however, that concept thinking is primarily a *creative* process. It does not always happen according to a linear, step-by-step method. Some of the steps we're about to cover may not even take place, at least not *consciously*. The entire process may seem to blend together into a fluid stream of ideas. Whatever the perception, however, concept thinking usually does involve a process that evolves in this manner.

The PNA and content information become the basis for a brainstorming session. Brainstorming produces visual sequences for memorable ways to communicate the key messages via visual media. These sequences are often based on descriptive analogies or thematic similarities between the content and the creative visual idea. Concept ideas are subjected to a client, design, producer (CDP) review that poses the question, "Does this idea work for the client, the design information, and the producer?" Based on the CDP review, many of the ideas are dropped. The few remaining ones are considered concept "finalists." Final concepts are "pitched" to the client or elaborated on in the form of a treatment.

This process involves a transition from the factual thought processes involved in developing the PNA and content outline to creative thinking skills as shown in Figure 8.1.

Before we begin to explore one result of concept thinking—the treatment—let's briefly look at several program concept ideas and discuss the types of content, design, producer, and client information from which they were drawn.

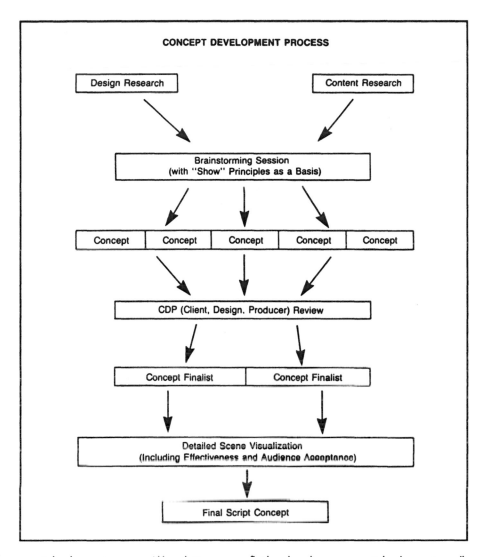

Figure 8.1 The concept development process. Although it may seem fluid and nonlinear, concept development usually evolves in a sequence something like this.

CONCEPT EXAMPLES

Host on Camera with Stills Transferred to Tape

A friend of mine once wrote a CD-ROM program for a client who wanted to train employees on the various functions an electronic calibration meter would perform. There was very little money available, and the client and producer agreed they needed something carefully structured but not flashy.

Because one objective of the program was to replace a supervisory presentation on the subject and because the audience was made up of blue-collar shop employees, the decision was made to go with an on-camera host in a shop-like setting similar to where the employees worked. The host, it was decided, would act as a peer-level instructor.

There was very little to see visually, however, and the non-host segments were written calling for extreme close-up still images of the meter's face. Superimposed titles were used as a means of support because the program objectives were primarily instructional. For instance, one part of the script read as follows:

ECU–RANGE DIAL. IT IS SET AT:

Times 10 (× 10)

HOST VO

However, when the range dial is set at the times ten position, all readings are multiplied by 10 on the digital readout window.

SUPER: "X 10" = TEN TIMES

READING ON DIGITAL WINDOW

The result was a very simple, economically made, but effective program. The producer shot digital stills and transferred them into a nonlinear editing system. These images were intercut with the host footage and used with extensive superimposed titles. The CD-ROM program didn't make for the most exciting use of the medium, granted, but a definite client need was successfully filled with a concept appropriate to the CDP factors at hand.

Music Video

The final awards banquet for a large sales force called for the production of what turned out to be a music video. The objectives called for excitement, fun, and motivation. Very little information and no instruction were required. The audience was made up of sales employees who had worked very hard during the campaign, and the client had a fairly hefty budget.

Because the theme for the entire 6-month campaign had been football, a Saturday football game and picnic was set up in a nearby park. Employees who had been involved in the campaign were invited to come with their families and play touch football. A multi-camera video crew also attended and videotaped the football game and festivities.

A motivational song lyric was also written, arranged, and produced. This musical soundtrack provided the basis for the final concept choice: a 3-minute, slow-motion montage featuring shots of all the employees and family members who had been involved in the celebration.

The completed program was played for these same employees three weeks later at the awards banquet. The viewing environment was a large auditorium. The lights were dimmed to signal the beginning of the meeting, and with no announcement the video suddenly played on a large-screen projection system. Seeing themselves, their family members, and peers playing football in slow motion to a very moving song had the desired motivational effect.

Documentary

Employees in a large company were suspicious of a new kind of decision-making process being introduced. Employee Involvement (EI) was based on consensus decision making in no-holds-barred meetings between management and hourly employees.

Both groups of employees were wary of EI. Management employees felt their decision-making powers might be robbed by the system, and craft employees felt they wouldn't be given more than token involvement in the real decisions made in the company.

To give the program audience credibility—a key objective designated in the PNA—it was written as a documentary based entirely on interviews with employees who had seen the system work successfully. Because the client felt strongly that audience members should see parts of an actual E.I. meeting in progress, the interviews were intercut with unrehearsed shots from actual meetings.

The result was a scripted but seemingly unscripted, very direct program that was extremely effective at convincing employees and managers alike to at least give the system a try.

Children Interviewed on Clean Air

A program was required to convince employees in a large company to begin to do their part toward cleaning up air quality in the Los Angeles area. This meant carpooling, biking, and riding buses and vans to work.

Both the client and the producer felt something memorable and motivational was called for because employees had seen several previous informational programs on the subject and, like most of us, they were procrastinating. Very little money was available for the project.

After much consideration, the program concept of children talking extemporaneously about the effects of smog and their future in the city became the basis. These shots were intercut with the following three other elements: (1) simple titles giving little-known harmful effects of smog on children, (2) smoggy slow-motion shots of cities and freeways, and (3) colored drawings by the children depicting their ideas of what smog was like and what it did to humans and animals.

The children were interviewed on a playground to show them vigorously exercising out in the air. Their off-the-cuff remarks, mixed with simple but powerful facts and pictures on the screen, made for a moving and effective motivational program.

CONCEPT SUMMARY

In each of these cases, the key point is that much thought was given to various program and segment concepts, and those decided on were arrived at after a process similar to the one we've been exploring—content and design information as the basis, brain-storming as the creative process, and finally applying the CDP factors—as a test of effectiveness.

As mentioned earlier, the conceptual process did not have to be executed in a linear, perfectly organized fashion. In whatever form it did happen, however, it used the types of information we've been discussing as a basis for an evolution of raw information into appropriate creative concepts.

Once this conceptual phase is accomplished, the writer "pitches" his or her ideas to the client and producer. This activity can happen verbally or in writing. The client and producer then pick the concept they feel will be most effective, which leads to the next step—to fully flush out the concept into a treatment.

9 The Treatment

Ideas are communicated in various ways. In a typical conversation, they are exchanged verbally in the form of words, gestures, and inflections. On the printed page, they are read. In sound media, such as radio, they are heard. In visual media, viewers actually see *and* hear those ideas created as "live" motion picture events. This motion picture element makes television and films powerful and popular communication tools. For this reason, the process of shaping a previously developed creative concept into a well-written treatment is also important.

There are actually two documented results of the concept thinking process. The first is the treatment, which is a simple but fully developed description of the concepts the script will present. The second is the script itself, which we will discuss shortly.

A DEFINITION

The **treatment** is a scene-by-scene narrative description of the program. It is written in the third person, present tense. This style means that instead of writing in typical third person, past tense: "John knocked on the door and Mary answered," the treatment is written as if the action were happening at the moment it is being written about: "John *knocks* on the door and Mary *answers*."

A treatment should convey the mood and tone of the concept as well. This goal is accomplished by using a simple descriptive writing style and by including short pieces of dialogue or narration.

In fact, the key to good treatment writing is clear, simple descriptions of well-conceived ideas. No matter how clearly a writer visualizes his or her concept, if it's confusing or vague to the client or producer reading the treatment, it will most likely be unsuccessful. I once saw a treatment, for instance, part of which read something like this:

PART I–SECTION 1: INT. SALES OFFICE
1. *CAMERA "DISCOVERS" two sales representatives working diligently. We DOLLY IN on one rep, MARTIN FOSTER, while he is talking on the telephone. We hear him say, "Yes, Mr. Johnson, that will be fine." The customer's voice is EQd as he responds to Foster, and we INTERCUT AS APPROPRIATE throughout this section.*
2. *When the conversation is completed, we CUT TO the second rep, SUSAN DARWIN, in the f.g. She has been watching Martin all along. Susan seems to be upset at Martin. An EXTREME CLOSE-UP reveals her fingers tapping on her desktop nervously. DISSOLVE TO:*
3. *INT. MARTIN FOSTER HOUSE. Later that evening. . . .*

This type of treatment would leave more questions in the client's mind than it answered. For instance, how does a camera "discover" something? What's a dolly? What do EQd and f.g. mean? What does *dissolve* mean? Just what is an INT.? Why number everything, including the paragraphs?

Even if the client knew the answers to many of these questions, these little bits of technical script terminology act as stumbling blocks that keep interrupting the flow of the written material. This treatment probably would have been much better received if it had been written like the following:

PART ONE: THE DISCOVERY
Two sales reps, Martin and Susan, are in their office working very hard. Martin talks on the phone with a client. As he says, "Mr. Johnson, that would be fine," we see that Susan is upset. She glares at Martin, tapping her fingernails on the desk. Later that evening at Martin's house . . .

This second version is simple and clear. That's because it's written in language we all understand, and the client is not forced to become a cameraperson or director to understand what's being described. A writer who keeps these ideas of simplicity and clarity in mind while writing treatments is more likely to please everyone involved with the project.

TREATMENT SUMMARY

The visual aspect of scriptwriting is really what makes it unique among all other forms of writing. A good writer capitalizes on this difference at every opportunity and makes his or her visual concepts, treatments, and scripts continually impress the clients, producers, and directors who read them. To achieve this goal, he or she must hone conceptual and basic writing skills to a razor-sharp edge.

Based on CDP factors, some projects will call for exciting, highly innovative concepts that allow the writer to challenge his or her concept thinking and visualization skills. Other projects are more technical and perhaps require more traditional concepts. In every case, the writer should strive to produce the most effective writing of which he or she is capable.

A COMPLETE PROGRAM TREATMENT

As you might expect, conceptualizing and visualizing the NuComm, Win the Connection program was a critical phase in its development. As the producer, the client, and I met to discuss the needs analysis and content outline, the following key words kept coming up: "fun, exciting, positive."

Because a presenter would be there with ample written material, and a live verbal presentation would follow every showing of the tape, the amount of content we had to include was minimal. Also, because Sell One Service had given the audience somewhat of a sour taste, we felt we needed either to honestly address it as a failure or to find a concept that would take the audience's attention completely away from it.

As for the requirement of displaying top executive support, we all agreed that the company president would do a typical talking head sequence to open or close the program. From his office, he would briefly state his personal support for Win the Connection.

In the final content meeting before I left to develop the concept and treatment, we reached a consensus: if we could leave the audience laughing and feeling excited about Win the Connection, the videotape would be a complete success. In addition, the following two other criteria had been set: (1) inclusion of the executive shot just mentioned and (2) a series of shots of an actual run through the warehouse, which had been sent to us from Klein & Associates. This run-through footage was so fast paced and exciting that we all felt a portion of it should be included in our program.

With these ideas uppermost in my mind, as well as one other key element that we will discuss a little later, I went to work. During the next week, I developed the treatment that follows.

Program Treatment
WIN THE CONNECTION
A Program Treatment
    As our program opens, we are amazed to see Allan Casey, the NuComm vice president known to us all, being hauled into a seedy downtown police station. As Casey is led through a cluttered office booking area in handcuffs, he looks tired and dejected. We see, from a distance, that he appears to be pleading for his release.
    From an adjacent office, Police Sergeant Davis, a grumpy, hardened, 30-year veteran of the force, and the arresting officer, Detective Parks, a chubby man, short on brains, look on.
    Davis asks Parks for the scoop on this arrest. Parks replies that Casey was picked up driving through town with five TVs, three stereos, and assorted other equipment in the back of his pickup truck. Robbery is suspected, of course, and Parks says Casey's alibi was quite bizarre.

(Continued)

As Davis chuckles at the absurdity of what he now hears, Parks goes on to tell him that Casey claims he is a vice president for a large communications company, NuComm, Inc. In addition, he swears he won all the equipment found in his truck through a company sales referral program called Win the Connection.

"Ha! Win the Connection. Sure thing," Davis says. "What does this guy think; we just fell off the turnip truck?"

Parks replies, "I know it sounds crazy, Sarge, but the guy is sticking to his story. He makes this Win the Connection sound like the greatest thing since electronic cell doors."

Although Davis is still skeptical, he asks to hear more. Parks now gets out his small, black notebook and begins to leaf through it, relaying what he has been told by Casey.

Win the Connection, he says, is an employee sales referral program with an 800 call-in number and an incredible prize package. Basically, employees talk with friends, neighbors, or people they meet on the job about services and equipment the company offers: custom calling features, intercoms, telephones, dialers, and so on. If one of an employee's contacts wants more information, he or she can arrange to get it through the employee. The employer simply takes the appropriate information down on a company-provided form and calls it in to the convenient 800 number. When the order is actually sold, the employee gets points based on a sliding-scale value system: the more valuable the sale, the more points acquired. Later, he or she can redeem the points for prizes displayed in a handsome catalog collection of items, everything from jewelry to small sailboats.

"Sailboats!" Davis exclaims.

"Yeah," Parks continues, "and that's not the best of it. They got luxury vacations, and the five top point earners, like that Casey guy, if he's on the level, that is, get what they call the 'run through the warehouse.'"

Davis chuckles and shakes his head in further disbelief, but he has Parks continue. Parks tells him the run through the warehouse is the grand prize. The five top-earning employees are given a 10-minute shopping spree in a warehouse full of incredible things like TVs, stereos, furniture, CD players, and much more. "They're given a huge storage tub to roll around, a cheerleader to follow them, and even a guy to help load whatever the employee wants!"

Davis then makes the assumption that it's this run through the warehouse that Casey claims to have used to fill up his pickup truck with the TVs and stereos.

Parks confirms this. He goes on to say, "And here's the kicker, Sarge. He's claiming his alibi can be backed up by his boss, the president of NuComm, John Crain. He also says the lady who actually runs the Win the Connection program, Rita Wallace, will back him up, too!"

When Davis hears this, his face lights up. He's sure he now has Casey cornered in the lie that will expose his entire bizarre scam. "Well, then," he says, "we'll just take him up on that. We'll call the president of NuComm right now and just see what he has to say!" With that, he dials the phone and calls John Crain's office.

As it turns out, when the call comes in, John Crain and Rita Wallace are seated in Crain's office discussing the recent results of the Win the Connection program. Crain's secretary passes the call on to him, and Sergeant Davis briefly explains the situation along with the alibi given by Casey. He does not, however, mention Casey's name yet.

When Mr. Crain hears this story, he realizes it's probably a legitimate call, but we can see that a light bulb has clicked on. He suddenly gets a fiendish idea. "And just what is the, ah, name of this person claiming to be a NuComm vice president, Sergeant?" he asks.

"Casey," Davis replies, "Allan Casey. Does it ring a bell?"

Crain looks at Wallace, covers the receiver, and says, "You'll have to excuse me, Rita. I've been waiting to do this for about 30 years now." He then replies to the sergeant, "Sorry, Sergeant, but actually the name doesn't sound familiar."

The sergeant chuckles and nods, thinking he has been right all along. Allan Casey is indeed a crook.

As our program nears its close, Casey is seen under the lights in an interrogation room with the sergeant. "I swear!" he pleads. "It's true! I've worked there for 30 years! I can't understand this! Did you tell him my name? There must be a mistake!"

The following message then appears over this shot of Mr. Casey pleading.

"John Casey was sentenced to 20 years of hard labor, loading prizes for NuComm employees at the Win the Connection warehouse."

As this picture fades away, we close the program with a series of exciting shots from videotapes of the first warehouse run-throughs. These were taped on September 16th by Klein & Associates. Master duplication copies are being sent to NuComm.

COMMENTARY

The additional key element I alluded to earlier was the reputation and personality of NuComm vice president Allan Casey. Although he was the top executive under the president, his personality was hardly stuffy or conservative. On the contrary, he was known as a likable prankster, an excellent impromptu speaker, and often the executive comedian. He had also earned great respect as a manager. In addition, he had come up through the ranks and was widely known, even by frontline craft employees. These qualities eventually made him the perfect choice to star in the Win the Connection videotape.

Before arriving at that idea, however, I spent a lot of time brainstorming concepts for this program. I remember sitting at a local coffee shop writing down many stream-of-consciousness ideas (initial concepts). Although I was coming up with ideas that I felt would generally work, they all seemed too standard. I was also having trouble finding a way to work in the run-through-the-warehouse stock footage. In general, the sense of fun and excitement we were after just didn't seem to be present in any of the concepts.

I kept at it, however, for two days. While I was considering who should do the executive talking head, the idea of using Casey as on-camera talent occurred to me. He was funny, everyone knew him, and using him might just be the way to incorporate that executive support into the program itself, rather than adding the usual talking head appendage.

Despite all these positive aspects, at first I dispelled the notion. I was well aware that using executives as actors usually meant poor performances and thus disastrous programs. There was also the problem of getting his time and even his agreement to do it.

The more I brainstormed, however, the more the idea kept occurring to me. If I could make his involvement minimal, I reasoned, he might agree to do it. If any executive would agree, in fact, Casey was the one. With very few lines, he wouldn't have to act much, and his time away from the office could be minimal, especially if it were carefully scheduled.

After a good deal of wrestling with this and other possibilities, the concept of Casey being thrown in jail after being caught with a load of run-through-the-warehouse prizes emerged. This idea seemed funny enough in itself, but the kicker was the idea of his boss,

President Crain, finally being able to get even with him for all the pranks he had pulled over the years. Audience members, all of whom knew of Casey's reputation and his relationship with Crain, would identify with it instantly. The two police characters also seemed like the perfect duo to get across the basic content of Win the Connection in humorous, naturally motivated scenes. As a bonus, the overall idea seemed funny enough to overshadow the prior Sell One Service failure without even having to mention it.

I felt that this concept had everything. Not only was it funny and exciting, but it was also unique, and it showed executive support simply by their involvement in the production of the program. The only real drawbacks seemed to be executive agreement and acting ability, but I reasoned that it could be pulled off if their parts were kept minimal.

I worked out the details, briefly listed the story points on a sheet of paper, and called the producer to make my concept "pitch." I took him briefly through the story and voiced my feelings on why I felt it was the best way to proceed. After hearing me out, he said he loved the idea and gave me the go-ahead. I went to work at once, carefully visualizing each scene, and had the treatment completed in a few days.

When it was complete, I presented it to the producer. He read it and requested a few minor changes. With the revised version submitted the following day, the producer called a client meeting, and we all sat down in a conference room.

The producer presented the treatment to the group very skillfully. He first made it clear that the idea was not what he usually produced, but he was sure it was the right way to do this particular show. He went on to say that he would explain why he felt so strongly about it after presenting the story. He then handed out copies of the treatment and read it aloud. He followed this reading by presenting everyone with a copy of the needs analysis they had previously approved. Using it as a reference, he reminded the clients of the program's purpose and of the objectives to generate fun and excitement, to include minimal content, to display executive support, to motivate employees to become involved, and most important, to leave them laughing.

After his presentation, everyone was convinced that we had hit the nail on the head. Tentative approval was given, and Casey was contacted. He agreed to do it, and I was on to the script.

10 The Script

The motion picture script is a very specialized form of writing that serves multiple purposes. First and foremost, it is designed to accurately communicate the writer's visualization to the director. This clear communication assures that the director will be able to faithfully reproduce the written scenes in live action.

Second, the script is an approval and budgeting tool for the producer. Regardless of all other documents that have been written for the project, not until the script is in his or her hands can the producer truly approve or disapprove the writer's concepts and visualization. Only in the script are the actual scenes and final **dialogue** or **narration** present as a complete communication entity. Moreover, only with the script in hand can the producer budget the production with complete accuracy. Although a treatment can tell him or her what types of locations and actors will be involved and provide a general idea of the extent of that involvement, only the script lays out those and all other aspects of the production in complete detail.

The script is also an approval document for the client. In no other document can he or she see the culmination of all research completely structured, with all dialogue, narration, visuals, and content in place.

For the other people on the production team, the script is also a specialized and very important document. For the assistant director or production assistant, it is formatted so that it can be easily broken down into numbered scenes, prop lists, shooting schedules, and so on. For the script supervisor, the script provides a standard format for notes that will offer the editor a directorial road map to the assembly of the different parts of the program.

As we will see shortly, there are a variety of script formats. Virtually all of them, however, have three elements in common.

Scene Headings are indications of *where* and *when* the scene is taking place. Scene headings are sometimes called *slug lines*.

Scene Descriptions are brief but inclusive descriptions of the visual action that takes place, at times including sounds and suggested music.

Dialogue or Narration are any words spoken by either characters or a **narrator**.

A brief example, including all three of these constants numbered in the order we have discussed them, would look like this.

1. *INT. OFFICE–DAY*
2. *John enters the office carrying stacks of paperwork. He's thrilled about something. He plunks the papers down in front of Bill, takes a deep breath, smiles and says . . .*
    JOHN
3. *You're not going to believe it, Bill! This is the fourth week in a row we beat the projections! We're in!*

FORMATS

The two primary script formats, both of which incorporate these three elements, are the **two-column format** and the **screenplay format**. Both formats are used in corporate media, but the two-column format is probably more common. Interactive scripts may be somewhat of a departure from the traditional forms. With the advent of CD-ROM and **Internet** training, however, they are becoming much more prevalent.

Other formats such as storyboards and documentary scripts are also used in corporate productions, but these formats are the exception rather than the rule.

The Two-Column Format

The two-column format divides the script elements into two vertical columns on the page. The **video** or picture part of the program is usually written in the left column, and the **audio** or sound part is written on the right.

The two-column format places the picture information conveniently beside the narration or dialogue to which it corresponds. This format was developed primarily for **multicamera** television production, in which a director must switch signals from several cameras on the fly with verbal cues. These switches are called *take points* because the director says, "Take 3," "Take 1," or whichever camera or source he or she has chosen.

The two-column format works well in this type of directing because the take points can be easily marked off in segments, with the action and the director's notes beside the narration or dialogue. Other information, such as superimposed title notations and special transition marks, can also be conveniently written in beside the words that cue them to happen.

The three constants—scene heading, scene description, and dialogue/narration—are present but separated into two vertical columns on the page. Aside from live productions, the handy placement of pictures beside words has made the two-column format a predominant and very effective style in the corporate world for video, film, and multimedia programs. A typical two-column format script for a live production looks like the example that follows.

FADE IN:

ROLL IN #1 -Graphic countdown (SOT)

with DISSOLVE to MAIN TITLE

ANIMATION:

"CENTRATEL: Power Selling!"

DISSOLVE:

INT. STUDIO

In this ESTABLISHING SHOT we see all members of the CentraTel sales panel: BILL DAVIS, JOHN PORTER, MARY MILES and DAVE DORMON. They are seated at a conference table having a round table discussion. As Porter turns to CAMERA we . . .

DISSOLVE:

SINGLE–PORTER–SUPER TITLE

          (MUSIC UNDER AND OUT)

                  PORTER

         Hello, and good morning. I'm John Porter, and I'm happy and excited to be your host for today's broadcast. As I'm sure you already know, we'll be talking about CentraTel, an important new product with exciting possibilities for the future. But before we get started, let me introduce the members of our panel. On my left is Bill Davis from product marketing. Beside him is Mary Mills, our resident advertising expert. . .

ON DAVIS–SUPER TITLE
ON MILLS–SUPER TITLE

The Screenplay Format

The screenplay format is the original Hollywood script format. It has traditionally been used to shoot film or single-camera productions, which often take place on location instead of in a studio.

In single-camera productions, the director is not working on the fly with multiple sources. Instead, one camera is moved from position to position, and the same action is repeated several times to create "coverage" of the scene. When edited together later, pieces of the scene from the various camera positions appear to be different perspectives caught in the same few moments.

The screenplay format does not split the sound and picture into columns. The scene descriptions are written across the entire page preceding the narration or dialogue associated with them. The dialogue or narration is then written in a wide column down the center of the page.

A typical screenplay format script looks like the following:

FADE IN:

EXT. INSTALLATION YARD–DAY

It is 7:45 AM. Trucks are getting ready to roll. Tailgate meetings are just breaking up. Two installers, DARRELL and JILL are talking beside their trucks as they straighten up some last-minute orders. Jill chuckles, turns to John, and says . . .

JILL

Ready for today's lesson in laziness?

DARRELL

Shoot.

JILL

How do you know when a field analyst dies?

DARRELL

Got me. How?

JILL

The donut falls out of his hand!

Both installers roar with laughter.

INT. FIELD ANALYSIS OFFICE–EVENING

A meeting is in progress. A group of about SIX FIELD ANALYSTS are gathered around a table. Sleeves are rolled up, collars are loosened. Crinkled coffee cups and stacks of papers are strewn around the conference table. A lot of tension is present in the room— pressure, urgency. ALBERT DALE, the field manager, steps to the front of the group. He pauses, looks the group dead in the eye, and says . . .

MANAGER

All other projects are on hold. We all hit the field tomorrow at six a.m.
I want to know exactly what we need to do out there . . . and fast . . .

Again, we have the three basic constants, but this format lends itself less to the multicamera, take point style of directing. It would be perfectly acceptable, however, for a single-camera breakdown.

Interactive Scripts

Interactive scripts typically incorporate either the two-column or the screenplay format or some version of either. They are typically much lengthier than standard scripts, however, because they include several branches of visual, audio, and text or graphic information. In addition to the typical scene information, interactive scripts must also make note of the branching options or cues and, of course, provide the scripted material for each of those options.

Because of this "layering," interactive scripts are presented in a variety of ways: several individual script segments or modules, which a producer can refer to at the appropriate cue points, is one method. Using different colored pages for individual segments is another means of clarifying what could easily become a very disjointed document.

Whatever the presentation style, organization and scene numbering are critical in interactive scripts because of their nonlinear form and multiple related scenes. In addition, an outlined structure or "navigation" guide may be developed as part of the nonlinear script package.

The introduction for an interactive script on verbal communications for instance, might be outlined as follows:

Scene 1–4:	*Introduction to Verbal Communications—Host on camera w/graphics and titles*
Branches/Icons	*"Stop the Show"—freeze*
1-4-a	*"The Right Way"—vignette*
1-4-b	*"The Wrong Way"—vignette*
1-4-c	*"Glossary"—text, graphics, audio*
1-4-d	*"Test Your Skills"—competency test, part one Text, audio*

In this case, scenes 1 through 4 deal with an introduction to the topic. The subheads indicate that in conjunction with scenes 1–4, a user may stop the program at any time or branch to any one of scenes a, b, c, or d. In the actual program, these events would be triggered by clicking on icons or perhaps touching an icon on the screen. The user could also branch back at any time to the primary scenes. As previously mentioned, scenes a, b, c, and d would each require an individual script segment using either the two-column or screenplay format. The "Stop the Show" icon would simply freeze the program at that spot.

Storyboard

The storyboard format is normally used for short productions such as commercials (see Figure 10.1). Its intent is to show the client and producer artwork or photographs of the intended visualization in relation to the dialogue or narration. To accomplish this goal, the storyboard is usually made up of a series of pictures or frames rendered by the writer, director, or an artist. Each frame suggests what would be seen on the screen, and corresponding narration, dialogue, or scene description information is shown beneath or beside it.

In larger productions, storyboards are sometimes used to graphically visualize certain important *parts* of a script, such as hard-to-describe graphic sequences or what a particular set might look like. Directors often develop simple storyboards as a personal visualization tool during the preproduction planning stages.

Because the screenplay and two-column formats are both common in the corporate world, a writer should be able to work in either style at the producer's request. Storyboards may not be as common, but the writer should also be familiar with this type of script presentation, should the need arise.

Narration Script

A narration script contains only the spoken words. It can be written either in the two-column format with no scene descriptions in the left column or as a single narration column down the center of a sheet of paper.

The narration script is often used for executive "talking head" shoots in which someone like the CEO decides to present a videotaped message to employees. Narration scripts may also be required for audio projects (usually audio training cassettes) or situations in which the producer has predetermined the visual part

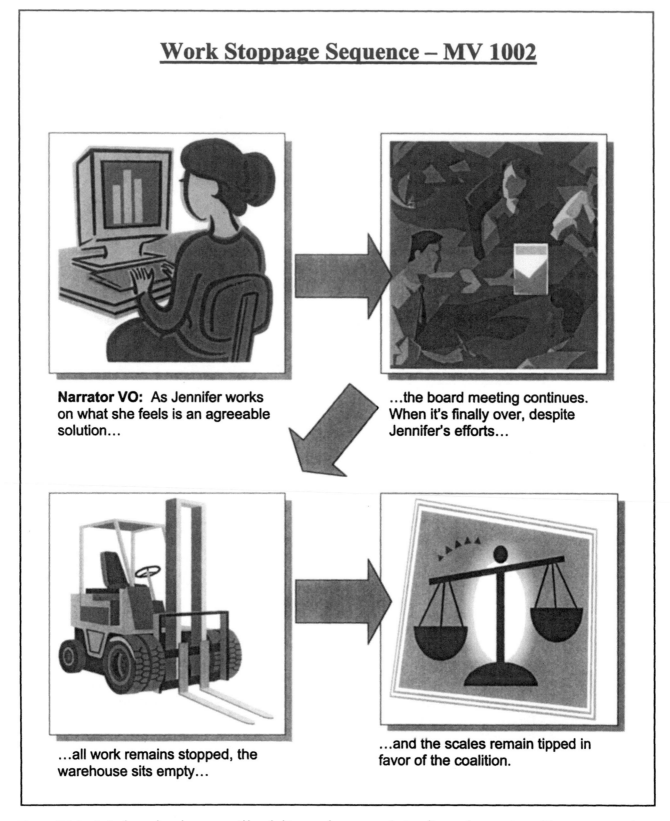

Figure 10.1 A simple storyboard sequence. Although this example was created using clip art, photos, artist renditions, or even simple stick drawings can be used.

of the script. Audio projects may also incorporate dialogue instead of narration.

Although the narration script has no visuals, it is a common requirement in the corporate world. Executives often want to appear on camera; when they do, they need scripts. For this reason alone, the corporate writer should be prepared to write a narration script whenever it is requested. The following is a short, partial example.

Now that we've had a chance to examine the standard script formats, let's move on to the terminology used in those scripts.

HARROLD AVRELL NARRATION SCRIPT

Opening Sequence for "Today and Tomorrow"

MR. AVRELL

Before you view the following program, I felt it was important that you first understand the general direction our company will be taking in the coming months. In addition, you should be aware of how our corporate mission statement has been focused on helping guide that direction. The decade ahead will bring exciting challenges and difficult times.

11

Script Terminology

Like the three primary constants, script terminology is common to nearly all scripts, regardless of format. This consistency is useful because it communicates important information to the production team in a language they use daily. Script terminology can be broken down into the following four general categories:

Editing terms

Camera terms

Scene heading terms

Sound terms

EDITING TERMS

These terms note how a program will be edited. Like most other technical notations, they are usually capitalized in the script. This format is used to make them stand out clearly for the director, producer, and editor.

Fade In/Fade Out

FADE IN and **FADE OUT** are used to note the open and close of a program or a major transition within the body of the show. They mean "fade the picture in from black" or "fade the picture out to black," respectively. These two editing cues are sometimes written as follows: FADE UP and FADE DOWN or UP FROM BLACK and FADE TO BLACK. All of these versions mean the same thing.

The black, by the way, can also be a different color. A script may call for a scene to FADE TO WHITE, for instance, for some dramatic or visual effect.

A typical FADE IN would be used in the following way:

FADE IN:

INT. OFFICE–DAY. JOHN MITCHELL is just pouring his first cup of coffee of the day.

Dissolve

This is a term meaning "dissolve one picture into another." In reality, a **DISSOLVE** is two fades, one picture fading in while the other picture is fading out. When this happens on screen, it causes an overlapping visual effect. A DISSOLVE is also a major transition second only to a FADE. It is meant to suggest a passage of time or a major change of location. For instance:

INT. OFFICE–DAY

Mel and Adrian both peek around the corner and suddenly spy each other. They walk forward, shake each other's hands, and, just as in their schooldays, both squeeze as hard as they can.

DISSOLVE:

INT. DOCTOR'S OFFICE–LATER THAT DAY

Mel is in the doctor's office getting a bandage put on his sprained hand.

Cut

A **CUT** is the most direct and frequently used method of getting from one scene or shot to another. A CUT happens instantaneously. It simply means one picture ends and another begins.

Although many writers include the word CUT or CUT TO between scenes, this direction is unnecessary in most cases. If one scene stops and another starts, the automatic assumption on the part of the producer, director, and editor will be that the transition is a CUT.

INT. JOHN'S HOUSE–DAY

John picks up the phone and dials.

CUT TO:

INT. DAN'S HOUSE–DAY

The phone on the kitchen counter rings.

This scene could just as effectively be written as follows:

INT. JOHN'S HOUSE–DAY

John picks up the phone and dials.

INT. DAN'S HOUSE–DAY

The phone on the kitchen counter rings.

Wipe

A **WIPE** usually means one picture is wiped off the screen while another picture is revealed behind it. Like DISSOLVES, WIPES suggest a major change of time or location. There are many different types of WIPES, however. CIRCLE WIPES form a shrinking or expanding circle usually emitting from the center of the screen. One picture is lost in the center of the circle and another is revealed around it. BOX WIPES perform the same effect in a box shape, CLOCK WIPES do it like a rotating clock hand, and there are many others.

A CIRCLE WIPE might be used this way:

EXT. OFFICE–DAY

John exits the building and gets into his car. As he drives off into the dead center of the screen...

CIRCLE WIPE INTO BLACK:

Digital Video Effect (DVE)

A **DVE** notation normally precedes the request for something like a picture that shrinks to a spot and flies away, splits into fragments, or warps into a cone and zips off the screen. There are numerous DVE "moves," as they are called, and, like WIPES and DISSOLVES, they are special effects. An example of a sequence of DVE script notations might be written this way:

ESTABLISHING SHOT–a desert landscape.

DVE–PAGE TURN:

ESTABLISHING SHOT–An expanse of snowy mountains.

DVE–PAGE TURN:

ESTABLISHING SHOT–A tropical coastline.

DVE–PAGE TURN:

CAMERA TERMS

Camera terms are also usually capitalized in the script. They let the director and camera operator know what type of focal length, camera placement, or movement you had in mind when visualizing the scene.

To keep your script as simple and effective as possible, camera terms should be kept to a minimum. The following are those used most often:

Wide Shot (WS)

This is a camera focal length providing a wide angle of the scene. **WIDE SHOTS** are usually used to establish locations or to accommodate a scene in which action is happening in a large area.

WS–OFFICE. Bill and Dana are seated to the left at their computers. Ellen enters from the right and sneaks up behind them.

Establishing Shot

This is usually a wide and often distant shot used to establish a major location for the first time; it is often an exterior. For instance:

EXT. COMPANY HEADQUARTERS–DAY
ESTABLISHING SHOT of the front door and parking area.

Long Shot

This is a shot made with a long focal length. **LONG SHOTS** actually magnify the scene, thus things can appear disproportionately large in the camera's frame. The writer might suggest using a long shot this way:

LONG SHOT–SEDAN. The car moves down the highway approaching us from a distance. Heat waves ripple up off the hundred-degree tar in front of it. Bill is behind the wheel, wiping his forehead with a towel.

Medium Shot (MS)

This shot is usually of one individual from about the thighs up. It is sometimes more generally referred to as a **SINGLE** or **ANGLE ON,** or sometimes simply as ON. A **MEDIUM SHOT** could be used following a WIDE SHOT to begin to move in on the action. It might also be used when the actor should be seen with a small part of the environment included in the shot.

> *MEDIUM SHOT–BILL. He gets up from his chair, walks to the corner, and stands beside the computer and printer setup. He tears out a sheet of paper.*
>
> *ANGLE ON DALE. He gets into the car.*
>
> *ON GARY. He pouts.*

Medium Close-up (MCU)

MEDIUM CLOSE-UPs are the bread-and-butter shots of most onscreen conversations. A **MEDIUM CLOSE-UP** is close enough on the individual actor to allow him or her to be the full focus of attention, but it is not close enough to create an overly dramatic or intense mood. A MEDIUM CLOSE-UP is a focal length that frames a person from the lower chest up. Like a MEDIUM SHOT, it is sometimes referred to as a SINGLE or ANGLE ON.

> *MEDIUM CLOSE-UP–JANE. She turns to Matt and speaks.*
>
> *SINGLE–ANNE. She smiles in recognition.*

Close-up (CU)

A **CLOSE-UP** places more attention and thus more importance on the actor. A CLOSE-UP fills the screen with that person's face. It is framed from about the shoulders up and is often used to reveal important expressions or facial inflections.

> *CLOSE-UP–MARK. He is shocked to hear Jane is angry. He stares for a moment, wondering whether Bill is behind this.*

Extreme Close-up (ECU)/Insert

This is just about as close as you can get on a person or thing without asking for a MACRO (microscopic) focal length. EXTREME CLOSE-UPs of people are usually used for dramatic impact. An **EXTREME CLOSE-UP** of an item might be used (and renamed) as an **INSERT** of some key item into a piece of action.

> *EXTREME CLOSE-UP–JILL'S MOUTH. Her chin begins to quiver. She is about to cry. CAMERA TILTS UP to her eyes. The tears come.*
>
> *INSERT–The pencil on John's desk. The tip has been broken off, proving that he could not have written the memo.*

Two Shot

This is a shot of two people, usually in a conversation. It can be a CLOSE **TWO SHOT,** in which the people would probably be seen from the lower shoulders up, or a LOOSE TWO SHOT, in which most of their bodies would be on screen.

> *LOOSE TWO SHOT–BILL AND DALE. They both look at the company manual held between them.*
>
> *CLOSE TWO SHOT–ANNE AND JENNY. They are arguing nose to nose.*

Over the Shoulder (OTS)

An **OVER THE SHOULDER** is similar to a TWO SHOT, but it favors one person. That means more of one person's face is showing, and most of the back or the back of the head of another person. OVER THE SHOULDER shots are often used in conversations in much the same way as MEDIUM CLOSE-UPS. They tend to give more of a sense of depth and relationship, however, because both parties are seen.

> *OVER THE SHOULDER–JAN. She and Bill talk quietly.*

Point of View (POV)

This is the **point of view** of some character without the character in the shot, as in the following example:

> *TWO SHOT–Jan and Dale. They continue to discuss the new sales policy. Suddenly the door starts to open. Dale turns toward it.*
>
> *DALE'S POV–The door swings open, and Dale's boss, BART MILLER, peeks in.*

If Dale were included in the shot of the door, the shot would then be an OVER THE SHOULDER or a WIDE SHOT INCLUDING THE DOOR.

Reverse Angle

This is a shot taken 180 degrees from the last one. It is not necessarily a POV shot because the character may be included in the frame.

MEDIUM CLOSE-UP–AL. He stands at the window looking outside. Suddenly, something catches his eye.

REVERSE ANGLE–OVER BILL'S SHOULDER. Through the window, we see a truck pulling up at the curb.

Rack Focus

This direction calls for a change of focus, usually radically and quickly. A **RACK FOCUS** typically changes the viewer's depth perspective and often juxtaposes visual elements in the frame.

For instance, we may be on a shot in which we are looking at the framework of a fire escape. In the distant background, we see something out of focus, moving through the frame. We RACK FOCUS bringing the thing—two employees walking down the alley—into focus with the now out-of-focus framework of the fire escape framing them in the foreground. This would be written as follows:

With CAMERA looking through the rusted framework of an old fire escape, RACK FOCUS, REVEALING two employees walking across the alley in the distance.

f.g./b.g.

These are abbreviations for **FOREGROUND** or **BACKGROUND.** They are used in the following way:

John steps past Lynn into the f.g.

Ellen moves behind the bush into the b.g.

Low Angle

This is an angle shot from a low position with the camera looking upward. A **LOW ANGLE** is sometimes used for a dramatic, overpowering sense or to convey a feeling of dominance.

LOW ANGLE–THE BOSS. He steps into the frame holding the faulty reports and looks down into the CAMERA.

High Angle

Obviously, this shot is the reverse of a low angle. A **HIGH ANGLE** can sometimes give a sense of eaves-dropping or an omnipotent perspective. It can also make the characters in the scene appear to be enclosed or trapped.

HIGH ANGLE–John. He paces in his jail cell.

Pan/Tilt

These terms call for the camera to rotate left (**PAN** LEFT) or right (PAN RIGHT) on its head or to tilt from looking down to looking up (**TILT** UP) or the opposite (TILT DOWN).

John moves to the door. CAMERA PANS with him. John climbs the stairs. TILT UP TO FOLLOW.

Dolly/Truck

DOLLYS and TRUCKS note a forward or backward movement of the camera (**DOLLY** IN or DOLLY OUT) or a horizontal left or right movement (**TRUCK** LEFT or TRUCK RIGHT). In both cases these moves are carried out by pushing or pulling the camera after it is mounted on a dolly with wheels.

Alice moves down the hallway. DOLLY IN past her to John seated at the table.

TRUCK LEFT following the customer into the warehouse.

SCENE HEADING TERMS

These terms set the stage for the scene description.

Int./Ext./Day/Night

INT. and **EXT.** are abbreviations for INTERIOR and EXTERIOR; **DAY** and **NIGHT** are self-explanatory. They are the first entries in a scene description because they are very important to the production crew. A film or videotape production is typically shot not in chronological order, but rather by logistical and other considerations. Two primary scheduling considerations are times and locations. Scenes that take place at night will require special considerations and will probably be scheduled together. Scenes that happen at the same locations will also be shot at the same time, although they may appear at different places in the script.

INT. JOHN'S HOUSE–DAY

EXT. GAS STATION–NIGHT

EXT. PLANT YARD–MIDNIGHT

SOUND TERMS

Sound Effects (SFX)

This notation tells all who read or work on the script that certain **SOUND EFFECTS** belong at specific points. For instance:

EXT. BACKYARD–DAY

John tests a line with the Olson meter.

CLOSE-UP–METER FACE–The needle on the meter suddenly jumps. SFX–HIGH-PITCHED TONE generated by the meter.

Music Up/Under/In/Out/Sting

Music terms tell the editor when to bring in music to emphasize scenes or transitions.

John turns quickly toward the door. Bill steps in looking angry. MUSIC STING.

DISSOLVE

Bill runs across the field. INTENSE, POUNDING MUSIC, UP SUDDENLY.

Sound Terms

The word **SOUND** or any type of sound written into the scene description is also capitalized. This, again, is to call attention to the fact that a specific sound effect will be required.

INT. OFFICE–DAY

John is startled by the SOUND of the RINGING TELEPHONE.

MASTER SCENES VERSUS DETAILED DESCRIPTIONS

As mentioned earlier, much of the technical terminology we've been discussing, especially camera terms, should be used sparingly in any script. Most times, especially in role-play scenes, the scriptwriter should be able to communicate his or her vision with the use of master scenes.

Master scenes are descriptions of the action in narrative terms rather than in terms of a camera's perspective. Master scenes have more of a sense of story and natural flow. They describe the scene with simplicity, clarity, a sense of the proper tone, pace, and mood. They leave the choices of angles and focal lengths to the people who are experts at selecting them: the director and the camera operator.

You may be tempted to write something like the following:

EXT. FIELD–DAY

CAMERA, looking through tree branches, REVEALS Bill in a LONG SHOT. Suddenly we RACK FOCUS to the f.g. REVEALING Jennifer watching John from beside her truck. MUSIC STING. CAMERA DOLLIES around to a CU of Jennifer, as she stares at Tom with curiosity.

REVERSE ANGLE–OVER JENNIFER'S SHOULDER. We see Bill turn and discover Jennifer watching him. Surprised, he moves toward her.

CLOSE-UP–Bill. He smiles.

BILL

Hi, what are you doing here?

MEDIUM CLOSE-UP–Jennifer

JENNIFER

Working. How about you?

MEDIUM CLOSE-UP–Bill. DOLLY IN to CLOSE-UP.

> BILL
>
> *I'm testing the cable feed in this area.*

But the scene should be written this way instead.

EXT. FIELD–DAY

Jennifer steps out from behind her truck and sees John moving along a sidewalk in the distance. Her eyes hold on him with curiosity. Suddenly, Bill turns and sees Jennifer. He seems surprised. He walks up to her and smiles.

> BILL
>
> *Hi, what are you doing here?*
>
> JENNIFER
>
> *Working. How about you?*
>
> BILL
>
> *I'm testing the cable feed for this area.*

The first version of this scene not only is cumbersome and difficult to follow, but it also places the director in a visual "box" that he or she probably will like.

The second version is a master scene. It is clear, simple, and descriptive. Better yet, it allows the director—the person hired to commit the script to tape or film—to make choices about the camera positions and visual aesthetics.

12 Dialogue and Narration

With a good grasp of basic script formats and the common terminology they incorporate, two other major script elements must be considered: *dialogue* and *narration*. Just as a writer's visualization is critical to the *picture* part of his or her presentation, dialogue and narration are the critical *sound* part.

Critical, by the way, is not an overstatement. If the visuals in a script are brilliantly thought out but the dialogue or narration is weak, the script will not work. In a well-written script, the audio supports the visuals and vice versa. In most scripts, the two elements should be interwoven like the tightly knit strands of a creative fabric.

With this word–picture relationship in mind, then, let's first establish a definition for **dialogue.** Dialogue is defined as words spoken in a conversation between at least two characters in a **role-play** situation.

Well-written dialogue adds credibility to a script. In other words, it is believable, and it gets the message across. Let's look at some examples of how these two factors result in effective dialogue.

DIALOGUE CREDIBILITY

Assume that a writer is scripting an instructional, role-play script on telephone sales. In one scene, he or she is working on a piece of dialogue between a new, somewhat timid female sales rep and a friendly, experienced male rep. The female rep is frustrated because she can't seem to get the hang of the work. She decides to confide in the male rep.

To provide credibility the dialogue should simply sound natural, as if it could really have been spoken between these two characters.

A *noncredible* way of handling this conversation might be scripted this way.

FADE IN:

INT. OFFICE—DAY

JIM, a friendly, experienced telephone sales rep is having a cup of coffee with JAN, a timid rep now in her third day on the job.

JIM

So, how are you getting along, Jan? Are your telephone sales skills effective yet? Sometimes with new people the skills need a little time to develop. I think if you are having trouble, a little experience will help you a great deal.

> JAN
>
> *No, I am afraid they are not. I just cannot seem to make a sale. I am not sure I know what I am doing wrong, but I think I am not showing enough initiative.*
>
> JIM
>
> *Try the three sales tips we all use here. One is pitch the sale. Two is overcome objections, and three is close the sale. I hope these help.*
>
> JAN
>
> *Thank you. They will.*

Obviously, this is a very stilted and unnatural verbal exchange. A much more credible version of the same interaction might be scripted this way.

> *FADE IN:*
>
> *INT. OFFICE–DAY*
>
> *JIM, a friendly, experienced telephone sales rep is having a cup of coffee with JAN, a timid rep now in her third day on the job.*
>
> JIM
>
> *So what's up, Jan?*
>
> JAN
>
> *(shakes her head)*
>
> *Problems.*
>
> JIM
>
> *Trouble making sales?*
>
> JAN
>
> *More like a sales disaster!*
>
> JIM
>
> *(chuckles)*
>
> *Well, don't get upset. Sometimes it takes a while to get up to speed.*
>
> JAN
>
> *(depressed)*
>
> *I don't know, Jim. Maybe I'm just not assertive enough.*
>
> JIM
>
> *Have you tried the three "golden rules" of telephone sales?*

(Continued)

>   *JAN*
> *"Golden rules?"*
>
>   *JIM*
> *Yeah. Sounds corny I know, but they work.*
>
>   *JAN*
> *I'll try anything at this point.*
>   *SUPER: PITCH, OVERCOME, CLOSE*
>   *JIM*
> *Pitch the benefits, overcome objections, and*
> *close the sale.*
>
>   *JAN*
>   *(thinks out loud)*
> *Hmm . . . Pitch, overcome, and close. Simple*
> *enough.*
>
>   *JIM*
> *Try 'em out. They'll help.*
>
>   *JAN*
> *Okay. Thanks.*

I think you'll agree that the second version is much more natural and credible. Why? What specifically are the qualities that make one version sound very unnatural and the other sound like a real conversation? There are actually three.

1. Natural speech patterns.
2. Believable character motivation.
3. Use of contractions and colloquialisms.

Natural Speech Patterns

Natural speech patterns mean that the conversation is kept moving back and forth between the two characters, often after only a sentence or two. At times, the sentences themselves are actually sentence fragments. This is the way people naturally express themselves.

In the first version, notice that the speech patterns are very unnatural. Jim's opening lines contain four separate thoughts clustered together. Rather than converse with Jan and allow these ideas to emerge naturally, he simply blurts them all out at once. Jan returns this unnatural delivery with her own thought cluster. The result is a very awkward exchange that actors would find difficult to say convincingly and viewers would find even more difficult to believe.

Believable Character Motivation

Volumes have been written on the intricacies of character development and motivation alone. Character is the basic personality of an individual, and motivation means purpose, a legitimate reason for doing something. This purpose can come to a character from any number of sources. It might be a phone call, a question, a hunch, or a headache. It could be an emotion, such as fear or love, a question about the future or a memory from the past, or just the type of personality the writer decides the character should have. The critical factors are that the motivation is believable in the situation based on the character's personality and that it helps move the story forward.

In the second version of our scene, both of these items are accomplished. The story is certainly moved forward by the dialogue and the friendship that is struck up as a result of it, and the characters seem motivated to speak as they do because of the situation and personality traits we've given them. I imagine Jan as somewhat timid, depressed, and probably wanting to do a good job, but feeling frustrated because she can't. I find it perfectly believable that a woman like her would probably be motivated to tell her troubles to a sales rep with a lot more experience who seems to have a sense of concern for her predicament.

Jim appears to be a friendly and open type. I can imagine him being very good on the phone as a sales rep. He also seems compassionate enough to be motivated to lend a hand to a new person in need of not only the "golden rules," as he calls them, but also a little kindness and support.

In the first version the characters seem lifeless and robotic, projecting almost no characterization. I can imagine them facing one another and simply letting their mouths mimic the words being spoken with no warmth or sense of human emotion at all.

Use of Contractions and Colloquialisms

The first version of this scene contains no contractions. This is another unnatural way of speaking. In casual conversation, most people usually don't say "I am," "do not," or "can not." They say "I'm," "don't," and "can't."

In the second version, both characters use contractions in ways that have human qualities. The John character also uses casual and colloquial phrases such as "Try 'em out" and "up to speed." These elements create natural human speech qualities that ring true (are credible) to our ears.

Besides this element of credibility, in corporate programs, effective dialogue must also provide content. It must make a point. If it doesn't, no matter how great it may sound, it boils down to wasted screen time at a very expensive price. In effective dialogue, the content is worked into the conversation naturally as in the case of the short exchange between John and Jan.

THE DIALOGUE TEST

A test of good dialogue would contain positive answers to the following questions:
1. When spoken out loud, does it sound natural?
2. Does it emphasize the proper content points in a way that is believable to the viewer?

3. Will the viewer believe that the actions and personality of the characters are credible and motivated?
4. Does it incorporate visual elements in the script to help convey as much content and characterization as possible?
5. Is it simple enough to convey the content clearly?

NARRATION

Much of the information an audience gains from a media program is communicated through words. In the case of **narration,** those words are not spoken by one character to another in a role-play situation. Instead, narration could be defined as: Words spoken by a voiceover narrator or on-camera spokesperson, directly to the audience.

Effective Narration Qualities

To be effective, narration should also provide content and credibility. Effective narration usually accomplishes this goal with three general qualities.
1. Conversational tone.
2. Content focus.
3. Simplicity.

Conversational Tone

Conversational means natural and comfortable. Conversational narration should sound as if it were being delivered off-the-cuff rather than as a prepared script.

The importance of this impromptu tone becomes clear when you consider that a narrator—especially an on-camera narrator—must establish a rapport with the audience if he or she is to be credible. The audience must like and identify with the narrator in order to accept the material being presented. If what he or she says sounds prepared or unnatural, it immediately becomes suspect. Once this happens, achieving audience rapport will become difficult at best.

What can a writer do to build this conversational tone into his or her scripts? The most important rule is simply to write to be heard, not to be read. Again, let's illustrate by considering two versions of the same script. In this case, the subject is how to become a successful purchasing agent. The first version is scripted this way.

FADE IN

A HOST steps into the FRAME in black limbo. He turns to CAMERA and says . . .

HOST

Purchasing is a difficult business in which to achieve success. Regardless of this difficulty, however, being a successful purchasing agent is indeed achievable if the proper preparatory steps are taken. This CD program will present those steps. They are: 1. Know the marketplace. 2. Shop for prices. 3. Bargain for deals. 4. Obtain the prices in contractual form.

A different version of the same material might be scripted like this.

FADE IN

A HOST steps into the FRAME in black limbo. He turns to CAMERA and says . . .

HOST

It's tough to become a successful purchasing agent. There's lots to learn, and it's a competitive business. But you can be good at it if you follow the right steps. Care to learn how? If so, listen up, because today I'd like to talk with you about those steps and hopefully get you started down that road to success. We'll be looking closely at knowing the marketplace, shopping for prices, bargaining for deals, and getting those deals written in a contract.

The first version of this piece is definitely formal and written more to be read than to be heard. It uses many formal, polysyllabic words like "difficult," "achievable," "indeed," "proper," "preparatory," and "however." It also uses no contractions, and it lists out the steps to be followed exactly as they might have been listed in some manual. In fact, this entire piece sounds like it might well have been lifted straight from the pages of a manual.

Because of these qualities, the host reading this script will have a difficult time making it work. No doubt the film or taping session will be stopped frequently for discussions between the actor, client, and director in an effort to make the material "sound bet-

ter." If it does get recorded as is, the audience will probably lose interest in it quickly and retain very little of what's been presented.

The second version, by contrast, has a warm, human tone. It uses much simpler, more commonplace words and informal phrases such as "lots to learn," "start down the road," and "be good at it." It also frequently uses contractions, and it addresses the audience directly with an occasional reference to "you."

The second version uses another natural speech quality we've already discussed: the use of questions. Besides sounding very "human," an occasional question helps draw the audience into the program.

The result of these qualities is narration that an audience will listen to and learn from—conversational narration written to be spoken and heard, rather than read.

Content Focus

We touched on the importance of focus in our discussion of dialogue. The same rule holds true for narration. It must not only sound good but also make the point. To accomplish this goal, you must focus on the proper content points at the proper times. For the most part, this means being sure that the points are present in the material, that they are clearly stated, and that the focus is on them versus other aspects of your script.

As an example, in the second version of the script passage on becoming a purchasing agent, the host makes a point that it's "tough to become a successful purchasing agent. There's lots to learn, and it's a competitive business." With this statement, an important point is made very briefly. In addition, the audience is set up for the subject about to be discussed. The narra-tion then moves on to the subject—learning the proper steps. This information represents what is called the "hard content" for this bit of narration.

If the narration had continued to focus on the subject of how tough it is to succeed in the purchasing agent business, however, whether it sounded conversational or not, it would probably have lost its value to the audience.

Simplicity

The need for clear, simple English can't be overemphasized in any form of writing. In script development, that need is even more critical.

In a videotape, CD, and program, words go by quickly. Granted, they are supported by pictures, but they are also heard for only an instant and then are gone. The writer should, therefore, strive for clear, simple word usage in every script. Although this rule applies to narration, it also includes dialogue and scene descriptions. Simplicity means reducing a subject to its lowest descriptive common denominator. It also means letting visuals support the spoken words.

13 Structure and Transitions

Corporate media is produced to train, motivate, and inform. To accomplish these goals, it must impart information in ways that make it easily understood. In other words, it must have what I refer to as a high clarity factor.

The level of that clarity factor is directly affected by all the script elements we've been discussing: concepts, visualization, dialogue, narration, format, terminology, and so on. Clarity is also affected by two other, perhaps more subtle, elements: the *structure* of the script and the *transitions* used to move the viewer through its scenes.

The relationship between these two elements might be thought of in terms of an analogy: An informational or instructional script could be thought of as a series of content islands a viewer visits that are linked by a string of transition bridges.

With this relationship in mind, script structure could be defined as: The arrangement of content information into logical, easily understood script segments. Script transitions are the sound or picture elements linking script segments.

TYPES OF STRUCTURES

There are many types of program structures. They are often based on storyline and the information being communicated. For instance, a story about a supervisor who gets reprimanded and nearly fired might include the events that led to his or her predicament. This *story* could be told effectively in a flashback *structure*. If so, it could have a back-and-forth, hopscotch type of structure. Information could be conveyed while transporting the viewer between the present and the past. In this type of structure, the transitions might be the special visual effects—perhaps slow dissolves—that mark our departures from one time frame to another.

Traditional dramatic structure usually follows a series of escalating crises that eventually lead to a climax and finally to a resolution. For instance, a male protagonist is typically faced with a conflict or dilemma. He overcomes this one, only to find another, perhaps even worse, barrier now in his way. Again he triumphs but is faced with still another crisis. The tension builds with each of these challenges until it eventually becomes a do-or-die situation. In the climax, the protagonist may overcome the final obstacle against all odds. Then comes the resolution—the antagonist's ruin as the protagonist is victorious. Although many dramatic stories incorporate different storylines, characters, and plot elements, most follow a dramatic structure similar to this one.

Transitions in such a structure are special effects, sound and music cues, dialogue, and combinations of these elements. For instance, in the story just mentioned, at certain crucial points the music might build to dramatic bridges as we dissolve to upcoming scenes. This music device would act as a subconscious signal that a dramatic change is about to occur.

STRUCTURE VERSUS STORYLINE

Structure should not be confused with storyline. The structure is simply the arrangement of the information, not the story "formula."

For instance, our story about the nearly fired supervisor might seem like a natural for a flashback structure, but it could also be told chronologically. In this case, the story formula—supervisor goes bad, gets caught, and is reprimanded—remains the same in both. The arrangement of how the story information is communicated; however, the structure is changed.

CORPORATE STRUCTURES

Corporate programs can utilize any script structure that is effective. The type of structure you choose for a project should be heavily influenced by the amount and type of information to be conveyed. Because information is usually of prime importance in corporate programs, some follow the simple, time-proven structure we discussed earlier in the chapter on content research.

The Tell 'em Structure

Tell 'em you're gonna tell 'em.

Tell 'em.

Tell 'em you told 'em.

This type of script structure is a very effective way to present material for training or informational purposes. It is by no means the only way to convey information in corporate programs, but you should be familiar with it, especially for writing technical or instructional scripts.

Tell 'em Example

We can best illustrate both the use of this structure and the basic value of good structure in general with another script example. In this case, we'll assume the content involves communicating a technical overview of a three-step process used to repair electronic work stations. The approach is a traditional voiceover narrator with example footage.

FADE IN:

INT. WORKSTATION–DAY

A REPAIR TECHNICIAN enters the station, removes his equipment, and begins to perform tests. SUPER TITLES: TEST, REPAIR, INFORM

> NARRATOR (VO)
>
> *Testing an electronic workstation involves three steps: testing, repairing, and informing the customer. All these steps are important, but let's start with the first one.*

DISSOLVE:

INT. WORKSTATION–DAY

The same station, later. The technician is just finishing testing the equipment as prescribed in the company manual. SUPER TITLE: 1. TESTING–PRIMARY AND SECONDARY CIRCUIT

> NARRATOR (VO)
>
> *Step one is testing. It involves running all appropriate tests on the primary and secondary circuits according to company standards. With this step accomplished, we can move on to . . .*

DISSOLVE:

(Continued)

INT. WORKSTATION–DAY

Later still. The repair tech has his tools out and is soldering in a new coil. SUPER TITLE: 2. REPAIR–ON THE SPOT OR REFERRAL

NARRATOR (VO)

. . . step two–repair. This involves fixing the bad circuit. Repair can be done on the spot, if time permits, or by referral to a later date.

DISSOLVE:

INT. CUSTOMER'S OFFICE–DAY

She is on the phone with the tech getting word that the electronic station is fixed. She is obviously pleased. SUPER TITLE: 3. INFORM CUSTOMER–PHONE, MAIL, OR FAX.

NARRATOR (VO)

Assuming we've done it on the spot, step three is next: informing the customer. This can be done by phone, mail, or fax.

DISSOLVE:

INT. WORKSTATION–DAY

ECU–Referral notice attached to an Electronic workstation.

NARRATOR (VO)

Obviously, step three is carried out later if repairs have been referred to a new date.

DISSOLVE:

EXT. HOSPITAL–DAY

At a company truck in the parking lot. The tech loads his tools into his truck and drives off to another repair job.

NARRATOR (VO)

By following these three steps–testing, repairing, and informing the customer–you can be a successful electronic workstation repair technician.

This topic obviously is not the most exciting to write about, but this short, instructional piece has a high clarity factor. The content is introduced with a brief overview. This introduction sets us up for what's to come, allowing us to become mentally prepared to absorb this subject.

Although this script also makes good use of titles and is written very concisely, a good deal of its clarity is based simply on the arrangement of the content (the test and repair steps) in the logical one-two-three order, as it would normally be carried out.

Finally, this script has a tidy little wrap-up, briefly summarizing what's been covered. It lets us know that what we've been discussing is now fully communicated and uses the moment to briefly reiterate the three steps.

Transitions are also provided in this piece. In this case, they are dissolves and simple verbal cues. The dissolves tell us visually that time has passed between the shots that take place at the same location, and the verbal cues move us smoothly from one idea to another.

The introduction and step one, for instance, are bridged by "Let's start with the first one." Steps one and two are bridged by "With this accomplished, we can move on to . . ." Between steps two and three, it's "Assuming we've done it on the spot . . ." The result is a comfortable, easy-to-follow, readily absorbed technical piece with a very high clarity factor and thus maximum instructional value.

Benefits Bookends

Another structure we previously touched on was the "benefits bookends." This structure tends to be more effective with motivational/informational content than with heavily instructional or technical material.

The benefits of becoming involved in some company campaign might be presented as an opening teaser—the front bookend. It might be something like this.

FADE IN:

MONTAGE—A series of exciting shots of people vacationing in areas offered in the company's "Sell-for-Sun" program—snorkeling, sunning on the beach, dinner on a beachside terrace, dancing by the surf at sunset.

HOST (VO)

Vacationing in paradise . . . Mexico . . .
Hawaii . . . the Caribbean. Getaways only for
the rich? Actually, they're waiting in the sun
for you. And in the next few minutes, we'll
show you how to get there!

Following this opening montage, our program title is perhaps superimposed over an exotic shot. We might then make a transition with a video effect and music to an on-camera host who, with the help of titles and cutaway footage, would take us through the program body. The body would consist of the steps to follow to win a cruise. Our host would cover them in much the same way we covered the electronic workstation steps, in a logical, straightforward order with appropriate transitions.

A close for this program—the back bookend—might then be handled like this.

EXT. LAGOON—DAY

The host has snorkeling gear on. He is standing under a palm tree with a group of vacationers who are ready to go diving. He stops his conversation with them just long enough to turn to the camera and say . . .

HOST

So, it's up to you. Spend your next vacation
trimming the hedges, or sell for sun!

He turns and heads for the snorkeling trip.
MUSIC UP.

DISSOLVE:

HIGH ANGLE—the lagoon from an overhanging cliff. The group, including our host, wades in and begins snorkeling. SUPER CLOSING CREDITS, MUSIC DOWN AND OUT, as we . . .

FADE OUT:

Contrasting Actions

Still another structure frequently used in corporate programs is what I call the "contrasting actions" structure. This method can be effective when communicating the right and wrong ways to carry out certain procedures.

First, the audience is shown, for example, the wrong way to try to make a sale. A host or narrator makes note of the mistakes, then explains that sales can be closed more often by doing it another (the right) way. We then see the right way, and the correct steps are noted. The customer is left much happier, and the sale is closed.

Creative Use of Structure

Remember that the structure of your material and the transitions you use to bridge it are critical to the clarity factor and thus to the success of your script. Also remember, however, that the concept or story into which you place your structure need not be boring or "educational" sounding. Provided your design calls for it and your producer and client are amiable, you are free to be as creative as you like within the parameters of whatever basic structure you choose. Your only guideline should be assuring yourself that the information is effectively communicated.

14 A Screenplay Format Script

The script for *Win the Connection* came very easily. I wrote it over a period of four days. By the time I sat down at the word processor, I had been over most of the visualization in my head until it was very clear. I could "see" the interior of the police station, the two officers, and the company president sitting in his office saying he'd never heard of Allan Casey. The other details were equally as clear and thus easy to convey.

As you look over the script, consider all aspects of the screenplay format we've discussed in previous chapters. Look at the way the script is laid out on the page and the amount of scene description and technical terms that have been included (and excluded). Is the script written in master scenes or using individual camera directions? Was the choice effective? Ask yourself if believable motivation is present for every word spoken and each action described. Does the pacing seem comfortable? Are the characters credible and humorous?

Above all, simply ask yourself if the script *works*. Given the development scenario you've been taken through, do you feel it's the right way to have produced the program? Do you feel it would accomplish the objectives outlined in the needs analysis? Maybe most important of all, if you had been the writer, how would you have handled this project?

WIN THE CONNECTION

A Screenplay Format Program Script

FADE IN:

INT. POLICE STATION–DAY

WIDE SHOT TO ESTABLISH A typical, seedy, downtown police station booking area: lots of clutter, dirty coffee cups, messy desks, and groups of overworked, gun-toting detectives at work.

An office, separated from this area by a glass partition, can be seen at SCREEN RIGHT. CAMERA PUSHES IN to this area.

DISSOLVE:

INT. SERGEANT'S OFFICE–DAY

A chubby POLICE DETECTIVE named PARKS is just coming into his sergeant's office to present the facts on a recent bust. The SERGEANT, a squat, harried man named DAVIS, is seated behind the desk, tie loose, busily doing paperwork. When he sees the detective enter, he stops and looks up. Parks hangs up his jacket and pulls a black notebook out of his shirt pocket.

(Continued)

NOTE: *During the following dialogue, SEVERAL POLICE ASSISTANTS can be seen in the b.g. through the glass partition. They are carrying in large boxes: TVs, stereos, tools, etc.*

SERGEANT

Okay, so what's the scoop on this guy you just picked up?

DETECTIVE

Pretty bizarre. Guy says he's from the phone company.

SERGEANT

The what?

DETECTIVE

Phone company. You know, NuComm.

SERGEANT

Yeah, well, he didn't look like no phone guy to me when they took him through a few minutes ago.

DETECTIVE

Me neither, Sarge. Looks a little too, ah, greasy to be a phone guy. But that's what he says.

The sergeant chuckles. He gets up, moves to a nearby shelf, and pours a cup of coffee.

SERGEANT

And pray tell what exactly is a phone company individual doing driving around town with a truckload of TVs and stereos?

DETECTIVE

That's what I asked 'im.

SERGEANT

And?

DETECTIVE

Win the Connection . . .

SERGEANT

(confused, flustered)
Win the what? You dummy, win what connection? I said, what's a phone guy doing with a truckload of TVs and stereos?

DETECTIVE

No, no, that's what he told me, Sarge! It's some company program called Win the Connection.

The sergeant moves back to his seat.

> SERGEANT
>
> (again, a chuckle)
> Yeah, sure thing. Win the connection with
> your fence, and if you get nabbed, tell the cops
> you're from the phone company.
>
> DETECTIVE
>
> He says it's on the level. Says their people can
> win lots of prizes or something.
>
> SERGEANT
>
> Truckloads of TVs and stereos? C'mon, Parks,
> when did you fall off the turnip truck?
>
> DETECTIVE
>
> Sounds bizarre, I know, but at least part of
> his story checks out.
>
> SERGEANT
>
> What do you mean?
>
> DETECTIVE
>
> Well, we made some calls. Seems the same
> kind o' thing's been going on in some other
> states, and those people've all checked out
> legit—NuComm folks who hit it big on this
> same kind of referral program thing.

This throws the sergeant a bit of a curve. He pauses, thinks, puts his coffee cup down, then leans forward.

> SERGEANT
>
> Exactly what is this Win the Connection
> again?

The detective now refers point by point, as if reading a script, from his notebook.

> DETECTIVE
>
> Let's see here. It's an employee referral
> program. Employees "win the connection"
> with friends and neighbors, that kind of thing.
> They tell people about products and services
> and make a call to a special 800 number.
> Then the salespeople call back. If they actually
> make the sale, the guy who first made the
> referral gets points.
>
> SERGEANT
>
> And?
>
> DETECTIVE
>
> And if he gets enough, I guess he gets a 10-
> minute free run through this huge warehouse
> where they got all this stuff.
>
> SERGEANT
>
> And he gets anything he wants?!

(Continued)

> DETECTIVE
>
> *Anything. Stereos, lawn mowers, CD players, TVs, you name it.*
>
> SERGEANT
>
> *And what if he doesn't, ah, "hit the big time?"*
>
> DETECTIVE
>
> *Well, I guess there's other stuff too. Watches, tools, gold jewelry, all kinds o' goodies.*
>
> *The sergeant is now realizing this all makes a certain amount of sense, but he's still not sure how much.*
>
> SERGEANT
>
> *(pondering)*
> *Hmmm. Sounds legit, I guess. But, you know, I just get a funny feeling about this guy, I don't know. It's just something about the way he came strollin' in here with all those cameras hangin' around his neck and remote controllers and stuff stickin' out of his pockets.*
>
> DETECTIVE
>
> *I felt the same way, Sarge. Gut hunch or somethin'.*
>
> SERGEANT
>
> *Can we check him out?*
>
> DETECTIVE
>
> *Well, he gave me this number. Says it's the president's office.*
>
> SERGEANT
>
> *The company president?*
>
> *A light bulb is now clicking on for the sergeant.*
>
> DETECTIVE
>
> *Right. He says all I have to do is call this guy, or some woman . . . (checks the notepad) named . . . Rita Wallace. I guess she's running this Win the Connection. He says either one'll verify his alibi.*
>
> *The sergeant chuckles and snatches the detective's notepad. He then sits down and reaches for the phone. He's got it all figured out.*
>
> SERGEANT
>
> *Well, what do you say we just take 'im up on his little game. We'll just give this president a call! Here, where's that phone number?*
>
> *Parks points out the number and sits down.*
>
> DETECTIVE
>
> *Second page, Sarge. Right there.*

> SERGEANT
> (dialing)

The president. Ha! Fat chance!

INT. JOHN CRAIN'S OFFICE–DAY

JOHN CRAIN and RITA WALLACE are seated at a small conference table discussing Win the Connection. Suddenly, Crain's SECRETARY'S VOICE comes over the SPEAKER PHONE.

> SECRETARY

Mr. Crain?

> CRAIN

Yes, Anne.

> SECRETARY

I have the police on line 2. They say they need to speak with you right away.

Crain looks at Wallace with concern.

> CRAIN

Excuse me, Rita. This sounds important. (To secretary) Put them through, Anne.

NOTE: We now INTERCUT between the sergeant in his office and Crain and Wallace.

> CRAIN

Hello?

> SERGEANT

Ah, hello. Ah, Mr. John Crain?

> CRAIN

Speaking.

> SERGEANT

Ah, yes, well, ah, Mr. Crain, this is Sergeant Davis down at the PD. We have a, ah, suspect here, who claims to be—get this now—an employee of NuComm.

> CRAIN

I see. So how can I help you, Sergeant?

> SERGEANT

Well, ya see, sir, we caught this guy driving down the street with a truckload o' televisions, stereos, tools, stuff like that.

> CRAIN

I see.

> SERGEANT

Right. And you see he claims he won all this stuff in some program called, ah, Win the Connection or something like that. And (chuckle) . . . are you ready for this one? He says all we have to do to verify his alibi is give you a call, the president!

Crain now realizes there's probably been a mix-up. He smiles at Wallace. She smiles too.

> ### CRAIN
>
> *Well, Sergeant, I happen to have Ms. Rita Wallace, the person in charge of Win the Connection, sitting in my office right now.*

> ### SERGEANT
>
> *So you do actually have a Win the Connection program?*

> ### WALLACE
>
> *Yes, Sergeant, we certainly do.*

> ### SERGEANT
>
> *Well, then, how about this character here? We're not quite sure about him, either. I mean, calling the president for an alibi?*

> ### CRAIN
>
> *Tell me, Sergeant, what's this person's name?*

The sergeant refers to his notebook.

> ### SERGEANT
>
> *Let's see here. Says here his name is, ah, Casey, Allan Casey.*

Crain and Wallace look at each other with surprise at first. Then Crain has an idea. He covers up the speaker and WHISPERS to Wallace.

> ### CRAIN
>
> *Rita, you'll have to forgive me, but I've been waiting to do this for about 15 years.*

He then uncovers the speaker and talks to the sergeant.

> ### CRAIN (CONT.)
>
> *Ah, Casey. Gee, I'm sorry, Sergeant, but the name doesn't ring a bell.*

We hold on Crain as he and Wallace chuckle quietly, then . . .

INT. POLICE INTERROGATION ROOM–DAY

ALLAN CASEY is seated across from a POLICE INTERROGATOR. The spotlight is on. Casey is sweating and pleading. The interrogator isn't buying his story.

> ### CASEY
>
> *. . . But it's the truth! I swear! I've worked for NuComm for 34 years! I'm a vice president!*

> ### INTERROGATOR
>
> *Right. Sure thing. And they've got this warehouse full of TVs and stuff for you people, huh?*

> CASEY
>
> *Yes! They do! And when people win they get
> to . . .*
>
> As Casey now continues, VOICE SLIPPING UNDER, we . . .
>
>

DISSOLVE:
>
>
> STOCK
>
> *Selected footage of the warehouse run-through.*
>
> CASEY (VO)
>
> *. . . walk through first, and then they get this
> big, ah, dipsy-dumpster, sort of, and they get to
> run up and down the aisle for . . .*
>
> As Casey's VOICE CROSS-FADES TO MUSIC, the following TITLE IS SUPERED:
>
> "John Casey was sentenced to 40 years of warehouse labor. He now loads prizes and awards for employees cashing in on Win the Connection."
>
> SUPER CLOSING LOGO. MUSIC STING AND OUT
>
>

FADE OUT:
>

COMMENTARY

As you may have noticed, the only real change that came about between the treatment and this script was the decision to have Casey revealed near the end of the program instead of up front. We made this change for two reasons. The first was Casey's time. To have him involved in a fairly complicated scene such as the program's opening might make for several hours of laborious shooting. These were hours the client and producer felt he could better spend on his own matters.

Second, it seemed even better to reveal Casey as a surprise during the latter part of the show. This placement offered the viewer two surprises instead of one. The first was the revelation that Casey himself was the person behind bars. The second was Crain's decision to say he'd never heard of Casey. We were convinced both would produce plenty of laughs.

Having read through this script once, you might reread it and think or refer back to our discussion on dialogue, structure, and transitions. Are those elements used as we discussed? If so, did their use make for what you consider to be an effective script? Maybe with some thought you can come up with an even more humorous or exciting approach. If so, why not write it as an exercise.

PART TWO SUMMARY

Now that we have explored the scriptwriting process, perhaps it's time for more self-analysis. Does writing sound like the creative media work you would enjoy most? Would you feel comfortable meeting with corporate middle managers and executives and helping to create a written framework to solve their media problems? Could you handle the sometimes unreasonable deadlines and multiple rounds of script changes? Are you open to the criticism of clients, producers, and directors—even though you may disagree with their reasoning?

Scriptwriting is extremely rewarding but also extremely demanding work. If you feel it's your calling, the following resources may offer more information worth your pursuit:

Van Nostran, William *The Media Writer's Guide Writing for Business and Educational Programming*, Focal Press, Burlington, MA, 1999

Dancyger, Ken *Alternative Scriptwriting Successfully Breaking the Rules*, Third Edition, Focal Press, Burlington, MA, 2001

Garrand, Timothy *Writing for Multimedia and the Web*, Second Edition, Focal Press, Burlington, MA, 2000

Iuppa, Nicholas V. *Designing Digital Interactive Video.* Woburn, MA, Focal Press, 1997.

part three

Preproduction: The Plan for Success

15 Preproduction

Once the script is written and approved by the client and producer, a new phase of the production process begins—preproduction. Like script development, the events that take place during this period are critical to the overall success of the media project.

DETAIL—THE KEY

Preproduction involves the organization, confirmation, and scheduling of all elements of production. It is both a foundation and a prerequisite to a smooth, productive shoot. That's because preproduction is the time for attending to details, and if anything will stop a shoot in its tracks, it's some silly, perfectly obvious, seemingly minor detail no one bothered to think about in advance.

For example, I once directed a corporate music video that required shooting employees running through a wooded area at night. We had no real woods close by, but I found a local golf course that, if lit and shot properly, would double nicely for woods. We made all the arrangements and attended to what seemed to be everything in advance. Who would open up? Where was power available? Could good-quality sound be recorded? At what times did golf course employees leave and arrive? Were there any restrictions? What was the phone number of the person in charge?

We arrived at the course at dusk ready for a full night of production. As the crew began unloading the vehicles, I got out my script book and walked with my videographer to the first camera location. As we arrived under a stand of oak trees and began discussing the shot, we both suddenly heard a loud hissing sound. We swung around in our tracks to find that the sprinklers—huge industrial, rotating, rain-bird types—had come on and were about to soak us!

It turned out the sprinklers were all on timers, preset to come on periodically in different places throughout the night. Fortunately, we were able to reach the superintendent in charge of the grounds, who turned them off for us. Had we not been able to reach her, however, the shoot would have been ruined. And had the sprinklers not come on until after we were in the trees actually shooting, not only would some very expensive equipment probably have been ruined, but the electric current being used to power the lights would also have been an extreme safety hazard to everyone close by. The lesson? Detail. Every *last* detail is important when preparing a shoot.

THE PLAYERS

Preproduction usually involves four key people: the client, the producer, the director, and an assistant director. In some cases, a production assistant is also brought in to help. In smaller facilities, this team of four may actually be a team of only two—the client and producer—with the producer switching hats continually in order to play the roles of director and assistant director. The number of people involved, however, does not change the fact that four key roles are required. Let's look briefly at each.

The Client

The client's role is most often one of support. He or she works closely with the assistant director or production assistant in arranging for things such as locations, props, and employees who may have roles in the program. Often, the client will also act as a liaison between the production team and various executives or departments in the company. He or she may also approve certain aspects of preproduction, including talent, locations, shooting schedule, and so on. The amount of client participation in preproduction is often dictated by work schedules and how excited he or she is at the prospect of watching the program take shape. Although client participation is a positive aspect in many ways, it can also become a hindrance if clients become so involved that they begin to usurp the creative responsibilities of the producer and director. Solid client–producer relationships usually alleviate this problem.

The Producer

The producer's job during preproduction is one of project management. He or she develops and monitors the production budget and oversees, guides, and approves the activities and elements brought together by everyone on the production team. This role means approving or disapproving locations, wardrobe, props, talent, and the like. It also means approving the director's shooting schedule and planned approach in terms of visualization, coverage, crew size, equipment needs, and so forth. Managing legal issues is also the producer's responsibility, and he or she is also the primary liaison between the client and the director—a job that can sometimes require great emphasis on human relations skills. This skill is most often needed when, as mentioned earlier, clients press for too much creative control or begin to dispute the needs of the production as determined by the producer and director.

The Director

After reading and visualizing the script, the director decides what elements and activities are needed and obtainable within the established budget and the producer's guidelines. The director also plays a key role in casting and establishing the basic studio or location plan,

as well as a **shooting schedule** and a **shot list** required to accomplish the production. The director becomes the person with the greatest creative impact from this point forward in the production, because only he or she can successfully bring the program to the screen.

The Assistant Director

The assistant director works with the director in making all the production arrangements. A good assistant director takes care of virtually all the details involved in bringing the production up to speed, while allowing the director time to work primarily with creative elements, such as the script, casting, studio or locations, blocking, and scheduling. In addition, a good assistant director assumes nothing; he or she confirms and double-checks everything prior to shoot day.

The Production Assistant

If a production assistant is brought in, he or she usually works for the assistant director attending to typing, orders, deliveries, certain phone calls, and other coordination efforts.

CREW COSTS

As previously mentioned, corporate budgets do not always allow for a full staff of people to carry out the preproduction process. Assuming the project does entail a full staff, the following are general cost figures for the preproduction team just discussed:

Position	Cost per Day
Director	$300–$500
Assistant Director	$200–$400
Production Assistant	$100–$150

Unless otherwise negotiated, these fees are usually payable in a lump sum after the production is completed. On longer projects, requiring weeks or months to complete, the fees are often broken up into installments or regular periodic payments.

RUN 'N' GUN SHOOTS

On smaller, "run 'n' gun"-type shoots, or those in which a producer or director must travel to a distant location, preproduction may be compressed into a series of rapid-fire phone calls, faxes, and perhaps e-mails. This situation occurs most often when a shoot involves only interviews or simple, news-style documentation of an employee work activity or a special event. In these cases, the producer or director must gain as much advance information as possible prior to the shoot and deal on the spot with any issues that arise on location.

This approach may sound like a risky way to execute a costly production effort, but unfortunately, it is frequently the case in large companies. The saving grace in this scenario is that it most often involves simple documentation versus dramatic, blocked scenes with actors, sets, lights, props, and so on.

PREPRODUCTION TASKS

Assuming that the production requires a full preproduction team, what exactly will their fees buy for the corporate media producer? The following is a general list of the tasks the team should accomplish during a typical preproduction period.

1. Budgeting
2. Reviewing and breaking down the script
3. Creating the Master File
4. Obtaining props and wardrobe
5. Scouting and confirming locations and obtaining permits and releases
6. Auditioning and selecting talent, professional and otherwise
7. Developing and writing the shooting schedule
8. Hiring the crew
9. Designing sets
10. Renting or reserving production equipment and vehicles
11. Designing and creating artwork, animation, and character-generated titles
12. Reviewing and selecting stock footage
13. Reviewing and selecting music
14. Blocking the script
15. Rehearsing
16. Conducting preproduction meetings
17. Preparing equipment for the shoot

Obviously, preproduction is a very demanding part of the overall production process. As I've mentioned, what happens during this time can literally make or break the production. With that in mind, let's cover each of these preproduction elements in greater detail.

Budgeting

Media producers have a variety of opinions about when a program should be budgeted. Some producers believe that budgeting should occur during the treatment stage, because this is when the visual foundation of the program is worked out. Others believe that budgeting should be completed even earlier by establishing a sum of money at the outset of a project and making the project fit that monetary mold.

Although this latter form of budgeting is an excellent cost-control measure, it can sometimes make programs less effective because they may be designed on the basis of cost rather than PNA factors such as audience, objectives, longevity, or potential monetary impact on the company.

Budgeting is probably most effective at the beginning of the preproduction stage. Only with a shooting script in hand can a producer accurately forecast the cost of a shoot and the subsequent postproduction required. Establishing a preliminary budget *range* following the proposal stage, however, is a common practice and a good one that has two benefits. This method allows for substantial cost control up front before the client's basic needs have been worked out, and it leaves room for justified increases (or decreases) as the proper design begins to take shape.

Assuming that budgeting is accomplished at the preproduction stage, the producer budgets a program by first breaking it down into basic elements: How many actors are needed and for how long? How much and what type of equipment will be required and for how long? What size will the crew be? How much did the script cost? Will CD or DVD authoring be required? What type of production is appropriate—Studio? Location? Or both? What type of postproduction is needed—a simple assembly of sound and images or a complex mix of graphics, special effects, and multiple soundtracks? With this information established, as well as a list of costs, or "rates" for the various crew members, facilities, and equipment, the producer can use a calculator or budgeting program to multiply out each "line item," resulting in the required totals. For instance, a director whose flat fee is $500 per day, used for seven days, will cost the producer (or client) $3,500. A percent or "load" may be added to this figure if a payroll company is used because they charge a fee for their services and deduct taxes and workers' compensation insurance.

The same type of simple multiplication is used on each "line item" to eventually arrive at totals. As you might guess from this process, the producers' keys to budgeting a program are to know *what* he or she needs, *how long* he or she will need it, and *how much* each item will cost. Figure 15.1 is an example of a typical production budget.

Creating the Master File

Though most people think of video production strictly in terms of cameras, lights and editing, a host of legal and organizational issues are also critical to the success of any production. Why critical? Assume a producer uses a piece of music he or she does not have rights to. After completing the program, 1000 copies are sent to company locations nation-wide. Then one day the producer's phone rings. It is the musician who composed the music, or perhaps the recording company that owns publication rights, or the company that owns distribution rights. They inform the producer that they have discovered the producer's copyright infringement and are taking his company to court to retrieve royalties, legal fees and damages.

This is only one of countless possibilities that point up the need for an accurately organized and thoroughly maintained Master File. Although that Master File is most often established by the Producer at the inception of the project, the majority of Master File documentation will be received starting in the preproduction stage. For this reason, now is a good time to cover this important producer management tool and his or her role in maintaining it.

As we will discuss shortly, the AD typically creates a production master file when he or she reports to work on the project. If both the AD and the producer are keeping their own separate master files, following production the AD's material should end up in the producer's file for archiving.

Figure 15.2 is one example of a typical Master File Checklist. Different companies may have different needs, but those shown in this figure are typically the primary items of concern to the corporate media producer. It's worth our time to briefly discuss each item, where it originates and it's importance.

Needs Analysis, Content Outline, Treatment, Shooting Script

As we have discussed in the writing section of this book, these are the critical elements of design, research, and writing. A final, approved copy of each should be maintained in the Master File for future reference.

Budget

As we have just discussed the budget is a critical financial documentation of what monies have been allocated for the production. Associated purchase orders, invoices and expense reports will show how those monies were spent. Budgetary documentation is another critical item that may be useful for future reference. How? It is not unusual at all for the financial executives in a company (those who may well determine the fate of the video production department) to request and scrutinize this type of information.

Agreements, Deal Memos, and Contracts

Agreements between writers, directors, producers, and crew members vary widely in the corporate media field. Many programs are written and directed on the strength of a handshake and perhaps a letter like the one shown in Figure 15.3.

Writers' and Directors' Contracts

Writers and Directors may require individual contracts since these are the two most critical positions on the production team. In addition, some writers or directors may view their creative work as automatically and indisputably owned by them. Automatic copyright ownership may be the case when no money is involved, however, the moment someone is paid for their written material or directorial expertise, he or she may relinquish ownership of it to the producer or company. And with that ownership typically comes the right to do as the company pleases with the work. A writer who feels her work has been damaged by a producer's revisions, however, may not agree. She may decide to take her case to court. And without a signed contract she may have a case.

Contracts vary widely, and for the reasons just mentioned they should be created or at least reviewed and revised by the company's legal team. If no legal team exists, an attorney should hired for this purpose.

DiZazzo Communications
Media Production Budget

PROJECT:	KTF Sales Training Video			DATE:	12/23/98
ITEM	**QUANTITY**	**RATE**	**DAYS/HRS.**	**EXPENSE**	**TOTAL**
SCRIPT					
CD-ROM Design					$0
Treatment					$0
Script	1	$2,500	1		$2,500
Rewrite					$0
Producer	2	$500	1		$1,000
			SCRIPT TOTAL		$3,500
PREPRODUCTION					
Producer	1	$500	1		$500
Director	1	$500	3		$1,500
A.D.	1	$350	3		$1,050
P.A.	1	$125	2		$250
Set Design					$0
Location Fees					$0
Props/Wardrobe	1	$100	1		$100
Set Materials					$0
D.P.					$0
Gaffer					$0
Grip					$0
Audio					$0
T.D.					$0
Prompter					$0
Graphic Artist					$0
Art System w/Artist	1	$1,400	1		$1,400
Tape/Film Stock	10	$36	1		$360
Permits	1	$350	1		$350
Insurance	1	$1,500	1		$1,500
Postage					$0
Miscellaneous	1	$500	1		$500
			PREPROD. TOTAL		$7,510
PRODUCTION					
Producer	1	$500	1		$500
Director	1	$500	3		$1,500
A.D.	1	$350	3		$1,050
D.P.	1	$350	3		$1,050
Audio	1	$250	3		$750
T.D.					$0
Grip					$0
Gaffer	1	$250	3		$750
P.A.					$0
Floor Manager					$0
Prompter	1	$250	1		$250
Make up	1	$250	1		$250
Studio					$0
Talent (On-Cam)	1	$2,000	1		$2,000
Talent (V.O.)					$0
Travel/Meals	15	$15	3		$675

Figure 15.1 Production budget lists and categorizes all elements of the production into line items. It also performs the required calculations to reach line-item and bottom-line totals. Line-item "loads" such as overhead and payrolling costs may be calculated in each line item or added at the end (as in this case) as a separate figure.

(Continued)

DiZazzo Communications   2

ITEM	QUANTITY	RATE	DAYS/HRS.	EXPENSE	TOTAL
Generator					$0
Camera Pkg.	1	$470	3		$1,410
Lighting Pkg.	1	$150	3		$450
Audio Pkg.	1	$75	3		$225
Other					$0
				PROD. TOTAL	$10,862
POSTPRODUCTION					
Producer	1	$500	1		$500
Director	1	$500	4		$2,000
On-line -Avid w/Editor	1	$1,800	2		$3,600
On-line w/Editor					$0
Avid - View & Log	1	$25	8		$200
Avid - Digitize	1	$110	7		$770
Duplication					$0
Avid - Laydown - D2					$0
Lab					$0
Telecine					$0
Preview Copies	3	$3	1		$9
CD-ROM Input					$0
CD-ROM Copies					$0
Music	1	$125	1		$125
				POSTPROD. TOTAL	$7,079
EVALUATION					
Informal					$0
Formal					$0
Focus Group					$0
Postage					$0
Other					$0
				EVALUATION TOTAL	$0
DISTRIBUTION					
Tape Stock					$0
Duplication					$0
Postage					$0
Other					$0
				DIST. TOTAL	$0
				SUBTOTAL	$28,951
				PAYROLL/ADMIN.	$2,895
				GRAND TOTAL	$31,846

Figure 15.1, cont'd

Crew and Non-Union Talent Deal Memos

Deal memos are simple contracts stating what will be expected of a crew member, the time frames involved and the compensation. Figure 15. 4 is a typical example.

SAG Contracts

The Screen Actors Guild (SAG) and the American Federation of Television and Radio Artists (AFTRA) both have very specific contracts that are to be used for their members. These spell out, among other things, exactly how the film or video recording may be used and what the rate of pay will be for the performer. SAG and AFTRA rates vary depending on the type of role the actor plays and how the program will be distributed. You can view comprehensive information on these associations at their Websites, www.sag.com and www.aftra.com.

Production Checklist

Note: Enter check or date when item is received. Include copies of all items.

Project #_____   Producer_____

Director _____   A.D._____

Editor_____   Date: Start_____ Complete _____

ITEM	RECEIVED
Needs Analysis	
Content Outline	
Treatment	
Shooting Script	
Budget	

Deal Memos and Contracts
 Writers and Directors Contracts _____
 Crew Deal Memos _____
 Sag Contracts _____
 Non-Sag Contracts _____

Rental Agreements

Releases
 Location _____
 Music _____
 Talent _____
 Other _____

Master Script(s)

Shooting Schedule

Shot list

Production Logs

EDL/Disk

Expense Log

Shot list

Receipts

Figure 15.2 Production Checklist. When the production is complete, the producer should have these elements in a Master File. This assures legal protection and an accurate resource for possible future reference.

June 2, 1999

Kirsten Mace
J. Marsh and Associates
30401 Andor Road
Agoura Hills, CA 91301

Dear Kirsten:

Following are the budget figures on the Larsen project. I laid them out according to the breakdown in the RFP.

PRODUCT TRAINING VIDEO PRODUCTION (5)	$300,000
SALES TRAINING VIDEO PRODUCTION (3)	$180,000
SALES TRAINING VIDEO EDITING/UPDATING (2)	$ 35,000
DUPLICATION (6,000)	$ 12,000
TOTAL	$527,000

Deliverables: 10 Digital Beta master tapes, plus 6,000 dupes (All packaging handled by J. Marsh and Associates)

Delivery date: 6/31/2000

A few notes:

I arrived at a rate of $2,000. per completed minute for the product and sales training videos. For the two programs needing updating, I assumed they would require little or no writing, shooting, etc. These I calculated at about $700. per completed minute. The duping I got at $2. per tape.

A few ideas I've used in my calculations that would save money: We would shoot all the host and voice-over material in *one* block of days with *one* host on *one* set (if that's okay with the client). All the walk-around shots and beauty shots could be done on a stage in the same way — one car after the other with essentially the same lighting setups, the same shots, and positioning. Any actors needed for role plays (sales consultants and customers) could be used in multiple shows. By the way, these could also be shot blue screen as I have done on previous projects for you, eliminating the need to tie up a dealership location.

As for the "...fun, upbeat approach..." comment by the client, I had a few preliminary ideas. One is LSU — Larsen Sales University. If this theme ran throughout, all shows could utilize the same or similar graphics and the college theme could be used in both the tapes and the written materials. Another idea is the Larsen 1,000 or Grand Prix. With this idea, we might even try to find a race track and shoot all the host on-camera material

Figure 15.3 An agreement letter states the parameters of the work to be performed and other critical elements. Some freelance producers use this format as a means of establishing a semi-contractual arrangement in writing.

Kirsten Mace
June 2, 1999
Page 2

and cars there instead of in a studio. This could save money (depending on how much the track costs were) and it would give the shows a sense of energy and competition. We could supplement this with rapid fire editing techniques, hot music and racing footage graphics.

As I mentioned to you several days ago, I'll be back east next week. I return on the 13th and I'd welcome the chance to dive in immediately and produce this project for you. In fact I could do some set-up work via telephone while I'm gone. And once I got more details I could also look for additional ways to trim costs and come up with more creative treatment ideas.

Thanks for calling me on this, Kirsten. As I said I'd like nothing better than to jump on it. If I can add or change anything, don't hesitate to call. And if you feel the rates I've quoted should be adjusted, please let me know.

Take care. I hope to hear from you soon.

Sincerely,

Ray DiZazzo

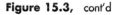

Figure 15.3, cont'd

Non-Union Contracts

Non-union contracts are created by an attorney or the company's legal department. Like the crew, writers' and directors' contracts, they spell out the services to be provided, the rights purchased and the total compensation. Typically, the ownership and control of all rights will also be included in this type of contract. Keep in mind that an actor can decide to sue for the same reason a writer might. He or she may feel the performance provided was used or edited in some way that is in dispute. Or, if the program is distributed to the public market and it becomes financially successful, the actor may show up one day asking for his or her cut of the profits.

Rental Agreements

Rental agreements are those established between the company and the equipment rental companies. This might include dollies, camera and sound equipment, lighting and often grip trucks equipped with a variety of production equipment.

Releases

The producer must have releases for all the material in his or her program to be assured someone cannot try, at a later date, to claim rights and require some sort of payment or legal action. Here are the most common.

Location releases (or permits) are the documents that allow the production to shoot on property other than the producing company's. This might be on a city street corner, in which case a location permit issued by the city will be required, or it may be the backyard of someone on the crew. In this later case, a release is important for liability reasons and to assure that at

Deal Memo – Non-Union Talent

This Agreement made this _____day of _____, 20____, between _____ _____ hereinafter called Producer and _____ hereinafter called Player.

1. PHOTOGRAPHY – Producer engages Player and Player agrees to perform services in a program tentatively entitled "Fitness for all Ages".

2. Start Date: _____ End Date: _____

3. LOCATION: Thousand Oaks, California.

4. TERM – Player's employment shall be for the completion of a script tentatively entitled "Fitness for all Ages." Producer will make every effort to complete principle photography and recordings in two days; however, Player is obligated to complete both scripts for the agreed rate. Additional pick-ups and/or changes after principal photography will be negotiated in good-faith at a rate **not greater than original offer**.

5. COMPENSATION – Producer employs Player for On-Camera Narrator/Spokesperson at a flat salary of $600.00. Payment will be made after receipt of invoice from Player or authorized Agency representing talent. There will be no additional compensation for supplemental use of material.

6. WARDROBE – Wardrobe will be furnished by the Player.

Producer: _____
by: _____
Title: _____

Player: _____
S.S. #: _____
Address: _____
_____
Agency: _____
Agency Telephone #: _____
Manager: _____

Figure 15.4 A typical Deal Memo outlining the parameters of a non-union actor's position. Crew member memos are very similar.

some later date the owner of the yard doesn't claim rights to, or payment from, the producer. Typically, before a city or business will sign a release, they will require that the production company be adequately insured for liability. This usually means to the tune of at least $1,000,000. Many companies or city agencies will also ask to be written in as a payee on a temporary policy rider. This may seem like overkill, but remember, a stunt person doing even a simple tumble could suffer severe injuries. Then the question becomes: will he or she sue the production company or, the company or agency that allowed the production, or both?

Music is used in most corporate media programs. And some companies simply dupe and use popular recordings with no regard for copyright. Musicians, music publishing companies, recording companies and musicians unions can all make legal claims against the producer or the corporation in such cases. These can get messy and very costly. The safest route is to always get releases. Companies exists that do only this type of work. They can be found on the internet in www.411publilshing.com and other such reference guides.

Models or extras are any people appearing in a featured manner in a video program. This might be considered something like an extra. It could be categorized as a separate function from actors or these types of participants may all sign one from created by the company. Figure 15.5 displays an individual and group release form.

Other

Other is the catch-all category for any situation that arises involving some legal release or situation. It may require revising an existing form or creating a custom form, specifying the services provided, the amount and from of remuneration or the fact that company is to be held harmless from all future claims.

Master Script(s)

One or more master scripts may be created during the shoot. Most ADs and producers make all notes on a single copy, but some prefer to create a master script for the live action portion of the shoot and, when a complete narration track is produced, a second script strictly for the audio portions. Both should end up in the master file.

Shooting Schedule

The shooting schedule, as we will discuss shortly, is developed by the director and a copy of it should become a part of the master file. It serves as a historic documentation of how the shoot was organized and where the crew was on specific days at specific times.

Shot List

Many producers require their directors to submit shot lists. These lists give the producer a good sense of how the director will "cover" the shoot and his or her priorities in terms of shot selection.

Production Logs

The Production logs are typically kept by the AD in conjunction with the DP or camera operator providing "In" and Out" times for every shot of the program. Production or "shot logs" as they are sometimes called are noted based on the time code recorded on the tape.

EDL Disk

As we will see in the chapters on editing, the Edit Decision List or EDL is a critical resource, typically contained on a floppy disk. A copy of it is a must for the producer's master file. The EDL is essentially the backbone of the entire edited program.

Expense Logs and Receipts

And finally, expenses and receipts. These are monetary documents used to record how the crew has spent money during the shoot. They are the types of records that any producer would be prudent to maintain as a kind of financial snapshot of the production days.

Reviewing and Breaking Down the Script

Just as the producer reviews and breaks down the script for budgeting purposes, so does the director, but for different reasons. The director must know the script not so much in terms of monetary detail, but rather in terms of *creative* detail. In order to be prepared to make crucial creative decisions, he or she must understand the script in terms of structure, informational quality, character profiles, and tone and pace. In the ideal situation, the director is left to these tasks during preproduction while the assistant director and the production assistant work on organizing and coordinating administrative tasks such as lining up props, arranging talent auditions, renting or reserving equipment, and so on. We will discuss the director's role in much greater detail in forthcoming chapters, so let's move on in the preproduction process.

A

Model Likeness Release
Granite-Collen Communications

I, _____ hereby assign and grant Granite-Collen Communications and its agents the right and permission to copyright and/or publish photographic portraits, pictures, motion pictures or electronic images of me in which I may be included in whole or in part, or in any composite or reproductions thereof, in color or otherwise, made through any media at their studios or elsewhere, for art, advertising, trade, education, or any other similar purpose whatsoever, indefinitely.

I hereby waive my right to inspect and/or approve the finished product or the advertising copy that may be used in connection herewith.

I hereby release and discharge Granite-Collen Communications, its successors and all persons acting under its permission or authority, or those for whom it is acting, from any liability by virtue of any blurring, distortion, alteration, optical illusion or use in composite form that may occur or be produced in the recording or editing of said images or in any processing toward the completion of the finished product.

Executed on _____, 200 __, at _____

_____

_____
Model's Name (Printed)

_____
Model's Signature

Figure 15.5 **A,** A standard individual model release. **B,** Same type of release used for groups.

B

Model Likeness Release
Granite-Collen Communications

I hereby assign and grant Granite-Collen Communications, Inc. and its agents the right and permission to copyright and/or publish photographic portraits, pictures, motion pictures or electronic images of me in which I may be included in whole or in part, or in any composite or reproductions thereof, in color or otherwise, made through any media at their studios or elsewhere, for art, advertising, trade, education, or any other similar purpose whatsoever, indefinitely. I hereby waive my right to inspect and/or approve the finished product or the advertising copy that may be used in connection herewith. I hereby release and discharge Granite-Collen, its successors and all persons acting under its permission or authority, or those for whom it is acting, from any liability by virtue of any blurring, distortion, alteration, optical illusion or use in composite form that may occur or be produced in the recording or editing of said images or in any processing toward the completion of the finished product.

Print Name	Signature

Date _____

Figure 15.5, cont'd

Obtaining Props and Wardrobe

This task normally falls to the assistant director or the production assistant, often with assistance from the client. It can be as simple as obtaining a set of work tools or as complex as visiting a wardrobe rental company to arrange costumes, take measurements, and so on. In corporate media, the former scenario is typically the case. But simple or not, obtaining props and wardrobe should never be treated as unimportant. A missing screwdriver can hold up a shoot for hours just as easily as an exotic costume.

Scouting and Confirming Locations and Obtaining Permits and Releases

In most cases, the director scouts locations early in preproduction, primarily because he or she must confirm that the locations will work to properly visualize the script. In addition, the director must be sure that the locations work logistically. Are parking places and restrooms available? Will a generator be required? How disruptive will the production crew be to employees or others? Is there a cost to rent the locations? Who will unlock the doors? Where are the electrical fuse panels located? And so on.

Whenever possible, a wise director scouts locations at roughly the same time of day that the shoot will take place. This process allows him or her to accurately gauge where the sun will be, the types of light and shadows the DP will have to deal with, how much traffic may be passing, how many pedestrians may be in the area, and so on. As an example, if shooting will take place in the vicinity of a school, the director will probably want to avoid shooting when students are arriving or leaving for the day.

As we have mentioned, shooting on public streets and even on private property often requires the production company to obtain a permit from the city and perhaps a release from property owners. In addition, police or firefighters may be necessary if traffic will be blocked or if some other hazard might arise as a result of the shoot.

The assistant director is normally responsible for obtaining the required permits based on the director's choices. As you might guess, advance location scouting and as much lead time as possible is often a critical factor.

Photographic or model releases are also managed by the AD. As mentioned earlier, a release should be signed by any employee or other person who is prominently featured or who speaks on camera. Releases should also be obtained for signs or businesses in some cases. As an example, if a host is being taped on a city street and a Burger King sign—along with many other signs—is visible in the background, no permit would be required. If the host is standing directly in front of the Burger King sign, however, and calls attention to it as an analogy for some aspect of the production, a release would be required. Most corporate video departments have standard release forms for these occasions that are approved by the legal department.

Auditioning and Selecting Talent, Professional and Otherwise

Preliminary casting is usually carried out by the assistant director, following a meeting with the director. Based on the director's requirements in terms of gender, age, look, and so on, the assistant director will often refer to in-house casting books, pictures, and résumés submitted by actors as well as to previous programs produced by the company. From this material, the director then chooses the actors he or she would like to audition. The assistant director makes the arrangements by calling the actors directly or speaking to their agents.

In the case of company employees, talent selection may take place by default; that is, the client may insist that certain of his or her employees participate in the production as a kind of perk. Or, the selection process may take place simply based on which employees in the media department may be available to be "stars" for a day. Whatever the selection process, all talent must be confirmed in advance for the days and times they will be required.

Developing and Writing the Shooting Schedule

This job is the director's and it, too, is a critical one. Based on his or her scouting and analysis, the director organizes the scenes into the proper shooting order (almost always different from the script order) and estimates the amount of time required to record each one. Once this process is completed, the director begins to schedule the scenes on the confirmed production days.

Scheduling is critical because it almost always requires juggling resources to make everything happen on the right day at the right time. Perhaps a location won't be available or an actor is booked on a different shoot or a company executive who must appear in the production will be out of town on the day most convenient to shoot him or her.

Also of prime importance is the director's sense of the amount of time required to record each scene. If his or her estimates are inaccurate, the shoot will either waste a lot of time and money with crew members in a nonproductive mode, or they may be scrambling for the entire shoot playing catch up and having to continually compromise the work into preparing the production.

Before it is finalized, the shooting schedule is approved by the producer and client. It is then often handed out to crew members on the first day of production.

Hiring the Crew

Some directors prefer to pick their own crews, whereas others simply leave the job to their assistant directors. Typically, a director will be most interested in the DP or videographer and the sound recordist. These two individuals have the greatest impact on the director's work and thus are critical to his or her success.

Crew sizes depend, of course, on the production's complexity. A small location shoot to document a company event or perhaps record a department in operation may need only a single camera operator. A shoot involving actors, props, complex blocking, lighting, and sound requirements may involve from 10 to 20 people.

Designing Sets

In corporate media, the producer or director typically designs his or her own sets. They are often simple arrangements consisting of a few flats and perhaps a company desk with typical props, a few plants, and a file cabinet or two. Corporate media programs are also often shot in what is called limbo—a black, seamless environment with a few set pieces used to "suggest" perhaps a company conference room or office. On larger shoots, requiring extensive art direction or a fully realistic look, a set designer may be brought in, but the expense often runs into thousands of dollars. Whatever the case, designing sets is important in much the same way as location scouting. It must be completed early in the preproduction process to leave time for blocking and scheduling.

Renting or Reserving Production Equipment and Vehicles

Obviously, a video production requires a camera, lights, microphones, monitors, cables, and so on. If a company has its own studio and production equipment, the assistant director can simply reserve it for the shooting period. If the equipment is to be rented, he or she must call a rental facility and arrange to have it delivered the afternoon prior to production. If delivery is not possible, a production assistant or crew member is normally sent to pick up the equipment and return it the day after the shoot.

Rental companies typically charge only for the production days but allow the equipment to be picked up on the afternoon of the day before and returned on the morning after the shoot. Many companies also offer reduced rates if the rental period is long enough. For example, if the equipment is to be rented for seven days, it is common to negotiate a four- or five-day rate. Experienced producers and assistant directors learn which rental facilities offer the best deals and usually become regulars.

Equipment Lists

An equipment list for a simple three-person shoot would probably look like the following:

Camcorder, power supply, and batteries.

Head, tripod, and spreaders

Several microphones with batteries

Portable audio mixer with batteries

Light kit

Several rolls of videotape

Video cables

Audio cables

A/C cables

Gaffer's tape

Dulling spray

An equipment list for a more complex shoot might include the following:

Camcorder, power supply, and batteries

Head, tripod, and spreaders

Video monitor with batteries

Waveform monitor

Several microphones with batteries

Portable audio mixer with batteries

Two light kits with gels/scrims/diffusion

Two reflectors

Several rolls of videotape

Video cables

Audio cables

A/C cables

Generator

Dolly

Several C stands

Sand bags

Assorted flags, scrims, and nets

Gaffer's tape

Dulling spray

Makeup kit

Slate

Felt tip markers

We will take a closer look at the purpose of all this equipment and the job functions of all crew members in the following production section.

Designing and Creating Artwork, Animation, and Character-Generated Titles

Many corporate television programs require some form of artwork, usually diagrams, charts, or specially designed still frames. Sophisticated three-dimensional (3-D) animation is also commonly used in corporate media. In some cases, this phase of preproduction may also include electronically generated titles, which must be designed, positioned, and in the case of live broadcasts, readied for use during the production.

In most cases, supervising graphic artwork is the responsibility of the director, with help from the assistant director. Artwork might be developed through an in-house graphics or animation department or by an outside company. Animation is typically storyboarded or sketched out by the director, who then sits with a graphic artist to develop the actual sequences. Whatever the situation, one of the most important things to remember in this area is lead time because the design and production of artwork can sometimes take several weeks.

Reviewing and Selecting Stock Footage

Stock footage—shots archived from a previous production—are often used in corporate media productions. The reason is simple—cost savings. Footage that can simply be retrieved from a video library versus going on location with a crew can save thousands of dollars. For this reason, most corporate media facilities maintain a stock footage library in which camera originals or program edit masters are stored. Many facilities also catalog their stock footage to make it easier for producers, directors, and assistant directors to locate.

In most cases, the assistant director or a production assistant retrieves stock footage based on the director's request. The director then views the selected reels or segments and chooses the exact shots he or she has decided to include in the program. These reels are given temporary reel numbers, making them a part of the program currently in production. After their use in editing, the temporary numbers are discarded and the stock footage reels go back on the shelf for use in another production.

Stock footage can also be purchased from news stations, production companies, and distributors who specialize in this service. It can be quite expensive, however, sometimes running hundreds of dollars per second. Some corporate facilities share stock footage as a means of cost control and mutual support.

Reviewing and Selecting Music

Virtually all corporate media productions require the use of at least one, and more often, several pieces of music. The director usually picks the music that he or she feels is most appropriate to match the tone and pace of the program. This job is sometimes left for postproduction, but it is often a good idea to take care of it in preproduction when all other preparation is taking place.

Music is typically maintained by a facility in the form of a CD library. "Network" is one of the most popular suppliers of both music and sound effects for corporate programming. Another popular supplier is "Killer Tracks."

The cost for use of library music can take several forms. A facility often pays the music company a yearly blanket fee for unlimited usage of all music in its library. Additional CDs are added to the library on an ongoing basis. "Needle drop" fees—individual charges for each selection used—are another means of payment. Needle drop fees can run $50 or more depending on the piece of music and the company offering it. "Buy-out" music libraries are also becoming popular, in which a single up-front fee is paid and the producer or facility owns the rights to use the music from then on.

Some very expensive corporate productions have music scored by an artist or band. Or, a producer can buy rights to existing hit songs. In the case of custom scoring, the fees are negotiated and paid to the musician or band, and a release is secured. When acquiring rights to existing music, an agency that specializes in this work is normally used because musicians' unions, music publishers, and producers may require varying contractual arrangements and percentages.

If research is required to negotiate rights and permissions, an assistant director typically does the legwork and reports his or her findings to the producer. The producer then typically decides if the budget will bear the costs of such a "requirement."

Blocking the Script

The director decides on **blocking,** which involves pre-planning how the actors will move in relation to the camera. Some directors block a script by storyboarding it scene by scene, as shown in Figure 15.6. Other directors prefer to make overhead sketches showing the position and movement of the camera and the actors. Figure 15.7 provides an example of this process. However it is accomplished, blocking should be carried out primarily in preproduction.

Blocking can sometimes undergo fine tuning once the camera and actors are in position on location. The director may decide that the way the host was going to exit does not look quite right against a certain background. Or, if he or she feels a higher or lower angle is better, the action may have to change to some degree. Also, blocking a dramatic scene is more complex than blocking a simple host scene or an employee at work. This type of blocking should be finalized on the set or location on the basis of how the scene plays out and its emotional content.

Blocking, however, is similar to any other preproduction detail. If a good deal of thought and preparation is not put into it in advance, it usually leads to costly, frustrating delays in production.

Rehearsals

Talent rehearsals are rare in corporate media production because they add up to extra time and actors' fees. But when the project is a dramatic program, involving role-playing actors and complex camera blocking, it is a good idea to rehearse if the budget will bear it. If a full rehearsal on the set is impossible, a meeting between the actors and the director to simply read through and discuss the script can be very helpful. If a brief meeting is not possible, the director should at minimum call each of the actors in advance to discuss their roles. Rehearsing company executives is also very beneficial if their schedules allow it. Whatever the type or extent of rehearsal, the result will normally be better performances and a faster, smoother production.

In the case of multicamera studio shoots, technical rehearsals are common, usually on the day before production. In a "tech" rehearsal, as it is usually called, the entire crew is brought in and all elements of the shoot—camera angles, lighting, audio, props, and so on—are checked during an abbreviated run-through. Tech rehearsals are also common to familiarize executives with their roles in corporate broadcasts.

In either of these scenarios, the director usually makes the decision to pick or negotiate the rehearsal day, and the assistant director schedules it.

Conducting Preproduction Meetings

Preproduction meetings tend to follow the same rule of thumb as many other elements of production: The more complex the shoot, the more meetings are needed to stay on top of details as they develop. On most corporate productions, a single preproduction meeting the day before the shoot, or even on the same morning, is adequate.

Typically, the entire crew meets, scripts and schedules are passed out, and the director briefly discusses the shoot scene by scene. This type of meeting allows crew members to get an advance overview of what the director wants on particular shots and how he or she plans to get it. It also allows for crew input, which in many cases can make for a faster, more efficient shoot.

Preparing Equipment for the Shoot

Following the preproduction meeting, or just before leaving for the first location, the crew checks over the equipment, repairs or replaces anything faulty, loads and gases up the trucks, and takes care of any other final details. This equipment checkout and repair process is important because of the nature of location television

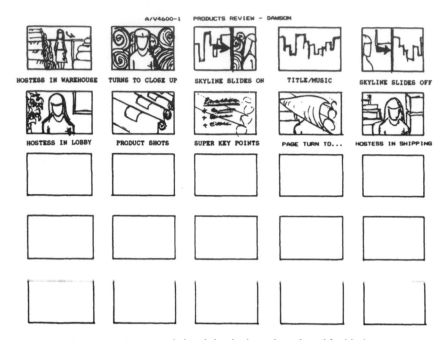

Figure 15.6 A simple hand-sketched storyboard used for blocking.

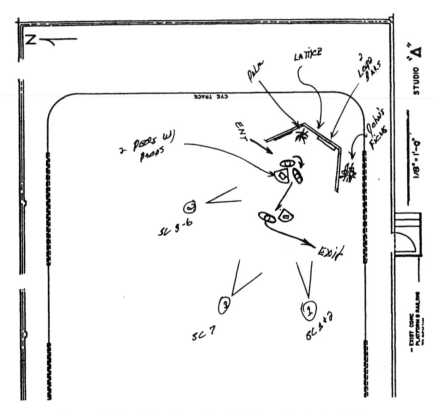

Figure 15.7 A director's overhead sketch used to develop blocking.

production. During a typical location shoot, equipment is loaded and unloaded at least several times. It gets carried, jarred, and piled up. It also endures a fair amount of bouncing around in the back of trucks.

When this type of treatment takes its toll and a piece of equipment turns up faulty during production, the tendency is to put it aside and quickly grab another piece that happens to be working. Unfortunately, the piece that was set aside on the last shoot is sometimes left unrepaired and ends up on another producer's shoot next time. This situation is most common in the case of camera registration, lights with blown bulbs, and weak or dead batteries.

If a corporate media department has maintenance engineers who continually repair equipment and "prep" it before each shoot, a production crew is less likely to end up with something faulty in the field. Rental houses typically prepare all equipment before it is sent out. Faulty equipment problems are still possible, however, and finding the problem before leaving the facility can save hours of frustrating downtime on location.

So, the equipment has been prepped and loaded, and all the other elements of preproduction have been attended to. Now, at last, the crew is ready (assuming the weather report doesn't predict rain) for production.

PART THREE SUMMARY

Attention to detail and the ability to quickly adjust to changing circumstances are keys to success in preproduction. Directors must consider every possibility when scouting, blocking, and scheduling their work. Assistant directors and production assistants must constantly keep the needs of directors, producers, and clients uppermost in their minds. Producers and clients must give their production teams the freedom to "flex" their creative muscles but also maintain a guiding hand in the overall process.

The initial rewards for such diligence? A shoot that moves seamlessly from scene to scene and location to location; a production that comes in on time and under budget; a satisfied crew and cast; and a client who is comfortable that he or she is truly in the hands of professionals. Also extremely rewarding are the days immediately following production when it becomes apparent that everything is "in the can," logged, and organized exactly as it was intended.

If you'd care to explore more details on the preproduction process, the following three resources should prove valuable.

BIBLIOGRAPHY

Simon, Deke and Wiese, Michael *Film & Video Budgets*, Third Edition, Burlington, MA, Focal Press, June 2001.

Lutzker, Arnold *Content Rights for Creative Professionals Copyrights & Trademarks in a Digital Age*, Second Edition, Burlington, MA, Focal Press, December 2002.

Cartwright, Steve R. *Pre-Production Planning for Video, Film and Multimedia.*, Woburn, MA, Focal Press, 1996.

part four
Production

16 Production Formats, Equipment, and Shooting Styles

Production is the process of recording all of the sounds and pictures called for in the script in a manner appropriate for use in the editing process.

GLAMOUR OR GRIND?

Undoubtedly, an image of glamour is associated with film and television production. Crowds gather quickly wherever a location shoot is in progress. Bystanders wonder aloud where the stars are or what commercial or movie is being shot. Children and adults alike attempt to slip into the background of a shot in hopes of later seeing themselves on television. Anyone who has actually worked on a production, however, will attest to the fact that the word grind is often a much more accurate description than glamour. Simply put, video production is work—long, hard, often frustrating work. At times, it also involves enormous amounts of pressure, especially for the producer and the director.

Before exploring how this work process actually takes place on a typical production, let's briefly review some basic but important preliminary information—the fundamental aspects of videotape, digital video, and film recording.

THE VIDEOTAPE, DIGITAL VIDEO, AND FILM RECORDING PROCESSES

Film recording is a chemical process as opposed to videotape and digital recording, which are electronic processes.

Film Recording

In film recording, an image is exposed to the emulsion on the film's surface for a specific, very short period of time. That exposure causes chemical changes in the emulsion, which, when the film is later developed, reveals a print of the image exactly as it existed for that instant. Frame after frame of these exposed images, projected rapidly on a screen, create motion pictures.

During production, the sound portion of a film scene is recorded separately on audiotape. This process is accomplished on a special tape recorder that is designed to run at exactly the same speed as the film camera so that the sound will later be "in sync" (synchronized) with the action.

Only in the final stages of the film postproduction process are these separate sound and picture elements combined to make the print we finally see projected on the screen.

Analog and Digital Video Recording

In video recording, an image is first exposed to a number of electronic circuits and "chips" (formerly tubes) in the video camera. These normally include three color chips—one for the color red, one for the color blue, and one for the color green. During this process, the red, blue, and green portions of the picture are separated into individual electronic signals, which can be adjusted independently. These color signals and other aspects of the video image, such as **luminance** (light intensity), are processed by the camera and sent to a videotape recorder (VTR), where they are recorded at a rate of approximately 30 (actually 29.97) frames per second. Unlike recording sound for film, recording the sound portion of a scene on video is not a separate process. Sound is recorded on an audio channel on the same videotape as the visual image.

If these video signals are analog—that is, electronic signals in their original wavelike frequency state—they must be recorded onto videotape. Digital video signals, however—wavelike electronic signals converted to binary information—may be recorded onto videotape or onto a computer hard drive. In the latter case, the need for videotape as a recording and storage medium is eliminated. With the advent of new technology, tapeless digital image and sound recording in the form of pure computer memory has become commonplace, especially in the case of animation and artwork. A typical video game, for instance, or animated sequence in a corporate program may never be recorded on videotape. They may originate in a computer graphics program, be edited in a computer editing program and be delivered for use exclusively on a computer via CD, DVD or the Internet.

Because electronic signals, unlike the chemical images recorded on film, do not require developing, these mediums do not have to be sent to a laboratory before they can be viewed. A video signal can simply be fed from the camera into a television monitor with the proper attachment and viewed in real time as it actually takes place. Once it is recorded on videotape, the video image can quickly be rewound and played back on the spot. If recorded onto a computer hard drive as digital information, instant access is achievable with the click of a mouse.

Obviously, the videotape and digital methods of recording sound and pictures are much more convenient and immediate than film. The editing process, as we will see in future chapters, is also much simpler with videotape and digital nonlinear systems. These factors have formed the basis for the phenomenal growth of video, in broadcast organizations, the business world and in private households.

With this basic foundation in place, let's look more closely at the different recording formats used in corporate media production and the types of equipment they require.

FORMATS

Most home video systems use ½-inch VHS or 8-millimeter formats. Half-inch and 8 millimeter refer to the width of the videotape, and VHS (video home system) refers to the cassette type. The following five primary formats are used in corporate and broadcast video: 1-inch reel-to-reel, ¾-inch U-Matic, ¾-inch D (digital), ½-inch camcorder, and 6-millimeter Mini DV (digital video).

The first two formats, 1-inch reel-to-reel and ¾-inch U-Matic, have been almost completely replaced with ½-inch camcorder and Mini-DV formats. This is because reel-to-reel and U-Matic recorders are much larger, more expensive and less effective than their modern counterparts. Because 1-inch and ¾-inch still exist, however, and the student or corporate producer may find him or herself working with them, we will cover them briefly in this chapter.

One-Inch Reel-to-Reel

One-inch reel-to-reel (see Figure 16.1) is what we *used* to see every evening on the network news and sitcoms. It provided very fine picture resolution; rich, true, color reproduction; and a very low signal-to-noise ("snow") ratio. The 1-inch reel-to-reel format was, and still is, used in both broadcast and corporate media studio productions. As we've mentioned, however, because of the smaller, more convenient, and cost-effective formats that have emerged, 1-inch has become the exception instead of the rule, especially in productions shot on location.

Three-Quarter-Inch U-Matic

Three-quarter-inch U-Matic (Figure 16.2) is a video cassette format, rather than reel-to-reel. Its picture reproduction quality is not comparable to 1-inch, but when

Figure 16.1 A 1-inch reel-to-reel VTR used for studio applications.

combined with a good-quality camera, it is better than the VHS format. In addition, because it is smaller than 1 inch and utilizes a cassette, ¾-inch U-Matic is much easier to use in the field.

For many years, these qualities made the ¾-inch format the predominant standard for non-broadcast video productions. The advent of ½-inch camcorders, however, and more recently, the Mini DV formats that produce better quality for a much lower price, have drastically changed this standard. In today's corporate media department, ¾-inch U-Matic is virtually a format of the past.

Half-Inch Camcorders

Broadcast-quality camcorders use ½-inch videotape cassettes (Figure 16.3) in a video tape recorder (VTR) that is built into the camera. The camcorder introduced two important benefits over its earlier counterparts: First, it eliminated the need for a separate VTR because the unit was built into the camera. This provided a cost savings as well as the ability to send out smaller and more mobile location crews. For instance, it virtually eliminated the need for the E.I.C. or Engineer in Charge, because this person was primarily responsible for operating the separate VTR.

Second, broadcast-quality camcorders introduced a high-speed, component recording system that exceeded the picture quality of 1-inch. This advanced recording system made professional units such as the Sony Betacam far superior in image quality to all other formats on the market.

Figure 16.2 ¾-inch cassette.

Figure 16.3 Sony Betacam made ½-inch tape cassette format an industry standard.

D (Digital) Formats

D-1, D-2 and other versions of the "D" format were an improvement even over broadcast-quality camcorders because they were digital. Once made digital, video signals could be manipulated in many ways and transferred with virtually no loss in quality. D formats use ¾-inch cassettes, which are larger than U-Matic cassettes (Figure 16.4). Because the D formats do not come in a camcorder arrangement, they are most often used in studio productions and online editing. With the advancements taking place in the smaller formats, however, such as Mini DV and Digital Beta, even the D recording formats are being replaced in many cases.

Mini DV (Digital Video)

The Mini DV formats utilize a small, 6 millimeter videotape that records digital video signals at what might be thought of as an upper-mid-range quality level (Figure 16.5). Mini DV is not quite comparable to the excellent quality of digital Betacam, for instance, or the larger D formats, but it is far better than ¾-inch U-Matic and the home VHS and 8-millimeter formats. This high quality level, combined with the small size and lower cost of Mini DV equipment when compared to other industrial and broadcast formats, makes it a resounding favorite of both prosumers (small independent producers) and many corporate facilities. Mini DV has also gained a wide reputation as a desirable format for news-gathering and documentary productions. In a few cases, industrious producers and directors have even used Mini DV to record feature films or portions of them.

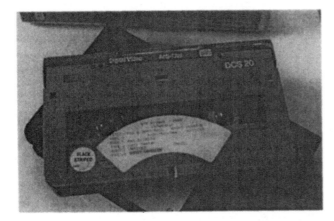

Figure 16.4 A D-2 cassette, used for studio applications.

Figure 16.5 A 6-millimeter mini DV tape compared to a ½-inch VHS tape. Mini DV tape is about 2 by 3 inches.

Custom Mini DV Formats

Though Mini DV is a standardized videotape format, there are several customized versions of Mini DV as well. Many producers consider these "professional Mini DV," stating that they produce better quality. Sony DV CAM is one (Figure 16.6). Panasonic's DVC PRO is another. These custom systems use Mini DV tape but incorporate proprietary technology and hardware that make their systems unique. DVC PRO for instance, uses a special Metal Particle videotape and both DVC PRO and DV CAM VTRs run at faster speeds than standard decks. Their cassette sizes are also different. It seems manufacturers gamble on the hope that their unique system will become the industry standard, allowing them to corner market. In the case of Sony DV CAM and the Panasonic DVC PRO, though both are used widely, neither has dominated the industry.

High Definition

High Definition is a growing format with excellent image qualities. It also boasts the popular letterbox film aspect ratio, 16 × 9, versus the television standard, 3 × 4. While this is a switchable feature on many other smaller format cameras, it is combined with pristine image quality in High Definition. In addition some producers claim that High Definition images produce the always sought after "film look." There's no debating, however, that traditionally high definition has been a very expensive format, in terms of both production and

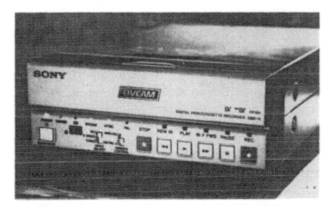

Figure 16.6 A, A Sony DV CAM videotape. Tape is Mini DV but cassette size is not compatible with other Mini DV systems. **B,** DSR-11 DV CAM record and playback deck.

Cameras

A video camera receives a live image through its lens; converts it into a video signal (these days almost exclusively digital); provides control over the signal, primarily in terms of color registration, light intensity, and contrast; and finally sends the signal to a videotape recorder or VTR. In the case of a camcorder, that VTR is attached to the camera itself (Figure 16.7).

As previously mentioned, cameras used in corporate and broadcast productions normally come equipped with three chips—one to process each primary color. These chips are actually charge-coupled device (CCD) circuitry. Three CCD Mini DV format, as seen in Figure 16.8, has become a popular and economical alternative to the ½-inch format. Although the images it produces are not considered Digital Beta quality, they are considered more than adequate for many types of corporate, news, and documentary productions.

The Canon XL 1S (Figure 16.9) is one of the most popular Mini DV cameras in the industry. Used by news, documentary producers, corporate producers and prosumers, its unique look and custom features make it a trendy and high quality unit.

Recording on standard Mini DV tape, and editable in any Mini DV system, the XL is a departure from the standard camera look, which no doubt lends to its popularity. It also sets itself apart from other cameras with a complete line of high quality, interchangeable Canon lenses. This ability to change lenses is not that much of

editing. For this reason, it was rarely used in corporate media when it first appeared. Small format, high definition cameras are now available, however, and costs have moved more in line with corporate media budgets. There's little doubt we'll see much more of this popular format in the future.

EQUIPMENT

In order to record in one or more of these formats, a video production requires certain pieces of electronic and digital equipment.

Figure 16.7 Sony Digital Betacam—an industry camcorder standard in all areas of broadcast and non-broadcast television.

Figure 16.8 Mini DV cam. In this case, the Sony PD-150. Image quality is not quite up to Betacam, but it is very good.

Figure 16.10 JVC GY-DV500 - With a high-end look and many industrial features, it, too, is a popular unit for producers in the Mini DV market. Like the Canon and most other Mini DV cameras it records on standard Mini DV tape which can be edited on any system.

benefit in the corporate media world, where standard zoom lenses are the norm. However, it is suggestive of the prime lens packages that come with many film camera packages. Add that to a "sexy" matte box, film camera look and a reputation of recording superior quality sound and images and it's no surprise the Canon XL line is a very popular mini DV camera. Also common in corporate media are JVC's mini DV camera (Figure 16.10) and Panasonic's innovative AG-DVX100 (Figure 16.12).

Figure 16.9 Canon XL 1S Unique look and film-like accessories make it one of the most popular in the Mini DV family.

Video Streaming

In order for footage to be streamed over the internet, it must be compressed using a system called MPEG. This typically requires a signal conversion between the camera and the Internet line. However, JVC's "streaming cam" (Figure 16.11) allows footage shot to be recorded in MPEG format and streamed directly onto the Net.

With Internet use growing exponentially in the business world, the use of streaming video is becoming common. Streaming video means digital video images and sounds which are "streamed" out onto the internet and viewed at distant locations with the use of virtual players such as Windows Media Player, Real 1 Player or Apple's Quick Time. This streaming technology eliminates the need to store a complete program on a hard drive before viewing. The video signal is converted to a stream, buffered in the system's RAM (Read Only Memory), played and then dumped out of the system.

Videotape Recorders (VTRs)

In production, VTRs receive video signals from a camera and audio signals from a microphone (Figure 16.13). They record each of these elements on separate parts of the same videotape. The video signal occupies the majority of the videotape surface. The audio signal is recorded on an audio channel near one edge of the tape.

Figure 16.11 JVC GY-DV300 "Streaming Cam" as it's often called, can stream footage directly onto the Internet.

Microphones

Microphones send audio signals from the live source—often the actor—to the VTR. They come in three basic types: shotgun, lavalier, and handheld (see Figure 16.14). **Shotgun** microphones are long and slender (like the barrel of a shotgun). They are extremely *unidirectional* in their pickup patterns. This means they pick up

Figure 16.12 Panasonic's AG-DVX100 records at 24 frames per second like film cameras. The jury is still out, however, on whether it provides a film look.

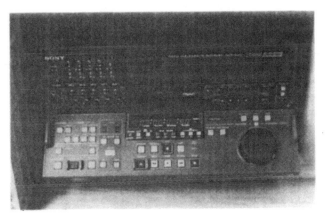

Figure 16.13 Sony Digital Betacam VTR used primarily in studio and editing situations.

sounds best from one direction—straight in front of the microphone. Shotguns are normally used on a **boom** (lightweight extendible pole) and are held *on axis* (in a direct line) with the actor's mouth, just out of the camera's range.

Lavaliers are very small condenser-type microphones, which clip to a tie or lapel. They are much less directional than shotguns and, therefore, record sounds well that come from most directions close to the microphone element. Lavaliers and other microphones that have comparatively broad pickup patterns are often referred to as *omnidirectional*. Pickup patterns that are most responsive in two directions (usually opposite sides of the microphone head) are called *bidirectional*.

Handheld mics are typically larger than lavaliers and usually also have omnidirectional or bidirectional pickup patterns. They are often used for on-camera host

Figure 16.14 Three types of commonly used mics, Left to right — shotgun, lavaliere, and hand held.

segments or are held by an interviewer in news-type pieces.

Although most audio signals are sent from one of these microphones to the VTR via audio cables, so-called wireless or radio microphone systems that transmit RF signals (audio signals converted to radio frequencies) are also common.

Wireless microphone systems have a transmitter and a receiver (Figure 16.15). They can be adapted for use with each of the different types of microphones just mentioned and are normally used when audio cables would otherwise be seen in the picture.

Mixers

Audio **mixers** are connected into the circuit between the microphones and the VTR. They provide two primary types of control over audio signals: (1) volume control and (2) the ability to combine signals. A typical field audio mixer (Figure 16.16) may have four inputs and two outputs. Sounds from up to four different microphones could thus be fed into mixer input jacks, combined internally into one signal, and sent via one of the output jacks to the VTR for recording.

Monitors

Two types of **monitors** are typically used in video production: standard video monitors and waveform monitors. Video monitors such as the one shown in Figure

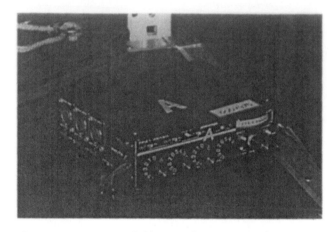

Figure 16.16 A Sure field mixer. Three inputs can be seen at left. Volume and other controls are on the front of the unit. Outputs are on the far side.

16.17 are connected into the circuit to allow viewing of a scene either live or during playback after it has been recorded. This is usually done to analyze picture quality and light levels, as well as the actors' performances.

Waveform monitors (Figure 16.18) provide a basic analysis of various elements of the video signal. The most important of these elements to the field production crew is normally luminance or light intensity. Use of waveform monitors on location shoots has diminished with the emergence of the camcorder and elimination of the Engineer in Charge (EIC) crew position.

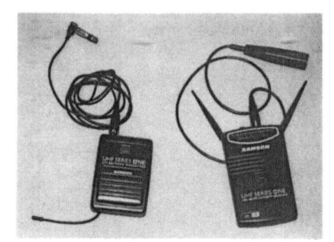

Figure 16.15 A typical wireless microphone system showing transmitter unit at left with a small lavaliere microphone attached and receiver unit at right with XLR plug which connects to camera.

Figure 16.17 Video field monitor used in both location and studio shoots.

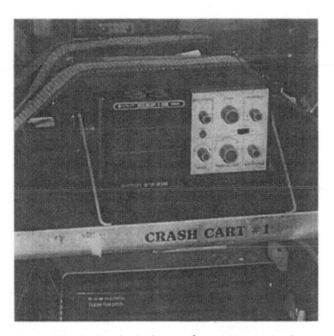

Figure 16.18 Standard video waveform monitor mounted on a "crash cart" for field use. These units are rarely seen in the field today.

Traditionally, it was the EIC's job to monitor all electronic equipment along with video and audio recording levels at the VTR. This required working with a waveform monitor continually. As field camcorders have become more prevalent and sophisticated, they have provided ways the DP can monitor light levels in the camera viewfinder. Waveform monitors are still used widely in studio production and editing applications, however. For this reason we will briefly discuss the waveform monitor to familiarize the student with a few of its basic functions.

On a waveform monitor, optimum light for recording video is measured on a scale of 7.5 to 100 units. The standard color black, often referred to in video as the *pedestal* or *setup*, has a correct intensity of 7.5 units. White, at the opposite end of the luminance scale, has a correct intensity of 100 units. If the white portions of a video picture are at 70 units on the waveform, the picture is said to be underexposed. If they are at 120 units, the picture, or at least that portion of it, is overexposed. Likewise, if the black portions are above or below 7.5 units, they are not considered true blacks but rather washed-out or "crushed" versions of the color black. With the use of a waveform monitor, then, the Engineer in Charge is able to view video luminance levels, discover overexposed or underexposed areas and

work with the DP to make the necessary lighting adjustments. The waveform monitor also analyses the video signal in a number of other ways which are far more technical and applicable primarily to the video engineer's job. The student who wishes to know more about these aspects should peruse technical books or other publications on video engineering or editing.

Lights

Although lights are not a part of the electronic system used in video recording, they are an important part of the overall process and thus deserve some basic discussion.

Production lights are so varied in size, shape, function, and output that it would take volumes to discuss each one in detail. Briefly, however, all production lights are used to do two things: first, they provide enough light intensity to enable the system to record a video image within the acceptable standards as measured on the waveform monitor. Second, they improve the aesthetic quality of the picture through the use of highlights and patterns, modeling with shadows, and maintaining certain color hues or temperatures.

Some lights have adjustable beams, which can be spotted or flooded for different intensities and areas of coverage. Others can provide direct, hard light or a softer bounce or diffused light. Still others provide different color temperatures (Figure 16.19).

Color temperature refers to the color of light on a standard scale. This scale measures the color radiated by a carbon filament when it is heated to different temperatures on the Kelvin scale.

As an example, when an exterior scene is recorded in typical daylight, it contains a naturally bluish tint, with a color temperature of approximately 5,500° Kelvin. This means a carbon filament heated to 5,500° on the Kelvin scale will emit this same tint or color of light. Arc-type and **halogen-metal-iodide (HMI)** lights provide this same color of bluish light and are thus used to imitate or mix with exterior light. Interior light, on the other hand, has a much more orange tint, with a color temperature of approximately 3,200° Kelvin. This color temperature of light is usually provided by **tungsten-halogen** light sources (a tungsten filament sealed in halogen gas inside the bulb) and is used for interior shooting. Unless it is done with skill and purpose, mixing lights of different color temperatures can result in pictures that look obviously lit and unnatural.

Gels, colored films placed over the light source, are used to change the color temperature of the light being

Figure 16.19 Production lights. **Barn doors**—fixtures that cut off area where light is unwanted—are attached to the Lowell 1K at left. On the right is an Arri 1K. Both lights have barn doors attached.

emitted. A tungsten–halogen light, for instance, with a specific grade of blue gel placed over it, will be "corrected" from 3,200° Kelvin to 5,500°, thus making it usable as an exterior light source.

Lighting Accessories

Gels are also used simply to color a light source for visual effect. One example would be an orange gel placed over a light to create the illusion of light from a fireplace out of the camera's frame. Cloth strips dangled and moved in front of the light can be used to create the flickering effect. Other lighting accessories (Figure 16.20) include **scrims** and **nets,** which, when

Figure 16.20 A variety of standard lighting accessories.

placed over the light source, decrease its intensity; **flags,** which cut off the light from certain parts of the picture; and **silk,** spun, and frost materials, which diffuse or soften the light on a scene or object.

Other Equipment

Some other common pieces of equipment used in production include tripods or *sticks* and *heads*, as they are called, on which the camera is mounted. Tripods were originally made of hard wood. These days they are made of tough, lightweight metals and plastics. They are built to provide sturdy, rigid camera placement. Heads usually have fluid workings that allow very smooth pan and tilt movements with little or no camera shaking. *Spreaders* are spoke-like pieces, usually metal, that are attached to the feet of the tripod to keep its legs locked in a spread position.

Dollies, on which the camera can be rolled forward or backward (called a dolly in or out) or sideways (called a truck left or right) come in a variety of forms. Doorway or western dollies are essentially simple wooden platforms with four wheels and a handle (Figure 16.16). The camera, mounted on its tripod, is secured onto the platform. The camera operator and perhaps a focus-puller also mount the dolly. As the shot is being performed, the dolly is pushed or pulled, normally in one direction, by a grip. With special wheels and sections of tubular track on which the whole system can ride, the dolly can be moved very smoothly. The more expensive dollies—Elemacs, Fishers, and Chapmans—are made of heavy metal. Most of these dollies also have pedestal or **ped** controls for up and down movements of the camera and **crab** mechanisms that allow the dolly to move in arcs, trucks, dollies, and combinations of these all in one shot.

Cranes and Jib Arms allow the camera to be moved high into the air often resulting in spectacular shots. In the case of cranes, the DP (and sometimes an assistant) "rides" up with the camera on a platform. The crane is counterbalanced with a group of heavy weights which make it very easy for one person to operate it (move it up, down or around) very smoothly on its fulcrum. Jib arms are much lighter units. They are used to hoist the camera, but not a crew member. When using a jib arm, the DP typically has a control unit and video monitor at is base, which gives him the ability to tilt, pan and in some cases even adjust focus on the camera as he views the shot taking place.

Video and audio cables are also standard items on any shoot that is recording sound as well as pictures. They are very different in makeup and, of course, serve different purposes. One cannot be substituted for another.

Batteries, generators, **A/C cables,** and power supplies provide power where none exists. Normally, the only pieces of production equipment that cannot be battery operated are lights. These require a generator because they operate at high voltage and amperage levels. In some cases, small lights are operated on battery belts or battery sources, but they usually can be used only for very limited periods of time.

C stands are three-legged metal stands used most often to hold flags or nets in front of lights. **Apple boxes** are wooden cubes of varying thicknesses (one-half apple, one-quarter apple, etc.) used for a variety of propping up or elevating jobs.

Finally, **gaffer's tape** is used for everything from dulling hot spots to sticking mics in collars. It looks just like duct tape but with a rough, dull gray finish. Gaffer's tape is considered an essential *expendable* (an item that can be used up) on most shoots. Legend has it that gaffer's tape will stick just about anything to anything else.

PRODUCTION STYLES

How is all this equipment actually used in a production? In the case of live action, involving real people at real locations, there are two types of television production styles: location and studio. Both have distinct characteristics, benefits, and drawbacks. In the case of digitally created sequences, what's called "virtual" production (the creation of sounds and images inside a computer) becomes the method of execution. Let's begin with a look at the real world.

Location Shooting

As a rule, a film or videotape crew goes on location for two reasons: to save costs or when they can't achieve what they must in the studio. Although location shooting often saves considerable expenses (studio time can cost thousands of dollars per day), it is more time-consuming, much harder work, and far riskier than studio shooting because the crew is at the mercy of so many unpredictable factors.

On the other hand, only location shooting can actually transport the audience to, say, an actual job site. No matter how well lit and dressed a studio set may be, it tends to look like a set instead of the real thing—an important factor in the credibility of the final program. For these reasons, shooting on location is a common occurrence for many corporate video units.

Single-Camera Style In some cases, a studio setup, including several cameras, a switcher, and multiple VTRs, is brought on location. Most location shooting, however, is done in what's called **single-camera,** or film style, because it makes use of a single camera that is moved from position to position for each angle—the same way films are shot. In this type of shooting, each actor's lines and action must be repeated for each angle. This coverage of the scene is cut together later in the editing process.

Typically, a director on location will first shoot a wide or master shot of the action. Next, he or she will shoot the same action in, perhaps, medium shots, taking in much less of the overall scene. He or she may then choose to shoot close-ups of certain parts of the same action. Later, when the editor gets the footage, he or she will most likely start by using several seconds of the master shot. At that point, he or she may cut to the medium shots and then, several seconds later, to the close-ups. Aesthetically, this method allows viewers to establish quickly where the scene is taking place and then move in closer for emphasis on the actors and key pieces of action. This process means that footage shot on location in the single-camera style is assembled after the fact from repetitions of the same action shot from different angles and focal lengths.

Studio Shooting

Studio shooting takes place in a much more controlled situation and, therefore, a much more consistently productive one. In a studio, a sudden gust of wind cannot ruin a host's monologue; cars do not come by and honk; and the lights are consistent and controllable, unlike the sun and clouds, which are constantly changing in ways that affect the continuity of scenes being shot. No breakers can trip, no generators can suddenly run out of gas, no bystanders can step into a shot and wave, and no equipment can turn up missing when a crew is 30 miles from the studio. For these reasons—ease and control—studio shooting is usually preferred over location shooting.

Multicamera Style

Although studio shooting can also be carried out with a single camera, in television it is often executed in **multicamera** style. In this style of shooting, rather than moving a single camera, the director simply switches the video images going onto videotape or on the air by choosing the signals from any of several cameras out on the studio floor. For example, he or she may fade up from black on camera 1, which is on a wide shot of the set and actors. Once their conversation starts, he or she may want a medium shot of the leading man. The operator on camera 2 has a medium shot, so the director switches to, or "takes," camera 2, getting the shot instantly.

Obviously, in this type of shooting, the program is edited on the fly, and studio shooting cuts down substantially on the editor's time in postproduction.

Studio shooting, however, does have several negative characteristics: First, as previously mentioned, well-equipped studios are very expensive to rent—often two to three thousand dollars per day. Second, studio shooting requires the time, personnel, and material resources to have sets designed and built in the days prior to shooting. Third, the ability to manipulate multicamera footage in editing can be minimal since the shots have been switched or "pre-edited" in advance.

"Virtual" Production

As digital technology has evolved, animated graphic sequences that were once very difficult and time consuming to produce have become commonplace in the corporate media world.

Originally, these sequences were used for things like visually depicting actions that could not otherwise be easily recorded, such as the internal workings of an engine. As corporate media became more sophisticated, animated sequences were also used to add colorful and dynamic visual elements that polished and stylized video programs. Today, with the growth of the Internet and interactive productions such as DVD and instructional CD-ROMs, both animated and still elements may provide the majority, if not all, of a production's visual content, and they often allow the user (not simply the viewer anymore) to interact with the content in highly effective ways.

Both still and animated graphics are developed on computer systems (Figure 16.21). Basic elements of a sequence are often created in what are known as paint or art systems. They are then composited or assembled

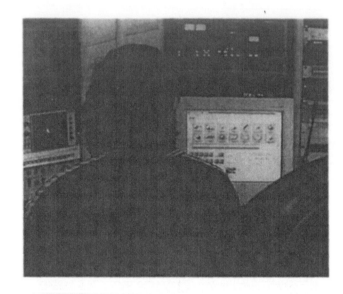

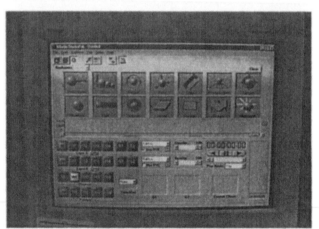

Figure 16.21 A, Graphic artist works on a "Pinnacle"—a powerful art and animation system used in both the corporate and entertainment capacities. **B,** Close-up of screen showing various graphic software applications.

into an edited piece and transferred into a nonlinear video editing or authoring system. In some cases they may also be developed in the interactive authoring system itself. These elements might include text as well as a variety of shapes, textures, perspectives, and movements. As one very basic example, a simple rectangle might be created and given thickness. It could then be given beveled edges and "filled" with a color. Its surface could also be shaded as if it had been placed in a light source and embossed with the word "Back" on it. When combined with voiceover narration and the proper programming or authoring commands, this graphic element could then "glide" onto the screen on cue and become a navigation button in a typical interactive program.

Another use of such shapes might be to develop a dynamic opening sequence consisting of shapes, text, colors, textures, and other elements that animate on the screen to a music selection.

Visual material for graphic sequences can also be scanned into computer memory or "captured" with the use of a camera or electronic system. This might include scanning a text document or capturing a live-action sequence from videotape to be integrated or "composited" with animated elements.

Compositing Systems

Adobe After Effects (Figure 16.22) is a powerful compositing system. It brings together various media elements allowing the user to creatively assemble them into a whole. Multiple video and audio layers can be created and easily combined in After Affects. These might include video clips, still images, scans and so on. Each element can be manipulated individually in terms of many preferences—placements in the frame, movement in the frame, duration, size, motion, speed, and so on. Graphics sequences created in After Affects can be transferred as digital files directly into many nonlinear editing systems. They simply become video sequences to be added to the program. One might ask why a producer would choose to use a program like After Affects when a standard Nonlinear system will do much of the same thing. The answer most often

involves time and complexity. While nonlinear editing system are capable of quite a number of effects, at some point, working with them in an editing system becomes slow, cumbersome and generally a pain in the neck to deal with. In these cases or when a particularly complicated sequence must be composited, it simply becomes much more cost-effective to make it in a program like After Effects and "drop" it into the show.

Modern Authoring Programs

As delivery systems such as the Internet, CD and DVD have evolved and improved, interactive media authoring programs such as Macromedia Director and Flash have emerged as powerful virtual production tools.

"Director" as it is most often referred to is an authoring program used to create interactive media programs for use on disc formats and the Internet. As an example, a user might insert a CD in his or her computer and "launch" a program such as the one shown in Figure 16.23. The "Buttons", developed in Director, are simply a graphic means for the user to interact with the program and move from sequence to sequence. The sequence might include video segments, text and still images.

Flash is a digital animation program. It is widely used in CD, DVD and Internet programs as a means of providing motion sequences. An example might be a

Figure 16.22 Adobe After Effects allows multi-layer compositing of a various sound and picture elements.

Figure 16.23 Interactive CD program authored using Macromedia Director and Flash. Images move on screen and allow the user to navigate through a multimedia presentation.

series of text and image titles that a producer wishes to "fly" onto the screen in a particular sequence and according to specific timing. The Flash software allows this type of creative production to be accomplished as shown in Figure 16.24.

Programs such as Director and Flash can also work in concert. For instance, animated text and graphic sequences can be created, composited, and timed in Flash. Those sequences can then be assembled in Director as one part of an overall program.

As covered in the writing section of this book, interactive productions must be carefully designed and planned, long before any of the authoring begins. Normally this is done by a producer-director and often working closely with a multimedia company or specialist.

The producer may start with a list of the program's learning objectives and from them develop a flow or sequence of scenes and perhaps tests that can effectively accomplish each one. This "Needs Assessment Design" is eventually translated into simple line sketches that illustrate the sequence style and progression which will take place on the screen. A meet is then arranged with a graphic artist, virtual developer or both. The intent is to discuss the most efficient way to develop the sequences or entire program. If the company the producer is working for has its own art system, there may be no monetary cost for this part of the work. If the work must be outsourced, however, the director will pay for the services.

The artist or developer often provides input that improves the producer's or director's initial ideas, and eventually all agree on how the program should play out. At this point, the artist and developer begin developing the sequence and the director checks in or visits periodically to approve the artist's progress.

Once the work is completed and approved by the producer and the client, if the result is to be edited on videotape, the sequence will be output or "dumped" to tape, at which point the director will take it back to be used as one of many other elements in the edit session. If the program is to be edited into a program on a nonlinear system, which we will discuss in future chapters, the sequence may never need to be output to tape. It can be copied to a CD or simply be transferred directly into the nonlinear editing system. Or if it is to be used on the Internet it may be uploaded and posted. If the use is on CD or DVD, duplicate copies of the program will be "burned" onto those mediums for distribution to users.

These are only a few of many authoring tools and processes used in today's multimedia production. The subject itself is a broad one that we have given only a cursory discussion. Producers wishing to prepare themselves for the media of the future should become conversant on these technologies and prepared to offer such skills to their clients.

With this basic foundation in place, it is now time to go on location and into the studio.

Figure 16.24 Text elements in motion on Flash sequence. In this case, the word Apex "flies" apart, revealing a set of navigation buttons.

17

A Day on Location and a Day in the Studio

LOCATION PRODUCTION

Location shooting days usually begin between 5:00 and 7:00 a.m., depending on the season and the type of shoot. When shooting exteriors, the objective is to have as much usable light as possible for actual recording. This means loading, unloading, travel and the initial setup can often take place very early in the morning. Whatever the call time, the crew arrives and either loads the trucks, or if this task was accomplished the evening before, completes a final equipment check and heads for the first location. Once the crew has arrived at the location, which we will assume is a large office area, the initial setup begins.

Set-up

During set-up, several things happen at once. The grips and gaffers begin to unload, while the assistant director (AD) gets the actors situated and makes the clients comfortable and attends to any other details that arise. Meanwhile, the director and the director of photography (DP) examine the area and discuss the first shot.

The director explains where he or she would like the camera positioned, what the action will be, and how close or wide the shot should be framed. The two also discuss how the scene should be lit—with a soft or hard look, contrasting or flat (lacking shadows), and so on.

Once the DP has a clear idea of what the shot involves in terms of lighting and blocking, he or she explains to the gaffer what lights to use and where they should be positioned.

Typically, the DP will want to light a scene with a **key light** that will appear to be the main source of light. For a "hard" look, this light might be a *1K Mole* (1,000-watt Mole Richardson) Fresnel—a light with a glass lens that is capable of spotting or flooding. For a softer look, it might be a Chimera—a 1K or 2K open-faced light inside a diffusion hood.

The DP will probably also want a somewhat dimmer and softer source of light on the other side of the camera as a **fill light**—to fill in the harsh shadows created by the key light. For this job, he or she might select a 1K "softy"—a less focused light that is bounced out of a reflective hood toward the talent. Or, if using the Chimera, he might simply use a reflector or white "bounce" card to reflect the key light back onto shaded part of the subject.

Finally, the DP may ask for a **back light** on the actor, which will make him or her stand out from the background. A 350 watt light placed behind and above the actor's head serves this purpose well. Depending on how wide the shot is and what else is seen, the DP may want more lights for the background or other objects.

The gaffer (Figure 17.1), whose job it is to know the electrical values and capacities of lights, fuses, breakers,

125

and so on, now talks to the grip about where the lights will be plugged in, how many can go on a particular circuit, and so on. The two then begin laying out A/C cables and setting lights.

Meanwhile the audio recordist, is setting up the mixer and the microphone to be used.

Because the teleprompter and the camera may end up mounted on the tripod as a single unit, the teleprompter operator may begin working with the DP to set this unit up. During this time, the director has discussed with the AD what shot this will be and to which scene it belongs. During this conversation, they will no doubt both refer to each other's scripts. They will discuss whether a master scene will be shot first, which actors or employees will be involved, and probably the type and extent of coverage the director plans to shoot. On the basis of this conversation, the AD prepares a slate with the proper scene number on it, finds a good spot from which to view the action, and handles any other details that come up.

The director now turns his or her attention to the actor or actress, in this case, the hostess. He or she explains what action will be performed and discusses the type of read desired—whether serious, light, formal, or some other tone. Once the actress is comfortable with what the director wants, they begin to rehearse.

Finally, the lighting is "tweaked" (adjusted) and looks good. Prior to this achievement, the DP and the gaffer have most likely met to resolve video-level problems such as *hot spots* (overexposed portions of the picture) or other lighting issues. No doubt the gaffer has placed various flags and/or nets on C stands to reduce light in certain areas to solve some of these problems.

The actress now appears to be reading well. The lavalier mic has been taped just under her collar, and the sound person has had the actress read several lines to verify that her level is producing a good audio reading on volume unit (VU) meters at both the mixer and the VTR.

The camera and prompter have been mounted together on the tripod, and the camera is white balanced and ready to go. *White balancing* properly references the camera's circuitry to the color white, thus making it able to accurately reproduce all colors. White balancing is accomplished by pointing the camera at something white, often the back of a script page, and activating the white balance circuit.

The DP now switches the camera to the *bars* circuit, which sends a standard pattern of colored bars to the VTR. At the same time, the sound person hits a switch on the mixer that generates a 1,000-cycle tone. With both the tone and the bars being sent to the camcorder's VTR, the DP puts the unit into record and "lays down" approximately one minute of this introduction.

This **bars and tone,** as it is usually called, is laid on the head of every tape that is recorded. Later, it provides a reference to set up the equipment used to duplicate the footage. In this way, consistent levels of light

Figure 17.1 Gaffer and sound recordist in a company location. Soft light at left is providing key light source. Reflector at right is used to bounce some soft light in as a source of fill.

intensity, color value, and sound can be assured between segments of recorded material. Roughly an hour has passed since the crew arrived. Finally, the director calls for a rehearsal on camera.

Rehearsal

The AD now calls for quiet, and the director says, "Action." Generally, this first rehearsal is rough, in several ways. If the DP has a "move", for example a dolly or zoom that must start and end on certain lines, he or she may need a few run-throughs to get the timing right. In addition, the actress's performance may have rough edges, or the background action may not happen just right. After several rehearsals, when all the bugs in the shot are fixed, it's time for take one.

Take One

Again, the AD calls for quiet. This time, however, the director tells the DP to **"roll tape."** The DP does so and, in a moment, tells the director he or she has **"speed."** This means the camcorder's VTR is up to speed and is now recording.

The grip now holds the slate he or she has received from the assistant director in front of the camera. On it might be written: Scene 15, Take 1, Roll 1, the title of the production, the date, and the names of the director of photography and the director. (We will see the importance of the slate in the section on postproduction.) The grip says, "Scene fifteen, take one." The scene now has a visual and audio *signature*. After the slate is pulled away, the director pauses for a moment and says, "Action." The scene plays out.

In all probability, something does not happen as it should. Perhaps the microphone rustles when the actress walks, or the zoom is late, or someone in the background looks at the camera, or a line is blown. The mistake could be any number of irritating minor occurrences; in any case, it means that the process must be repeated for a take two. After anywhere from two to perhaps fifteen takes, everything plays out to the director's satisfaction, and he or she says, "That's a buy."

During this process, the AD has been noting the number of each take and writing a brief description of it, including anything that went wrong, on the master script. He or she continues to take notes for every shot of the production. Now, however, upon hearing the director declare that scene 15 is a *buy*, the AD draws a circle around the number of that take.

Figures 17.2 and 17.3 are examples of master script pages. As with the slate, we will see how the master script becomes important in the section on postproduction.

Once this first scene is recorded on tape, the director may or may not want a close-up or medium shot of the same action. If he or she thinks it is necessary, the director will explain to the AD what is about to occur and then ask the DP to reframe the same scene with a new focal length or angle. A new slate is then produced.

If the new shot is an alternate enactment of the scene, the slate is marked A15. This marking indicates to the editor a different version of a scene. For example, the hostess might gesture to the left instead of to the right. If, on the other hand, the new take is a close-up of the same action or a part of that action, it is marked 15A. This marking indicates an insert into the existing scene rather than an alternate version. An example of this type of shot would be a close-up of the hostess's hand picking up a tool just as she did in the master scene. A second insert of a different part of the scene would be 15B, a third 15C, and so on. Whatever the slate marking, the same recording process takes place again and very likely several more times before the director buys it.

The Strike

After perhaps an hour and a half from the time the crew first arrived, the director has the shots he or she wants and instructs the crew to *strike* the location. That command means it's time to pack everything back up and move to another location to do the same thing over again. If the next location is nearby, it may mean simply moving some equipment a short distance and relighting. If the next location is not close by, it probably means putting all the equipment back into cases and boxes, loading the trucks, and driving to the new location.

This process is repeated perhaps 2, 4, or even 10 times during a typical 10-hour shooting day, again depending on the complexity of the shots, their distance from each other, and any other complications that tend to arise during location production.

Roughly 10 hours after they began, the crew, thoroughly exhausted, rolls back into the yard. If this production was only a one-day shoot, all the equipment may then need to be unloaded before anyone leaves. If the production is a two-day shoot or longer, the equipment may stay loaded in the trucks, and the crew heads home immediately.

The AD will probably stay behind to catch up on paperwork or notes left unattended to in the heat of

3 R1 6/13	MASTER: WIDE SHOT. HOST GETS UP FROM DESK, WALKS TO FRONT. Z.I. ON GRAPHIC.
1.	N.G. HOST MISSED LINE
2.	N.G. ZOOM SHAKEY
3.	HOST STUMBLED
④	GD -
A3 R-2 6/13	ALT. MASTER. NO ZOOM IN TO GRAPHIC
①	GD -
3A R-2 6/13	SAME ACTION AS MASTER IN CLOSE UP
1.	N.G. HOST MISSED LINE
2.	N.G. "ROUGH" READ
3	STILL ROUGH
④	GD. -
4 R-4 6/14	MASTER: MED. SHOT, JENNIFER @ DESK ON PHONE W/ CUSTOMER
1.	N.G. POOR PERFORMANCE
2.	N.G. MIC RUSTLE
3.	EMPLOYEE STOOD UP IN B.G. (1ST. PART GD)
④	GD -
4 R-4 6/14	C.U. SAME ACTION
①	GD -
4B R-4 6/14	HOST V.O.
①	GD -

Figure 17.2 Back of previous script page is used for note-taking that relates to the facing page seen in Figure 17.3.

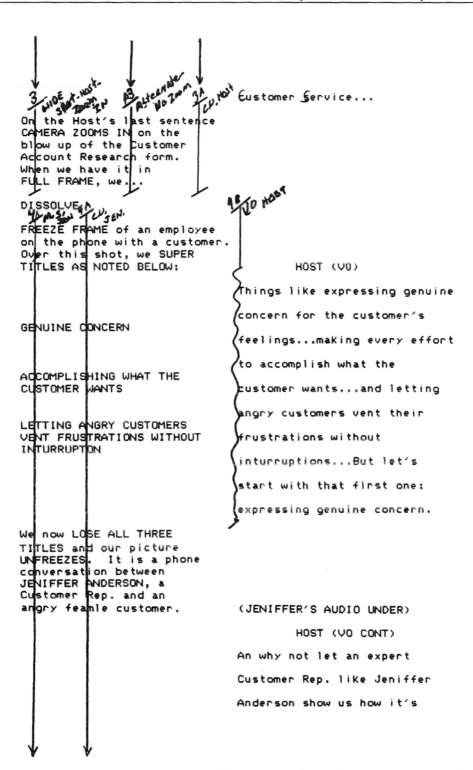

3 /WIDE Shot-Host-Zoom IN   A3 /Alternate No Zoom   3A /CU. Host   Customer Service...

On the Host's last sentence
CAMERA ZOOMS IN on the
blow up of the Customer
Account Research form.
When we have it in
FULL FRAME, we...

DISSOLVE
4/MS   4/CU. Jen.

FREEZE FRAME of an employee
on the phone with a customer.
Over this shot, we SUPER
TITLES AS NOTED BELOW:

4B /VO Host

HOST (VO)

Things like expressing genuine

concern for the customer's

GENUINE CONCERN

feelings...making every effort

to accomplish what the

ACCOMPLISHING WHAT THE
CUSTOMER WANTS

customer wants...and letting

angry customers vent their

LETTING ANGRY CUSTOMERS
VENT FRUSTRATIONS WITHOUT
INTURRUPTON

frustrations without

inturruptions...But let's

start with that first one:

expressing genuine concern.

We now LOSE ALL THREE
TITLES and our picture
UNFREEZES. It is a phone
conversation between
JENIFFER ANDERSON, a
Customer Rep. and an
angry feamle customer.

(JENIFFER'S AUDIO UNDER)

HOST (VO CONT)

An why not let an expert

Customer Rep. like Jeniffer

Anderson show us how it's

Figure 17.3 Front of each script page is marked with a series of lines, scene numbers, and take numbers, which are later used by the editor to determine the type and amount of "coverage" shot for that particular scene.

production. The director will also stay behind and probably view many of the shots recorded that day. The DP and the producer will probably also attend this review session to ensure that the footage brought in is acceptable. Later, the director will take his or her script book home to look over what has been accomplished so far and the next day's schedule.

SMALL LOCATION SHOOTS

The corporate shoot just described would be considered a relatively large production. Corporate shoots are often much smaller, less complex, and in some ways more challenging. For instance, a shoot may be more difficult when an executive or employee must be recorded or documentation footage must be gathered on a particular department or event. In these cases, the crew may consist of only a single camera operator or perhaps the cameraperson and the producer. These types of smaller shoots are often recorded in what is called an electronic news gathering (ENG) or "run 'n' gun" shooting style.

A single camera operator may be sent out to document a warehouse operation, for instance. In this case, he or she would bring along only the bare essentials—a camera, head and tripod, videotape, batteries, perhaps a microphone, and a small light kit. While shooting, he or she would act as producer, director, sound recordist, and assistant director, changing hats as necessary.

Following the shoot, the cameraperson would return with several reels of tape and perhaps a few sheets of sketchy notes on what was recorded. This material might then be used as cover footage, or what is called "B-roll," for a video news magazine story being developed by the producer.

When interviews or staged action using employees must be shot, a director and sound recordist are more likely to be involved. Small setups are usually the norm in these situations, and much less emphasis is placed on preproduction planning, scouting, blocking, and so on. These aesthetic decisions are simply made on the spot.

In the case of an employee interview, the interviewee might be asked to take a seat at his or her desk, and a few lights might be set up to complement the fluorescent or other existing lights. The director would then quickly decide on camera placement and compose the shot, and the minimal crew would go into action with each member focused on his or her specific function.

In ENG situations, it's important to note that although the crew size may be smaller, the emphasis on shooting quality footage and credible performances is still critical—therein lies the challenge. If an employee demonstrating the proper way to handle customer calls, for instance, is nervous and self-conscious, his or her performance may require directorial input by the camera operator or producer, or perhaps even the client. If he or she does a fine job of handling customers, but the shot is framed wrong or the sound is poor, the producer may have to adjust the microphone, change its battery, or reposition the tripod.

As mentioned earlier, this type of video shoot may require wearing several hats. and it often involves much harder work. Nonetheless, these types of shoots are the norm in many corporate video departments. They are also the norm with many smaller broadcast productions such as news and news magazine programs. For this reason, knowledge of multiple skills and the ability to adapt on the spot is essential for aspiring producers or directors.

Location television production often means hours of loading, unloading, rehearsing, lighting, adjusting, and so on to produce minutes or even seconds of usable footage. The experienced corporate producer, recognizing this fact, learns to weigh the positives and negatives of different types of shooting against the needs of the project and the resources at hand. Some common considerations are: (1) Does it need to be shot on location? If so, can it be a location close to the facility or offices? (2) Can what the script describes as multiple locations be combined into one location, which is redressed to look like others? (3) What are the costs for the locations?

The experienced producer also knows that considerations of the number and types of locations that arise in production are too late to be economically helpful. Ideally, these decisions should be made in the script stage or preproduction.

STUDIO PRODUCTION

Studio in the shooting tends to be much less strenuous than location shooting once the sets have been built and lit. It also tends to be much more controllable and hence more efficient. This improved productivity, of course, is the reason sound stages were originally built.

On the morning of the studio shoot, the crew will have a call time roughly one hour before the director plans on rolling tape. This preparation time allows the cameras to be turned on, registered, white balanced, and so on. It also gives the TD time to put a reel of videotape up on the production recorder, turn on and set up all the house equipment, recheck video and audio levels, and help with camera adjustments.

During this time, the actors will have arrived and probably will have been shown to the dressing room to get made up and dressed. The director will most likely visit with them, pump them up a bit for the day's performances, and discuss and choose wardrobe for the various scenes.

The AD, meanwhile, prepares the script, helps the actors with their needs, and works with the crew and clients or other dignitaries who are also arriving. The camera people, besides preparing their cameras, are probably adjusting lights at the insistence of the DP.

Rehearsal

When everything is set, the actors are called to the stage to discuss the first scene with the director. The process is basically the same as on location, with the exception mentioned earlier: The director may now have several cameras at his or her disposal. Assuming this is the case, coverage of the scene can be shot with a single pass—a single good pass, that is.

Once the scene has been walked through a few times and the director is satisfied that the action and performances are close, he or she generally leaves the stage and goes to the booth—an adjacent control room equipped with banks of monitors, scopes, controllers,

and a video switcher. Here the director takes a seat between the AD and the TD and, just as on location, he or she calls for rehearsals and, finally, "action."

Switching Live-on-Tape

This time, as the actors go through their paces, the director watches the camera angles and focal lengths he or she has on the monitors and calls out takes to the TD, who switches the show "live-on-tape" (Figure 17.4).

During this process, everyone on the crew is connected via a private line (PL) on headsets. All crew members act in response to the director's commands.

The following list shows examples of typical director's calls during an opening portion of a show, along with the action that takes place and who does what.

Director says . . .	. . . and this happens
Roll tape.	The TD puts the production recorder into "record." He or she acknowledges that the machine has "speed."
Slate it.	The TD switches to a camera or electronic source with the proper slate. He or she, or the audio engineer, calls out the scene and take number into an open microphone.

Figure 17.4 Director in the "booth" during a live-on-tape production.

Ready to fade up on one.	The TD sets camera 1 to "preset" on the switcher and grasps the fader bar.
Fade up.	The TD pulls the fader bar, and the picture on camera 1 appears on the program monitor. This image is being recorded on tape.
Lights up, please.	The floor manager slides one or several dimmers, which cause the lights on the stage to "come up."
Mic up and . . .	The TD or sound engineer "opens" the proper mic for the actor who is about to speak. Sound is now being recorded.
. . .cue talent.	The floor manager points a finger at the actor whose job it is to walk on and start the scene. The actor does so.
Camera 2, give me a close-up, please.	The operator on camera 2 zooms in quickly to a close-up of the actor he or she is focused on.
Ready two.	The TD sets camera 2 to the preset position on the switcher.
Take two.	The TD "switches" to camera 2, and the program monitor instantly shows the picture on camera 2.
Ready three.	The TD sets camera 3 to the preset position.
Take three.	The TD switches to camera 3. Its image now appears on program.

This process continues until the scene ends or someone makes a mistake, which, of course, is when the familiar "Cut!" is heard.

Similar to on a location shoot, the chances of everything going right the first time are slim. A camera operator may miss a shot, the TD may switch to the wrong camera, an actor may blow a line, or the director may miss a call and have the TD switch to the wrong source.

Chances are good that a take two will be called for, and the scene will be repeated. Later, when everything has played out to the director's satisfaction, he or she will call the scene a "buy." The AD will circle that number on the master script, and the crew will move on to the next scene.

The typical corporate studio shoot of this type is shot in large chunks or scenes, which the editor later cuts together into the final program. As for time, if the action isn't too complicated, the crew can hope to accomplish about 15 pages of script per day. This rate means that the average corporate script can be shot in a single day in the studio. Because of the setup time and other complications usually inherent to a location shoot, this same amount of shooting on location would probably take two or three days.

NONDRAMATIC STUDIO SHOOTS

In nondramatic studio shoots, such as live executive broadcasts, corporate talk shows, and product roll-outs, the same process is followed. In these types of shoots, however, preproduced roll-in tapes are more likely to be used at various times, requiring the assistance of a tape op (tape operator). Unless the production is live—in which case everything must happen right the first time—there will undoubtedly be retakes to adjust microphones on executives, reset lights, or reshoot some action that failed to happen exactly as planned. A graphic artist and character generator operator may also be used on live productions of this nature to provide titles and artwork for immediate inclusion in the program.

SMALLER STUDIO SHOOTS

Just as on location, ENG-type shoots can take place in the studio as well. Employee interviews or simple demonstrations are often shot in corporate studios using much smaller crews and much less complex setups. A company executive may visit the in-house studio, for instance, to record a videotaped message that will be distributed on its own or attached to another program currently in progress. If not an interview, the shoot might involve simple scenes shot with minimal or no sets and employees instead of actors.

To accomplish such shoots efficiently, video and audio control rooms are often eliminated, and the footage is taped on a camcorder just as it would be in the field. The producer may also be the director, the camera operator may be the sound recordist, and both together may serve as grip, gaffer, makeup artist, and engineer in charge. In these situations, much the same as on smaller location productions, the minimal crew must wear the appropriate hats when called for and exhibit the flexibility and knowledge to get the job done quickly, efficiently, and appropriately.

Whatever the shooting style or situation, with footage "in the can" from locations, studio, and the graphic department, it may seem as if we are ready to explore the next step in program development—postproduction. Not quite. Before postproduction, one more assignment often must be accomplished—an audio recording session.

18 Audio Production

When producing a program with a voiceover narrator or other voices and sounds that do not actually synchronize or "sync" with specific pictures, some of the production may involve recording only audio.

AUDIO RECORDING IN THE STUDIO

Audio production can be accomplished either on location or in the studio. If the audio is recorded in the studio, it will most likely take place in the area called production audio or voice-over booth.

THE PRODUCTION AUDIO BOOTH

Production audio usually consists of two adjoining rooms separated by a glass partition (Figure 18.1). The first room is an announce or narration booth. This is the soundproof room in which the actor sits when reading his or her lines. It is equipped with a microphone, a simple seating arrangement, and usually a video monitor on which a program can be viewed as the voiceover recording is taking place.

The second room is the control booth. This is the room on the other side of the glass partition in which the audio engineer, the director, and usually the AD are seated. As the name implies, the recording session is actually started, stopped, recorded, and played back from the control booth.

A typical control booth is equipped with a multi-channel audio mixing board (Figure 18.2), two sets of speakers (a large, high-quality pair and a small pair that together simulate sound as heard through a typical television), a reel-to-reel audiotape recorder or nonlinear recording system, and other sources of sound that can be fed into the system for recording. These sources might include an audiocassette player, a turntable, and a compact disc player.

THE RECORDING SESSION

Before a recording session, the audio engineer usually sets up the room by patching the sources to be used through the audio board on individual channels and routing them into the audiotape recorder. If music and sound effects are being recorded, the source might be the compact disc player. For an actor's narration, the source would simply be the microphone in the announce booth.

Thirty or sixty seconds of thousand cycle tone may also be recorded onto the tape or digital source being used. This will act as a calibration setting to assure accurate transfers of the recordings or matches with other recorded segments.

Assuming that the microphone is the source for this session, once the room is set up, the actor is invited into the announce booth. The director and AD sit with the engineer in the control booth. Typically, a level check is run by asking the actor to speak into the microphones. As he or she does so, the engineer checks the volume and tone of the actor's voice passing through the system and sets the equipment to the proper recording levels. At this point, recording can begin.

Figure 18.1 An audio production control room or "booth." The "talent" sits in a soundproof booth separated by a glass partition seen at upper left, or a program in progress can be viewed on monitor. Mixing board provides audio control.

Figure 18.2 A skilled audio recordist or mixer can operate many "faders" on the fly, while simultaneously using the various control knobs to adjust the quality of sound.

The director now gives the actor final instructions concerning the type of read desired. The engineer puts the audiotape recorder or digital system into "record," he or she signals the actor with a hand gesture, and the session is off and running.

Like video production, multiple takes are usually required for various reasons. Frequently, the director may want to hear playback of some segment just recorded in order to make a determination. Just as in video production, the AD listens intently and takes continual notes on which readings are good and which are bad, why, and which the director buys.

THE AUDIO SCRIPT

The same script used for production may be used in audio production or the director may want to use an unmarked copy of the shooting script for audio use only. In this case, when the program moves into postproduction, the editor would use this audio master script to perform the necessary voiceover edits and the video master script to edit pictures under that narration.

TRANSFER TO VIDEOTAPE

Production audio is usually recorded onto ¼-inch audiotape, digital audiotape (DAT) or directly into a nonlinear audio system. The ¼-inch tape recording is then transferred to videotape for use in the editing sessions. If a nonlinear editing system is used, however, the sound may simply be transferred into the nonlinear system as an audio file—in which case it may never be recorded or transferred to tape.

If any audio transfers are required, it is best to turn them in for duplicating along with the video footage shot for the program in order to keep all the elements of a particular show together. A new producer soon learns how easily audio and video reels can be misplaced when they are not well organized.

AUDIO RECORDING ON LOCATION

If audio production for voiceover segments is done on location, it is best recorded wherever the on-camera portions were done, assuming that acceptable audio can be recorded at the video location. On location, audio segments are recorded directly onto videotape instead of onto ¼-inch audiotape. This process is accomplished by turning on the camera and either pointing it at the slate for that scene or switching it to the color bar circuit. The camera's VTR is then put into record, and sound is recorded onto the videotape just as any other scene might be, except that the visual part of the picture is not for use.

FIELD OR STUDIO?

Recording voiceover on location is a good idea whenever parts of the script are on and parts are off camera. Using the same microphone placed in the same location on the actor and, if possible, recording in the same general area means that the audio ambient quality of

individual segments will match well when they are edited together later. This setup also saves a later transfer session of ¼-inch audiotape to videotape.

On the other hand, if part of the audio for a program is recorded in an audio booth and part in the field, the general quality of those audio segments will be clearly different when they are edited together. Although ambient background sounds, can be added later in the postproduction process, the booth audio usually has a noticeably different quality than the audio recorded in the field.

THE IMPORTANCE OF SOUND

One final note on audio recording: Whether it is audio only or audio in sync with video images, sound is often given a back seat to the visual aspect of a program. Many directors and producers have had the "fix it in postproduction" mentality come back to haunt them later. The reason is simple: The pictures turn out great, but a sound problem overlooked in the field actually ruins the circled take—and it cannot be "fixed in post."

Poor sound can destroy a program just as easily as poor pictures, acting, or scripting. The experienced producer understands this correlation, as well as the importance of avoiding the temptation to overlook sound problems in the heat of production. The producer should insist that the proper microphones be used, that competent sound recordists be hired, and that proper care be taken in production to ensure that the quality of the sound is top-notch, along with the rest of the program.

PART FOUR SUMMARY

Production is the short but crucial time in the media production process when everything must happen exactly as planned. A well-written script and a thorough period of preproduction are both critical factors in making production successful. Other critical elements are the creative skills of the cast and the director. Regardless of the amount of care and preparation that goes into any media project, things inevitably change. As one producer put it, "In production, Murphy's Law is the rule rather than the exception." Obviously, then, those individuals with the flexibility and presence of mind to make valid creative decisions under the often extreme pressures experienced on the production "roller coaster" are true professionals.

If you feel you have the stuff to produce, direct, or play a support role in the production process, you can expand your knowledge by exploring the following resources.

BIBLIOGRAPHY—AUDIO

Lyver, Des *Basics of Video Sound*, Second Edition, Burlington, MA, Focal Press, 1999.

Watkinson, John *Introduction to Digital Audio*, Second Edition, Burlington, MA, Focal Press, 2002.

Kindem, Gorham, Ph.D., and Musburger, Robert B., Ph.D. *Introduction to Media Production From Analog to Digital*. Burlington, MA, Focal Press, 1997.

Medhoff, Norman J., and Tanquary, Tom. *Portable Video: ENG & EFP*. Burlington, MA, Focal Press, 1997.

Part 5

The Director

19

The Director's Role

We have now followed the production process from a detailed perspective focusing on the involvement and responsibilities of the client, producer, director, crew members, and the equipment utilized. At this point, we must focus more closely on one person in this group—the director. This in-depth look at a single key player is critical because the director's work is the most complex and challenging from a creative standpoint. In fact, most producers would agree that regardless of the extent of equipment, technical elements, and support people involved, *directorial decision making* ultimately determines the quality of the final program.

ILLUSIONISM: THE DIRECTOR'S ART

Webster's Collegiate Dictionary defines the word illusionism as follows: *The use of artistic techniques (such as perspective or shading) to create illusions of reality.* This phrase describes very closely what a corporate director does. To make the definition fully correct, we would revise it to read as follows: *The use of artistic techniques (such as performance, videography, lighting) to create illusions of reality in a media presentation.*

The illusions referred to here are situations such as two actors cast as sales reps discussing a new technique over lunch; or a host actor cast as a first-line supervisor presenting customer-handling tips directly to viewers; or an employee working at his or her craft as if no camera or lighting setup was present.

In order to make these media illusions appear to be unrehearsed moments captured on the screen that engage a viewer's interest, the director works with the following five aesthetic elements:

Script aesthetics

Human aesthetics

Audiovisual aesthetics

Technical aesthetics

General aesthetics

Each of these elements has a profound effect on the illusory credibility of the director's work. In fact, even the most subtle aesthetic faults can destroy the credibility of a shot, scene, or entire program on the spot. Keep in mind as we discuss them, however, that the critical importance of each one can sometimes be deceptively unassuming. Many manifestations of the aesthetic qualities we are about to discuss can be extremely easy to misjudge or overlook. The shaping and guiding of these aesthetic subtleties is one facet that makes the director's work so challenging.

SCRIPT AESTHETICS

A script is a transitional document. A writer creates the script as a detailed representation of how his or her vision should appear on the screen. Because the writer has worked with a client and producer while creating the script, and because his or her work has probably been approved by both of these individuals, we can assume that they fully agree with the writer's vision.

If the director is to successfully transform the script into live action on the screen, his or her first task is to carefully *analyze* it and gain an intimate and multifaceted understanding of what the writer has attempted to communicate. A thorough understanding of these elements is critical on the director's part because he or she could never hope to guide actors, videography, preparations, editing sessions, and so on without making specific judgments about how the material should play in front of the camera. Those specific judgments cannot be made without an intimate understanding and analysis of every nuance in the script.

In feature film and primetime television production, that analysis means careful exploration of characters and their development, plot structure, conflicts, crisis tension levels, and many other dramatic elements. In corporate media, complicated plots, pronounced character development, and intense emotional conflicts are not often used. When they are used, they are often much less complex than those in dramatic presentations because corporate media programs are not made strictly to entertain or gain a viewer's dramatic involvement. These programs may contain some degree of drama, but they are produced primarily to convey either specific information, such as five steps on how to make a sale, or a general concept that will motivate viewers to follow those five steps.

This lack of complex dramatic elements does not change the fact that a corporate director must analyze the writer's script; it simply means that his or her analysis is usually focused on somewhat different priorities, including the following:

Informational clarity

Character profiles

Plot

Structure and transitions

Tone and pace

Informational Clarity

On any directing project, one of the first questions a director must ask is this: If shot as the writer has described, will this script create for its viewers the same informational clarity it has for its readers—the client, producer, and any technical experts who may have read and approved it? In other words, will it work on the *screen* the same way it works on the *page?* The director makes this assessment by carefully reading the script scene by scene, applying his or her experience and judgment as a director of visual media and continually asking that same question.

If the answer continues to come up "yes" with each scene, the director can proceed with the script analysis feeling comfortable that, from an informational standpoint, the script is sound. This positive analysis is most often the case because the producer and client have no doubt carefully scrutinized and revised the script in terms of content. If, at certain places, however, the answer to the "will it work?" question comes up "no," the director must bring those areas that fall short, along with his or her suggested solutions to those shortcomings, to the attention of the producer and the client.

For instance, let's assume that a director is reading a script that he or she feels is informationally sound, and one section suddenly appears problematic. The information being communicated in that section pertains to two specific aspects of quality service: *focusing* on the customer's problem and being *courteous*.

The troubling script section looks like the following:

INT. AIRPORT TERMINAL–DAY

John walks up to the ticket counter. The TICKET PERSON approaches with a courteous smile.

NARRATOR (V.O.)

*Quality service is important in any job
because it's critical to customer satisfaction.*

The ticket person takes John's ticket, focuses on his problem, remains courteous, keys the information into the computer, makes a change to the ticket, and gives it back to John, corrected. John exits the shot perfectly happy. He has just had an encounter that displayed these two specifics of quality service.

DISSOLVE:

At first glance, this scene might appear to be effective. The ticket person seems to act in a courteous and focused manner, and the scene certainly talks about focus and courtesy. The writer even closes the scene by confirming this with the line, "He has just had an encounter that displayed these two specifics of quality service."

But viewers will never read the writer's scene description, including the closing line. They will only see the ticket person approach wearing a smile and go through the motions of writing out John's ticket. What they will *hear* will be the scripted narration.

Given these two elements, will they understand that focus and courtesy are the key instructional elements being displayed on the screen? Probably not. They will undoubtedly get a general sense of quality handling from this scene, but they will retain no knowledge of the specifics because, although the writer has included the key items in his or her scene description, neither action titles nor dialogue have been included to support the message.

What, then, is the director's solution to this type of problem? In this case, several possibilities are available for correction.

One solution would be to add action and dialogue that display a sense of focus and courtesy. For instance, several telephone calls or pesky fellow workers might act as distractions to the ticket person. If it became visually clear that the ticket person was consciously ignoring these distractions to keep *focused* on the customer, the point would be made.

The *courtesy* idea could also be conveyed through additional dialogue and action, such as several courteous lines delivered by the ticket person. Another possibility would be to add narration and perhaps superimposed titles. For instance, the narration might be rewritten this way:

NARRATOR (V.O.)

Quality service is important in any job because it's critical to customer satisfaction. In this case, even in the face of constant distractions, the ticket rep keeps her attention focused squarely on John's problem. She also remains courteous every step of the way.

This additional narration would certainly help make the point. If the scene were also supplemented with superimposed titles that read "Focus" and "Courtesy" as they were mentioned in the narration, its informational clarity would be further enhanced.

A Rule of Thumb

This example is only one of many types of informational problem areas a director may have to work out, but in each case the general rules remain the same: Analyze each scene. Determine if it is informationally sound, not from a print standpoint but from an audiovisual one. If the scene will not be clear when taped, determine what revisions are needed. Revise or suggest revisions to include action, dialogue, narration, and, where appropriate, support titles.

These suggested revisions should be presented to the producer and possibly the client at the outset of the director's work. If the producer agrees with the suggested changes, they can be made, often by the original writer, and the project can move forward. If the producer disagrees, the director must either disregard the problems or decide whether he or she wants to continue with the project, knowing that it may not meet its objectives in the end.

Character Profiles

Characters are the human elements in a program and thus the most important to audience identification. The director's challenge is to make characters appear real and engaging. To achieve this goal, he or she must get to know the characters intimately through script analysis. In future chapters, we will explore these human aspects of the director's work in much greater detail. Strictly in terms of the script, however, the director should consider the following two important elements of character profiles: (1) the appearance or "look" and (2) the personalities of the actors who will appear in the program.

In corporate programs, the director will work most often with host and dramatic or humorous profiles.

Host Roles

A host is a common role in corporate media. He or she is a tour guide of sorts, leading the viewer through parts or all of the information being communicated. The director should remember that, although the host looks directly at the camera and talks to the audience, he or she is still a character that must be cast and played accordingly.

A host personality often needs to be friendly, warm, and conversational. His or her appearance or look should complement the content being delivered and the setting established in the script. For instance, if the content of the program concerns instruction on how to supervise service order writers, the host character might be a supervisor of these types of employees. This role would allow audience members to identify with the host character and view him or her as a credible source of information.

Here's another example.

EXT. TRUCK YARD–DAY

Our HOST steps down from the cab of a shiny new semi. He is a hard-looking, middle-aged man dressed in blue jeans and a plaid shirt. He wears a weathered ball cap. Gesturing over his shoulder toward the truck, he steps forward and says . . .

HOST

You and I both know that a rig weighs close to a hundred thousand pounds. And we also know that stopping it on a dime isn't easy.

This writer's description seems to create an appropriate appearance for this character. His personality would seem to be tough, road wise, and no nonsense but also considerate enough to want to pass along what he knows about truck safety to his viewers.

Obviously, a host cast as a bank teller or an executive would require different considerations on both the writer's and the director's part.

Dramatic or Humorous Roles

Actors and actresses cast in role-play scenes have dramatic or humorous profiles. Unlike a host, they act out their parts as if neither the camera nor the audience were present.

A good scriptwriter will have developed characters that work naturally to enhance the message being communicated. In doing so, he or she will have given them effective dialogue and actions that fit their character profiles and simultaneously move the story toward its objective.

During script analysis, a director must clearly visualize how these characters will act on the screen and cast them accordingly. As you might guess, the director has many choices in this area, and the implications of those choices can be critical to the program's success. If characters are miscast, the result can be distracting at best. At worst, less-than-credible performances can "stop the show" for the viewer, thus breaking the program's illusive quality.

For these reasons, the director must conduct a thorough character profile analysis for every character in the script. He or she must know what the actors look like and how they would think and act in all situations established in the script. Only with this knowledge can the director cast appropriately and develop the right kinds of character traits and motivated actions during rehearsal and shooting.

Plot

Few, if any, corporate programs have heavily dramatic or complex plots. This is the case for two reasons. First, corporate programs are usually too short to allow for adequate plot development. Second, the focus of corporate programs is informational or motivational, not dramatic.

Simple plots, however, are often used in corporate media. I once directed a program that used a story about an employee and her spouse attending a weekend company outing to reveal information about the company's mission and its benefits.

The plot was simple. As the couple arrived, it became obvious that the employee's husband was very uncomfortable. He was positive he would have absolutely nothing in common with his wife's "techie" phone company friends. His wife was irritated by his stubbornness and closed-minded attitude. As the husband began to meet people, however, he found them warm, their conversation enjoyable, and the party more and more fun. With each encounter, his negative attitude slowly diminished. By the end of the program, not only had the information about the company been communicated, but the husband had also discovered that his wife's friends were just like him—a good-natured and friendly bunch of "regular" people.

Although this video was not high drama, it did involve specific plot turning points, conflicts, and character development. As the director, I had to pay careful attention to these elements during my script analysis in order to ultimately make the program work on the screen. Because the program was shot completely out of script order, I had to remain continually conscious of where we were in the husband's character development and the overall plot.

Therefore, just as the director must be aware of character profiles, he or she must also be closely attuned to every plot twist and turn in the story, and this attunement can only come through in-depth script analysis.

Structure and Transitions

Corporate programs are carefully structured to impart information in logical, simple-to-follow segments. As we have discussed, part of this careful structuring is the inclusion of appropriate transitions between segments.

This structural aspect often replaces dramatic or humorous plot elements. For example, when a host and general cover footage are used to impart information, a detailed understanding of the structure of the narration and the cover material replaces the director's need for the same knowledge about story elements.

In some cases, both story and informational structure become important; for example, in a program in which the host introduces a story and returns periodically to provide transitions.

Similar to other aspects of script analysis, the director must become closely attuned to these structural and transitional elements. This process allows him or her to use the appropriate visual and sound techniques to help clarify the material for the viewer. If the structure of a script is confusing or unclear in the director's mind and the confusion is not resolved, he or she will have great difficulty making the script play well on the screen. One subtle example follows:

INT. STUDIO–LIMBO SET

We come back to the host leaning against her desk.

HOST

So, you can see that safety isn't always determined by the attitude of an individual or their mood. In this case, Helen was a good employee, her attitude was positive, and she was in a jovial mood, but she still got hurt badly. The story of John Bell, on the other hand, shows us that attitude does, indeed, play a part in developing safe work habits.

Although this segment is scripted as a single monologue, two separate thoughts are included. The first is what appears to be the wrap-up of a story focusing on an employee named Helen. The second thought is the introduction to the new story of John Bell. This juncture is a good place for the director to consider doing one of several things that could enhance the program. He or she might want to shoot this scene having the host turn to a new, closer angle immediately after the words, " . . . she still got hurt badly." This simple turning motion, combined with the closer angle, would provide a comfortable visual transition for the viewer. A second choice might be to dissolve away from the host to a shot of John Bell on the job as the host introduces

him. This visual clue would add a sense of finality to the previous segment and provide a comfortable transition into the new story.

After the director has carefully analyzed the script, he or she will find many of these structural stops, starts, turns, and signposts. Becoming aware of them will enable him or her to direct the program in a way that helps make the content perfectly logical and clear to viewers. The visual elements that eventually become the manifestations of these structural characteristics, such as dissolves, wipes, and DVE transitions, are subjects we will cover shortly. For the moment, let's move into the final two elements in the director's script analysis.

Tone and Pace

The tone of a script might be thought of in terms of the mood it evokes. A script may contain varying tones. For instance, consider a script about an executive who falls prey to substance abuse, loses everything, and eventually recovers. This script might begin with a suspenseful tone as the executive is shown trying to hide his problem. Later scenes might reflect sad or depressing tones as he sinks into the horrible reality of what substance abuse does to people. Later still, the script may reflect a hopeful tone as he seeks and gets help. And finally, we might experience joy as he succeeds and begins a new life.

During script analysis, the director must carefully analyze these tonal elements, both in the individual scenes and the story as a whole. In doing so, he or she will be prepared later to make critical directorial decisions that will create these qualities as each scene is prepared and shot.

A host program may not be dramatic, but the host is still a character who should reflect certain tones during presentation. In a program on company security, the host's tone might be serious. In a program on company benefits, however, the host might be warm and friendly. In a program on new products or company achievements, the host might be energized and excited.

Pace is linked to tone in that one quality often affects the other. Pace, too, can vary in different parts of the script. In sad or suspenseful areas, the pace may be slow and lethargic. In energized areas, it may be fast-paced and dynamic. In basic informational areas, it may just be easily conversational and relaxed.

Similar to all other elements, the director must gain an accurate sense of the script's pace to use in preparing and shooting the program. Energized segments might be recorded with short, rapidly moving camera shots. A slow or suspenseful pace might call for long, static shots, and so on.

In each of the cases we've discussed, casting, props, coverage, music selections, and many other aspects of the production would be determined by these pace and tonal script interpretations and the director's decisions.

SUMMARY

Analyzing the script is the director's first and one of his or her most important tasks. Attempting to direct a script without careful analysis of all the aspects we have discussed is analogous to trying to play a piece of music without understanding how the notes on the page interrelate to create rhythms, tempos, moods, and varying paces. After careful script analysis, however, the director gains a precise vision of what must be accomplished. He or she is thus well prepared to move into preproduction with confidence that he or she is guiding production of the script toward a successful finish.

20 Human Aesthetics

If a film or television program is skillfully written, carefully prepared down to the tiniest detail, and lit and shot with great professionalism, but its actors lack credibility, viewers will "turn off" to it at once. By contrast, a talented cast performing in a program prepared and shot by mediocre standards may be not only acceptable but actually gripping to its audience.

Actors are the human part of the director's illusion. They are what viewers identify with most and, as such, are without question the most critical elements on the screen. It stands to reason, then, that the most important tasks a director performs are those involving human aesthetics.

IMAGE AND PERFORMANCE—THE CRITICAL INGREDIENTS

Human aesthetics are those pertaining to actors' images and performances. To create a convincing performance and thus sustain the director's illusion, both of these qualities must appear to be natural characteristics of a scene and the actors in it.

One of the director's primary roles is to ensure that this true-to-life quality is present before he or she "buys" or accepts any scene being recorded. With professional actors—or "talent," as they are often called—the director accomplishes this goal by paying great attention to the following four critical areas of human aesthetics: *casting, rehearsal, execution,* and *communication*. With *non*professional talent, such as company employees, the director's concerns are basically the same but with a somewhat different emphasis.

CASTING

Casting is the process of contacting, auditioning, selecting, and hiring actors and actresses. Its purpose is to assemble a cast that fits the director's vision of each role based on his or her previous script analysis. Like every other aspect of human aesthetics, proper casting is essential to a successful program.

AUDITIONS

In feature films and commercial media productions, auditions are often an extensive process involving weeks of interviews and readings, hundreds of actors, and multiple callback sessions. These "casting calls" are often set up and administered by casting services and casting directors who do much of the initial weeding-out process before the film or program director ever gets involved.

In corporate television, casting is handled on a much smaller scale. Actor selections are usually accomplished based on the previous experiences of the producer or director or a one- or two-day audition in which perhaps 10 to 40 actors are seen.

A corporate director may have only a host role to fill that requires no unusual look or physical characteristics. In this case, the director may cast the role with a person with whom he or she has recently worked, or based on a request by the producer or sometimes even the client. If the program has multiple roles, however, or if those roles require special characteristics or particular "looks," an audition is usually needed. As an example, a program produced for a primarily Hispanic audience will most likely require a Hispanic host since viewers would identify more closely with this person. Likewise, a program aimed at secretaries who are predominantly female would call for a female host.

Typically, the audition is set up by someone like the AD during the initial phases of preproduction. The AD calls casting agencies and views previously produced programs in which the director may remember some actor who impressed him or her. The AD also looks over photo "composites" and "head shots" kept on file. From these sources, he or she develops a list of potential actors and some visual representation of each. The AD and the director review the list and decide which actors to call in for "readings." Auditions are often videotaped, allowing the director to review performances again later during final decision making.

During auditions, the director carefully scrutinizes the following four basic qualities in each actor: *appearance (look), performance capability, ability to take direction,* and *personality.*

Appearance ("Look")

In any corporate program, the actor's "look," as it is often called, is very important in a somewhat paradoxical sense. That is, it should appear so natural to the role that it does not call attention to itself. If the script calls for a gymnastics instructor, for instance, a lean, well-built individual could do the role looking perfectly natural in a gym environment. If such a role were cast with an overweight individual, however, the audience would immediately notice the actor's physical makeup as being odd or unnatural.

An actor's look often does not need to be physically specific in corporate programs. For instance, a role may call for someone like Bill Moller, in the following scene:

INT. LOBBY–DAY

John walks around the corner and finds BILL MOLLER, a communications systems sales rep, spreading his brochures out on the desk.

If Bill Moller's role is a minor one, he could be tall or short, overweight or thin, and the audience probably wouldn't notice much difference one way or the other. In this case, his wardrobe and makeup would be more important. If he were clean-shaven in a suit and tie he would appear natural as a sales rep. Three days' worth

of stubble, on the other hand, and a pair of sweats or jeans would look noticeably unnatural.

An actor's look may also be determined based to some degree on the audience makeup of the program. For instance, a program on cosmetic application would probably be shown mostly to women. A female host would identify best with and seem most natural to the audience. A program on backhoe operation, on the other hand, would probably be shown to mostly male construction workers; thus it should be hosted by a male.

Following careful script analysis, a director should have a keen sense of the types of looks he or she is after before auditions begin.

Performance Capability

While an actor's look is important, his or her ability to perform is the most critical element considered in an audition. Unfortunately, the time constraints and logistics of most corporate auditions are not the most conducive to quality performances.

Facilities are typically small and makeshift—perhaps a conference room or corner desk; actors get only a short time to review the script pages to be performed—often 5 minutes—and the time available for the actor and director to spend together is usually only 5 to 10 minutes. Add to this situation the fact that actors are often sensitive to rejection, and you can imagine why auditions can be extremely tense interactions for them.

The director, however, does not want tension. He or she wants a relaxed, comfortable atmosphere in which the actors can deliver their best under the circumstances. To achieve this atmosphere and encourage solid performances, a director can take a number of steps.

1. Give the actors minimum material and maximum time. If the amount of material an actor is given is kept to a minimum (a well-chosen single page or part of a page is often enough) and as much time as the director can allow is provided, a better performance usually results.

2. Briefly discuss the role before the reading. An actor given a page or two of a script will have no sense of the "big picture" that might give him or her a better grasp of the role. A quick overview covering what the program is about and how the role fits into that big picture is often a good enough framework to prompt a more accurate and comfortable reading.

3. Give the actor someone to perform with—when possible, another actor. Actors work best when they have someone else to play off who has a good sense of timing and delivery. For instance, a scene in which an actor must continually interrupt another person would be difficult to do when played off a person with no sense of when to start and stop speaking. One way to get this type of interplay is by auditioning two or more actors at a time, letting each work different roles and perhaps even switching roles midway through the audition.

4. Never play the other part. A director who plays the opposite role cannot hope to accurately judge an actor's performance—at least, not during the initial audition. If due to budget constraints, you must read opposite an actor, be sure to videotape the auditions and save your judgments until you can view the tapes uninterrupted.

5. Give direction and a second chance. If an actor does not deliver what you're after on the first read, unless you happen to be in an extreme time crunch or unless it is painfully obvious that he or she couldn't hope to get it right, offer direction and give the person at least one more opportunity. Sometimes a little encouragement and a second try can work wonders.

Although auditions can probably never be truly comfortable meetings between directors and actors, the director who follows these steps can at least make them as comfortable and productive as possible.

Ability to Take Direction

The ability to take direction means the ability to change a performance based on the director's wishes. A director can quickly find out how well an actor takes direction in an audition by asking him or her to change delivery.

For instance, if an actor is doing a role as a customer service representative on the telephone and her initial direction was to *please* the customer on the other end, the director might follow her performance by saying something like, "That was very nice. Now let's approach it a little differently. Instead of pleasing the customer, let's do the same lines but try to insult her."

This direction requires a completely different treatment of the same words. Tone, inflection, pace, gestures, and facial expressions would all change.

If the actor does this well but the director is still not convinced, he or she should follow by asking for some *degree* of change. For instance, "Great. That would insult anyone. Nice job. Can we try it once more, though, and take it only half that far? I wouldn't want this customer to be given a reason to hang up and call the boss. I'd just want her to leave the conversation with a bad taste in her mouth." If the actor can deliver again, the director can feel comfortable that the actor is able to take direction quite well.

Personality

A director and production crew must sometimes work closely with an actor for days. This relationship means eating together, taking breaks together, traveling together, collaborating on the set or location to create credible performances, and, most of all, maintaining a productive working relationship through difficult and at times extremely tense situations.

If, during an audition, an actor appears to be the type who might be difficult or overly demanding, it's a good bet he or she will be even more difficult in a production situation—when lunch is late, rain is on the way, and the shoot is an hour behind schedule.

In feature films, the needs of actors and actresses are often seen to by staffs of people whose jobs are simply to keep the actors content and ready to perform when their scenes are shot. These people provide everything from massages and portable Jacuzzis to decks of cards and shoulders to cry on.

In corporate television, these luxuries are rarely the case. In many instances, besides having no frills whatsoever, actors must apply their own makeup and provide their own wardrobe.

All these factors point out the need for a director not only to be sure that actors are able to perform and take direction but also to remain positive and helpful under the sometimes uncomfortable situations that are part of the media production process.

Audition Review

When the auditions are finally over, the director will review the performances of those actors whom he or she is strongly considering. As the director does this, he or she will either consciously or unconsciously refer back to script analysis. What should the person in the script look like? How should the actor move in front of the camera? What tone of voice, facial expression, or gestures should he or she use? Which actor is best able to do those things most convincingly? When the director's decisions are made and the actors are booked, the next step in the human aesthetic process is rehearsal.

REHEARSAL

Rehearsal in network television means gathering the actors together at the studio in the days before production. Working with the director, the actors read, revise, and eventually "block" the script, working out entrances, exits, and other movements in front of the cameras.

In big-budget feature films, the same process is carried out but often on a far more elaborate scale. The cast may assemble in Spain, Japan, or whatever other country the film happens to be shot in. Actors visit locations weeks or months in advance to get a "feel" for them. They may also study local history and culture as part of their research. When rehearsals take place, they might happen on the bank of a river, in the tower of a castle, or on top of a mountain—wherever those scenes are to be shot.

In corporate media production, a rehearsal rarely happens on a soundstage or in a castle tower, but some form of rehearsal (at minimum, a brief discussion) should take place. The reason is simple—even a short period of rehearsal between only the actors and director can save considerable time on the set or location while a full production crew stands by looking on. Depending on the budget and time available and the size and type of the cast, rehearsals can take place either before or during a corporate shoot.

Before the Shoot

Full advance talent rehearsals are rare in corporate media for two primary reasons. First, enough time or money is rarely available for full rehearsals. Second, the roles are usually simple enough to negate the necessity for a rehearsal. In many cases, however, some degree of talent rehearsals does get scheduled, in which the director usually works in three steps: *script discussions, readings,* and *blocking.*

Script Discussions
Simple script discussions between the director and the cast often take place over lunches or sitting around conference tables. Topics include character traits, motivation, difficult dialogue sections, and plot elements. Informal as they may be, these types of meetings often clear up many minor questions that would later have proven costly.

For instance, an actor's interpretation of how a character should display a certain emotion may differ from the director's. If these differences aren't discussed and resolved in advance, they will have to be worked out on the set. At this juncture, however, they will become apparent only after at least one unsatisfactory run-through, and the ensuing discussion will hold up a full crew of perhaps five to ten people while the actor and director reach an accord.

Readings
If the director is allowed more time than is required for an informal script discussion, his or her next step would be to have the cast read through the script several times. This process allows the actors and director to talk about how performances might vary and to test those variations.

In addition, rough spots in the script are often discovered in read-throughs. On-the-spot revisions can often take place before they become stopping points on the set or location.

Blocking
The ideal, although rare, situation for a director is to have rehearsal time set aside with the cast on the set or location on which they will work. When this scenario is possible, the entire performance, including any nuances, rough spots, and even blocking, can be worked out. When the actual set or location is not available, blocking can still be worked out to a large degree by using prop furniture and similar rooms or areas.

As the actors read, they also walk through each scene and get a feel for things such as when to turn, when and where to walk, and how to gesture and glance. The director watches such a rehearsal and stops it with comments like, "The way you turned on the spot and faced him was powerful. It worked well. But I don't think it's time yet to walk up to him. In a few minutes, you're much more upset. That would seem to be the time to move toward him. Let's try holding that move until page five." Because it may be impractical to go through the entire script with all the actors, scene by scene, a common practice is to rehearse and block the most complicated scenes or those that will require the most time to get right in production.

If the director is not given time to meet with the actors face to face, he or she should still insist on some rehearsal preparation for the cast. This goal can be accomplished in a few ways.

Call at Home

Most actors and actresses are delighted to receive an advance call from the director to discuss a particular role. A face-to-face discussion with the rest of the cast is obviously preferable, but a phone conversation can still clear up *lots* of little questions.

E-Mail or Fax

If a telephone conversation won't do, try corresponding by e-mail or fax. At the very least, a director can write up a short overview of how he or she envisions the character to be played, including nuances or special instructions and perhaps a general interpretation of the role as it relates to the other characters or the overall script. Fax or e-mail correspondence can sometimes be carried out via the actor's agent.

Rehearsal on the Set

The amount of advance rehearsal a corporate director gets is usually minimal. In these instances, it becomes necessary to rehearse on the set just prior to each take. A few hints can help streamline this process and make it more effective.

Give an Initial Scene Overview

It always helps to be given a framework within which the performance should take place. For instance, imagine that the scene to be played is the "open" of what the director knows is a very positive program. The action involves a host entrance, delivery to camera, and an exit.

The director might tell the actor something like the following: "This is the open, and I'd like to set a positive tone right away, so we'll try an entrance from over here; a nice, conversational, upbeat tone; and when you get to the lines 'Let's find out,' just turn and exit to your left.

This type of quick overview would set the stage nicely. The director should next elicit any questions that might be on the actor's mind. Once these questions were answered, a rehearsal in front of the camera would follow.

If the scene is a dramatic one, for example, involving two role-play actors having an argument, the direc-

tor should still offer his or her sense of the scene in an overview fashion and should still have suggested blocking. Final blocking for dramatic scenes, however, often must be worked out as the actors actually perform the scene.

In such a case, the director might say, "So this is the scene where Andrea blows her top. My sense of what's happening here is that since she's been holding it in for months, now she's ready to just punish William with everything she's got. I think we'll start with a master shot with the camera over there. I thought it would work out naturally if you're just turning back from the window, Dale, as she rushes in the door. That way, you're both suddenly thrust face to face. What do you think?"

At this point, the actors might have questions or suggestions. The director should listen to these comments, explore the reasoning behind them, and reach a consensus on what to include or not. When an agreement had been reached, the scene could be rehearsed.

Be Specific

When an actor is performing in a way the director does not like, it's very important that the director clearly identifies what's bothering him or her and why, using examples and analogies. Both the director and the actor can then set about changing the performance as needed.

For instance, in the scene mentioned above, if the Andrea character were being overplayed, as the rehearsal finished, the director should not say something vague and confusing like, "Good. The emotional content is great. That's what I'm not positive about. The level is pretty intense. I mean, it's intensity I'm after, but, well, I'm not sure about the content and the level of that intensity."

Instead, she might say, "Very nice. Well done. But I'm a little uncomfortable with the intensity you're giving it, Joan. My sense is that Andrea would feel a more controlled, seething kind of anger. What do you think?"

If the actor disagreed or had questions, more discussion would follow. If the disagreement remained, the director should be democratic as much as possible. In the end, however, he or she is the one responsible for what goes on the screen and thus is the final decision maker. Most actors realize this and are generally willing to go along with the director's wishes.

Give Specific Changes Immediately

When a performance requires changes, the director should not wait four or five takes before communicating these adjustments. As actors go through a scene over and over, they become more and more attuned to its flow and pace and certain key events or pieces of dialogue. They may mentally "connect" a turn of the head with a certain line, or perhaps tie a gesture to a specific inflection.

The best directors make sure their criticism is heard *before* this ingraining process makes it increasingly difficult for the actor to change. As with any rule, however, there are always exceptions. One exception is when a scene is rough in general and the director feels that a few more rehearsals will smooth it out. Another exception is when an actor delivers some tone or inflection that the director feels was just a quirk on that particular take. In these cases, the director might simply say, "OK, a little rough around the edges, but I think we just need to warm up to it. Let's try it again."

Provide Encouragement

Acting is an extremely vulnerable profession. Actors are often very sensitive and keenly perceptive individuals who are sometimes hurt by rejection and virtually always motivated by recognition.

With this personality trait in mind, the director should always provide immediate recognition and encouragement to cast members when it's deserved. Such praise can come in the form of a sincere but brief comment such as "Very nice," "Well done," or "Convinced me!" With this type of professional "applause," an actor will be eager to please and much more likely to accept constructive criticism when it's offered.

What the director should *not* do, however, is patronize an actor or overplay his or her sense of satisfaction. Actors are quick to see through and lose respect for "syrupy" directors who are manipulative and insincere.

Break for Discussion if Needed

If your scene simply is not working, it's best to break and take five minutes to think it over or discuss it with the actors. It can also help in these cases to ask the AD or another trusted crew member for an outside perspective. At times, even the best directors and actors can get too close to their material, and an objective point of view can provide a new sense of focus.

It also helps during these times of confusion to focus on the word *motivation*. A lack of true motivation is often what makes a scene seem unnatural or uncomfortable.

To alleviate any improperly motivated material, the director should go over the scene carefully in his or her mind, analyzing each line and movement and asking, "Is this called for?" or "Would this character really do or say *this*, in this situation?"

Be Decisive

Finally, remember that a wishy-washy director usually gets little respect from either the crew or the actors. A director with a clear sense of vision, on the other hand, is prepared to provide the leadership and direction that both the crew and the cast require.

Even more admirable to the crew is a director who knows what he or she wants but is willing to let the crew and actors have input into how the vision is to be accomplished.

EXECUTION

If a director's casting and rehearsal have been productive, the actual execution of the scene on the set or location is normally as simple as saying "action" and "cut" several times while waiting for the perfect take to occur. By this time, the rough spots have been uncovered and dealt with, the actors and director are both clearly focused on what they must accomplish, and the crew is in place and ready to do its part.

Distractions

The most frequent problems during a well-rehearsed execution come from irritating distractions or frustrating circumstances, at times beyond the control of the director. For instance, if a scene being played out on location is going extremely well but three times in a row a plane flies overhead, ruining the take, both the director and the actors will become frustrated.

Another irritating distraction that sometimes hampers corporate media shoots is equipment absence or failure. Nothing is more frustrating than having a performance fine-tuned and ready to record, only to have a camera break down or a generator run out of gas. The negative impact these types of problems can produce is multiplied as other complications, such as time constraints, also become factors.

Many of these types of distractions can be alleviated in preproduction. Careful choices of locations and thorough planning and organization before the actual shoot days can make the production days much more enjoyable and productive.

A director's golden rule, however, whether or not distractions occur, is to remain calm, confident, and in control. As previously mentioned, crew and cast members look to the director for leadership. When frustrating times occur, if the director tends to lose his or her temper or composure, it will create a negative tone on the shoot that could seriously affect its outcome.

Directing Nonprofessional Talent

In feature films and commercial work, a director has the luxury of working with consistently professional and often highly paid talent. In corporate television, however, due to budget restrictions, this luxury is not usually possible.

Although many corporate programs rely on professional actors to perform key roles, such as hosts and principal characters, the corporate director still often works with company employees. These nonprofessionals are typically used when shooting employee interviews, executive messages, and employees involved in some form of work activity.

Under some circumstances, this type of footage can work quite well. In other cases, it can be disastrous to the program's credibility. A director should remember several basic rules that will greatly improve his or her chances of success when working with nonprofessional talent.

Use Employees to Demonstrate, Not to Act

The most credible roles employees can play in corporate programs are those of people similar to themselves. A telephone installer, for instance, stands a good chance of doing a credible job in a scene that calls for someone to greet a customer and repair her phone. A company secretary would be well equipped to fill the role of a clerical employee going through, perhaps, the four steps involved in proper records retention. Likewise, a warehouse worker could probably do a convincing job of demonstrating how to safely stock shelves.

In each of these cases, the key is the fact that the employee is *demonstrating* rather than acting. Because these types of demonstrative scenes are common in corporate programs, employees can often fill them successfully. Two primary cautions apply, however, when using employees even in this limited "talent" capacity—*overdirecting* and *stilted dialogue*.

Overdirecting means requiring an employee to do anything more than simply be him or herself and demonstrate the job at hand. Some examples are asking the employee to hit the DP's camera mark on an entrance or exit, telling him or her to lean or turn a certain way to accommodate lighting or framing, or encouraging him or her to gesture, glance, or motion in some way that is not normally part of the job activity being performed. In each of these cases, the result is almost always a stilted, obviously staged performance.

Stilted Dialogue When an employee is required to speak dialogue, he or she is immediately removed from the demonstrative role and placed into a character role. As we will discuss shortly, virtually all attempts to make this work will fail. One compromise, however, is to use an employee's dialogue as audio *under* a host's narration. When used in this way, although the dialogue is present, stilted or not, it simply provides a background "bed" of audio ambience under the host's predominant voice.

Do Not Cast Employees in Character Roles

Acting is a highly complicated skill. It is amazing that a client would invest thousands of dollars in a company video program but allow—and, in fact, sometimes even request or insist—that one of the most critical elements in that program be left to people totally unprepared to deliver what will be expected of them.

It takes years of hard work, study, and dedication to become a credible actor. Employees have none of this background. They are totally unfamiliar with the production process and are often dazzled by the "glamour" of lights, camera, and so on. As a result, when they are put in this position, what normally ends up happening is the following:

Laughable performances are the best that can be recorded.

The employee is embarrassed.

The program loses all credibility—if the material ever gets used.

The client is left unhappy, and the director's and producer's work looks terribly unprofessional.

Ideally, the producer with whom the director works will have explained this situation to the client and he or she will never be placed in such a position.

Do Not Give Employees Scripted Information Lines

This situation sometimes happens when an employee is to be interviewed or must look directly at the camera and convey specific information.

When specific information is delivered by an executive, such as the CEO, scripted information lines become an unavoidable necessity. Such messages must contain only certain points, often stated in specific ways. Thus, they are prepared in advance. The talking-head CEO, however, is forgivable to a large degree because employees expect such presentations and realize that his or her remarks require the advance preparation just mentioned.

On the other hand, when the information is delivered by a regular employee who is supposed to be sincerely making a point or explaining some job function, the result is usually a complete loss of credibility. Employees are not actors, and scripted lines that are delivered to either a camera or to another person require solid acting skills.

The answer to this dilemma is often what's called the news-style interview.

Employ the News-Style Interview

In the news-style interview, the employee is asked to face just away from the camera, looking at an off-camera interviewer—normally, the director. A series of ideas or topics are suggested to the employee, in the form of either questions or statements, and he or she articulates answers in his or her own words. Later, the material is edited to remove redundancies, pauses, stumbles, or extraneous comments. News-style interviews allow employees to maintain their dignity and composure while still communicating important information. Just as important to the corporate director, the interview format also adds credibility to most programs.

Meet with Employees Before Taping Interviews

This meeting is sometimes not possible on corporate shoots due to time or budget constraints. Usually, however, it *can* be arranged, and when the luxury is extended, the director should take advantage of it.

When conducting such meetings, the director should make the employee feel as comfortable as possible and simply talk about the subject of the video interview. As the discussion gets under way, the employee's look and *ability to articulate* ideas are the critical considerations.

If both of these elements appear positive, especially the ability to articulate and express ideas, the on-cam-era interview will probably go well. Keep in mind, however, that even after a successful preproduction interview, some employees freeze up when the lights and camera actually arrive.

Play Down the "Hollywood" Image

One sure-fire way to make an employee nervous is to play up the fact that he or she is about to "become a star." Employee segments or interviews are best handled on a business level. Employees should be encouraged to forget the lights, crew, and camera as much as possible.

Be an Involved Listener

If an employee being interviewed believes that the director is really listening, he or she will tend to forget about the situation at hand and become involved in making credible points.

The director can be an involved listener by, first, sincerely caring about the subject at hand and the employee's opinions or ideas. Second, the director can encourage the employee to continue speaking by nodding often or saying things like, "I see," "Yes, I understand," "Right, right," or "Now I get it. So tell me more about. . ." Third, the director should always ask open-ended questions that cannot be answered with a simple yes or no. These questions encourage thought and discussion rather than single statements. A few examples of both open- and closed-ended questions are the following:

Open-ended questions   Tell me, how would this happen? I'd like to hear more about that? What kinds of steps are involved?

Closed-ended questions   Would it happen like that? You would say that's good, I assume? There are three steps involved, right?

Prepare Interview Questions in Advance

A good way to keep a discussion moving while getting at the key issues involved is to carefully think out and write down the questions employees will be asked. As part of this preparation, the director should first consider not the question but the *responses* he or she hopes to elicit. The questions should then be determined accordingly.

For instance, if an employee is to be interviewed about a new work policy, and the director hopes to hear that the policy is well accepted and was easy to implement, he or she might ask:

Tell me about the new policy. What does it entail?

Just how does it affect you and the other people on the job?

Is it a good policy? If it is, tell me for what reasons?

Overall, tell me why the policy's implementation will be a positive change for your department?

How about your own personal feelings, or anything else you'd like to add?

These questions cover the areas of concern several times from slightly different angles. They would thus give the employee plenty of chances to find positive things to say about the new policy. Asking for a personal opinion as a last question often elicits good ideas that may previously have slipped the employee's mind.

Be Patient

Last but not least, be prepared to let the tape roll, if necessary, or wait for the employee to relax. Many poor interview pieces could have been considerably improved simply by allowing the employee a chance to become oriented enough to the surrounding crew and equipment to begin to *forget* them.

The director can help those processes by assuring employees that plenty of time is available and encouraging them to gather their thoughts before speaking. I usually follow such a statement by saying something like this:

> To be frank with you, when we do these interviews, we use only a few seconds of what the person says. You may talk for 10 minutes, but we'll end up using maybe 30 seconds or so. Oh, and by the way, we can edit out any stumbles or mumbles, so don't worry about getting it all out in one breath. Just take your time, think about it, and say it however you like.

In the final analysis, a director's ability to shape the human aesthetics of a corporate media production are directly related to his or her ability to communicate with, empathize with, and guide the efforts of the cast, crew, and the company employees with whom he or she works.

21 Audiovisual Aesthetics

The director has now carefully analyzed the script and, based on this analysis, formulated character roles. He or she has also begun the delicate process of guiding the cast toward credible performances. These elements he or she has executed thus far could be thought of as one side of a director's aesthetic balance.

Now comes the other side of that balance—the task of making sure the actor's performances are recorded in a way that will not only maintain but also heighten their impact and credibility. The first element on this second side of the balance is audiovisual aesthetics.

In a dramatic scene, however, the audiovisual elements would change. For instance, the set might be something like a darkened room. If so, dramatic, high-contrast lighting would probably be used; more extreme close-up focal lengths might be incorporated; and perhaps nonstandard camera angles, such as overhead or low angles, would be employed as well.

When these types of audiovisual elements are shaped and guided properly and added to the performances the cast puts forth, the two separate sides of the director's balance blend as one solid, audiovisual entity—a shot, scene, or entire program that is credible and captivating to its audience.

PICTURES AND SOUND

Audiovisual aesthetic qualities are those pertaining to the **audio** (sound) and **video** (picture) elements of each scene. They are elements such as lighting, focal lengths, frame composition, camera movement and placement, and sound recording. The use of audiovisual aesthetic elements often changes depending on the type of program being produced.

As an example, the audiovisual elements in a simple "host on camera" program might include an office set, lighting with little contrast or modeling, typical mid-range focal lengths, and camera positions such as eye-level medium shots. It would probably also include standard sound recording systems and techniques.

SCRIPT ANALYSIS AND VISUALIZATION

Similar to human aesthetics, audiovisual aesthetics are at first based on script analysis. As the director reads and visualizes each scene, he or she begins to "see" the audiovisual elements it incorporates: angles, lighting, locations, and so on. This visualization process continues throughout the preproduction phase of the director's work. As production nears, this visualization gains focus and detail. Finally, during production, the audiovisual aesthetic qualities of every scene must be shaped, guided, and judged acceptable by the director on each take.

Audiovisual aesthetics fall into the following two general categories: *visual elements* and *sound elements*.

VISUAL ELEMENTS

Visuals mean pictures, and when it comes to pictures, the director of photography (DP) is the director's closest collaborator. The DP's job is to help bring the director's vision to the screen with photographic—or, in the case of video, videographic—impact and credibility.

In big-budget feature films, the DP typically does not operate the camera. His or her main functions are to plan, create, and supervise the lighting of each set or scene and guide the camera crews in such areas as the use of appropriate film stock, camera positions and movement, and filter and lens usage. The DP often has a full staff for these purposes, and their single overriding objective is to accomplish what the director asks for in terms of the mood and look of the pictures.

In corporate media, the DP (often called the videographer or lighting director, LD) usually handles lighting *and* camera operation. He or she may have one or two people, perhaps a grip and a gaffer, to help place cables and lights and to move the camera and lighting equipment. On many smaller corporate shoots, the DP is on his or her own—setting up lights and camera alone.

Although the scope of the DP's job may be smaller than in features, his or her objective remains the same—to give the director the visual aesthetic quality envisioned. The DP accomplishes this task by orchestrating four elements under the director's supervision: camera placement and movement, frame size, frame composition, and lighting.

The DP and staff may be physically executing these elements, but the director is the overall guiding force and the final decision maker behind them. For this reason, the director must have a complete understanding of the DP's role and responsibilities. He or she must also know how the elements just mentioned affect the audiovisual aesthetics of the program. In order to gain that understanding, let's examine each of these critical areas in greater detail.

CAMERA PLACEMENT AND MOVEMENT

When considering camera placement, the director should first and foremost remember that it is the perspective he or she chooses to give the audience. This perspective can be singular, as in the case of one camera shot that records an entire scene, or it can have multiple perspectives, as in the case of an event recorded from several angles that is later edited into one scene. The perspective can also be stationary or moving.

In order to arrive at a decision on camera placement and movement, the director once again reflects on his or her script analysis, the blocking or movement worked out with the actors during rehearsal, and the resources available. With all these issues considered, the director must ask, "What is the best place or *places* for the audience to view this action? Should the camera be at eye level? Should it be fixed in terms of position or focal length? Should it follow the action by actually moving along with it, or simply pan left or right as the action takes place?"

As you might guess, many technical ramifications are involved in this decision, including: What type of camera equipment is available? Is there a dolly? What type of lenses are being used—a zoom or fixed focal lengths? How much time is available on the schedule? Is the camera operator capable? Is the talent capable?

STANDARD COVERAGE

The safest way to record a scene is to shoot the identical action from a number of typically accepted camera angles and focal lengths. This method is referred to as shooting "standard coverage."

Standard coverage normally calls for the director to first record a *master scene*. This perspective is usually a wide angle that encompasses all action and all actors in the scene.

After a satisfactory take or "buy" of this master, the camera is moved in for medium shots or medium close-ups. These shots are much closer angles that encompass each individual actor's part in the scene. They are recorded with each actor repeating lines and action identical to that of the master scene. When a "buy" of each of these shots is recorded, close-ups of certain parts or "inserts" are recorded in the same way. These shots are still closer angles that encompass very small parts of the same action.

The result is a scene recorded identically from a number of angles. Later in the editing process, this coverage allows the director to provide the viewer with a series of effective and aesthetically pleasing perspectives as the scene unfolds.

To illustrate, let's use a very simple example.

INT. SERVICE OFFICE–DAY

JEAN, a customer rep, is talking to a customer on the phone.

> JEAN
>
> *Yes, ma'am, we do provide a warranty for the
> first two years . . .*

CAROL, her supervisor, enters and sits down. Jean can see that Carol wants to say something important.

> JEAN
>
> *Excuse me, ma'am. Could you hold for one
> second, please? Thank you.*

She places the customer on hold.

> CAROL
>
> *Sorry to interrupt, Jean. I just need to know
> right away if you're signed up for the first
> training session. The sign-up cards have to go
> in by three today.*

> JEAN
>
> *I did sign up. Donna has my card.*

> CAROL
>
> *Great. I'll get it off, then, with the rest of ours.*

Carol now gets up and exits. Jean releases her hold button and continues with her customer.

> JEAN
>
> *I'm back, ma'am. Thank you for waiting.
> Now, about that warranty, you can sign up
> for it by phone . . .*

DISSOLVE:

As shown in Figure 21.1, we could shoot standard coverage of this scene as follows: The camera is positioned at approximately eye level for a seated person. It is mounted on a dolly and rolled in to a point where it can begin the shot by giving the viewer a close-up of the telephone the representative is talking on.

The master shot is recorded beginning with this close-up of the phone. As the representative starts her dialogue with the customer, the camera is rolled (dollied) back to a position in which both the representative at her desk and a second chair beside her desk are visible. A small part of the surrounding office can also be seen. As this "dolly back" is nearing its end point, the supervisor enters the scene and takes a seat. She and the representative talk, after the representative puts the customer on hold. The supervisor finishes and leaves, and the representative releases the hold button and begins talking again with the customer.

This initial angle would provide a profile view of both actresses during the entire scene, as well as an "establishing" perspective of their immediate surroundings—a service office. The shot would begin, however, with a close-up of the phone that would "reveal" the scene to us and perhaps allow for a comfortable transition from the previous shot—possibly a host on camera.

Once a "buy" of this master has been recorded, the director might ask that the camera be kept at the same level but moved to a position looking over the supervisor's shoulder at a *medium shot* of the representative. This shot would allow the viewer to see the representative

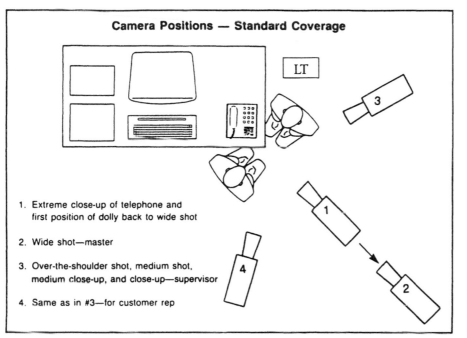

Camera Positions — Standard Coverage

LT

1. Extreme close-up of telephone and first position of dolly back to wide shot

2. Wide shot—master

3. Over-the-shoulder shot, medium shot, medium close-up, and close-up—supervisor

4. Same as in #3—for customer rep

Figure 21.1 Camera positions for a typical corporate setup—supervisor on right and customer representative on left. Camera angles 1 through 4 will provide standard coverage.

completely and some of the desk and computer in front of her. The scene would then be acted out again, identically as it had in the master shot.

As the representative began to talk, we would see the back of the supervisor move in from camera left to right as she entered the shot. She would take a seat, remain there with her back to us as the scene played out, and move out of the frame when the conversation had ended. Again, the representative would hit the hold button a second time and continue her conversation with the customer.

The director might now ask that the camera stay at the same or a close by position and be zoomed in to a medium close-up shot in which only the face and upper body of the representative were visible. The scene would again be played out and a "buy" recorded.

The camera would then be moved to the other side of the desk, looking over the representative's shoulder at the supervisor. It would remain in basically the same focal length as the previous over-the-shoulder angle—a medium shot. The scene would again play out completely and identically to the master until a buy had been recorded. The camera would again be moved in to a close-up—this time, of the supervisor—and the scene would be recorded a final time.

Finally, the director would ask that the camera be moved to a position where it could provide an extreme close-up of the hold button on the telephone. From this

position, the director would record the operator's finger entering the frame and pushing in the hold button and a second version, this time of the representative's finger entering the frame and releasing the button.

I should note that in an actual shooting situation, these final inserts might have been shot in the very beginning, when the camera had been dollied in for the opening close-up of the master shot. I've placed this piece of the coverage last in this instance for the sake of clarity and simplicity.

Having accomplished this sequence of shots, the director would have recorded standard and very adequate "coverage" of the scene for use in editing.

EDITING COVERAGE

Perhaps days later when the editor had finished cutting this footage together, the scene would begin with the close-up of the phone. As the camera dollied back, the wide master shot (including the representative) would be revealed. We might hold onto this shot until the supervisor entered, took a seat, and began talking. At this point, the editor would most likely cut back and forth or "intercut" using the over-the-shoulder and close-up shots. This approach would allow us to see the supervisor and the representative individually as each one spoke.

When the rep put the customer on hold and later released her, the editor might briefly use the extreme close-ups of the rep's finger to show us that action taking place. Finally, the editor would probably cut back to the master shot just as the supervisor was getting up to make her exit. This type of shooting and editing would provide the audience with an establishing sense of where the scene was taking place and a series of comfortable perspectives of all the action as it played out.

NONSTANDARD CAMERA PLACEMENT AND MOVEMENT

Standard camera placement is usually at eye level to the actors, in a position that will provide a clear view of the action. This type of standard camera placement is appropriate in the vast majority of corporate shooting situations. In some situations, however, the scene might be enhanced by what could be called nonstandard camera placement. This method is typically used when a nonstandard view of the scene or a part of it would heighten its visual impact.

For instance:

FADE-IN:

INT. LIVING ROOM–DAY

Bill and Genie are face to face, arguing angrily.

> GENIE
>
> *I've had it with you! You're never on time, and all you ever do is complain once you get here!*
>
> BILL
>
> *Yeah, well, I figure why should I be on time when you don't really care anyway!*

Genie has had it. She slaps Bill in the face.

This scene could be shot with standard camera placement and work fine. It could also be shot, however, from a low, close camera angle that would in effect place the viewer in a somewhat vulnerable position under and among the actors. The viewer would then become more affected by and involved in the anger and slapping action that takes place in the scene. This perspective would add tension and a sense of reality.

The same scene shot from an *overhead* angle, on the other hand, would tend to provide a voyeuristic or omnipotent perspective, in which the viewer would feel safely removed from involvement in the action. Depending on what the director wanted to accomplish, either choice or a combination of both could be quite effective.

When nonstandard placement is used in this way, it becomes a seemingly natural perspective that goes unnoticed by the viewer. When such placements are used improperly, however, the viewer may become aware of the camera's presence—which is something the director rarely, if ever, wants to happen.

Besides heightening tension and dramatic impact, nonstandard angles can also be used simply for a fresh perspective or to enhance the visual aesthetics of a shot. For instance, I once shot a host in front of a building with a large, attractive, logo-type sign on it. When the camera was placed at eye level, we could not frame the shot so that the actor could be seen in conjunction with the logo—something I wanted to accomplish. After some discussion with my DP, we lowered the camera to about chest level and brought it in closer to the actor. This positioned us looking up at him. The shot then framed very attractively with the logo sign just over his shoulder.

On another project, I was once scouting to shoot a morning meeting between a supervisor and roughly ten of his employees standing at the rear of the supervisor's truck. From eye level, I knew the shot would be acceptable, but it would not give a sense of the circular, almost powwow-type arrangement in which the men would gather. I found a nearby second-story balcony that I knew would provide a more attractive perspective. That's where we placed the camera during production, and the shot worked quite well.

MOVEMENT

Remember, the director's intent is to never let the audience become aware that a camera is present in the midst of this action. When he or she is successful at this intention, the full illusory quality of a scene keeps its integrity and the audience never questions how or why they are able to eavesdrop on the events.

Camera movements, including zooms, can ruin this illusory quality if not executed properly and with motivation. Unmotivated moves can make the audience aware that the camera is present and that the director is "doing something" with it for dramatic effect. Keeping this effect in mind, remember that, in most cases, camera movement should be used only to emphasize, reveal, or create a needed sense of motion to enhance a shot or scene.

For instance, consider the following scene:

INT. KITCHEN–DAY

Marian is on the phone. As she hears the words of the police sergeant, her face registers total shock.

SERGEANT (V.O.)

I'm sorry to tell you this, ma'am, but your son has been involved in a severe motor vehicle accident. He's in critical condition at St. Martin's Hospital . . .

If the director decided to zoom or dolly rapidly in from a medium shot of Marian to a close-up as these lines were being spoken, it would certainly emphasize the shock Marian is feeling, and because the audience would, in a sense, be sharing that shock, they would never stop to realize the camera was moving. This is a well-motivated camera move.

Suppose Marian were having a conversation with her son, however, about what to fix him for lunch that day. If the same zoom or dolly were used as she was asking "Mustard or mayo?" it would break the illusion rather than emphasize it. The move would have no purpose and would appear obviously unmotivated to the audience.

Let's consider another example.

FADE IN:

INT. FITNESS CENTER–DAY

An aerobics class in action. Feet hammer at the wooden floor, faces bead with sweat, and arms swing up and down in time to MUSIC. The instructor stops working out and moves among the exercisers.

INSTRUCTOR

Stay with it . . . and two and three and four and . . . good! Knees high . . . arms to the sky. Let's go!

While a moving camera might not reveal or emphasize any specific thing or person in this shot, a sense of motion is definitely appropriate. In this case, the director might want a handheld camera to move among the exercisers or a series of rapid zooms, pans, or dollies.

The general sense of motion this shot would create would be a natural enhancement to this type of footage. Because it would be motivated, the audience would never realize it was happening. Camera moves can also be used to emphasize transitions. For instance:

INT. OFFICE SET–DAY

The host turns to the CAMERA and says:

HOST

*So, the way you treat your customers can have
a definite effect on the mood you take home—
as we're about to see.*

Because this shot is signaling a transition to what will probably be a vignette, a zoom or dolly in to a close-up—or even the reverse, an outward move—would act as a subtle cue to the audience that we are about to "leave" for some other location.

As long as these types of zooms are not overused, they work fine. If the director starts zooming or dollying on every shot, however, the transition "signal" will be replaced by an awkward, forward-and-backward sense of motion that will more than likely distract instead of enhance the scene—and probably also become apparent to the audience.

FRAME SIZE

Frame sizes refer to the amount of area seen in a shot. Because frame sizes are directly related to the focal length of the lens being used, let's first consider this aspect of the subject.

Short Focal Lengths

Lenses with focal lengths of approximately 10 to 25 millimeters produce wide angles and sometimes a distorted sense of distance between foreground and background objects. A wide-angle lens, for instance, can make a set piece, perhaps 5 feet behind a host, appear to be far behind him in the distance. Extreme wide-angle lenses produce fish-eye perspectives that severely distort the images. These lenses are normally used only for special or noticeable effects.

Mid-Range Focal Lengths

Lenses with focal lengths of 30 to 50 millimeters produce images of average size and background–foreground relationships. They also produce the least amount of image distortion. These focal lengths are most commonly used for recording master and medium shots.

Long Focal Lengths

Lenses with focal lengths of 75 to 100 millimeters and above produce narrow angles. They also tend to magnify images and distort the distance between foreground and background objects in the opposite way wide angles do.

Long lens shots are those in which, for example, a person is seen running across a boulevard and a fast-approaching car nearly runs her over before swerving to one side at the last instant. In reality, a great distance exists between the person and the car, but the long lens tends to "squash" or "flatten" the apparent distance between the two objects.

PRIME LENSES

In feature film production, an assortment of lenses called "primes" are typically rented as a part of the camera package. A set of prime lenses usually consists of five to seven lenses, each with a set focal length ranging from short, perhaps 15 millimeters, to long, perhaps 150 millimeters. Because prime lenses contain a minimal amount of lens surfaces, they produce top-quality pictures with minimal light requirements.

ZOOM LENSES

A **zoom lens** has multiple focal lengths and is adjustable by rotating a lens barrel either by hand or with the use of a small motor called a "servo." Zoom lenses are often described by the ratio between their shortest and longest focal lengths. For instance, a "10 to 1" zoom lens with a minimum focal length of 15 millimeters will have a maximum focal length of 150 millimeters.

Zoom lenses are often more useful than primes because changing a focal length simply entails rotating a lens barrel instead of removing and replacing a lens. Feature film directors and DPs often stick to primes, however, because zooms have more internal lenses or "glass." Each additional glass surface slightly reduces overall picture quality and increases the need for light.

In corporate media, zoom lenses are the norm and primes are the exception. Today's zoom lenses produce images of more than adequate quality for high-resolution video and digital production. In addition, zooms are much simpler to work with, especially when the DP does not have one or more camera assistants to quickly retrieve and mount the proper lens.

For the director, each of these lenses with their varying focal lengths means different types of frame sizes and thus different visual qualities for his or her shots.

SHOT DESCRIPTIONS

The frame sizes used most commonly in corporate media describe the following types of shots: *wide shot (WS), medium shot (MS), medium close-up (MCU), close-up (CU),* and *extreme close-up (ECU).* Variations of these frame sizes also make up other commonly used shots, such as two shots, over-the-shoulder shots, point-of-view (POV) shots, and reverse-angle shots. Since a director must be knowledgeable about these shots, let's briefly discuss each.

Wide Shot (WS)

A wide shot is normally made with a mid-range focal length, often around 30 millimeters. It usually encompasses all of the action within a scene and establishes the area or location in which the action is taking place. A wide shot normally also keeps everything in the frame focused.

A wide shot might allow us to see a complete den or kitchen, a full set, or a work area in which employees or actors are working. In our previously diagrammed shot of the service representative and her supervisor, camera position 2 would produce the wide shot shown in Figure 21.2. It would serve the purpose just mentioned.

Medium Shot (MS)

A medium shot most often frames one actor from about the thighs up. A medium shot can be framed nicely with a 50-millimeter focal length. Its purpose is often to feature an actor but not to call dramatic attention to him or her.

A medium shot is also used when a director wants to single out an actor but still keep the audience aware of their immediate surroundings or set elements. Similar to a wide shot, the medium shot may keep the entire frame in focus (Figure 21.3).

In our representative and supervisor scene, the over-the-shoulder angles, such as the one pictured again in Figure 21.4, are also medium shots. In this case, they might be called over-the-shoulder medium shots or just over-the-shoulder shots; either distinction is correct. In both cases, if the foreground actor were removed, the remaining actor would be featured in a medium focal length.

Medium Close-up (MCU)

Medium close-ups frame an actor from the lower chest up. A 75-millimeter focal length is often about right for a medium close-up. In this focal length, the background often begins to go "soft" or lose focus because the depth of field is shallower than with a wide angle.

A medium close-up singles out the actor (Figure 21.5) and reduces the viewer's awareness of the surroundings. Medium close-ups are frequently used by directors to intercut individual dialogue segments between actors in conversations. Similar to medium shots, medium close-ups usually do not call dramatic attention to an actor, but they do bring audience focus strictly to him or her.

Figure 21.2 Wide shot establishes actors and surrounding area.

Figure 21.3 Medium shot singles out an individual but still gives a sense of the surrounding location.

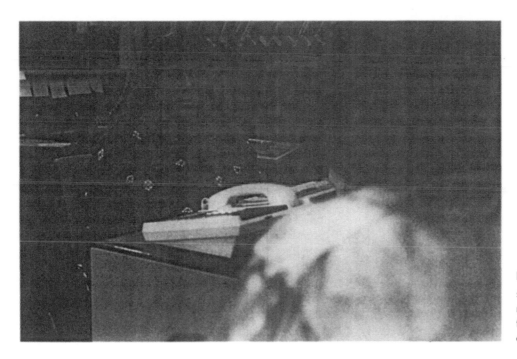

Figure 21.4 Over-the-shoulder shot (OTS) provides more depth and perspective than medium shot, since both actors are seen in the frame.

Figure 21.5 Medium close-up features an individual and begins to lose the background.

Close-up (CU)

Close-ups should be reserved for dramatic emphasis. A close-up might be shot with approximately a 100-millimeter focal length. It fills the entire frame with the actor's face and perhaps upper shoulders (Figure 21.6). Close-ups typically also cause what little of the background is still seen to lose complete focus, so that the actor is separated still more from the surroundings. Little motivation usually exists to bring the audience into this intimate a perspective on an actor unless something he or she is saying must be punctuated or a subtle facial expression must be emphasized.

Extreme Close-up (ECU)

An extreme close-up fills the frame with the actor's face or part of it, as in Figure 21.7. It is normally shot at about 100 millimeters. Its purpose is to create dramatic effect or unquestionable emphasis.

An extreme close-up can be used to see fear, anger, or perhaps tears welling up in an actor's eyes. It can also call attention to a lip quiver, a twitch, or a toothpick being rolled over a tongue.

As with close-ups, extreme close-ups should be reserved for those few instances when the audience will not become aware or be made uncomfortable by being placed, in effect, nose to nose with the actor.

Insert

Extreme close-ups of objects or special actions are often called *inserts*. Inserts are typically shot to highlight some small or important action or element of the scene.

For instance, in our representative and supervisor scene, when the representative presses and releases the hold button (pictured again in Figure 21.8), the coverage includes an extreme close-up or insert showing this action take place. If part of this program's purpose were to instruct employees on when and when not to put customers on hold, use of these insert shots might be appropriate to ensure that the audience had noticed whether the representative followed the procedure correctly or not.

By contrast, if the scene had nothing to do with putting customers on hold and the action were simply incidental, the insert would be unnecessary.

AVOIDING "JUMP CUTS"

Another frame size consideration the director must keep in mind when shooting coverage of any scene is to avoid what are referred to as "jump cuts."

A *jump cut* is an unsightly edit that occurs when two similar pieces of footage shot from basically the same focal lengths and usually the same camera positions are

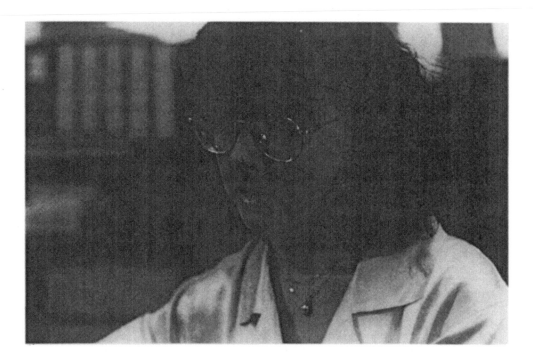

Figure 21.6 Close-up commands full attention.

Figure 21.7 Extreme close-up is often used for dramatic emphasis.

Figure 21.8 Extreme close-up of an object such as a telephone is often labeled an "insert." This is the case when the shot will be inserted into the main action of the master shot.

cut together. These junctures create pictures in which the elements in the frame, such as people or objects, appear to jump suddenly from one position to another. Jump cuts can be avoided by keeping the following basic parameters in mind when shooting more than one angle of any scene or shot.

Change Focal Lengths

Never shoot coverage of the same action from the same position without at least a 15 millimeter change in focal lengths. For instance, let's assume a host faces the camera in a medium close-up (approximately a 50-millimeter focal length) and records scene one. Before the camera rolls for scene two, the director has the DP change the focal length to a wide shot featuring the host's entire body. This is approximately a 20-millimeter focal length. When these two scenes are cut together, the host will not appear to suddenly jump from one position to another because the focal length was changed more than 15 millimeters. Had both segments been recorded in the initial 50-millimeter focal length, however, the result would have been an unsightly jump cut.

Change Camera Positions

Try to change camera positions by at least 40 degrees when shooting coverage of the same action—even in addition to the change of focal length. Using the previous host example, we can assume that with just the change of focal length the footage will cut together acceptably, but the direct cut from the narrow to wide focal length won't make for the smoothest transition. On the other hand, if the host had turned to a new angle between scenes one and two, the camera could record not only the change of focal length, but also a changed background, which (provided the continuity of the turning action matched) would result in a very comfortable transition.

Plan Edits Carefully

Plan your edits so that not only shots within scenes, but also transition edits between scenes are made with a substantial change of focal length or camera angle. For example, leaving one scene on a shot of a person looking just past the camera and beginning the next scene with a person framed and facing the same way would create a similar uncomfortable visual jump.

A director who has a good sense of camera placement and movement and who then becomes comfortable with the proper frame sizes for his or her subject must next address what will appear in those frames and how it will be arranged—in other words, composition.

FRAME COMPOSITION

To compose means to create. Frame composition is exactly that. The director, working closely with the DP, arranges actors and foreground and background objects in the frame to create an overall visual effect that enhances or provides credibility to all other aspects of the illusion.

Frame composition is a subtle skill that usually involves the following three primary elements: *balance, depth,* and *lighting.*

Balance

Balance refers to how people and objects are arranged in the frame. In Figure 21.9, the actor's face and upper body are at the right side of the frame. This placement leaves a lot of empty space at frame left. In addition, his eye line is directed toward the edge of the frame to which he is *closest.* This focus creates an uncomfortable or unbalanced feel that is distracting to the viewer.

In Figure 21.10, however, the frame is comfortable to the eye. The actor is framed slightly to the left of center, facing screen right. He appears naturally positioned in the frame, and his eye line is given a bit of "lead" space, rather than being "up against" the left frame. The viewer will have no trouble at all watching this picture.

Understanding this type of balance gives us some sense of composing the left and right sides of the frame, but what about the top and bottom? These areas, too, help make up the sense of visual balance.

In Figure 21.11, the frame is unbalanced because far too much headroom is left in the picture. Comfortable headroom can normally be achieved by keeping the actor's eyes roughly one-third of the way down in the frame. This placement usually leaves a small but very visually comfortable space between the actor's head and the top of the frame. In extreme close-ups, the top of the actor's head is often cut off. This shot is called giving the actor a "Warner Brothers haircut."

Figure 21.9 Unbalanced image. The face is too close to the leading edge of the frame. Distracting space is left behind the actor.

Figure 21.10 Balanced frame. The frame has lead space in the direction of attention, and the actor is comfortably placed slightly to the left of the overall frame.

Figure 21.11 Too much headroom creates a displeasing and uncomfortable composition. Eyes should normally be one-third of the way down the frame.

Figure 21.12 Horizon in middle of frame creates a flat and uninteresting image with no emphasis on foreground or background.

This one-third rule, like most others in the art of directing, is not without exception. For instance, an actor might be shown in relation to an area or object that requires him or her to be at the bottom or perhaps the top of the screen. This situation is often the case when logos, buildings, or other elements must also be framed in the shot. Shots of places and objects should also follow the rules of balance.

For instance, a horizon should almost never be made to fall in the middle of a picture, as in Figure 21.12. This tends to flatten the image and destroy the viewer's sense of perspective and depth.

In Figure 21.13, this imbalance is corrected by placing the horizon in the upper third of the frame, thus making the foreground appear much more interesting and comfortable to the eye.

Figure 21.13 Horizon at lower, or in this case at upper, third of the image is much more pleasing to the eye. Foreground becomes area of emphasis in this case.

Depth

With a basic feel for the sides and top and bottom of the frame, a director must consider depth—the foreground and background. Foreground or background elements, or the lack of them, can make a picture seem flat and uninteresting or can provide an aesthetically pleasant feeling of depth and texture.

For instance, in Figure 21.14, an employee being interviewed in front of a flat, pale wall produces an uncomfortable and even somewhat unnatural composition. If a small tree is placed in the background over her right shoulder (screen left), the picture becomes a bit more interesting and pleasing to the eye. If we also add a globe and several books on a shelf partly in the frame over her left shoulder, even more texture is added. Finally, if we position several out-of-focus fern leaves at the corner of the frame in the foreground, we end up with Figure 21.15. Instead of being a single uninteresting plane, the image has become a multiplaned composition that is visually balanced to the eye.

By contrast, you may be shooting a host in **limbo** (a totally featureless environment), presenting a very serious subject. In this case, a stark black or white background might be appropriate to the content being delivered.

Depth can also be created simply by not shooting against flat surfaces. In an office or set, it is often visually more interesting to shoot so that the corner can be seen in the frame or so that wall areas are framed diagonally. Again, this shot adds a pleasing sense of perspective and depth.

This sense of depth often motivates directors to shoot over-the-shoulder and "two" shots instead of individual medium close-ups of actors. A medium close-up may focus in on the actor, but as in Figure 21.16, an over-the-shoulder shot can also establish a visual sense of relationship between the two actors—in other words, a feeling of depth (Figure 21.17).

Depth can also be controlled by lens usage and light levels. Lenses with long focal length tend to flatten a background and foreground, making distant objects appear much closer to each other than they are. Wide-angle lenses do the opposite.

F-stop also affects depth by changing the depth of field. When a camera's aperture or iris is fully opened, in low light conditions, the depth of field is sharply reduced. This means that foreground and background objects lose focus if they are not close to the actor. A nearly closed F-stop, on the other hand, used in bright lighting conditions, increases the depth of field so that background and foreground objects appear in focus, even if they are quite a distance from the actor.

Figure 21.14 Employee interview composed with a flat, uninteresting background.

Figure 21.15 When plant and other items are added, more depth and visual interest is created. Image becomes much more pleasing to view.

Figure 21.16 Medium close-up.

Figure 21.17 Over-the-shoulder shot.

Lighting

Lighting serves two important purposes for the corporate video director. The first is simply to make the scene being shot bright enough to achieve the proper video levels. This illumination ensures that the technical standards are met and that the visuals are of adequate quality to be reproduced, edited, and, of course, viewed by an audience. The second purpose of lighting is to enhance the images being shot and to create moods and tones that support the director's illusion.

Achieving the Proper Video Levels and Values

As mentioned in the section on production lighting, a video scene's brightness is measured in terms of luminance. Luminance is measured on a waveform monitor that is either taken to the field or mounted in a studio control room.

The brightest parts of a video picture—usually the whites—should register at approximately 100 units on the waveform monitor. The darkest parts of the picture—the blacks—should register at 7.5 units.

In addition, the overall video image being shot should not contain severe contrast between these two extremes. Instead, a good video image normally contains a *range* of levels between 7.5 and 100 units. A human face, for instance, normally registers between 60 and 70 units. A dark shirt or suit registers perhaps 30 units. A pale wall may register 90 units.

If a part of the picture becomes overexposed or registers more than 100 units, the video signal becomes distorted and that portion of the image loses detail and seems to "bloom" unnaturally. These overexposed portions of a picture are usually called "hot spots."

If too much of the picture is extremely dark, it may appear acceptable on the high-quality broadcast system that is recording it, but later, when it is duplicated to a viewing format such as standard VHS, the darks begin to break down, creating grainy or "noisy" images.

Achieving these technical standard levels while creating moods and textures with lighting can sometimes be difficult. The director must understand these issues because they directly affect how he or she might plan to shoot a scene. For instance, consider the following scene:

INT. CEO'S OFFICE–DAY

The CEO is standing at his large window, gazing out over the city, as he carries on a conversation with one of his VPs.

CEO

John, I'm convinced we should up the stakes
on the Waite project. They're going to blow
this thing sky-high unless we get in on it now.

Remembering what we just said about not having too much contrast in a video image, would it be a good idea to plan on shooting this scene with the window as a backdrop for the CEO? It's doubtful. The outside light would probably be much too "hot," surrounding and overpowering the most likely dark-suited figure of the CEO in front of it.

If forced to shoot such a scene, the DP would probably start by closing down the f-stop of the camera until the outside light registered 100 units on the waveform and did not "bloom." At this point, the background luminance level would be proper. But with the camera's iris shut down this far, the dark-suited image of the CEO would probably appear only as a silhouette because this portion of the picture would be severely underexposed.

To balance the overall image, the DP would have to focus a good deal of light on the CEO to "pump him up" to match the background level. Although this method would probably produce the proper recording levels, there's a good chance it would also make the CEO look very lit and unnatural.

A better solution would be for the director to choose a camera position that does not juxtapose the CEO in front of the window. Shooting him from the side, for instance, with a small portion of the window in the frame and using a hard key light that appears to be outside light, would no doubt create an effective look. This approach would also save time and result in a much more natural and aesthetically pleasing shot.

The same types of problems can develop when dealing with a *lack* rather than an overabundance of light. The director should, therefore, be well aware of the capabilities and restrictions of his or her lighting needs.

Creating Mood, Tone, and Textures

Lighting also helps create moods that strengthen the director's illusion. Here's one simple example.

INT. SET–DAY

We see only a dark wall. On it is a shadow pattern that appears to be light shining through bars in an open jail cell door. HOST ENTERS under what appears to be a harsh, single light source.

HOST
(Gestures to shadows)
Life under lockup. Not a very settling thought.
But is it really that bad? This is "Newsline,"
and in this issue we'll find out.

As host exits, the shadows on the wall begin to move, suggesting that the cell door is sliding closed. It slams shut with a METAL CLANK.

Obviously, the dark walls and cell door shadows help create the tense mood the director wants for the "open" of this program. The "single" light source on the host also helps reinforce the dark, harshly lit conditions that might exist in a real jail cell. Both elements, in concert with a convincing performance by the host, would create a very credible opening segment that would no doubt keep viewers waiting for more.

Standard Three-Point Lighting

In many corporate programs, a dramatic mood is not needed. What is needed, however, is an attractive image, complementary to the actors or employees being shot. This might be the case when shooting a videotaped message by a company president who must look very cor-

porate and polished. Or it might make an employee interview in a supply room or manhole appear natural but aesthetically pleasing for the location. When this is the case, variations of a standard three-point lighting setup become the tool used by the DP.

Three-point lighting refers to a "key" or primary source of light, a "fill" or weaker source used to fill in shadows created by the key light, and a "back" or "rim" light used to separate the subject from the background by creating a thin rim of light on the subject's head and shoulders. Figures 21.18 through 21.22 show several variations on standard three-point lighting setups, and diagrams explain how the different looks are produced. Again, the director must be aware of these lighting options as he or she considers how the various segments of the program will be shot.

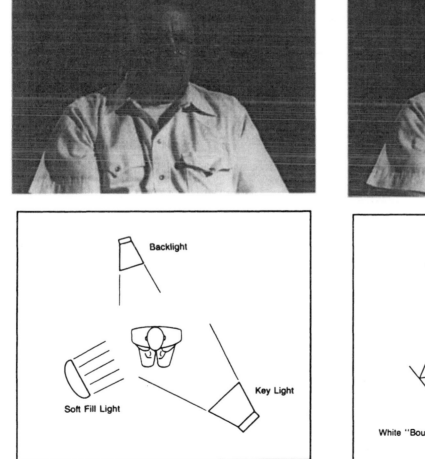

Figure 21.18   Interviewee lit with standard three-point lighting setup.

Figure 21.19   Same setup, but fill light has been replaced by a bounce card, producing slightly more shadow.

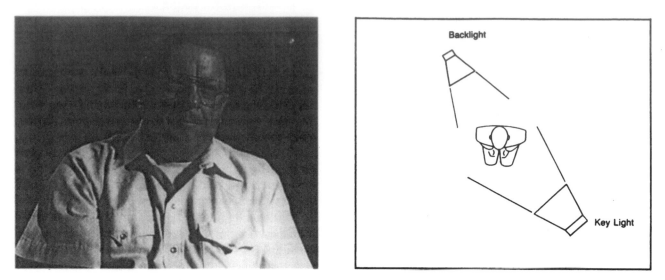

Figure 21.20 Same setup, but in this case with no fill light. Shadows are now becoming dramatic.

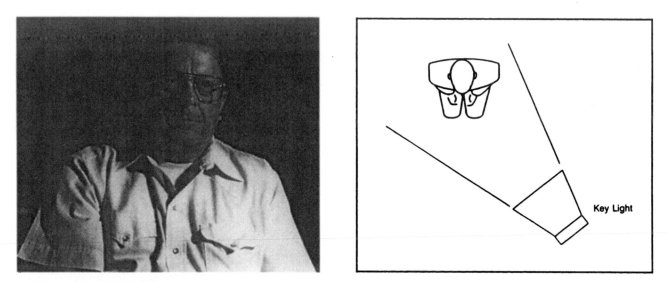

Figure 21.21 Now only a single hard source of light is being used—the key light.

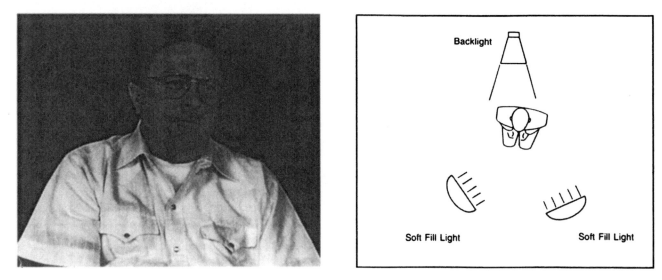

Figure 21.22 Flat lighting (no shadows) is created by using a wash of soft, equally balanced light.

SOUND

The audio or sound portion of a production also has a profound effect on its aesthetic quality and audience impact. The right sounds, creatively placed and appropriately enhanced, can wake up an otherwise "flat" scene.

Unlike lighting and camera work, however, the majority of sound enhancements on a typical production happen after production, in the editing or audio "sweetening" rooms. These processes enhance existing recorded sounds and add sound effects and music at the director's or producer's request. During the production process, the director has two primary considerations in relation to sound: the *quality* and the *types* of sound being recorded.

Sound Quality

Recording sound in a studio situation is usually a fairly routine matter that involves the proper microphone arrangement in the hands of a skilled sound recordist and perhaps a boom operator. On location, sound recording often becomes complicated and frustrating due to elements that are out of the production crew's control.

As an example, I once shot several host scenes in a house in a residential area. In one scene, the host was to step into a kitchen and introduce the subject of home security systems. Due to a camera problem, we had started out behind schedule that day. Next, a conference about a wardrobe change between me, the actor, the producer, and the client held us up even more. In addition, the lighting design was fairly time-consuming because we were shooting day for night (a scene shot during the day that has to appear as if it were happening at night).

When we had at last managed to iron out these problems and rehearse the scene a few times, we were more than an hour behind schedule. I finally decided we were ready and said, "Let's roll tape and try one."

The actor prepared. The crew settled. The slate was held in front of the camera. Just as the camera rolled, however, the whine of a distant lawn mower suddenly started up. I looked at the audio recordist, who had on a set of earphones to monitor the sound being recorded. She returned my glance and shook her head. This meant there was no way we could record the scene. The whine was prominent enough to be recognized and also to affect the sound continuity of any editing that might take place later.

What did we do? The AD located the gentleman mowing his lawn and offered him $20 to put off his yard work until the afternoon. Luckily, he accepted.

This example is just one of numerous types of sound problems that can and often do arise when shooting on location. Whether in the studio or on location, a director should remember a few common rules of thumb and concerns.

Microphone Choices

First, shotgun mics mounted on "fishpoles" generally produce high-quality audio, but they typically require a two-person sound crew—a mixer and a boom operator. The boom operator follows the actors around, holding the fishpole, so that the mic is "on axis" with the actor speaking. The mixer or recordist monitors the sound at a mixer and makes the necessary adjustments to the incoming levels to ensure that the recording is technically acceptable before reaching the VTR.

In some cases, the boom operator is not needed if the actor remains in a single spot. In this case, the fishpole can be mounted on a "C" stand or light stand and locked into position just out of the camera's frame.

Another possibility, if the actors are to remain fairly immobile, is to use lavalier mics on hardwire cables or RF transmitters. Lavaliers are small capsule mics that can be easily hidden under a collar or inside a shirt. They, too, produce high-quality audio, but they sometimes begin to make rustling noises when actors move about and their clothes shift. This situation is especially true when the actors are wearing clothes made of silky materials, such as ties and thin blouses.

A hardwired lavalier clipped to a tie or lapel and used in an "exposed" fashion is often excellent for employee interviews and host scenes when a wide angle will not reveal the attached audio cables to the audience. When audio cables may end up being seen in a shot, lavaliers on RF transmitters usually solve the problem by eliminating the cable.

Types of Sounds

A director should always plan to record ample, good-quality dialogue and narration, as well as ambient sounds. To the video or film sound recordist, **ambience** means sounds present in or characteristic of the location. In a gym, ambient sounds would be weights clinking, the chatter of voices, and perhaps the sounds of people straining or breathing heavily. On a city street corner, ambience would be traffic sounds, horns, and perhaps pedestrian chatter. Even rooms have ambient sound characteristics—often called "room tone" or "room ambience." At least a few minutes of ambience should be recorded at every location the production crew visits.

These ambient sounds should be recorded separately, as should dialogue and narration, so that all recordings are kept totally isolated or "in the clear." This allows the different sounds to be edited together later with maximum effect and flexibility.

The aesthetic qualities that well-recorded sounds bring to a production can't be overemphasized. They add a subtle level of enrichment and an underlying texture to a scene that, similar to all other audiovisual aesthetic qualities, provide still more credibility to the director's illusion.

SUMMARY

If we take a moment to consider what we've covered up to this point, we should recall that the director first analyzed the script and from this analysis made numerous initial decisions about actors, locations, camera positions, lighting, and so on. Next, he or she chose actors and guided the cast in rehearsals toward the performances visualized. Through the use of audiovisual aesthetic qualities and with the support of the crew—in particular, the DP and sound recordist—the director then ensured that the proper visual and sound elements were utilized to give the scenes maximum credibility.

It would seem that all of these elements are already enough creative responsibility for any one person. For the director, however, quite a few technical and general aesthetic qualities are yet to be considered.

22 Technical Aesthetics

We have examined how important human and audiovisual aesthetics are to the corporate director. Just for the moment, let's assume he or she has done an excellent job in these two areas. The performances in the program are perfectly credible, as are all camera, lighting, and sound elements. But suppose some other, seemingly minor details are not so perfect—a prop is wrong for a job situation or a piece of wardrobe doesn't fit the setting or location.

Assume, for example, that an employee was supposed to have been using a specific, company-approved drill when he was taped. As it turns out, however, he was actually recorded using a different drill—one he had brought from home. Or instead of the company-mandated, steel-toed, leather shoes, he wore tennis shoes. Or, even worse, suppose he was wearing leather shoes in the opening scenes, but later, because certain scenes were shot on a different day, he wore loafers.

What effect could these kinds of errors have on the completed program? They could easily negate all the other positive things the director had done and ruin the entire production. Even minor technical inaccuracies or continuity problems can break the director's illusion and result in an instantaneous lack of program credibility.

AVOIDING TECHNICAL INACCURACIES

Avoiding technical inaccuracies most often begins by paying great attention to several important details in preproduction.

Props

The job of lining up props for a corporate production is usually left to the AD. The director, however, must approve the acquisition of these elements, oversee the acquisition process, and make key decisions as to how, when, and where the props will be used. This process begins in the very first phases of preproduction and often continues through the production days themselves.

For instance, consider the following scene:

EXT. ALLEY–DAY

The installer dons his climbers and work gear and starts up the pole.

HOST (V.O.)

Having no luck in locating his line trouble in the house wiring, the installer may try the pole terminal . . .

The "work gear" referred to in this scene might include special kinds of tools. Neither the director nor the AD, however, would be made aware of these special needs by reading the script.

The wise director realizes this omission and makes careful and detailed notes during his or her script analysis. He or she then heads off such potential problems by asking the client or producer about any questionable items or areas. Or, if the director is too busy taking care of other issues, he or she assigns the AD to research the questions and report back the findings.

Based on this research, the director then makes carefully thought-out decisions regarding the props required for each scene and their use. He or she (usually through the AD) also verifies that everything that has been requested will be the correct, company-approved make, model, and issue, and that it will be delivered to the proper location on the right day and time.

The corporate director who does not take full responsibility for these details often regrets it later. When he or she is sitting in the rough-cut meeting and the client brings up the fact that the type of screwdriver used by an employee or actor was not in accordance with company policies, the resulting decision may be to scrap the footage. This decision usually means a reshoot, which equates to additional time, money, and headaches for the producer.

Makeup

In corporate media, makeup artists are often the exception rather than the rule. In many cases, the actors are asked to apply their own makeup, which usually consists of a simple cosmetic base and perhaps a thin coating of powder to smooth out wrinkles and eliminate any sweat or "shine" as it is usually called. When a makeup requirement does exist on a corporate shoot, it often becomes another of the AD's tasks, especially with executive shoots or employee interviews.

The director should be conscious of and prepared to handle makeup needs as another technical aesthetic responsibility. This job includes assigning the task to the AD if it is simple enough, or actually hiring a makeup artist if the situation calls for it. In either case, this task is important for the same reason the director must approve props and wardrobe—because regardless of performance, camera work, or even very skillful lighting, a lack of proper makeup can sometimes ruin the credibility of a director's work.

To understand how this problem can occur, consider two inherent elements of the production process: lights, which generate a lot of heat, and employees' nervousness when sitting in front of a camera. This combination of heat and nerves often leads to sweating, or getting "shiny." When an employee or, heaven forbid, the CEO begins to sweat, that "shiny" forehead or upper lip quickly becomes a damaging distraction in the audience's eyes. The accomplished director avoids this and other makeup problems by being conscious of makeup needs in preproduction and making absolutely sure those needs will be met when on location or in the studio.

Wardrobe

Employee wardrobe is often not a problem in corporate television if the employees are acting in their own job roles. An executive being interviewed or shot as an executive in a scene will most likely wear the appropriate dress. A customer representative or telephone installer will likewise usually be dressed appropriately for the job.

In these cases, the director must simply be sure the wardrobe meets all safety and company standards. The telephone installer, for instance, who shows up on the shoot wearing shoes or boots that are not company approved for climbing telephone poles will surely become a (possibly very expensive) problem later if he is not corrected on the spot. The trouble is that correcting him on the spot could result in an hour's downtime for the entire crew while the employee runs home to change his boots. Making the correction in preproduction, however, by having a brief telephone discussion with the employee or perhaps his supervisor, would head off this problem before it materializes.

When actors are involved in the shooting, the director must decide on wardrobe, which is done in two ways. Initially, the director usually speaks with the actors in preproduction and gives them a sense of what types of wardrobe will be required. This instruction often happens in phone conversations between the two or by instructions given to the AD to pass along to the actor. In addition, the actor is expected to bring several choices of wardrobe on the first shoot or rehearsal day, and from these the director (often with help from the client and producer) makes final decisions.

In most corporate video productions, the rule of thumb regarding these decisions is conservative and pastel. In keeping with their physical appearances, actors' dress should typically be unnoticeably natural for their surroundings and the situation. In addition, if they are to be shot in a location of predominant colors, the director may ask that they dress to complement the overall color scheme. Actors dressed differently from the corporate norm, especially in bright, highly saturated colors or detailed patterns, often cause problems with lighting or video levels.

If these technical issues do not result in trouble, the actor may simply become noticeably out of place and thus distracting to watch. The actor would not be distracting, however, if the program being shot called for outlandish or bright wardrobe as part of the director's illusion—perhaps in the case of a comedic approach or a festive party scene. As a general rule, the director should make it his or her business to be absolutely sure that all props, makeup, and wardrobe considerations are researched, confirmed, and scheduled in preproduction.

CONTINUITY PROBLEMS

Another element that can have a distracting and often devastating effect on a program is a lack of continuity. There are two primary types of continuity a director must be concerned with: physical continuity and performance continuity. Both require maintaining close similarities between shots, scenes, and program segments. These similarities trick the audience into believing that two shots recorded hours, perhaps even days, apart actually happened at the same instant.

Physical Continuity

To illustrate, let's briefly return to our scene in which the supervisor and a customer representative were having a discussion. Let's assume that throughout the shooting of the master scene, the supervisor was wearing a white blouse. Sometime after the master scene had been recorded, the crew and cast went to lunch, and it was not until the afternoon that the over-the-shoulder and medium close-ups of the supervisor were shot.

But suppose she had gotten a spot of mustard on her blouse at lunch and had changed to a red one. She had then forgotten to clean the original white blouse and put it back on when these later angles were shot. For whatever reason, no one on the crew had realized it either.

When the coverage of this scene is edited together later and the editor cuts from the wide shot to the medium close-up, the supervisor's blouse will appear to change colors. This visual break in physical continuity will be so distracting that either the master scene or the subsequent coverage will be unusable.

Instead of a piece of wardrobe, it might have been a simple hand-position problem. Suppose the representative had her right hand curled under her chin in the medium close-up, but it was on her lap in the other angles. Later, in editing, every time a cut is made to this shot, her hand will appear to instantly jump to her chin.

These examples are only two of countless physical continuity problems that can be sources of distraction in and even ridicule of a director's work. When audience members become aware of physical continuity problems, the director's illusion is broken and the distraction may become the butt of audience jokes.

The corporate director can avoid physical continuity problems in three ways. One is by keeping a close personal eye on all sources of physical continuity during shooting. This includes how the actors are positioned, what they are wearing, their physical actions in relation to dialogue in each scene, and basically all other elements within the camera's frame. The problem with this solution is that it can keep the director so busy that he or she may be distracted from other aesthetic issues, such as performance and composition.

The second solution is to assign the responsibility for physical continuity to someone dependable, such as the AD or a person taking script notes. In this way, the director can focus on the other elements just mentioned and feel secure that someone with a keen eye for detail is watching physical continuity. "Keen eye," incidentally, is the critical phrase here; the person who watches continuity must realize its importance and maintain strict vigilance throughout the shoot.

A third possibility is to review some visual reference of the scene. This might be video playback or Polaroid pictures of actors and sets taken by the AD at key points. For instance, in the mismatching blouse situation just mentioned, if both actors had had Polaroid pictures taken of them just before lunch, or if the director had watched playback of the master scene immediately following lunch, the mismatch probably would have been discovered before shooting continued.

In feature film production, "continuity," as it's called, is usually a job in itself or a part of the script supervisor's responsibilities. In corporate media, when both the director and someone like the AD or a trusted PA work together to watch continuity, problems usually can be avoided.

Performance Continuity

Maintaining performance continuity involves focusing the same attention on similarity but in a nonphysical sense. Consider the following two angles in the same host scene:

FADE IN:

EXT. PARK–DAY

A company picnic is in full swing. There are tables and umbrellas; badminton games, as well as horseshoes and croquet, are in progress. The HOST steps into the frame and looks first over his shoulder and then at the CAMERA.

> HOST
>
> *Well, here it is, at last–picnic day! The games are under way, the hamburgers are on the grill, and everyone's having a great time. C'mon, let's have a look around.*

Host steps into ANOTHER ANGLE. We see that he is standing beside a table. Members of the Johnson family are laying out paper plates, plastic forks, cups, and napkins. Mrs. Johnson pours soft drinks.

> HOST
>
> *Here at the Johnsons' table, it's strictly soft drinks. No alcohol–even for the adults.*

Host exits.

Imagine the host entering the first angle in this script with a smile on his face and an energized sense of excitement in his delivery. This attitude seems appropriate for the picnic setting.

But suppose when he stepped into the second angle, the smile was gone. Assume too that his tone had suddenly become serious or subdued. The result would be a break in performance continuity that would be extremely jarring to the audience.

This continuity break might seem like something the director simply would not let happen, but remember, like our previous scene, the second angle of this shot might not be recorded for several hours after the first one—maybe not until after a large, heavy lunch and 30 minutes of napping in the shade. If this were the case, unless someone had remained keenly aware of the tone and energy level the host had used in the first angle, the second angle could easily be recorded differently.

The director is responsible for performance continuity. To maintain it, he or she watches and judges each scene carefully, committing what has been seen to memory. Then later, when a second angle is shot, he or she must recall the first performance and compare the two, making sure the proper continuity is present. In the case of video, the director may also watch playback of the previous scene as a memory refresher. As an additional bit of "insurance," he or she might also show playback to the actor as they discuss the proper energy level of the next shot.

These same precautionary steps, incidentally, apply to audio recording. Performance continuity is often broken between on-camera and voiceover segments recorded at different times in different places. Working from memory and playback and enlisting the help of the audio recordist to match microphone and location qualities, the director must take careful precautions to ensure matching tone and energy levels between all recorded segments.

Physical and performance continuity problems become increasingly complex and difficult to manage with longer schedules and out-of-sequence shooting. The experienced director is aware of this situation and takes the necessary steps in preproduction to ensure that continuity remains intact throughout the shoot.

SCREEN DIRECTION

Although screen direction problems are not often thought of as continuity faults, they are. In the case of screen direction, however, the lack of continuity relates to the logical sense of motion on the screen instead of performance or physical mismatches.

To understand the importance of this logical sense of motion, keep in mind that the viewer of a film, videotape, or CD develops a subconscious sense of relationship between people and objects moving on the screen. This relationship is often described in terms of something called *screen direction*.

For instance, if a scene establishes a train going from one city to another and the initial direction of travel is screen left to right, the audience will subconsciously expect to see the train traveling in that same left-to-right direction anytime it is shown en route. If we suddenly cut to a shot of it going in the opposite direction—screen right to left—a momentary disorientation occurs for the viewer as he or she reestablishes that the train is still headed for where it had originally set out.

The same visual relationship is developed between people in terms of their movements, gestures, focus of attention, and dialogue. For instance, if two people are having a conversation and the director chooses to inter-cut back and forth between medium close-ups of each person, the audience will expect them to be facing toward each other. If one person is facing screen left to right, the other must be facing right to left, as shown in Figure 22.1. This placement will give the appearance that both people are facing properly. If one actor is shot so that he faces the same screen direction as the person opposite him, he will appear to be looking away from the other person, as shown in Figure 22.2.

Again, this juxtaposition creates an immediate sense of disorientation in the viewer's mind. He or she will subconsciously wonder something like, "Wait a minute. Is he still talking to the same person? Why did he turn away? Or did someone move?"

These types of screen direction discontinuities occur due to camera placement on the wrong side of what is called **"the line,"** "the stage line," or "the screen direction line." The "line," as it is most often called, creates an imaginary, vertical plane through objects moving in any shot. In order to maintain consistent screen direction in a scene, a director cannot cross this line with the camera except under certain circumstances and only with great care given to how the resulting footage will cut together. To illustrate, let's imagine shooting a very simple sequence involving several elements.

EXT. HOUSE, IN THE DRIVEWAY–DAY

An EMPLOYEE is seated in his truck preparing to leave. A CUSTOMER is leaning in at the driver's side window.

CUSTOMER

Thanks a lot. Nice work.

EMPLOYEE

*Don't mention it. Call again if you run into
any more problems.*

CUSTOMER

You bet. Drive carefully, now.

The employee and the customer shake hands. As the customer walks away, the employee starts the truck, backs out into the street, and pulls away.

As we first begin to view this scene, the line is established, as shown in Figure 22.3. As long as the director shoots on the A side of this line, the eye lines of the customer and the employee will keep a consistent and properly established screen direction. The customer will always be facing screen right to left, and the employee will always be facing screen left to right.

But suppose the director has the DP move the camera to the B side of the line and shoot a close-up of the customer. If this shot is now cut into the conversation sequence, a reversal of screen direction will occur, creating an immediate disorientation for the viewer. The customer will suddenly appear to be facing away from the employee.

Figure 22.1   Two medium close-ups facing properly.

Figure 22.2   Two actors facing the same screen direction creates the illusion that one person is facing away from the other as they speak.

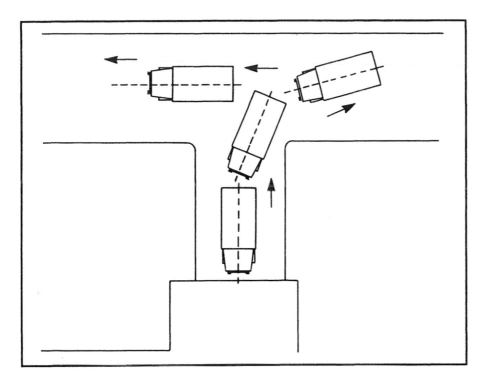

Figure 22.4 When focus of attention changes after the customer leaves and the truck begins to back out, the line also changes. Direction of movement is now focused on the truck.

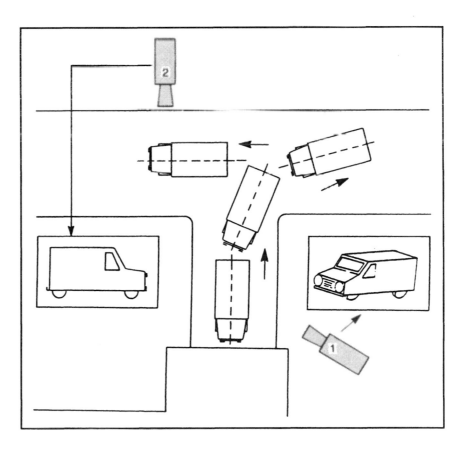

Figure 22.5 Backing truck shot from opposite side of the line (positions 1 and 2) will reverse the screen direction, disorienting the viewer.

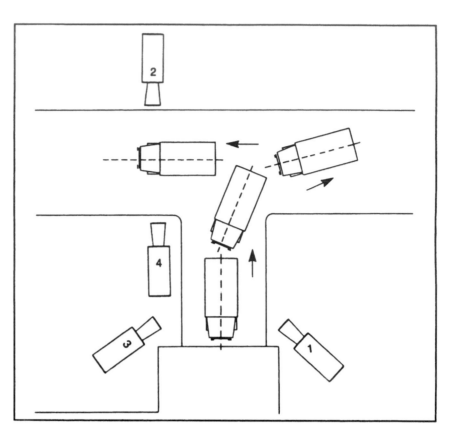

Figure 22.6 Several new camera positions. If shots from each are cut together at different times during the backing action, they will have varying effects on screen direction and continuity.

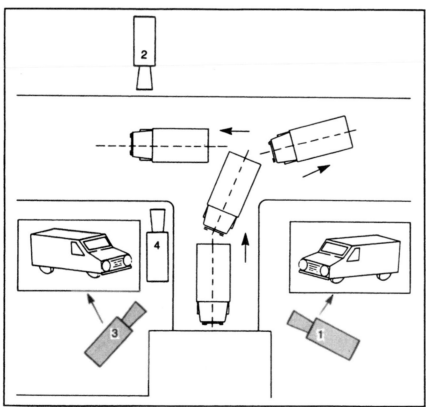

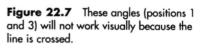

Figure 22.7 These angles (positions 1 and 3) will not work visually because the line is crossed.

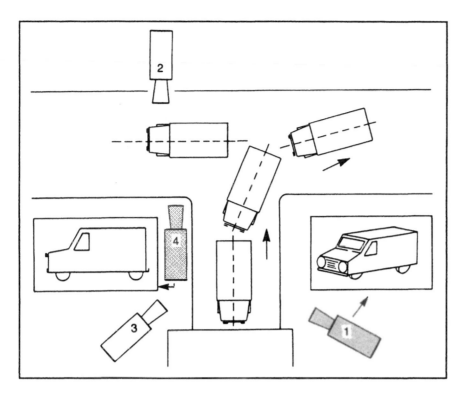

Figure 22.8 These angles (positions 1 and 4) keep the continuity of motion intact.

same direction of travel and the continuity of motion remains intact.

What happens if we intercut positions 1 and 2? We again cross the line and disorient the viewer. In the first shot, the truck appears to be moving screen left to right; then, as we go to camera 2, it suddenly changes to right to left (Figure 22.9).

Now consider a two-shot sequence in which we begin with a shot from camera position 2 as the truck is backing out. Before it reaches the end of the driveway, we cut to camera 3. Since, at this point, we are still on the same side of the line, the truck continues to move in the same direction—screen right to left (Figure 22.10). If we stay with camera 3, we see the truck reach the end of its backing trajectory and start forward in a right-to-left motion. The viewer is still kept perfectly oriented because we never crossed the line.

But suppose we had cut to camera 3 after the truck had started forward. At this point in the motion, the camera positions are on opposite sides of the line, so a reversal of screen direction would have occurred (Figure 22.11).

Thus you can see that the stage line creates an imaginary plane running down the center of motion of any object. As that center of motion changes direction, so does the position of the line. Whether it's objects or people, the director must remain aware that the line exists in every shot. Constant attention must be paid to ensure that the people and objects in those shots are moving logically and consistently.

"Sneaking" Across the Line

With so much talk of staying on one side of the line, you might wonder if crossing the line is ever acceptable. The answer is yes, and the rule of thumb is simply to be sure the change is not disorienting to the viewer.

To illustrate, let's return to our truck backing out of the driveway. In Figure 22.6, we established that camera positions 1 and 3 were on opposite sides of the line and that intercutting between them would cause a discontinuity of motion for the viewer. This scenario assumes that both camera positions are nearly perpendicular to the truck's backing motion and that the focal lengths and levels are roughly the same.

If we move the cameras to the positions shown in Figure 22.12, however, since in angle 2 the direction of motion is directly away from the camera, the change of

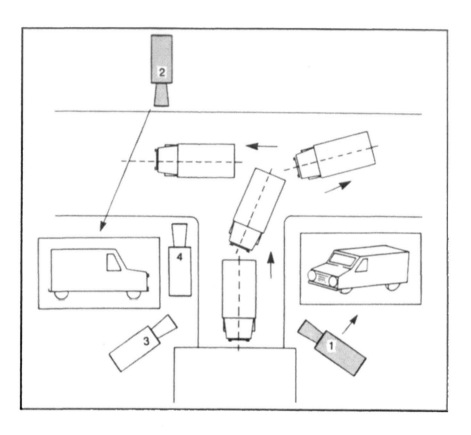

Figure 22.9 Positions 1 and 2. Again, a screen direction reversal.

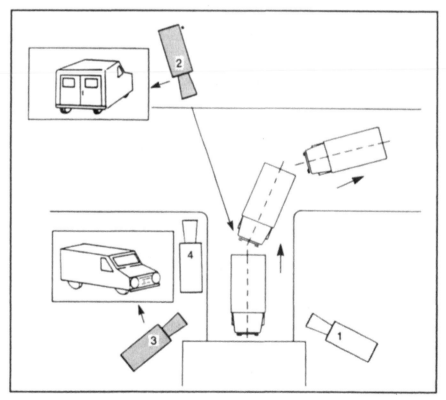

Figure 22.10 Screen direction will remain proper as long as the cut to camera 3 is made before the truck reaches the end of the driveway. After this point, positions 2 and 3 are on opposite sides of the line.

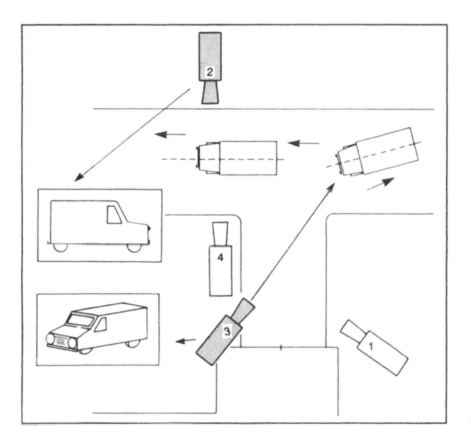

Figure 22.11 Reversal of screen direction.

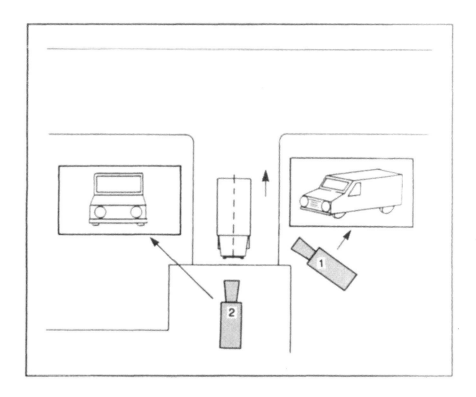

Figure 22.12 Cutting from an angle on the line (camera position 2) to one side or the other will not be visually disorienting.

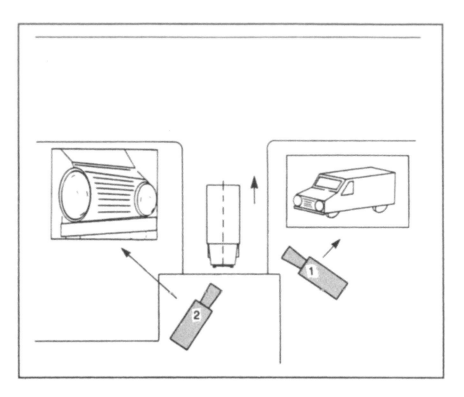

Figure 22.13 "Sneaking" across the line is done often. If shot properly, it works fine because the viewer is not disoriented.

motion from a perspective on the line to one on either side would be less jarring to the viewer. In addition, even if we actually cross the line (Figure 22.13), if we make the camera 2 focal length a close-up—of the grill, perhaps—and the focal length of camera 1 a wide shot, once again the disorientation is reduced. We might also make camera 1 a high angle looking down on the truck.

In each of these cases, the changes of motion are made much less noticeable by other changes in the frame, such as focal lengths and camera positions. Intercutting these types of shots leaves the viewer feeling comfortable with the continuity of motion on the screen. Thus these examples represent acceptable ways to "sneak" across the line if the director finds it necessary to do so.

Using these techniques and dealing with the stage line in various situations can be confusing for a new director. After considerable time behind the camera, the director begins to develop a "feel" for screen direction; he or she can simply look at a scene or shot and

sense that a discontinuity of motion will result from using it.

In any case, the director should always pay careful attention to the idea that a continuity of motion must exist between any shots in which objects move. The director should remain equally aware that although the DP or AD may assist in this area, the director only is ultimately responsible for maintaining this continuity.

SUMMARY

Avoiding problems that negatively affect the technical aesthetics of a director's work is also extremely important to a credible final illusion on the screen. As a new director, you should become very familiar with the ramifications of technical and continuity elements of your program and continually strive to achieve a sense of technical aesthetic perfection.

23 General Aesthetics

Again, let's make an assumption that the director has carefully analyzed and appropriately handled all the aesthetic elements we have discussed so far—the script, performances, camera, lights, sound, and technical elements such as screen direction and continuity. Is he or she now able to relax and assume that everything for which he or she is accountable has been taken care of? Not quite. One more critical area must be considered—general aesthetics.

A DEFINITION

General aesthetics refers to the broader and often more subtle aspects of the program—*tone, pace*, and *transitions*. The subtle nature of these elements does not reduce their importance. Like so many other subtleties under a director's control, these elements can have a profound impact on the aesthetic quality of any show.

Although we have previously discussed tone and pace in terms of script aesthetics, it's worth our time to reexamine their importance as they relate to production.

TONE

You may recall that some words that describe program tone are positive, negative, inspirational, informational, sad, happy, uplifting, depressing, and so on. Although a program may have a single overall tone, it may have multiple tones throughout.

For instance, a program that explores the process of striving to achieve one's aspirations might begin with an informational tone as a host sets the stage by explaining the subject. The same program might then follow with a series of sad or negative scenes as a main character is seen trying to excel but continually failing at what he attempts. These scenes might lead to a series of additional informational scenes as the host explains what the character must do to succeed. They are eventually followed with several positive scenes in which the character takes the proper steps and finally makes good. The end result of all these scenes might be an overall program tone viewers would call uplifting.

As mentioned previously, during the initial script analysis, the director carefully considers these types of tonal elements. He or she then strives to create the tone the writer intended and the producer and client approved. In production, this task translates into decisions about such things as lighting, wardrobe, camera positions, and so on.

For instance, the first host scenes might take place on a dark limbo set with random light patterns thrown on a lattice or cyclorama in the background. This setup would maintain the informational tone needed to start the program, but it would also hint that the subject matter was serious, thus setting the stage for the sad or negative scenes. These scenes might also be lit darkly with an accent on shadows. The character's makeup and wardrobe might reflect frustration and sadness. His clothes could be rumpled and askew, and perhaps he could be made up to appear tired. Camera positions could also be adjusted to help achieve the tone of sadness or frustration by being slightly tilted or oblique in perspective.

When the host is seen again, if what he says begins the sequence that changes the tone, he might appear in a new position on the set or under lighting that is brighter and more upbeat. Perhaps the initial dark shadows could be brightened and softened. These changes could also be accented by the host's performance, which might be more positive and upbeat.

Later, when the character is seen achieving his goals, he could appear fresher and more positive in his dress and makeup. The lighting, camera positions, and, of course, the actor's performance could also reflect this change. The sum of these many individual tonal elements would help create the final, overall tone mentioned earlier—a sense that the story was uplifting.

Corporate Tone Considerations

In many cases, a corporate program is expected to achieve a general positive tone because executives and corporate clients often believe that stressing the positive aspects of any subject they wish to communicate is critical.

This expectation can sometimes create a dilemma for the corporate director if the subject matter does not appear to warrant a positive treatment. Usually, however, the writer must fight these battles as the script is being developed. By the time the director is brought in on the project, the written scenes reflect what the client and producer have agreed will work. The director's job is then to deliver the scenes as scripted. While this task may seem simple enough, it can sometimes be difficult due to the subtle nature of tonal elements.

I know of one director who was given a script with what could have been called a "serious informational" tone. It consisted of a tour by an on-camera host through a typical residential home. While on this tour, the host discussed the dangerous chemicals that many of us unknowingly keep in our homes. He also talked about ways to handle and dispose of them.

To give the program more interest and add what he considered a "light touch," the director decided at the last minute to include a youngster in many of these scenes. As the scenes were shot, the host would occasionally pass the boy during the tour and find him in humorous situations—eating cake in the kitchen, wearing headphones, playing loud rock music in the den, leaving a mess in the garage, and so on.

The addition of the youngster succeeded in doing exactly what the director had wanted: It added a light touch. But it also changed the tone of the program. Instead of informational serious, the program became informational light. This result was something the producer had not wanted, considering the seriousness of the subject matter. As a result, the youngster's scenes were cut before the program was completed.

This outcome is just one of many possibilities, but the caution is always the same. Be conscious of the tonal elements of any program you direct, and consider how you can support or enhance what the script strives to achieve. Do not, however, change the program's tone without the full prior knowledge and approval of both the producer and the client.

PACE

Pace might be thought of in terms of "life speeds." These speeds are manifested on the screen through three elements: *shot content, shot length,* and *editing.*

Shot Content

Whatever is contained in a shot has pace. If actors are seen moving carefully and methodically, the pace will be slow. If actors are seen rushing about, the pace will be fast. These same shot content rules hold true for dialogue and narration.

Consider the following scene:

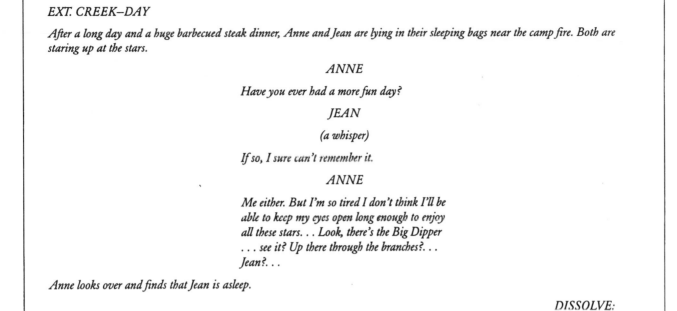

EXT. CREEK–DAY

After a long day and a huge barbecued steak dinner, Anne and Jean are lying in their sleeping bags near the camp fire. Both are staring up at the stars.

ANNE

Have you ever had a more fun day?

JEAN

(a whisper)

If so, I sure can't remember it.

ANNE

Me either. But I'm so tired I don't think I'll be able to keep my eyes open long enough to enjoy all these stars. . . Look, there's the Big Dipper . . . see it? Up there through the branches?. . . Jean?. . .

Anne looks over and finds that Jean is asleep.

DISSOLVE:

It's obvious that a slow, relaxed pace is called for here, in terms of both movement and dialogue delivery. If these actors were fidgeting about nervously or the lines in this scene were delivered with a rapid pace, it would ruin the tone and the credibility of the scene.

Shot Length

By necessity, shots that are short in length dictate rapid editing, which will lead to a more energetic pace. To illustrate, imagine that the campfire scene just described is being shot by two directors.

The first director starts by shooting a wide establishing shot in which we see the two sleeping bags lying on a forest floor with the campfire nearby. Next, he moves the camera in for a two shot in which the perspective is looking down on both Anne and Jean. From this position, he records all dialogue. Next, he shoots a close-up of Anne only, performing all dialogue and following this shot, a close-up of Jean. Thus, he has covered the scene with four shots.

The second director shoots only one shot. He mounts the camera above the two women and begins with a shot of the campfire alone. After several seconds, he begins a slow pan revealing Anne and Jean in their sleeping bags. As Jean begins to talk, the camera zooms in or lowers slowly, moving first into a two shot as the women exchange their first lines and finally to a close-up of Anne's face alone. This camera motion ends just as Anne is about to look over at Jean. As she does so, the camera pans a final time to reveal that Jean is asleep.

To see what effect these two shooting styles would have on the finished piece, we must consider how each will be handled in editing.

Editing For Pace

Editing affects the pace of a program primarily in terms of the frequency of edits. Short, rapid cuts typically create a jumpy sense of speed and excitement or tension. Long takes with infrequent cuts, however, often create a slower, smoother pace.

In the coverage shot by our two directors, you will recall that the first director chose to cover the scene with a series of short, static shots. His version of the scene might then be edited as follows: The establishing shot of the fire is used for a few seconds of silence until Anne begins her first line. As this line begins, cut to the two shot to establish both women. As Jean says, "If so, I sure can't remember it," cut to her close-up. As Anne speaks again, cut to her close-up. As Anne looks over and sees that Jean has fallen asleep, cut to Jean's close-up showing her eyes closed. Finally, cut back to the establishing shot before dissolving to the next scene.

The first version of this scene thus cuts together five short segments. Although the editing pace this approach creates could certainly work, it is somewhat inconsistent with the smooth, relaxed tone the scene should be communicating.

The second director's coverage of the scene consisted of one long, slow-moving shot that would require only a single edit. This version accents the calm, relaxed tone of the scene and thus enhances the overall illusion.

Tone is a subtle aesthetic element that is often affected by other elements, such as actors' performances, lighting, sets, and props. Additional considerations are the production schedule and budget. It can sometimes take more time and equipment to get a long single shot than it takes to cover a scene with several standard shots. In short, hard-and-fast rules about tone are difficult to establish. Every scene is different, and the director must create the proper tone by shooting scenes effectively. The experienced director realizes this dilemma and analyzes all production elements when considering the type of coverage that will be required.

TRANSITIONS

With the tone and pace of a program established in the director's mind, he or she must also consider the transitions between shots and scenes, which also involves editing.

Four primary edits are used to provide transitions from one shot or scene to another: *cuts, dissolves, wipes,* and *digital video effects (DVE).* Because each of these edits can also have important effects on the general aesthetic quality of the program, it's worth taking the time to briefly discuss them.

Use of the Cut

A cut is the simplest way to get from one picture to another. A cut simply means that one picture ends and another begins instantly. In many cases, a cut is the preferred transition because it makes no "statement" about the program's content. A cut is usually meant to happen without audience recognition; thus it lets the pictures and sound carry the complete message.

When a conversation in a sitcom cuts from one person to another, as viewers, we are unaware of these cuts. They happen subliminally and seem to coincidentally transport us to the most logical viewing per-spectives as they become appropriate. This same subliminal quality is in effect when cuts are used as transitions between *time frames, locations,* and *general subjects.*

In some cases, however, a director can use a cut to make a statement. Instead of going unnoticed, it can punctuate a transition. Consider the following scene:

INT. OFFICE–DAY

Lots of PEOPLE, business, and office SOUNDS. Janice is rounding the corner by her desk. Her foot catches on an electrical cord. She trips and falls toward another, close-by desk. On the desk is a large, acrylic square decorative piece. Janice's face is headed straight toward its pointed corner.

JANICE's POV–The CAMERA ACCELERATES straight toward the corner of the piece, and suddenly . . .

CUT TO BLACK/SILENCE.

In this case, the cut to black and silence at the moment of Janice's impact with the sharp corner heightens our awareness of the transition. In doing so, it drives home the point—both visually, by going to black, and through the use of sound (in this case, a lack of it)—that Janice is, at best, left unconscious. The previous cut, however, from our view of Janice to her point of view (POV) would happen with no awareness on our part.

Use of Dissolves

A dissolve overlaps one picture onto the next during the transition; therefore, it is a slower and usually softer way to transition from one picture to the next.

Dissolves often do make statements. They tell the viewer that time has passed or that some other major change has taken place. Sometimes they say both.

EXT. HIGHWAY–DAY

The company truck moves off on a long, flat, empty country highway, toward a setting sun. MUSIC UP–A RAMBLING PIECE.

　　　　　　　　　　　　DISSOLVE:

EXT. MOUNTAIN ROAD–DAY

The truck rounds a corner on a steep, snowy mountain road.

　　　　　　　　　　　　DISSOLVE:

EXT. OCEAN HIGHWAY–DAY

The truck winds along the sunny Pacific Coast Highway.

　　　　　　　　　　　　DISSOLVE:

EXT. FREEWAY–DAY

CAMERA starts on a shot of a freeway sign for the exit to Hollywood Freeway. As the shot widens, the company truck moves into the frame. With its turn signal on, it heads toward Hollywood. MUSIC CONTINUES.

                                      DISSOLVE:

EXT. WAREHOUSE–NIGHT

Starting on a shot of the "Benson Furniture Warehouse" sign, CAMERA WIDENS to reveal the company truck pulling up in front. As it comes to a stop, MUSIC STING.

In this case, the dissolves help tell us that time is passing, as are major locations. Supported by the rambling music piece, they help carry us across the country—again, totally unaware of the camera or the transitions from one scene to another.

The length of a dissolve can also have varying effects on the segments it is used to bridge. A very slow dissolve, for instance, can make one picture appear to be superimposed over the next. This technique can create an eerie or dreamlike effect. Faster dissolves, sometimes referred to as "soft cuts," can be used to take the hard edge off an otherwise rough or jarring cut.

Use of Wipes

Wipes cause one picture to "wipe" off the screen as another appears. This edit is usually done with the vertical edge of one picture traveling from right to left or vice versa across the screen. Wipes can also be made in circles, squares, or various other shapes and patterns. Similar to dissolves, wipes usually signify a passage of time or a major change of some sort. They also call immediate attention to themselves, however, and thus should be used sparingly.

The following humorous scene is one example in which a wipe might be used:

INT. WIZARD'S CASTLE–NIGHT

Merlin looks into the crystal ball and smiles.

MERLIN'S POV–The ball. Deep in its glass, something is moving. From the ball . . .

                        CIRCLE WIPE OUT TO:

INT. WITCH'S CAVE–NIGHT

Ingrid stands over the boiling caldron.

A circle wipe would probably work in this situation for three reasons. First, it suggests a major change of location. Second, it would punctuate the transition from the POV shot of the circular-shaped crystal ball. Third, and perhaps most important, it would enhance the humorous tone the writer intended. In this type of tongue-in-cheek application, if an effect such as a wipe calls attention to itself, so much the better. In a similar scene with a serious tone, a cut or dissolve would probably be more appropriate.

Use of Digital Video Effects (DVE)

DVE, as it's often called, can do virtually anything to a video picture—make it curl up like a piece of paper, turn into a ball, and bounce off the screen, become one side of a spinning box, or do any number of other, often very flashy visual effects.

Digital effects often call attention to themselves on purpose. They are often used in corporate magazine-type shows and marketing programs that require a high-tech production look. They are also often used simply to give corporate programs an expensive, broadcast appearance. Producers reason that today's typical corporate viewers are very visually sophisticated because of what they see continually on their TVs at home. If corporate programs don't match up to this level, producers reason that they will be considered inferior.

Some truth to this argument undoubtedly exists, but it should not be considered a license for unrestricted DVE use. Many other ingredients affect the quality of a corporate show—primarily good scriptwriting, credible performances, and audiovisual aesthetics.

SUMMARY

We've found that the tone, pace, and transitions in a corporate program, like so many other subtleties a director must deal with, are critical to the show's illusory quality. The wise director remains aware of this fact throughout the entire production process and strives, as with all other aesthetic elements, to keep them totally credible to the viewing audience.

24 People Skills

One of a director's attributes might be called aesthetic sensitivity. This sensitivity enables a director to consider all of the aesthetic elements we have been discussing and to make basic judgments about their credibility or aesthetic quality. When all is said and done, however, no matter how much aesthetic sensitivity a director may have, he or she cannot achieve the goals of creating and maintaining a media illusion without a strong ability to work with *people*.

The actors must deliver sincere performances. The DP must light with speed, skill, and creativity. The AD must take accurate script notes and remain alert to possible continuity problems. The sound recordist must constantly monitor audio quality and levels. The grips and gaffers must hustle to keep the shoot on schedule. The client must support and approve the work, as must the producer.

For these reasons, good people skills are not just important but also an inherent part of any director's role. People skills allow the director to act effectively in the following four basic capacities: as *consultant, manager, supervisor,* and *coach*.

THE DIRECTOR AS CONSULTANT

When first brought in on a project, the director is a consultant to the producer and the client. He or she advises both on how the script will manifest in visual form and suggests possible changes if he or she believes they will improve the end product. Two key words in this statement are *advises* and *suggests*. These words are important

because they leave the final decisions on script changes up to the producer and client.

Similar to any other consultant, the director's job in this early phase of preproduction is simply to make these two critical players aware of any aspects that could have a negative impact on the project. If, having heard the director's opinions, the client or producer decides to go ahead with the script as is, the director should then set about doing exactly that to the best of his or her ability. The exception to this rule, of course, is a script that the director feels is simply too bad to attach his or her name to it.

Some directors find this process of conceding to client and producer wishes difficult. If you think you may fall into this category, the important thing to remember is that if you are hired to direct a corporate program, you are certainly involved in an important project, but you are not directing an epic. You are being paid to meet the client's and producer's requirements. Directors who become obstinate about making changes or overly possessive about their creative control usually end up becoming too much trouble for the corporate producer to deal with.

When a new project arises, rather than "fight" over changes he or she would like made, the producer will probably just hire another, more agreeable director. Or, if the friction has been between the client and the director, there's a good chance the client will make it clear to the producer that he or she chooses not to work with that individual again. In most corporate environments, the producer will be obliged to go along with the client's wishes, whether he or she agrees or not.

THE DIRECTOR AS MANAGER

A manager oversees a project, its people, or both. In the director's case, the word *both* is accurate. From the time a director begins to prepare a project for production, he or she will be entrusted by the producer with managing *people* and *resources*.

The people include the entire production team, the cast, and perhaps the offline editor. We will discuss these relationships in more detail shortly. The resources include all other elements of the production, such as props, locations, permits, equipment, and schedules. Because each of these elements also involve money, the director is a manager of anywhere from a few thousand dollars on a very small shoot to $100,000 or more on a big-budget corporate shoot.

The director's managerial skills apply mostly during preproduction and deal with the general aspects of the production, such as *planning, organizing,* and *confirming* all aspects of a shoot.

Planning

The director plans by applying his or her specialized knowledge to a script and judging the time, people, and resources required to get the project "in the can." In order to accomplish this goal, the director must first decide how each scene will be shot. Will the video require a dolly rental at $300 a day? Or can the camera record the action from a tripod? Will paid extras be required to move about in the foreground and background to create a sense of reality? Or will friends or employees perhaps be available? Will lights be required on location, making the rental of a generator necessary? What type of mics will be required, and do they involve the rental of special equipment or accessories?

These questions and many other similar ones must be answered by the director in preproduction in order for the *production plan* to be accurately formulated. That plan usually consists of the following documented items:

1. A script breakdown itemizing all elements, both human and otherwise, required to be recorded in all scenes of the shoot.

2. A shooting schedule outlining the shoot scene by scene and hour by hour.

3. A crew list showing all crew members and their roles, workdays, and "call times."

4. A shot list of the types of shots the director plans to record to cover each scene.

5. An equipment list showing all equipment needed for the shoot, the days it will be required, where it is to be obtained, and perhaps its total cost.

6. A talent booking sheet listing all actors and actresses, either professionals or company employees, along with the dates and times they will be required.

7. Various other departmental documents required by the producer, client, or director.

As we mentioned previously, although the AD or PA may do much of the legwork on many of these items, the director is the guiding, approving, and thus managing force behind them.

Organizing

The director then organizes by bringing together all of the people and elements just mentioned and arranging them in a way that will allow everything and everyone to be utilized in the most cost-effective manner. For instance, he or she will carefully choose locations considering costs, travel time, logistics, and other factors. He or she will then schedule the use of each location to get as much shooting accomplished as possible in the shortest time and consider crew and talent in terms of what job requirements are needed on what days. For instance, on the days with the dolly work, will an extra grip be needed to push the dolly, lay the track, or perhaps pull focus for the DP? Is makeup needed only on the days with principal talent? How many trucks must be rented or reserved on each day to accomplish this? And so on.

Confirming

Confirmation of all elements brought together in preproduction is extremely important, especially if the shoot is a large or complex one. Planning and organizing effectively is key, but the director must be absolutely sure that everything has been arranged and will arrive when, where, and how it is supposed to.

The feature film and primetime television director has less to worry about in these areas because staffs of people are specifically dedicated to being certain that all loose ends are taken care of. In corporate television, however, such luxuries are rare. These responsibilities usually fall squarely on the director's shoulders. If they are not carefully attended to with great attention paid to even the smallest details, the shoot can be stopped short for hours.

For instance, a bolt that attaches a camera plate to a particular type of tripod head is essential to shooting. Sometimes, however, such bolts may not be stored with the camera. Or, the missing key to an office building that is located 40 miles from the studio may be the only possible way to get into a location on a weekend. Or, in a scenario described earlier, if shooting will occur in a business lawn area, the possibility of automatic sprinklers coming on during shooting and how to turn them off must be considered.

Preproduction Meetings

The easiest way for the director to confirm the elements involved in his or her shoot is by having one or more preproduction meetings with the AD and perhaps the entire crew. In such meetings, the director can simply go down the "to do" list and get updates and confirmations on various aspects of the production as they develop.

One effective way to perform a final confirmation is to sit with the AD and "walk through" the shooting schedule point by point and scene by scene, discussing exactly what will physically take place in each case. The beginning of such a walk-through conversation might go something like this.

DIRECTOR: At 6:45 tomorrow, who will be showing up and in what order?

AD: Crew call is 6:45; talent call is 7:30.

DIRECTOR: OK. Let's confirm the crew and positions.

AD: John Martin, DP; Bill Davis, sound; Darla Orren, gaffer; Rudy Gomez, grip; Tom Arton, prompter; and me.

DIRECTOR: OK. And the crew will get busy right away loading the trucks?

AD: Right. The equipment was delivered today.

DIRECTOR: Everything checked out?

AD: Right. It's all in the prop room. The truck reservations are on your desk.

DIRECTOR: Good. And the cast?

AD: Host, Dorothy Miles; installer, Gina McCoy; and customer, Marvin Aganell—all booked and confirmed for 7:30 tomorrow.

DIRECTOR: You're meeting them and showing them to wardrobe?

AD: Yes. And I have coffee and rolls arranged.

DIRECTOR: OK. And how about the client?

AD: She'll be here after lunch. She can't escape a morning meeting.

The conversation would continue in exactly this way until the two had talked their way through every aspect of the shoot. Notes would be made to follow up on any items found needing attention.

Preproduction meetings with the full crew are still another confirmation check. The director should bring in the entire crew half an hour early to go over each scene and any special aspects of the shoot. Again, if the shoot is a simple one, a brief discussion will be adequate. If the setups are complicated, however, flip charts, photocopies of blocking diagrams, or storyboards may be necessary. For instance, the director might stand next to a flip chart and easel and say:

DIRECTOR: We plan to finish with the host material at noon, so after lunch, Tom, you become a dolly grip. I've got two dolly shots set for the afternoon. One scene involves about 20 feet of track, and there are seven extras. Here's generally how it's blocked. The actor moves across this way, and the extras cross back here. It's going to be a tough one. On scene 4, Bill, it's going to be real hard to get a boom mic in. There's a low ceiling, and it's a confined space. Should we think about using a lavalier?

BILL: A lavaliere will probably be fine if it will match your other audio. If there's a direct cut to a scene mic'd with a shotgun, though, I'd say let's try to get the boom in low or go with a lavalier on the other shots.

Discussions like this allow the crew to gain valuable insight into the coming day's activities. They also provide a forum for input that may help the shoot run more smoothly. For instance, based on this exchange, a plan could be formulated that might save a good deal on time at the location and result in better quality recordings.

THE DIRECTOR AS SUPERVISOR

Although his or her administrative and supervisory skills may overlap, a director tends to become less administrative and more supervisory as preproduction ends and production begins. At this point, the planning and organization are complete and all that remains is execution.

The effective director supervises the crew by setting the pace, establishing a positive tone, and demanding the best from everyone involved. He or she avoids the temptation to become aloof or prone to tantrums or irrational behavior. The best directors are simply hard-working individuals who inspire their crews by gaining respect. And just how, you might ask, is this done? With plain old hard work, talent, and the use of a few basic supervisory steps.

Communicate

Nothing is more frustrating for crew members than being left in the dark. Always tell crew members *why* what they are doing is important and *how* it fits into the overall production plan. Besides leading to much more motivated crew members, this communication will also cut down on rework due to mistakes or misinterpretations.

Just as crew members dislike being left in the dark, a director dislikes returning to the set from a meeting with an actor to find the wrong setup in place. Clear, simple communications will help alleviate these types of frustrating and often costly problems.

Be Accessible

Never create an egotistical or a standoffish air. Some directors I have met appear to believe this attitude is important to maintain their sense of control or importance. Actually, the opposite is true. If crew members feel uninhibited in approaching a director about a possible change or potential problem, a much more productive shoot usually results.

If the director decides not to take a crew member's suggestion, it is usually enough to say something like, "That's a good idea, and it would work if I had something else in mind. But this sequence is going to play out a little differently in the final cut. Thanks. Keep the ideas coming."

Usually such a response is accepted by the crew member, and the productive, open channels of communication remain intact.

Be Decisive

Crew members, especially DPs, quickly lose respect for a director who is unsure of what he or she wants or who is generally wishy-washy.

If a DP approaches a director on their arrival at a new location and says, "OK, so what's happening here?" he or she would most likely respect a director who replied: "We'll do this scene in a single shot. I want to start with a close-up of the calendar here on the desktop. The actor will start talking, and we'll tilt up to a close-up of him. After a few seconds, we'll dolly back and reveal the second actor coming in from back here. I'd like to get a nice smooth master shot we can use for the whole piece, but I'll want a little coverage too; maybe an over-the-shoulder shot from back here and a reaction shot."

That same DP wouldn't have much respect for a director who responded to his or her question with an answer like this: "Well, we need to shoot the two actors here at the desk. I guess one could be sitting. What do you think—would that work out? I'm not sure if they should be sitting or walking, actually. Maybe he could walk and you could follow him—how would that be?"

This second director not only has not taken the time to think out and plan the shoot but also seems to have no problem placing his or her own responsibility for blocking the scene on the DP.

Be Reasonable

A director who wants a $10 million feature on a $10,000 budget is just as bad as one who has no idea of what he or she wants.

A director who knows his or her craft knows what a crew can and cannot accomplish in a reasonable amount of time. The director may challenge the crew if the budget is tight or time is constrained, but he or she will also do everything possible to plan the shots so that they can be accomplished successfully with the resources at hand.

A DP, grip, or gaffer would quickly become demoralized after a few comments like, "OK, we've only got half an hour here, but I need a handheld shot where they walk through the door, down the hallway, and into the restroom. We'll follow along from the rear and then get another angle from the front. Oh, and we need to shoot an overhead shot in the bathroom from a ladder, and I want a few cutaways. We also need to light this really carefully. I want it to look nice."

Recognize Good Work

Recognition is a sure-fire motivator in just about any situation. When people go above and beyond their job description or do excellent work, let them know you appreciate it—and by all means, mention it in front of the rest of the crew.

If the director is respected, the crew members look up to him or her. A pat on the back and a mention of a job well done from someone we respect can be worth an entire day's paycheck. By contrast, the director who never has a nice word to say will soon discourage people from putting out that extra effort that can often bring a shoot in on time or make the difference in getting a particularly complicated or difficult shot.

Have Fun

Corporate media production can be a highly rewarding profession. It can also be a tough one, due to constant pressures, frustrations, and numerous other difficulties. Whatever else it is, it should be fun. This means that no matter how far behind your shoot may be or how hard a scene may be to get, it never hurts to take a break and crack a joke or make light of the situation.

Relieving the pressure in this way can often revitalize a cast, crew, and the director in a difficult production situation. Aside from all these reasons, no profession is worth a heart attack or ulcers.

Say Thanks

I make it a point to thank my crew members after each shoot. Again, a simple word of acknowledgment lets the grip or gaffer who worked particularly hard know that you saw what he or she did and appreciated it.

You will probably want to book the same people again at some time, and of course, you hope they will work hard for you again. A parting thank you can help ensure that this will be the case.

THE DIRECTOR AS COACH

The director supervises the crew, but he or she coaches the talent. These two activities have similar means and ends, but the differing factor springs from the word *performance*.

Crew members work on an ongoing basis throughout the day. Their labors are certainly important and by

no means easy, but those labors are also spread out over many hours. Crew members might be thought of as operating on a labor plateau that rises to one level in the morning, stays there throughout the day (with the exception of break periods), and drops off as the shooting day comes to a close.

An actor, on the other hand, is only "on" for a short but extremely intense and critical period of time—much like an athlete. Like an athlete, when his or her performance is over, the actor retreats into a resting or replenishing mode, waiting for the next call for his or her brief, crucial delivery. This process means that the actor's day is more like a series of radical peaks and valleys. He or she is either operating at a pinnacle or in a very sedentary state.

In an athletic sense, coaching means encouraging and inspiring a team or individual to deliver an excellent athletic performance for a short but sustained period. In an acting sense, remove the word *athlete* from this statement, and the same definition holds true.

The coaching techniques the director uses are also similar to many used by athletic coaches. He or she *communicates, encourages, demands excellence, recognizes worthy efforts,* and *knows when an actor has reached his or her limit.* In doing these things, the director also gains actors' respect.

Communicating with Actors

Communicating means making your ideas clear to another person. This task is especially critical for the director because he or she is communicating what the actors must then manifest before the camera. Communicating can also be especially difficult for the director because he or she is often explaining or exploring intangible elements, such as emotions and personal opinions.

A director overcomes these difficulties by learning (1) to articulate feelings with clarity and (2) to speak the actor's language.

Articulating

Articulating Feelings with Clarity
To cite an example of clear articulation, I remember a voice recording session I once directed as a newcomer to the field of corporate media production. The actress I was working with was a very talented woman, but she was not providing the delivery I was after. I had a clear idea in my mind of how I felt the delivery should change, but I had no idea of how to explain to her what I wanted.

The sound engineer I was working with was an old pro, and he saw my frustration. He listened as my conversation with the actress went something like the following:

> *ME:* It's not quite right. I mean, it sounds good, but it's, well, I'm not sure.
>
> *ACTRESS:* Am I missing some inflection or tone you're after?
>
> *ME:* I'm not sure. I think the tone is fine. There's nothing specific, but it's too, well, too abrupt or something.
>
> *ACTRESS:* Too abrupt ... OK, let's see ...

This vague conversation went on for awhile and although I was stuttering and stammering, the engineer seemed to sense what I was after. Finally, as I was saying, "Try to be ... um ... a little more ..." "Intimate," he said.

As soon as he said the word, both the actress and I knew he had managed to articulate what I had been trying to say. Intimate was exactly right. The actress was then able to deliver what I wanted, and the session moved along fine from that point.

How do you learn to articulate such subtleties? One way is simply by observation and practice. Think about the feelings and emotions you ask actors to evoke, and search for the precise word choices that would describe those emotions to you.

Remember, too, that the description of how a line should be delivered need not always match the visual aspect of the program. For example, in the situation just mentioned, the pictures being shown as the actress delivered her lines were not intimate at all. They were actually visuals of a small town in the days following a destructive earthquake. The intimacy in the actress's voice, however, registered very appropriately when heard with the pictures.

Speaking the Actor's Language

This process often involves having an awareness and basic knowledge of the type of training the actor may have had. Most professional actors have been trained in variations of two primary schools of discipline. They are either *method* actors or *character* actors.

Method acting refers to the Stanislavsky method originally developed by Konstantin Stanislavsky, a Russian actor, director, and teacher. In the late 1930s

and early 1940s, method acting took root and grew in America, thanks to a small group of revolutionary actors and teachers—most notably Sanford Misner, Lee Strasberg, and Stella Adler.

Method acting requires that actors vividly recall events, people, and moments in their lives through sensory exercises. When getting "into the moment," an actor meditates on details of this past event. He or she then brings those true original emotions into the present and applies them to the scene being acted out.

For instance, an actor doing a scene in which he must display sheer joy on receiving a gift might recall the actual moment in his life when his mother presented him with a new puppy. To convey those emotions with true credibility, the actor would get "into" that moment by recalling the type of day it was, the look of the room he was in, the smell of his father's pipe, how the puppy first licked his hand, what its fur felt and looked like, and so on.

Method actors usually prefer a more relaxed and quiet environment on the set. They also like the time to be able to meditate on past experiences, even including smells, touches, room sizes and characteristics, and the like.

Character acting, on the other hand, means essentially developing a character profile based on the script. Rather than being offered a quiet place to get "into the moment," a character actor might require a detailed description of the character, along with an account of his immediate and perhaps distant past history—where he was born, how he was raised, and what his attributes, faults, drives, and fears are.

Allowing Flexibility

Whether it is method or character acting, the director should, first and foremost, be able to talk the actor's language and, second, give the actor as much flexibility as possible in creating the performance. This consideration allows the actor to use his or her creative talents in developing a performance that he or she will be truly proud to present.

Giving an actor flexibility means not demonstrating how to deliver a line or express an emotion, but rather giving the actor certain guidelines and letting him or her develop the detailed aspects of the performance on his or her own. For instance, it is not advisable to say, "Do the line like this," and then read it the way you want it. This direction limits the actor to mimicking rather than creating true character traits and emotions.

To avoid this limitation, the director might offer a general comment like, "I think when you deliver this line, 'Well, you finally made it,' you're really congratulating him for all the good he's done." Asking the actor to use a congratulatory foundation allows him or her to develop his or her own means of delivering the line in accordance with the director's wishes.

Clarifying Motivation

Motivation is another common word in the actor's and director's vocabulary. It refers to the purpose for a line or action. For instance, in blocking a scene, the director may say, "I think you should turn away from him at that point and start for the door." The actor may then ask, "What's my motivation?"

The director would probably respond with something like, "You've been wanting to get out of the house all through this argument, haven't you? This is the first moment you could actually seize to go. Do you think you'd grab it?"

Motivation should always correlate with the character makeup of that person. For instance, in the example just mentioned, an argumentative type of character might not want to leave the room. He or she might be motivated to stay and argue. A timid or less verbose character, on the other hand, might want to do what the director has suggested.

This interplay of motivation and character is often the subject of repeated discussions between the director and actors as they develop and execute performances.

Recognizing The "Real World"

As much as a director may want to follow the accepted creative etiquette, corporate media time constraints or the production situation may limit his or her ability and sometimes willingness to use this method. If he or she is behind schedule, rapidly losing sunlight, and needs only a single line from an actress, it may simply be easier and quicker to say, "If you don't mind, I'd like to give you the reading for this line so that we can move on," rather than going into a long dissertation about character, motivation, subtext, and so on.

Actors who work in corporate media usually have no problem with this direction because they understand the types of pressures the director is often under. In this case, if the line were "Andrew is really growing up," the director could then say something like, "Put more emphasis on 'really' and less on 'up.' I'd prefer that the line read, 'Andrew is *really* growing up,' instead of 'Andrew is really growing *up*.'"

Whatever the case, try to give the actors as much time and creative flexibility as the situation will allow. Not only does this approach permit them to truly practice their craft for you; it also shows your confidence in them. Both of these elements are positive motivators.

Encouraging Actors

Encouraging actors usually means either spurring them on to deliver exceptionally difficult performances or encouraging them to take a chance by going further with an already adequate performance.

Encouraging an actor can often be accomplished by taking five minutes away from the set to discuss ways of overcoming some difficult aspect of the performance. Together, the director and actor might focus on the difficulty and find a way the director can help. Maybe it means shooting the scene in two or three shots instead of one long take. Or maybe it means changing a line or two in the script. It may also mean eliminating a line or movement the actor feels is unnatural.

I once had an on-camera host who had a very difficult time saying the word "terminal" in a line he was supposed to deliver to the camera. Although it may sound absurd, we spent 15 minutes and went through 11 takes trying to get the word right. In every case, would pronounce it "terminal."

Because the program dealt with telephone terminals, I was hesitant to consider changing the line. As the takes mounted, however, I could see that the frustration was wearing on the actor. Finally, I asked that the crew take a break, and the actor and I carefully went over the line several times. It turned out it was not the word terminal itself that was causing a problem but the alliteration of the "t" sounds in the line, "Trying out every telephone terminal in the area could be the answer."

We found that by changing the word telephone to phone, the actor had much less trouble with it. I made a decision to change the script and told the actor I was perfectly confident he could do it. He read the line with no problem, and we were on our way.

In another situation, with a few brief comments, I once encouraged a woman who was doing a dramatic role for me to go beyond what she felt she was capable of. Although her performance was working, I felt she could do more with it. After the fifth take, I said, "That's a buy. Very nice. Now I want an alternate—a totally loose read, just for the hell of it. I want you to really let go on this one, Meredith. No holds barred. We've already got the keeper on tape, so just have some fun with it."

We did the scene again, and her performance was better but still not there. "You're going halfway," I said. "Pull out the stops! Don't worry. If it's overbaked we just won't use it!"

She did it again, and this time it was brilliant. Her emotional range and all the animation and inflections that came with it blossomed into a truly rich and credible performance.

Finally, a director can encourage actors simply by displaying confidence in them. If a performance is not working, a comment like: "I know you and I know what you're capable of. You can do this scene perfectly," can go a long way toward bolstering an actor's ego at a particularly delicate time. You might then go on to say, "Let's just take a minute to sit down and figure out what's holding you back."

Demanding Excellence

An actor often knows when a director is accepting a performance with which he or she is not totally happy. Unless the conditions are extremely difficult, the actor usually loses some respect for a director who gives up in this manner. The director should be prepared to work with the actors to achieve solid performances, and should not give up too easily if they don't happen right away. To do so is to "rob" the actor, in a sense.

A director can encourage excellent performances in several ways. I often have short, tone-setting meetings with my casts before a shoot begins. In them, I say something like: "We have an extremely talented crew and cast. I know everyone here is capable of excellence, and that's what I'm going to be after. We have the time and the resources to create a truly excellent program, but we'll all need to put out the extra effort to achieve it. If something isn't working and we start getting into high take numbers, just try to bear with me. I think if we hang in there until it's right, we'll all be much more proud of the outcome."

Recognizing Effort

When the actor does put forth that extra something that results in a wonderful performance, don't hesitate to let him or her know how pleased you are. Remember,

however, that some actors can sometimes be extremely sensitive. If one sees you showering accolades on another, he or she may get jealous or resentful. This potential reaction shouldn't restrict you from recognizing a worthy effort; it just means you should be aware of the temperaments of the actors on your set and spread the recognition around.

I once worked with an actress who delivered very consistent, excellent performances. She was so good that as the shoot went on for several days, I found myself forgetting to give her much attention. She was so rock-steady and credible at what she did that I began to take her for granted. During that same period, I congratulated several other actors for delivering performances that weren't even up to this woman's level.

On the fourth day of the shoot, I noticed that she seemed a bit more reserved than normal, although her performances remained excellent. Realizing that her quiet mood might be the result of my lack of attention, I called her aside during a break and said, "I just want you to know you're providing the foundation and the example for this entire cast. I realize I'm not saying much to you, but that's because I'm busy trying to get some other people up to your standard. You're really excellent at your craft, and a delight to work with."

She beamed and, I knew at once, understood. Her happy mood returned, and she finished the shoot with even more flawless performances.

Knowing When to Let Up

Regardless of all your efforts and those of the cast and crew, you may still have times when you think it is best to simply accept what you have "in the can" and move on. It may become obvious that a performance cannot be improved and that time or other constraints are becoming negative factors. Or, if you simply have no more sunlight, for instance, and you have a performance in the can that is adequate, you may be forced to buy that performance and aim for better casting or perhaps rehearsal on the next production.

Because achieving true flawlessness is a rarity, this process of knowing when to let up and buy what you have is not an exception but rather a continual pressure for any director. Remember, that similar to all other creative activities, there comes a point of diminishing returns. When the extra time and effort you may be about to put in will probably not pay back enough to make it worthwhile, you must have the presence of mind to simply let go and move on.

Letting up for the moment is another strategy. If your take numbers are getting into the double digits and you sense that an actor is becoming frustrated by his or her inability to get it right, you might just say, "Let's take five and have a cup of coffee." Often, with the pressure off for a few minutes, the actor can gather his or her thoughts, brush aside the frustration, and garner new levels of confidence. Then another take or two will often be the one you were looking for.

Gaining Respect

Every coach should have the respect of his or her athletes; the same is true for every director. If your cast respects you, they will give you the 110% effort required to achieve excellence. If they don't respect you, that level of effort will be the exception rather than the rule.

How, then, do you as a director achieve respect? Mainly by doing all the things we've been discussing in this chapter—communicating with your cast, supporting and encouraging them, and guiding and challenging them toward excellence. In addition, however, you can also know your craft extremely well and give 110% yourself.

Having exceptional craft knowledge breeds admiration and respect among both crew and cast. If you are truly a professional, they know they can trust your requests and decisions as the right ones for the good of the project. They can also feel secure that their efforts will be guided properly and used correctly later in post-production. In other words, they will feel secure that you will produce a show that will create a positive reflection on their efforts and abilities.

Giving 110% yourself should be self-explanatory. If you're not willing to put in your very best effort, the project isn't worth the time and effort on the part of your cast and crew either.

Coaching Employee Talent

The director's coaching techniques for company employees should be much more attuned to creating a warm, friendly work environment than a professional dialogue. As we have established, employees have no acting skills. Thus, to talk with them in terms of character traits, motivation, sensory perceptions, and so on would be useless as a means of changing their performances.

What does tend to work with employees, however, are three simple techniques: *downplaying the production*

mystique, creating a relaxed environment, and *using simplified acting skills.*

Downplaying the Production Mystique

In most cases, focusing on the mystique of the production process creates tension for employees. When an employee "actor" steps onto a set or location for the first time and suddenly finds him or herself among lights, cameras, monitors, flags, nets, cables, and so on, the sheer enormity of what he or she is about to do may leave him or her virtually speechless. The director who plays up the production mystique usually heightens this sense of awe. The end result is almost always a tense, obviously staged performance—even if the employee is simply performing some demonstrative job function.

What is the proper approach when an employee walks on the set?

Creating a Relaxed Environment

I typically welcome employee talent to my sets with a warm smile, a friendly handshake, and a comment like: "Hi, you must be John. I'm Ray, nice to meet you. Let me introduce you to the crew."

Following these informal introductions, the initial awe of stepping into a production situation often begins to wear off. I might then follow with something like, "We've got a few simple things you can help us with, John, but we'll have you out of here in no time. So how's it going? You folks as busy in your department as we've been out here today?"

This type of inquiry often starts a brief work-related conversation that helps put the employee even more at ease. Once I see this happening, I then begin to ease into a discussion of the employee's role as talent. I might do this with a statement, such as, "Well, what we've got here is a part where we need someone like you to just step up and greet this customer like you normally would. That's really all it boils down to—doing what you do on the job."

I would then walk the employee through the part step by step and perhaps follow with a remark like, "I really don't want any acting. Honestly, what I hope to get is just exactly what you do, the way you typically do it. Nothing corny or set up."

If I've been placed into an unavoidable situation in which scripted lines are a necessity, I might show them to the employee and say, "Is this the way you'd normally greet a customer?" If the answer is "No," we would set about changing the lines as needed. If the answer is "Yes," I would follow with, "Okay, good. So show me how you'd do it. If these lines are close, you can go ahead and say them, but if you'd normally say something else, or add anything, just do that."

Through a process like this we would soon arrive at a situation in which the now relaxed employee would, as much as possible, demonstrate what he or she normally does versus trying to act. If the resulting performance is acceptable, the shoot can progress as planned. If the employee begins having difficulty, a few possible options are still available to the director.

Using Simplified Acting Skills

In some cases, an employee can actually be directed like an actor. I've found this technique most successful when the employee is relaxed and comfortable in front of the camera, but he or she can't seem to make the lines work naturally. In such cases, the performance might be improved by using a simplified version of a method acting technique.

The method actor concentrates on past events in his or her life and applies these sensory perceptions to the scene at hand. Keeping this process in mind, the director might say to the employee who was having difficulty greeting the customer naturally, "I'll tell you what. Think back to a specific customer you recently greeted. As you remember that person, try to remember what you said and how you felt when you met her. I mean, you were probably feeling positive and relaxed, and maybe she had a pleasant expression on her face or a nice voice or something."

If the employee can be gently coaxed into recalling a situation like this, as long as the action is kept simple, there's a good chance the performance can be improved. I have used a similar technique in coaxing employees to perform better in interview situations as well.

In one case, the employee was doing a fine job of answering my interview questions in a pleasant and articulate manner, but her voice and presence were extremely flat and monotone. After several takes, I said,

"Okay, very good. Now I'd like you to do me a favor. Ever had a situation where you're talking to someone, like maybe a friend or neighbor, and what you're saying is important, but it just doesn't seem to be sinking in? And you know how you kind of wanted to lean forward and say, 'Hey, listen up here! This is important!' Well, as you answer my questions this time, consider me someone like that. I'm just not getting it, and you have to drive the point home a little harder to make me understand. Okay?"

Again, this simplified technique, if properly handled, can boost an otherwise flat delivery.

Coaching employee talent into delivering credible performances can be one of the corporate director's greatest challenges. The wise director handles such situations with care and sensitivity. He or she realizes that employees are not actors and that to attempt to fit them into such a mold is most often embarrassing for the employees and detrimental to the production. The wise director also knows, however, that with careful, insightful handling, employees can add a level of credibility to corporate programming that few, if any actors can supply.

SUMMARY

The director's people skills are really what make or break him or her. All the technology and special effects in the world cannot make a good program out of bad writing, poor acting, and technical mediocrity. But when the director is able to work with people on a challenging, positive, and productive level, he or she is given the ability to take the program to great levels of excellence at both a technical and a human level. Once the director is capable of achieving this goal, he or she need only be concerned with one more critical skill—the ability to make sound, creative judgments under some of the most difficult circumstances imaginable.

25 Judgment Skills

So far, we have looked closely at the business aspects of corporate directing, the aesthetic qualities the director must concern him or herself with, and the people skills he or she must master. In all these cases, we have talked about *quality* performances, *excellent* composition, *perfect* tone, and so on.

But what exactly are the manifestations of such words? What separates excellent composition from good or mediocre composition? What elements could be construed as being intrinsic to a quality performance? And how do they differ from those of a bad performance or a pretty good one? What is perfect tone compared to acceptable tone?

Ultimately, much of what separates these definitions is subjective *judgment*. It is in the eye of the beholder and is different for each of us, depending on our personal tastes and opinions. If three, five, or ten people on a production crew watch a scene, all of them may have different opinions about whether or not it works and, if not, what is wrong. These differences, of course, mean that someone must make the final judgment. This final judgment responsibility is the director's, and it may be the single most important artistic skill he or she brings to a shoot—the ability to know what works.

This one critical element often separates a director from other members of the production crew. He or she has the ability to watch a scene play out, visualize how it will look when edited, and decide whether it will successfully convey the script interpretation to the intended audience, while simultaneously keeping the client and producer happy.

Although this judgment skill may be the most important of the director's abilities, because of its sub-jective nature and because it seems to be a product of experience and personal sensitivity, it is also one of the most difficult elements to explain in the pages of a book. We may not be able to define it exactly, but on the following pages we will explore some of the sensitivities that seem to be intrinsic qualities in directors who know what works.

SENSITIVITY TO THE PEOPLE AND THE WORLD AROUND US

Any director who must judge an actor's performance must know how people might act in a similar situation. For instance, if a married male employee is being fired from his job, how would the typical wife react when she was told? Would she cry? Get angry? Become panicky about the future? Would she want to call the boss and yell at him, or go sit in church and pray? Or would she simply sit down and begin to laugh?

Each of these reactions to a situation a corporate director encounters in a script might be possible. Each reaction is also related to the character development and motivation mentioned earlier.

For instance, is the wife proud of the husband or cynical? Is she a confident woman or a very negative and skeptical person? What does she think of the company for which her husband works? Has she wanted him to quit for a long time anyway or was this job the very best thing that has happened to him and her in years? You can see that the possibilities are numerous, and the director must be sensitive to how this wife character might react with any one of these character profiles.

Besides human aesthetic judgments, countless other audiovisual judgments must also be made. Will a close-up have more impact shot in a long focal length or a short one? Is a close-up even needed or appropriate? Will a dolly shot heighten a sense of tension by following the action, or would a zoom or a series of lock-off shots be just as effective? Is hard, dramatic lighting called for, or is flat lighting?

The ability to make these and many other similar judgments is at least partly an intrinsic skill that comes from the continual observations of a person sensitive to the people and the world surrounding him or her. He or she either has seen and pondered how persons in real-life situations act or is sensitive enough to the emotional content of a scene to visualize a simulation of those actions accurately enough for it to become a credible part of the illusion.

SENSITIVITY TO AUDIENCE TASTES

The director must also be keenly aware of how the audience feels about what he or she is directing. Consider the director who has been charged with the responsibility of shooting a short, year-end recap by the CEO on how well her roofing supply company has done and how bright the future looks.

If the audience for this piece is crafts workers who drive forklifts all day, would the CEO be more effective giving this message in a warehouse situation or from the executive boardroom at the head of a large oak table? The warehouse setting would probably be most effective because it would bring the executive to the audience's level, placing her in familiar territory. On the other hand, if this same message were being presented to a group of executive board members, the CEO would probably be most effective in an executive setting familiar to them.

Although such location decisions are often made in advance by the scriptwriter and producer, sometimes they are not. When they are left to the director, he or she should be sensitive to the audience's likes, dislikes, and opinions about the subject being shot.

Another example in this same area is wardrobe. The director normally decides on the actor's wardrobe. If he or she is directing a company news program featuring an on-camera host, how should the host be dressed? Again, this judgment comes down, at least partly, to the director's sensitivity to the audience.

Would the host appear most credible to the audience in a three-piece suit or wearing a tie and white shirt with the sleeves rolled up? Or should he perhaps be in a V-neck sweater with no tie or a waist jacket? Should he wear semiformal slacks, such as corduroy or expensive slacks? Tennis shoes or boots?

Each of these questions is a judgment the corporate director will be called on to make, and each of them can either enhance the illusory power of the program or detract from it.

SENSITIVITY TO THE CLIENT'S AND PRODUCER'S TASTES

When the director has satisfied his or her own sensitivities and those of the viewing audience, the final test is, in a sense, the client and the producer. Failing to take their preferences into account can be as damaging to the program as choices inappropriate for the audience.

For instance, if we return to the CEO year-end wrap-up mentioned earlier and consider it from the client's point of view, the director's first choice might change. This situation could be the case if the client is a conservative corporate executive, such as the public affairs vice-president. This individual might be very concerned about the CEO's image, and although the director may feel strongly that a warehouse setting would be appropriate, the client may object on the grounds that the image is too "rough" for a CEO.

Although the director may totally disagree with this observation, he or she may have to concede to the client as a matter of basic **corporate politics.** As long as it is done tactfully, there is no harm in the director voicing his or her opinion about why the "rougher" image is considered appropriate. In the end, though, if the vice-president disagrees, the director will have to change the location to please the paying client.

This same type of sensitivity "reading" must be taken on the producer. Is he or she comfortable with what the director has decided? If not, why, and is a compromise that satisfies both parties possible? Like the vice-president, if the producer is open to suggestions, there is no harm in presenting reasons why the director feels he or she has made the right choices. But if the producer is unwilling to budge, the director has little choice but to give in.

Remember that giving in to either clients or producers should not be considered a major artistic disaster.

A corporate program is an important creative effort, but it is not a work of art worth damaging a career or reputation over.

Further, regardless of the director's intuition, the client or producer may have some larger perspective that may be valid. For instance, suppose the CEO finds it personally awkward to be seen "acting" in front of employees. The public affairs vice-president may know about this quirk but be unwilling to pass the information on to the director. Or the producer may know that a union disagreement is developing in the warehouse and that bringing the CEO in at this time is not appropriate.

These types of situations are not uncommon in corporate media production. They demonstrate the need for the director's ongoing sensitivity to the clients' and producers' needs.

OTHER JUDGMENT CALLS

What other judgments must a director make? Consider these: What crew members will work best together? Which actor should be cast in the role? Is a set best in this situation or a location? Is the CEO presenting his message credibly, or should he be told that he sounds nervous? Should a technical expert be invited along on the shoot? Should the client be sent an audition reel or simply be told what choices you've made? Should the producer be told that the budget is too small for what she wants? Should three angles of coverage be shot or a single angle? Should the camera be low or high, close or far? Should sound be recorded or not? Should lunch be catered, or should the crew be released and told to be back at the shoot in an hour? Should the day go longer than 10 hours, resulting in considerable overtime costs?

The director's judgment calls play a critical role in every aspect of the production. As mundane or minuscule as some of those judgments may seem, they can be the very factors that make or break an entire production—and sometimes a director's career.

If the CEO's footage is brought back from the warehouse and the public affairs vice-president doesn't like it, chances are it will be scrapped and a new shoot will be arranged. Not only does that cost extra money, create extra pressures, and make the producer look extremely bad, but it also seriously decreases the chances that the same director's judgment will be trusted again.

JUDGMENT UNDER PRESSURE

Pressure is a familiar word to any director—corporate or otherwise. In a sense, it is also the "kicker" with regard to all the judgment issues we've been discussing. Making the many types of decisions we've explored with no pressure applied would be difficult enough, but this case is rare for the corporate director. In production, pressure virtually always exists, and it is sometimes excruciating.

VISUAL VERSUS CONTENT

Directors can sometimes be greatly tempted to buy a scene on the strength of its visual quality alone—even if an actor's performance is considerably less than perfect. For example, consider a scene that requires the camera to start in a wide shot, dolly into a two shot as dialogue begins, and dolly in again to a close-up as one actor exits. From a camera operator's standpoint, this setup can be difficult to achieve. Not only must the camera move to specific marks at a set rate of speed, but the focus must also be adjusted at critical points along the way, and frame edge marks must be found and hit by the DP on the fly. In addition to these requirements, if the scene is being recorded on location, other extraneous elements—airplane sounds, the sun passing behind a cloud, or wind rustling into a microphone, to name a few—can ruin an otherwise good try.

Such a scene may require ten or more takes. During this time, the actors begin to get tired, the crew becomes increasingly frustrated, and the director, producer, and client become more and more tense with each failure.

Now imagine that the camera move is suddenly achieved with absolute perfection. As playback of the scene is viewed, those who are gathered around the monitor resound with a cheer, and the DP lets out a sigh of relief, at the same time shaking hands with the gaffer.

There is one problem, however. The performance does not work for the director. A line was delivered with a weak inflection, a momentary stumble occurred in another spot, and one actor looked stiff and unnatural as he moved to his second position. As the director realizes these problems and looks up from the monitor, he is surrounded by 5 to 15 people who want nothing more than to hear, "That's a buy."

The sound recordist says, "Worked fine for sound. Not a rustle!"

The DP declares, "I'll *never* hit it that good again."

The client chimes in with, "Boy, three o'clock. . . it's getting late!"

The director checks his watch. Sure enough, on top of everything else, the shoot is an hour behind schedule, and with the onset of afternoon sun, the quantity and quality of the light are changing rapidly. The director therefore has a tough choice. He can buy the scene because it's technically perfect and then look for a way to cut around the poor performances. Or he can say, "First positions. We're going for take 16."

This scenario, of course, is only one of countless similar examples. And what should the director do? Contrary to what you may think, it is not always prudent to go for that take 16. The director's decision should be weighed based on a number of factors. How far behind time is the shoot? Can the loss of time be made up the next day? How bad was the performance? How easy will it be to cut around the bad parts in editing? What extra coverage must be shot to achieve this? Again, the choices are too numerous and diverse to list.

CONTENT VERSUS VISUAL

The same thing can happen in reverse. A performance may suddenly play out absolutely exquisitely after 14 takes, just when the director is sure the actor is nearing exhaustion. At first, the director breathes a sigh of relief. She has it! It was brilliant! She can move on, thank heaven, and maybe still make it in with only an hour of overtime!

But when the shot is played back, the balloon is burst. The shotgun microphone had dipped into the edge of the frame at a critical moment.

The director will no doubt hear comments like, "It'll be cropped in duping," "They'll never see it," or "Even if it doesn't get cropped, if you didn't know it was there, you'd never catch it." Again, the decision must be weighed. Will it really be cropped? The person who said that will not have to sit in the screening room with the client and producer and take responsibility when someone says, "Did I see something for a second there?" Or is there a way to cut around it? Does the actor have enough left in him to do it one more time?

How is the producer feeling? Can a "pick-up" of only a portion of the scene be used?

While you're busy weighing out that dilemma, here's another typical corporate situation—the familiar CEO message. Assume that the director is shooting the top man in the company, who is in a great rush. As the CEO enters the studio, he says, "I need to be out of here in 10 minutes."

He sits on his stool in front of a prelit flat, and a microphone is pinned to his lapel. He speaks to provide an audio level check, and the microphone isn't working properly.

The second recordist goes to work, frantically changing the batteries and checking the cable connections. Meanwhile, an entourage of dark-suited executives crowd around the CEO, the producer, and the director. All of them look extremely important, terribly rushed, and highly irritable to boot. In fact, the CEO himself has a particularly distasteful look on his face.

The mic is fixed in five minutes—record time. The director is ready to say, "Roll tape," when the DP realizes he forgot to set his backlight. There is virtually no separation from the background flat. The shot doesn't look good at all. Six of the ten minutes is gone as the DP scurries up a ladder into the grid to set the backlight.

Five minutes later, every executive in the place is checking his watch. The producer is developing a nervous twitch. The CEO looks downright angry. The director finally says, "Roll tape," and the copy on the teleprompter is wrong.

It is fixed in a flash. The director rolls again, and *finally* the CEO is able to present his entire message. There is only one problem. The performance is noticeably staged and nervous. The CEO looks plain old bad. The five executives gathered around the director, however, immediately start spouting compliments like: "Great, J.B.," "Very sincere," "Sounded right on to me," and "I'm convinced!"

The producer looks at the director, and he is sweating. The CEO is checking his watch.

If you are this director, what do you do now? Do you go along with everyone else who is scared stiff, even though you know this executive will be laughed at later when viewed by employees? Or do you risk both his and the producer's wrath by saying, "I'm sorry, but that one was a bit rough around the edges. If you don't mind, Mr. Billings, I'd like to do it again." Your answer may seem easy now, but believe me, it will not be easy when you are sitting in the director's chair.

SUMMARY

These types of decisions made "under fire" are a constant part of the corporate director's life. If he or she is a sensitive and observant person, critical judgment skills will most likely be sound and he or she will find ways to come away from each shoot with human and technical aesthetic qualities that produce credible scenes and programs.

By contrast, if the director is insensitive to his or her world and the people in it, he or she will have a difficult time attuning to viewer's, client's, and producer's tastes. In this case, judgment skills will almost certainly be faulty, and the director will run into continual problems as the footage shot is subject to producer and client scrutiny. This issue is so important that, in the latter case, it's highly likely that the director will soon find him or herself in a different job market.

PART FIVE SUMMARY

As we noted at the beginning of this part, the director is undoubtedly the most critical player when it comes to making the script into an effective visual entity.

Without his or her professional creative skills in the areas of human, audiovisual, technical, and general aesthetics, the program is doomed to mediocrity or failure. The director's people and judgment skills, however, are equally important. Of course, the director's critical foundation for all of these skills is his or her ability to see through the eyes of the audience.

Similar to writing and producing, successfully directing a corporate media production also takes plain old elbow grease and a great personal desire to achieve excellence and true-to-life credibility on the screen. You can gain further knowledge in this area by exploring the following:

Fairweather, Rod, *Basic Studio Directing Focal Press,* Burlington, MA, 1998.

Kagan, Jeremy, *Directors Close Up: Interviews With Directors Nominated for Best Film By the Directors Guild of America,* Focal Press, Burlington, MA, 2000.

Comey, Jeremiah, *The Art of Film Acting A Guide For Actors and Directors,* Focal Press, Burlington, MA, 2002.

Rabiger, Michael. *Directing the Documentary.* 3rd ed. Burlington, MA, Focal Press, 1997.

Weston, Judith. *Directing Actors.* Studio City, CA, Michael Wiese Productions, 1997.

part six

Postproduction

26 A Postproduction Overview

TRADITIONAL VERSUS NONLINEAR

Postproduction is the process by which the footage shot or digitally created is edited together into a completed program. It is also the phase of the production process that has undergone the most change in recent years, largely due to the evolution of digital technology. What was once a time-consuming, laborious, and highly technical sequence of electromechanical events has evolved into a digital process that is much more user friendly and as simple as the click of a mouse.

Because traditional **editing** systems are still used in corporate media and because students of media production should understand the evolution of the editing process, we will begin with a brief overview of traditional video editing. I will use the present tense in explaining this process because, although traditional editing has become the exception versus the rule, it still takes place, and in fact is the standard in some organizations.

TRADITIONAL EDITING OVERVIEW

The traditional video editing process normally starts with two elements: (1) duplication of the original footage into a format the "rough cut" or "offline" **editor** can work with, and (2) preparation of what is called a *master script package*.

Duplication

Different formats of original footage, along with a variety of offline editing systems, have created a need for various kinds or combinations of footage duplication, or "duping". This is because the editing process may take place on videotape recorders (VTRs) with formats different from that of the original tapes. For instance, a program might be shot on one inch, then duped to ¾-inch U-Matic for rough cut or offline editing, and online edited on D-2.

To keep things simple, let's assume that our original footage was shot on a common videotape format—Betacam SP. We will also assume that the program is to be offlined or rough cut on a three-quarter inch offline system and onlined on Betacam SP. Typical duplication requirements for the footage will then be as follows:

1. Three-quarter-inch window dubs of all the footage: These are workprints of the footage, used in the offline editing process. They have a small window area burned in on the picture in which SMPTE time code (which we will discuss shortly) appears visually as a series of numbers. This time code is copied from, and thus is identical, *frame for frame*, to the time code that was recorded in the Betacam SP on the original footage as it was being shot.

2. "B" rolls or duplicate Betacam SP copies of any parts of the footage, which may be used for special effects such as wipes or dissolves. These copies are required because on traditional editing systems, effects such as dissolves require *two* source reels—the original and a duplicate of the original.

The Master Script Package

As the name suggests, the master script package is the documented history of the shoot containing all notes and paperwork required to perform the edit and present the finished package to the producer. The primary source of information in the master script package is the master script. The AD made notes on this script (or scripts) all during the production, which we discussed in Chapter 17. This script now becomes an informational tool for the editor, explaining every shot that took place and highlighting the "buys" (circled takes) that he or she will need to assemble the show.

Along with the master script should be a shot report, usually noted by the AD or camera operator. This report simply lists the "in" times of the various shots, according to a time code display on the camcorder itself. The shot report also helps the editor locate certain footage by telling him or her specifically where the shots are located. A typical shot report would look like Figure 26.1.

Also included in the master script package should be paperwork such as listings of any stock footage that is to be used and where it is to be obtained; specifics about any animation, artwork, or titles to be used; notes on where to locate music picked by the director; and any other general notes the director or AD may have wanted to pass on to the editor. In short, the master script package should contain any and all written elements as well as the duplicate footage the editor will need to proceed with the job.

Once these elements have been assembled (usually by the AD immediately following production), the program is ready for editing.

The Editing Process and Time Code

In film, the editing process is manual; that is, the footage is physically cut and spliced together piece by piece. In videotape, this process is accomplished electronically. In order to control the electronic machines that actually perform the edit functions, engineers have come up with something called time code.

Time Code and Control Track

Several types of time code are used in videotape editing. The most common is called SMPTE time code. (SMPTE is pronounced "semptee," but it is often referred to simply as *time code* or just **code.**) Time code is a series of digital signals that translate visually into segments of time based on a 24-hour clock. The format of these signals has been standardized by the Society of Motion Picture and Television Engineers, or SMPTE, hence the term SMPTE time code. Visually, a typical time code number looks like this: 01:05:18:28.

The "01" in this code number refers to the videotape hour, the "05" refers to the minute, and the "18" to the second. The "28" refers to the video frame. (As you may recall, there are approximately 30 video frames per second.) So, 01:05:18:28 is an exact point on the tape that is 1 hour, 5 minutes, 18 seconds, and 28 frames from the beginning.

This time code is usually recorded onto an audio channel or what is referred to as the "address track" on a videotape using a **time code generator.** On a window dub (the workprints we just mentioned) the code is *burned in;* that is, it actually shows up on the screen for the editor.

The edit **controller** then allows the editor to select very specific segments of time on the videotape for transfer onto another tape. For example, if an editor wants to transfer a scene that runs a total of 10 seconds, beginning at 01:22:18:10 and ending at 01:22:28:10, he or she uses the edit controller to shuttle through the footage and stop at those two exact points: first, where the edit should begin and, second, where the edit should end.

At each of these points, the editor enters into the controller the time code numbers appearing in the window—the first as an "in" point and the second as an "out" point. Next, he or she enters two numbers into the controller that tell it where this ten second piece of footage should be recorded on the *record tape,* which has been stripped with time code as well. Finally, the editor performs the edit.

At this point, the controller electronically locks in on the specific numbers the editor has chosen. It then synchronizes the playback and record VTRs to roll at the exact same speed. As this process takes place, the

VIDEOTAPE SHOT REPORT

# 7616l-3	TITLE THE SUPERVISOR		REEL NO. R-6	DATE 5/18

PRODUCER McPHERSON   DIRECTOR ALBERT   A.D. MARTIN

FOOTAGE IN	OUT	SCENE NUMBER	TAKE NUMBER	DESCRIPTION
001	019	—		BARS AND TONE
019	151	8A	1	JOHN @ TERMINAL -C.U.
	160		2	
	171		3	
	190		④	
191	277	9	1	HOST ENTERS @ JOHN'S DESK
	280		2	
	284		3	
	290		4	
	295		5	
	302		⑥	
303	516	9A	1	C.U. HOST
	521		②	
522	711	14	1	SUPERVISOR TAKES CALL -W.S.
	900		②	

Page _____ of _____

Figure 26.1 Typical shot report showing scene numbers, time code "in" times, and circled takes.

video and/or audio signals between the two time code numbers selected are transferred *from* the playback tape *to* the record tape.

Another, less effective system used for videotape editing is known as **control track**. Control track is a series of identical pulses (one per frame) recorded on the videotape. While control track provides basic editing control because the pulses can be used as "in" and "out" point markers, it does not provide a *unique address* for each frame—a factor that makes the editor's job much quicker and simpler. As an example, imagine that an editor has been given 15 60-minute reels of three quarter inch dupes, and he has no time code addresses, only control track. When he wants to locate a shot, he may know that it is on, say, reel three, but exactly where on reel three he can only approximate. This means he will have to shuttle back and forth on the tape until he locates it. On the other hand, if he were using time code, he could place the reel in a VTR and automatically fast-forward to the exact frame address he is searching for.

With this brief explanation of time code, control track, and the basic elements involved in the editing process, we can now continue with two more processes that are very important for the student to understand—the a traditional offline and online edit.

27

The Traditional Offline and Online Edit

THE OFFLINE EDIT

As with the previous chapter, we will discuss the traditional editing processes in the present tense. Keep in mind, however, that many aspects of these traditional processes are negated by contemporary, nonlinear editing systems. In the next chapter, having laid the foundation for understanding the editing process, we will move on to modern systems and the student will clearly see how much of a revolutionary improvement the new systems are.

The Editor

If the producer is not the person offlining the program, at this point he or she will want to hire an editor. Editors, like writers, directors, and crew people, are available on a freelance, per-project basis.

Editors' rates vary depending on the complexity and variety of the equipment they work on, their level of skill and their track record. An offline editor who works in the type of edit bay described in Chapter 26 (two videotape machines and a controller) will cost approximately $150 to $300 per day. An online editor, who usually works with more sophisticated systems and has an outstanding track record, will cost approximately $400 to $500 per day.

The Offline

The offline edit usually begins after the editor has met and discussed the program with the producer or director. During this pre-edit meeting, the editor receives any guidelines, preferences, or special instructions he or she must follow. He or she also receives the master script package and window dubs.

Once the editor is in the edit bay (Figure 27.1), his or her first act will probably be to read the script and get a feel for it from an editing standpoint—whether it is fast-paced, light, dramatic, and so on. At the same time, he or she will look over the AD's notes to get a feel for the type and amount of footage that was shot to cover the various scenes.

Once the editor has completed these tasks, if time permits, he or she will view the footage. Sometimes an editor will even log in a personal shot list using time code numbers. In many cases, the director will also sit in on this logging session, discussing the footage with the editor and making known his or her preferences for how certain scenes should be cut.

With these two chores completed, the editor has a very good feel for the script, the producer's and director's preferences, and the available footage. Now, either with or without the director present, the editor begins to edit.

Figure 27.1 An offline editor prepares in a typical offline bay.

The Editing Process

The editor starts by loading a three-quarter-inch cassette tape that has been *stripped* (prerecorded with time code and black) into the *record* machine. Next, he or she looks at the master script and determines the first shot of the program. Let's assume that the editor finds in the script notes that the first shot is scene 101, that it has been recorded on reel 4, and that take 7 was the buy since it has been circled.

The editor loads the three-quarter-inch window dub of reel 4 into the *playback* or source machine, refers to the videotape shot report taken by the EIC to find its approximate location, and shuttles through the footage to that spot.

When the editor has found the slate for scene 101, take 7, he or she looks over the shot and decides what seems to be the right "in" point or place to begin the edit and the right "out" point or place to end it. These in and out points are specified by the time code numbers visible on the screen in the time code window. At this point, the editor also decides on in and out points on the record tape—the tape onto which the footage is recorded.

The editor now enters these numbers into the controller and most likely pushes the preview button, this lets the editor view what the edit will look like without actually performing it. The preview function is useful because the first in and out points that the editor chooses often have to be *trimmed* (adjusted slightly) before the shot is exactly right to edit into the program.

After trimming a few frames at either the head or the tail of the shot, the editor gives the controller the "perform" command, and it does the following:

1. It rolls the record machine to a spot usually five seconds prior to the *exact* time code number on the tape the editor chose as an in point.
2. It rolls the playback (source) machine (with the three-quarter-inch window dub footage) to a spot five seconds prior to the exact time code spot that the editor chose as an in point.
3. Once both machines have pre-rolled and stopped, it rolls both at identical speeds (in sync) and records the piece specified on the source tape onto the record tape.
4. It ends recording at the exact spot that the editor selected as out points.

With this task is done, the editor has laid down his or her first edit on this program. Now, depending on the system being used, he or she may do several different things.

If the system has what is called an *automatic list management function,* the time code numbers that the editor has just chosen will automatically be stored in memory and later recorded onto a computer disk for use in the online editing session. In this case, the editor is now free to move on.

If the system that the editor is using does not have such an automatic function, the editor keeps a manual list by writing down the time code numbers. Whether manual or computerized, this list of time code numbers, often called the *edit decision list (EDL),* later becomes the backbone of the online or final editing session.

Now, working within the parameters of this system and according to the desires of the producer and director, the editor moves through the program repeating what he or she has just done—selecting shots using the master script and log sheets; entering the specific time code numbers of the ins and outs of those shots into the controller; and previewing, trimming, and finally performing edit after edit until the offline or rough-cut version of the program is complete.

At this point, the editor returns to the producer the original package containing window dubs and master script, with the following two additional elements: (1) a completed rough cut of the program and (2) either a manual list of edits or a computer disk with the numbers stored on it. Now, with the rough cut complete, it's time to call the client.

THE TRADITIONAL ROUGH-CUT SCREENING

If your client has never been involved with the production of a videotape program, he or she will probably be waiting impatiently for a first look at what you have developed. That first look normally comes in the rough-cut screening.

It is very important to make sure the client understands that the program, at this point, is exactly what the name implies—a *rough* cut. If, after weeks of anticipation, the client comes to the traditional rough-cut screening expecting music, dissolves, and special effects—a perfectly polished program—he or she will probably be disappointed.

Another equally important point to clarify is that this screening is the client's last real chance to make changes in the program. If this point is not made clear, the producer could be in for some headaches and, as we will see, some added online expenses.

To keep from running into these problems, each rough-cut screening should open with an informative introduction, which might go something like this:

What you're about to see is what we call a rough cut. Basically, that means a rough assembly of your program, shot by shot. What it doesn't include is the music, titles, any special effects we may add, certain basic effects like dissolves, and the general fine tuning and polishing that come in the online—the final editing process.

Today's screening, then, isn't so much for aesthetic reasons but more for content approval. Is all the information there? Is it placed in the right order? Has it been visualized correctly? And so on. Once we've established these things or noted any changes we need to make to accomplish them, we can then move the program into online for those final touches I mentioned.

Another key point to remember is this—after today it could becomes very expensive and complicated to make even little changes. So, whatever questions or concerns you may have, by all means, bring them up in this meeting.

At this point, the producer might explain to the clients that they will be seeing the time code window and numbers at the bottom of the screen, and that these will be gone in the final version.

During the rough-cut screening, it is important to pinpoint any specifics that need to be added, deleted, or changed in any way before the program moves ahead. It is equally important to take very specific notes on these changes because, if the program needs more changes after it has been onlined, depending on the type of system that was used, the cost can multiply dramatically.

ADDITIONAL NOTES

The following are a few additional notes on rough-cut screenings. It is beneficial to have the editor or the director attend this meeting, if time and money allow. These two people, especially the editor, are much more familiar with the footage than the producer.

If the client is concerned about a certain shot, for instance, the editor will know if another take or shot could be substituted. The director, who carefully planned the visualization and, in many cases, got extra coverage of scenes as backup, should also be able to help in these situations.

After this meeting, the producer must decide whether to send the program on to online or hold it back for more offline work. That decision is usually based on the types and amount of changes that have been determined. Another factor in the decision will be whether or not the producer has an in-house online system.

The rule of thumb is to make virtually all changes in offline editing because a traditional online system rented from an outside facility can cost well over $300 per hour.

THE ONLINE EDIT

Earlier, we established that the term *online* refers to the final editing process. In a few cases, the online is accomplished on a system as simple as the one used in offline editing, sometimes even the same system. Much more often, however, an online takes place using a sophisticated, computerized editing system, as shown in Figure 27.2.

All the various types of traditional online editing systems do basically the same thing: They control multiple videotape machines; interface with switchers, special-effects generators, audio mixers, and other equipment; and, in doing so, allow the editor to assemble the final program from original footage (not workprints) and usually first-generation duplicates (B rolls) of the originals.

You will recall that in the offline edit, a rough cut was made from duplicate footage with a time code window superimposed. Because only a single playback or source machine was used in the offline edit bay, the system was capable of cutting together shots from *only one source*. This is called *cuts-only* editing. During that rough cut, the editor, either manually or via the system, developed a list of time code numbers that corresponded exactly to each edit.

As previously mentioned, these time code numbers correspond *exactly* to the same pictures on the original footage—not in the form of a visible window but, rather, as a series of digital signals on the address track.

Figure 27.2 A traditional, tape-based online editing system.

This process, as you may recall, was accomplished during the initial duping after production.

AUTO ASSEMBLE

Using these numbers for reference and control, then, a sophisticated online system can control multiple playback or source machines and it is capable of incorporating many special effects, depending on its associated interface equipment. Further, the online can perform edits *automatically* once it has the list of time code numbers entered into its processor. In an ideal situation, then, the editor could have an online edit session that proceeds as follows:

1. The edit decision list from the rough cut is fed into the online machine and stored. This process is accomplished by disk input if the automatic list management system was used, or, if the list is manual, by entering the numbers on the system's keyboard.
2. Anywhere from two to four, or even more original footage cassettes are then loaded into individual videotape machines connected to the online editing system.
3. The editor gives the system a series of commands that tell it to "auto assemble."
4. As the editor looks on, the online system synchronizes and rolls the proper machines at the proper times to edit the entire program together with frame accuracy, automatically.

This situation is ideal; in the real world, it rarely happens this way. It is much more likely that chunks of the show will be auto-assembled, whereas other parts will be assembled manually, edit by edit. The amount of editing that can be done in the auto-assemble mode is determined by how closely the time code list developed by the offline editor reflects the final version of the program. In other words, if the offline of the program reflects *exactly* how the final program should look, and the editor's list accurately shows each of the edits performed, then the online session could be done strictly in the auto-assemble mode. But if the rough cut is *close* but not in exact agreement with the written list, the changes required will negate the auto-assemble process.

Obviously, then, from a producer's point of view, it pays to have the program as close to the final version as possible before taking it into the online session, especially if he or she is renting the online facility.

SPECIAL EFFECTS

Special effects such as dissolves, wipes, fades, and so on are also put into the program during the online edit. As mentioned previously, accomplishing these effects requires the use of more than one playback machine because two sources are being mixed visually during one edit.

A *dissolve*, for example, is made up of two pictures—one fading out and the other fading in—at the same time. Both these sources, often called *A/B rolls*, must be identical reels and must be recorded at the same time from two different source machines onto a third one—the record machine. The online system is designed to accomplish this task with its expanded machine control capabilities and use of the video switcher to generate the effect.

A *wipe* is a similar transitional effect in which, usually, a line crosses the screen, bringing in a new picture as it passes. A wipe does not require fades, but it does involve two pictures at once—one already on the screen as the other wipes it off. For this reason, a wipe also requires A/B rolls, two source machines, one playback machine, and the video the switcher.

Digital video effects (DVE) are also normally an online function (Figure 28.1). These effects are accomplished with special pieces of equipment that digitize the video image and then manipulate it in many ways. The picture can be shrunk, expanded, flipped away off the screen, posterized, and so on. DVE, used in conjunction with the switcher, adds even more capabilities to the system.

Titles will now be added as well. Usually, they are developed on a character generator, either in the online edit bay or nearby. The titles will be "keyed" (chromakeyed) over the proper pictures, again using the video switcher.

When the program is totally complete visually, the final step in the traditional postproduction process is often to "sweeten" its audiotrack. Before we get to that, however, let's now move from the traditional editing processes and equipment to today's nonlinear systems. As you will soon discover, the changes that have taken place in this area of the production process are quite remarkable.

28 Nonlinear Editing

As mentioned in Chapters 26 and 27, the editing process has undergone major changes during the past decade. The basis for these changes has grown out of the ability to digitize video signals, compress those digitized signals, and store them on computer hard drives. With this ability, analog signals that are bound by the laws of electromechanical physics have become, to use a well-worn computer term, "ones and zeros." And what advantage has that given us?

A NONLINEAR ANALOGY

To understand the answer in editing terms, let's first use an analogy. Imagine a writer who authors large documents. He works on a typewriter. In order to transfer ideas from his mind onto the paper, he first threads a sheet of paper into the typewriter's carriage. But probably not just one piece of paper. In many cases, he will insert at least two sheets with a piece of carbon paper in between. Next, he starts to type. To do this he pushes the arm on the carriage, and the entire carriage unit moves to the right. As he begins typing, the metal arms connected to each letter key pop forward and strike through the ribbon making imprints of letters of the alphabet on the paper as the carriage slowly moves back to the left. After typing one line (roughly ten words) and before every line thereafter, he must push the carriage again to the right and continue typing. If he gets every stroke right, he ends up with a sheet containing the work he set down to write. But rarely is every stroke right. More than likely, he will make mistakes and have to use white out, erasures, or some other means to cover

those mistakes. This quickly becomes a complicated matter because covering or erasing on the top sheet may be difficult enough, but doing the same to the carbon copy is virtually impossible, especially without getting ink all over one's hands, not to mention clothing. Eventually, however, this writer will finish his first draft.

Now, in order to edit what he has written, he removes the papers from the typewriter and begins to make marks with a pencil. He crosses out some words and letters, modifies others, and circles passages he will want to move to another area when he types his next draft. Eventually he does just that—he inserts two new sheets of paper and a carbon and moves through the same process to include his changes. Chances are he will edit once again with a pencil and retype still again—perhaps several times.

Now imagine that same writer is given a word processor. Instead of a sheet of paper in a moveable carriage, he views a screen that displays a *digital image* of a piece of paper. As he starts to type, no lettered keys pop up to strike a ribbon. Instead, his letters simply appear on screen before his eyes! As he types, the lines automatically "wrap around" so he does not have to reset the cursor position each time. When he makes a spelling error, it is automatically highlighted on the screen and in many cases the software corrects the error for him. No more need for erasures, Whiteout, etc. When he is finished and wants to edit his work, he doesn't remove his paper and begin to make marks, he simply deletes on the screen, changes words and lines at will, and moves the passages he is concerned about with a few clicks of the mouse. Perhaps five or ten digital "drafts" later, when he is satisfied with the work, he selects one or more font styles and sizes he likes and does some special formatting to visually polish and enhance the work. Then he prints out flawless, professional looking sheets, without the use of carbon paper, but receiving the number of copies he wants—collated per his instructions.

What's happened? In moving from a typewriter to a computer, a once cumbersome, *mechanical* part of the writing process has become a simple, *nonmechanical* process of using "ones and zeros" to represent his writing in digital form. And with the appropriate word processing software to manipulate those ones and zeros, the writer's work has become much easier—allowing him or her to spend a good deal more time on the most important part of the process—creative thinking. This example of moving from a typewriter to a word processor is very similar to the process of moving from a traditional, tape-based editing system to a modern, nonlinear system.

With the sound and images of a video recording session digitized and stored as ones and zeros on a hard drive, cutting, pasting, expanding, shrinking, and manipulating in countless ways, becomes a simple matter achievable with the click of a mouse and a few keystrokes.

This new nonlinear method of editing caused quite a stir when it was introduced to producers in the early 1990s. As amazing as it seemed, however, there were several significant problems in those early years. First,

although pictures and sounds could be converted into digital information, they required such large amounts of disk space (one uncompressed frame of motion video and sound requires roughly one megabyte of space) that they had to be digitized and compressed at a very low resolution level. This process meant that the images displayed were not nearly good enough to use as completed programming. Second, manipulating the sound and images in certain ways, for instance creating a dissolve or other special effect, was not a "real-time" process. Such effects had to be *rendered* or created by the computer, which in some cases took inordinate amounts of time.

For these reasons and the fact that buying a nonlinear editing system required a very large capital investment, systems such as the Avid shown in Figure 28.1 and the Media 100 shown in Figure 28.2 were first used only as offline or rough cut systems. In this capacity, they replaced the cuts-only tape-based systems used in many corporate and broadcast shops. For offline, the nonlinear systems were excellent. They allowed editors, directors, producers, and clients to quickly assemble pictures and sound and instantly make changes that would have been much more time consuming and cumbersome on tape-based systems.

One example of this ease of use can be illustrated by considering the replacement of a single shot in a rough cut with a longer or shorter one. In the world of

Figure 28.1 Avid is a popular nonlinear editing system.

Figure 28.2 Media 100 is a nonlinear editing system very similar to Avid.

tape-based systems, if a program with one hundred edits required placing a longer shot at, say, edit fifty, the editor had three choices. He or she could lay the new shot in, covering up part of the preceding or following shot (which usually destroyed the program's pace), he could re-edit the entire show from edit fifty on, or he could make a copy of the half of the show following edit fifty, lay in the new longer shot, and then re-lay on the back end of the show, following edit fifty, in one long edit.

Not only did this process take a lot of time and extra videotape, but the copied part of the show was also two generations lower in quality than the first part because it had to be copied *off* to another tape then back *onto* the rough cut. As a result, the sound and image quality suffered greatly. In addition to the picture and sound denigration, the edit decision list also required adjustment because the long single edit now perhaps comprising the second half of the show would not be workable in the online session to follow.

In the nonlinear world, however, placing a longer or shorter shot at any place in the program became as simple as inserting a word or sentence in a word processing document. It was a "virtual" insertion, and thus a simple matter of a quick cut-and-paste-type operation. The edit decision list, which the nonlinear system kept up to date automatically, was always maintained in a

frame-accurate state from start to finish—with no adjustment needed by the editor.

The result? During this early period, many producers began cutting offline edits on nonlinear systems and with a frame-accurate EDL, going back to tape-based editing systems for online.

Over the next 10 years, however, many of the "online" problems associated with nonlinear editing systems were solved. Compression technology improved to a point where higher levels of resolution could be achieved in the same storage space, "larger" storage devices were developed, and the speed of computer processors increased dramatically. In addition the special effects that took so long to render at first became considerably faster.

The result? Today, nonlinear editing is widely used in both an offline and *online* capacity.

This progress means that the term "offline," as it was originally defined, is disappearing. Because newer nonlinear systems can place in music and effects such as dissolves virtually in real time and because artwork and titles can be created *inside the editing system*, a typical program is essentially onlined the first time around!

These days, then, the traditional rough cut screening process is also disappearing. The client sits in the edit suite and in the first viewing sees what the producer considers a completed (or nearly completed) show.

Because the process is digital and computerized, in many cases the editor is able to make any changes required on the spot. When the program is truly completed, it is simply output or "mastered" to a high-quality tape source such as Digital Beta, which becomes the edit master or duplication master of the program.

There is one caveat to this advancement that modern producers still deal with. In some cases, especially with very long programs, a first cut must still be created at a much lower resolution than the final cut. This "low res" first cut is necessitated by simple mathematics; the lower the resolution level the more information (pictures and sounds) that can be stored in and edited by the system. When one considers the fact that with all of the selected takes digitized into the nonlinear system a large amount of non-program footage is taking up space, you begin to see the problem. If a typical editing ratio is a very conservative five to one (five minutes digitized into the system for every one minute that will end up in the final show) you can understand how a large amount of "extra" space will initially be required.

Once the program is finished and approved, however, only the final clips appearing in the program are needed. At this point, everything but the timecode list of those final clips is "dumped" out of the system. Reinserting the original reels, the editor then re-digitizes from the original tape *only* the program clips in the timecode list. And these he brings in at a *top quality* resolution. He also instructs the system to automatically re-assemble the program, creating the final "high res" version for output to tape.

THE NONLINEAR EDITING PROCESS

Because nonlinear editing systems have become the standard in modern editing, it's worth our time to follow the nonlinear editing process just as we did with traditional editing methods—step by step (Figure 28.3). For the sake of consistency, let's assume the same parameters as in our first example—that the original footage was shot on the Betacam SP tape format. We will also assume that although logging and digitizing can (and often does) take place on the nonlinear editing system itself, this production facility has a separate workstation strictly for logging. The obvious advantage of this setup is that the logging process we are about to discuss can take place without tying up a complete editing system.

Logging and Digitization

In preparing for a nonlinear edit, instead of duplicating the footage to a workprint format such as three-quarter inch, the director may take his or her original reels to a logging room with a monitor and a Betacam SP VTR connected to a media logging system. When placed in the VTR, the footage can be viewed on the monitor, and the media logging software displays a graphic control panel that allows the producer to move through the footage as the corresponding, time code is displayed.

When the director arrives at a spot he or she knows will be used in the upcoming edit, he or she simply places an "in" point with the click of a mouse, then moves forward until the end of the shot to be used is reached and places an "out" point. He or she then instructs the logging tool, again with the click of a mouse, to store these time code numbers.

A

B

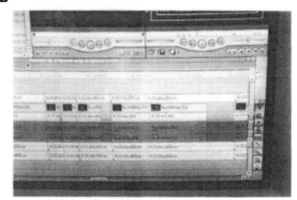

Figure 28.3 A Final Cut Pro nonlinear editing system. **A,** Final Cut Pro has become a very popular editing system with Mini DV producers. Its impressive list of features, and reputation as a system that's simple, effective and easy to use have made it an industry standard. **B,** Controls are intuitive and easy to learn.

Having chosen the first piece, the director continues through the taped material repeating this logging process. When he or she has logged all the reels, he or she inserts a floppy disk into the media logging system and requests that the list of timecode numbers be transferred to disk. The system does so, and the director has a complete, frame-accurate list of the material to be submitted for digitization and editing.

With original reels as well as the disk in hand, the director may now submit the material to an editor or digitizer. This person sits at the nonlinear editing system and begins the process of inputting or digitizing the material. To do this, the editor inputs the director's list, originally on the floppy disk, and places the system into the digitizing or "capture" mode. Following this step, he or she places the director's first original reel into a Betacam SP VTR connected to the nonlinear system. Then, with a few clicks of the mouse, the system is instructed to begin digitizing. It now begins a process of automatically shuttling through the tape to each time code in and out point on the list. When it reaches a section noted, it automatically switches into digitizing or "capture" mode and begins transferring the sound and images from tape onto the system's hard drive as digital information.

When reel one is completed, reel two is inserted and so on until all of the material is contained on the hard drive. It now exists in much the same way word processing information exists—in bins, folders, and files as virtual, randomly accessible digital memory (Figures 28.4 and 28.5).

Editing

When the scheduled edit session begins, the director or producer and the editor open up the bins and folders containing the material and begin transferring pieces of it—time code numbers corresponding to the sounds and images digitized—onto what is called a "program timeline." For instance, the director may say he or she first wants to lay down scene 1, take 3. The editor finds this listing in the bin. With a click of the mouse, the editor and the director are able to "call up" that shot. The two review the shot, then the editor clicks an "in" point where the director wishes to start using the shot and an "out" point at the end. With another click of the mouse, that piece of digital sound and image information is transferred instantaneously onto what is called the program timeline.

The same process is repeated shot after shot. If, at a certain point, the director or editor feels a special effect is needed, such as a dissolve, the editor simply highlights or selects that point on the timeline and clicks on a graphic icon providing access to an effects palette. After selecting the effect, the editor clicks on a series of options, such as the rate of the dissolve in

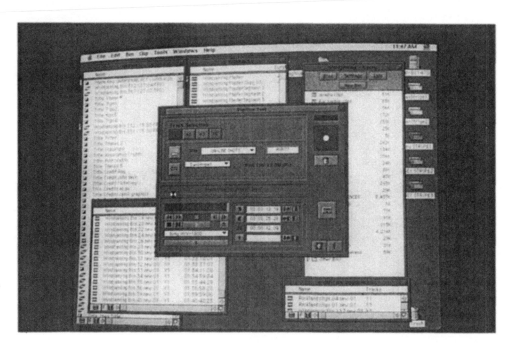

Figure 28.4 Avid in digitizing mode. Panel at center of screen is the digitizing tool. Bins and clips are visible behind it.

have several layers of video displayed or mixed at various points in the program. Sounds are layered in the same way. The director and editor may choose one layer for host narration, a second layer for music, and perhaps a third layer for sound effects. The sound signals can be manipulated individually on each layer since these layers can be mixed at any time during the edit session with a click of the mouse.

Titles and Artwork

When the initial program timeline is in place, the director may want to add instructional and perhaps identification titles at certain points. This process, too, is simple in the nonlinear editing world. The editor simply "clicks" into a mode that is similar to that of a standard word processor. He or she types in the titles, choosing colors, drop shadows, fonts, positions, and so on and instructs the system to superimpose or **"key"** them over the appropriate shots for the length of time desired. The editor also decides whether to have the titles fade onto the screen or perhaps move on and off using some sort of effect. As with the dissolve mentioned earlier, the rate and position are easily changed at any time.

Simple art and animation can also be created in nonlinear editing systems and inserted in much the same manner as titles. Or, if sophisticated sequences requiring an art and compositing system are needed,

Figure 28.5 Adobe Premier is also a widely used editing software in the corporate and prosumer world. With user friendly interfaces and controls, the system allows simple "drag and drop" techniques for most editing functions.

frames and its exact position. Having told the system to create this effect, it quickly does so and inserts a representation of it on the timeline between the two specified shots. The editor and director can then watch the transition and decide if it works as they intended. If so, they leave it and move on. If not, they simply remove the effect with a click of the mouse and either modify it or try something else—perhaps a wipe or page turn. This process continues until the entire program timeline is created.

The timeline is created in sound and image layers, as shown in Figure 28.6. For instance, the editor may

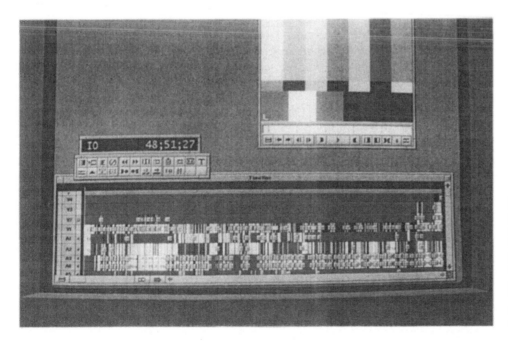

Figure 28.6 A very busy program timeline. Bars extending across the bottom of the screen represent the entire program. Various levels indicate the type of media being used and its position. For instance, V1, 2, 3, and 4 are video components. A1, 2, 3, 4, and 5 are audio channels or tracks.

those items are created outside of the editing system and imported as digital files.

Client and Producer Review

When the program is completed to the editor's and director's satisfaction, the producer and the client are brought in for viewings. If they like what they see, the program is considered completed. If they request changes, the process of adding or removing information can often be carried out immediately. In most cases any audio sweetening the program might need has also been handled by the nonlinear editing system, so the traditional, lengthy and complicated final processes of laydown and layback (which we will discuss shortly) are also eliminated.

Rendering Effects

Although special effects such as dissolves, wipes, titles and so on can usually be viewed virtually in real time, in most cases these effects still require rendering time before the program can be finalized and output. Once the program is approved, the rendering process often takes place at night. The editor will simply place the system into rendering mode when everyone leaves for the day and allow it to complete the process overnight for final viewing and mastering the next morning.

Output

After rendering, the entire program is output to high quality videotape. At this point, two masters are often created. The *edit master* with audio channels separated in case future editing is required, and a *duplication master* or *dupe master* with the audio channels mixed down for the distribution format, such as VHS.

As we have discussed, in the case of CD, DVD, or Internet productions, the edited program or individual segments may never be transferred to videotape. They may simply be used as digital elements along with artwork, titles and animated sequences.

THE FUTURE OF NONLINEAR EDITING

It appears that nonlinear editing and digital production will continue to evolve, simplifying and improving the corporate media process. Systems that allow video shot in the field or studio to be recorded in its original form as digital information onto hard drives instead of videotape are now in use. The same systems allow nonlinear editing in the field using the camera's VTR as the editing tool. In the case of news, material is now sometimes being shot in the field without videotape, edited in the camera and sent as digital information via satellite to the studio for broadcast.

Increasing size and speed of memory and processing systems have given way to nonlinear edit systems that capture and edit uncompressed video direct from high quality tape sources. When you consider the fact that uncompressed, high quality video footage requires roughly one gigabyte of memory per one minute of footage, and when you add to this the fact that many corporate programs are shot on ten 60-minute reels, you can begin to get a feel for how much memory these systems require.

Real-time logging and digitizing systems that allow a director to make "select" choices while in production are also in use. Selected segments are automatically listed and "logged" on a laptop computer for digitization or direct input to a nonlinear editing system. These systems eliminate the logging and digitizing step the director has typically gone through following production.

And laptop computers are now available which house complete professional editing systems. This means the producer, director or editor does not even require an edit suite! Programs may be edited in hotel rooms, on planes, perhaps even in the producer's back yard under an umbrella while sipping a cool soft drink.

SUMMARY

What does all this progress mean to the new producer or director? It means that digital, nonlinear technology has revolutionized the production and to a larger degree the postproduction processes. It also means these advancements will play an important part in the future of the media field—both in the corporate and the entertainment worlds. This revolution, of course, means that knowledge of these systems, including their advantages and disadvantages, is critical to working in the industry.

Producers and directors do not need to be accomplished nonlinear editors, but they must be highly conversant in the basics of nonlinear system operations. Only with this knowledge can a director make accurate decisions about how to shoot certain sequences and how artwork or other elements will eventually converge in the editing process to make up the final program.

The following URLs are just a few of the many Internet resources the student may want to take advantage of:

www.avid.com

www.apple.com/finalcutpro

www.media100.com

www.adobe.com

29 Audio Sweetening

Audio sweetening means enhancing a program's sound. When the enhancements required are simple, they can often be accomplished in the online or nonlinear edit session, working with the audio channels available on the existing videotape or timeline.

If complex enhancements are required, however, such as adding multiple sound effects or filtering and equalizing sounds, the audio mixing capabilities in the edit suite may not be the most economical or effective way to accomplish the work. Mixing sound in an online editing suite can become quite expensive, especially when the mixing requires more than a simple addition or change. When such requirements exist, by virtue of either volume or complexity, an audio sweetening session is normally arranged and takes place in a room dedicated strictly to sound.

THE SWEETENING ROOM— TRADITIONAL AUDIO SWEETENING

The traditional sweetening room (Figures 29.1 and 29.2) normally contains an audio mixing board with several individual audio inputs and a multichannel audio recorder. Also present are a television monitor and a VTR. Finally, the room contains various audio sources, such as turntables, cassette recorders, disk players, and assorted pieces of equipment used to modify the sounds in the program in different ways. This equipment might include filters, compressors, reverberation units, and so on.

THE LAYDOWN, MIX, AND LAYBACK

The first step in a traditional audio sweetening session is to *lay down* the existing audio channels onto audiotape. All channels from the online edited version of the program—the edit master—are laid down off the original videotape onto a multichannel audiotape that may have up to 16 or more separate channels. Time code is also recorded onto this tape on one of those channels. Simultaneously, a videotape copy of the entire program, with identical time code in the form of a window dub, is also made.

With both of these items in hand, the audio engineer and the director or producer now head for the sweetening room. There, the audiotape is placed on a special audio recorder (Figure 29.3), which, like the tape itself, has multichannel recording capability. The program dub is placed into a VTR to be viewed on a monitor.

Normally, the multiple-input mixing board is prepatched so that each of the 16 channels from the audio recorder is routed into a separate board input. This setup allows individual control over each channel with regard to volume, filtering, equalization, and so on.

Once any necessary patching of sources has been accomplished, audio reference levels are set to ensure that the volumes remain consistent on all channels. At this point, the room is set. Now, because the audiotape and window dub have identical time code and are *interlocked* (able to roll together in sync) to the same shuttle control, the audio recorder is "slaved" to follow the visual copy of the program. This function allows the

Figure 29.1 Typical audio sweetening room.

engineer to shuttle back and forth through the program, visually locating places for music, sound effects, and other changes that will perfectly match the pictures. These elements are recorded onto the audiotape on separate channels in a series of passes, and using the frame-accurate time code as a reference, each is placed in perfect sync with some visual part of the program on the window dub.

Once all the effects recording and manipulation has been done, the actual mix takes place. Using the mixing board skillfully, the engineer begins combining all the channels on which he or she has recorded,

Figure 29.2 Audio recordist mixes an audio track.

Figure 29.3 Sixteen-channel audiotape recorder loaded for use.

adjusting various volume, tone, and filtering characteristics along the way. In the end, the entire mix, consisting of perhaps 15 individual channels, is combined onto only a few channels—typically one for music and effects and one for dialogue and narration.

As a final step, this mixed audio recording is now re-recorded, or *laid back*, onto the original edit master of the program from which it was removed. Because this process was accomplished in sync with the time-coded window dub, all sounds remain in perfect sync with the pictures on the edit master.

NONLINEAR AUDIO SWEETENING

If the sweetening session is being carried out in a nonlinear fashion, just as with editing pictures, the electromechanical parts of the process are contained "virtually" in word processor-type cut-and-paste functions.

The sounds are stored on a computer hard drive as digital information files; therefore no audio recorder is needed. The equalization and manipulation controls are also computer based, so the need for a mixing board is eliminated as well. These two pieces of equipment are replaced by a computer screen with a layered timeline very similar to the program timeline.

Because digital information can be transferred online or stored on disk, the soundtracks can either be sent from the nonlinear editing system directly into the audio sweetening computer or saved on disk as a file and read in. Sounds imported from other sources such as CDs and tapes are encoded and input as digital files as well.

Once inside the sweetening computer system, just as with pictures, these sounds may be quickly placed in any spot required. A virtual mixing board appears on the screen and the engineer is able to adjust rows of virtual "sliders" and controls using a mouse. The effect is the same as the electromechanical process – the sounds are manipulated as needed to enhance the program. Once this task is done and the sweetening session is completed, the tracks can be mixed as desired and transferred back via disk or direct input to the program.

Once the program is output to tape, the result is a completed edit master videotape with a sweetened soundtrack, from which an edit master and dupe master are made. Duplicate copies can then be struck in any viewing format for use in the field. Or, if the viewing format is DVD or CD-ROM instead of videotape, a master disk is "burned," from which distribution disks are struck.

PART SIX SUMMARY

The areas of postproduction and delivery systems are undergoing the most radical changes in the field of corporate media. As we have noted, the advent of digital, nonlinear editing systems has revolutionized the editing process.

The cumbersome and often complicated ritual of sorting through stacks of videocassettes has become a simple process of selecting images and sounds with the click of a mouse. Even with these technical advancements, however, the craft of assembling pictures into a coherent whole remains—as it always has—the editor's traditional art form. That art form is, in many ways, kin to directing. The process takes keen visual, audio, and timing skills, and an ability to sense how the audience will "see" the work after it is assembled.

Editors relate to directors in somewhat the same way as writers. Writers hand a framework to directors, from which directors then create the elements of an audiovisual entity. Directors in turn hand those audiovisual elements to editors, who fit them together, thus creating a media whole. One difference in these relationships lies in the fact that directors remain much more involved than writers or editors in the preproduction and postproduction processes. Directors also work closely with people to achieve their vision, whereas writers and editors spend most of their time working in isolation.

If you believe you have an affinity for editing, the reading suggested below will offer you a more in-depth perspective on the process and its various facets.

Lyver, Des, *Basics of Video Sound*, Second Edition, Focal Press, Burlington, MA, 1999.

Watkinson, John, *Introduction to Digital Audio*, Second Edition, Focal Press, Burlington, MA, 2002.

30 Why Evaluate?

Many producers consider evaluations one of those tedious administrative chores that they must deal with, like it or not. Most times, they don't like it; and that's understandable, for two reasons. First, evaluations mean more work—paperwork, fieldwork, phone work, and mental work—on top of what is probably an already overloaded schedule. Second, evaluations typically are not considered part of the production process. They do not involve writing, producing, or directing—the things a producer tends to see as his or her purpose in corporate life. If the producer wants to eliminate the feelings of annoyance that may accompany an evaluation assignment, he or she simply needs to ask a simple question, why evaluate?

THE EVALUATION PAYBACK

Evaluating programs pays back two important elements to any corporate television department. The first is obvious—feedback on the effectiveness and audience acceptance of the work being distributed. The second may be less obvious, especially if the producer has not been in the corporate media business very long. Media managers or administrators might call it *documentation,* but a better word is probably *ammunition.* That's because favorable evaluations provide some form of proof from the people on the line that the programs being produced are worth *the company's expense.*

Let's consider these two ideas one at a time.

FEEDBACK AND THE NEED TO IMPROVE

The employees in any company are to the corporate media department what the general public is to the producers of broadcast programming—the single most important ingredient in their survival—the audience.

If the audience isn't happy, they're not going to watch. And if the audience doesn't watch . . . well, we all know what happens then. In the entertainment industry, the advertisers don't buy time, the show goes off the air, the production company goes out of business, and the employees are laid off. In the corporate world there may not be any advertisers, but the department will certainly "go out of business."

By evaluating what the audience likes and dislikes and acting on those evaluations, the corporate media department is able continually to improve its product and its image and thus remain valuable to the company employees.

This latter statement might seem to imply that once your department becomes very good at borrowing programs, the need to evaluate goes away. No such luck. I have yet to meet a corporate producer who feels he or she cannot improve on the quality of their product. This is because the nature of production work and the technology it is based on are constantly improving. Writers and directors are continually looking for a better theme or a more interesting shot. Directors of photography are continually striving for just the right contrast ratio and lighting mood; engineers are continually looking for higher resolution or an ingenious way to transmit or receive a video signal.

As we have discussed in this book, the equipment with which all of these people make a living is also constantly improving. Cameras, recorders, editing systems, and sound systems are getting smaller, lighter, more sophisticated, and capable of delivering better quality.

Achieving constant improvement then becomes a way of life for the corporate media department that wants to stay in business. And evaluations are the quickest and easiest way to find out exactly what needs improving.

But audience feedback, as important as it is, is still only half of the big picture.

DOCUMENTATION: AMMUNITION AGAINST EXECUTIVE ATTACK

Although corporate media departments are a vital part of the corporate world, they are also a very vulnerable part, for two simple reasons. First, executives who know little or nothing about what the department really does tend to see it as a luxury that can be pared down or even eliminated at budget-cutting time.

Second, it can be very hard to disprove what these executives believe because it is difficult to prove just how much help the media department is to the bottom line.

For example, how much money would an excellent program on how to use a new test meter actually save company X in a year if all 100 craft employees who will use the meter see the program? Is there a way to calculate how much more time it would have taken these employees to do their jobs or how much rework might have resulted if, instead of viewing a videotape, they had simply been given the user's manual and told to use the meter? Unfortunately, such benefits are difficult, if not impossible, to quantify. Provided the media department really is helping out, however, properly designed and executed evaluations can add up to an impressive showing.

On one occasion I had the pleasure of being involved with a program on which the payoff could not be disputed.

I was approached by the human resources and employee assistance departments in a large corporation to produce a video program on drug abuse. The plan was for both departments to contribute support and expertise. The result would be a single program, aimed at all employees, exploring the terrible results of drug and alcohol abuse.

Together we decided to do a program that would be a frank exploration of drug and alcohol addiction. The program would also send the message that the company would not tolerate drug use, but it was there to help any employee who showed that he or she really wanted to break an addiction and start a new life.

Over a two month period the program was made and distributed to all employees. Shortly after this, our department was undergoing a particularly rigorous period of grilling by the finance department. Finally, in an attempt to gather support from our clients, my boss came up with an idea. He asked that each producer get on the phone and see if any clients had information on ways our programs had paid for themselves in concrete terms.

One of my calls was to my client in the employee assistance department who had worked on the drug abuse program.

"Concrete terms?" she asked.

"Right," I responded. "Dollars and cents."

"I can't offer that kind of 'concrete,'" she said, "but how about this. Since our drug abuse program has been implemented, over twenty people have called our Employee Assistance Hotline as a result of watching the videotape."

I was ecstatic. Twenty people! How could anyone possibly measure the value of twenty lives? Yet how could anyone ignore the value of a program that had helped save them!

I told my boss immediately. First his jaw dropped, and then he went to the budget committee. They left us alone for the rest of that year.

With that background in mind, let's first consider a few evaluation basics and then discuss two of the many types of evaluations you might choose.

WHICH EVALUATION?

Evaluations can be formal or informal, written or verbal. They can be pre-or post-evaluations. They can be given in person, given on-line or sent in the company mail. But whatever format and medium you choose, a good evaluation should accomplish several things. It should do the following:

1. Tell the producer if the program accomplished the objectives originally established in the PNA.
2. Tell the producer if those objectives were the right ones to solve the problem on which the program was focused.

3. Tell the producer how acceptable the program was aesthetically to its audience.
4. Give the producer input on ways to improve those areas that fell short of the audience's expectations.
5. Be simple enough not to intimidate either the audience or the producer who is developing and administering it.

As an example, assume you produced a program on customer handling. The objectives in your PNA were as follows.

Having viewed the proposed program, the audience will be able to do the following:

1. List the following three proven customer-handling techniques:
   a. Express genuine concern for the customer's needs or problems.
   b. Make every effort to accomplish what the customer wants, or follow up as needed.
   c. Let the angry customer vent his or her frustrations without interruption.
2. State the main reason that proper customer-handling techniques are personally beneficial to them.
   a. Handling customers properly means less frustration and therefore greater job satisfaction.

A written evaluation of this program that would satisfy the five criteria just stated might look like Figure 30.1.

Obviously, this evaluation uses various formats—true or false, multiple-choice, and essay responses. All however, are focused on one objective: revealing whether the program was effective and, if not, what could have been done to make it effective.

The first three questions, for instance, are extremely important. Employee opinions on what is a good or bad use of their time, whether the characters were believable or not, and whether the program was helpful to them are key *general* indicators of its credibility.

The next two questions explore whether the program actually taught the audience what it was supposed to. Even if they indicated they had a great time watching the program, the following question remains: Did they *learn* anything?

Question 6 asks for a frank "will/will not" response. If the preceding answers were generally positive and this one is "will not," something is definitely wrong.

Question 7 explores another key issue—program length, and question 8 gives the audience a simple way to rate the program's overall look and feel—both crucial indicators.

Finally, the essay question allows the employee to express his or her feelings about the program in freeform. At the same time, it encourages employees to offer suggestions or make statements about anything you might have missed in designing the evaluation. And, of course, closing with a "Thank You" is essential.

ADMINISTERING THE EVALUATION

The administration of an evaluation can be handled in a number of ways. For example, 100 forms like the one just discussed can be mailed with a videotape to the person who will present the program. He would then pass out the evaluations after the audience had viewed the program, gather up the completed forms, and send them to you by company mail. E-mail is another simple way to accomplish the same result. The forms could be completed electronically and returned via e-mail, or printed out at the viewing location and sent back by mail or company dispatch.

Although these are certainly effective ways to accomplish an evaluation, time permitting, the best way is to go to the field and do it in person. There are two main reasons for this. It allows the producer not only to explore the impact of his or her work on paper, but also to see it in the live reactions of the people it was intended to help. This can be a very rewarding or, sometimes, a very embarrassing experience. Further, a field visit usually allows a little time for informal discussion in addition to the written evaluation. This, too, can be an important eye opener, as some employees may be better able to express themselves verbally than in writing.

WHAT NEXT?

Once an evaluation is completed, the producer has many options, but in one way or another most of them boil down to this. The producer should tally the results and look for the trends that seem to indicate either very good or very bad *common opinions* from a substantial number of viewers. Then the producer should take action and change something in the production process to improve things.

Program Evaluation

"Professional Customer Handling: How it's Done"

In order to evaluate the program you've just seen, we would like your frank, anonymous opinions and thoughtful answers to the following questions.

	TRUE	FALSE

1. In general, watching this program was a
   good use of my time. _____   _____

2. The characters in this program, or the program
   host, were believable. _____   _____

3. The customer handling techniques taught in
   this program will help me do a better job. _____   _____

4. According to this program, three techniques I can use to deal effectively with
   customers are:

a. _____

b. _____

c. _____

5. Handling customers in a professional manner can benefit me by taking some of the
   _____ out of my job.

6. I **WILL/WILL NOT** use the techniques shown in this program   (circle one).

(If you circled **"NO"** could you tell us why? _____

_____

7. The program was: **The Right Length**   **Too Long**   **Too Short** (circle one)

8. On a scale of 1 to 10, how **professional** did the program look and sound?_____

9. What could we have done to improve this program? (Please use the reverse side if you'd like to share additional suggestions or ideas with us.) We are always anxious to hear from the employees who view our programs, and we are always looking for ways to do a better job.

_____

_____

_____

_____

_____

THANK YOU!

Figure 30.1 A simple written evaluation using the following types of questions: true or false, multiple choice, fill in the blanks, and essay.

In addition the results should be documented as ammunition for that day in the future when a key executive wants to know if the "video people" are really doing the company any good.

INDICES EVALUATIONS

The evaluation just outlined is only one of many types. Another type worth exploring is what is called an *indices evaluation*. An indices evaluation looks not so much at what the audience felt or learned from the tape but, rather, at what the program actually did to the bottom line.

An indices evaluation might be applicable to the back injury problem discussed in Chapter 6. You may recall that in that case, the client said the company had lost $90,000 as a result of back injuries in the preceding year. Obviously, then, this safety representative is documenting the number of back injuries occurring and their cost. If this is the case, one of the objectives for that videotape might have read as follows:

Provided this program is properly administered to all employees, a 20% savings in back injury expenses will be realized by the company during the year following its distribution.

This would be evaluated simply by looking at the records or *indices* kept by the safety department for the following year, documenting the results, and comparing them with that $90,000 figure from the previous year.

CONSIDERATIONS

There are three considerations to keep in mind when doing this type of evaluation. First, since the results tend to be longer-term than audience evaluations, they can require more persistent follow-up after the program is long out of sight and out of mind. Second, indices evaluations are riskier because there is no gray area. The program either does or does not affect the bottom line, and the results are there in black and white for everyone to see. Finally, such evaluations tend to be extremely credible to those executives who seem oblivious to everything but the bottom line.

For this last reason alone, if a producer is confident that his or her work is really making a difference, it is well worth the time and effort to do this type of evaluation.

A FEW FINAL NOTES ON EVALUATIONS

A sampling of only about 1% or 2% of your entire audience will usually give you an accurate evaluation, provided you evaluate a random cross-section. If 1,000 company employees will see a program, and you manage to gather 20 of them and do an evaluation, your responses should generally reflect the reactions of all 1,000.

In the final analysis, evaluations should be considered valuable departmental marketing tools. Marketers use evaluations and surveys to explore audience feelings and target specific likes and dislikes. They rely heavily on what those evaluations and surveys reveal because history has proven them to be very effective. The corporate producer should think about evaluations in this way.

With all this in mind, then, we can ask once more: Why evaluate? And now we have a valid answer: Because evaluations are crucial to the growth and survival of any corporate video department.

31

The Future of Corporate Media

As technology advances, the uses for corporate media advance as well. What began more than 50 years ago as the training films we highlighted in the first chapter of this book have evolved into a much more sophisticated and effective means of communicating and training. Where that evolution will lead us in future years—some of which we are experiencing as you read these words— is certainly speculation, but general directions seem imminent.

NETWORK MEDIA DELIVERY

Delivery systems for our current day media programs have progressed from large cumbersome film projectors to VCRs and compact disc players. The viewing apparatus has likewise gone from the large, silver screens on three-legged stands to television monitors and more recently to computer screens.

The next step in the process (and indeed this is happening on a limited scale) would seem to be media programs delivered via networks such as the Internet, the Web, private Intranets, and local area networks (LANs). With the large amounts of digital information contained in media programs becoming continually easier to store, and with the speed of network delivery systems increasing on what seems like a weekly basis, media programs *on demand* will likely become commonplace. Employees will simply be able to choose their media programs from a menu and have that programming "stream" to their personal computer or be stored for offline use.

INTERACTIVITY

A high degree of interactivity in these programs will also be commonplace. The typical employee will be able to branch through material in a nonlinear fashion, take virtual tests, and operate training simulators that will automatically send the results of their efforts to databases for scoring, archiving, and use by various departments within the corporation.

GOING GLOBAL—AND WIRELESS!

With the advent of low earth orbit (LEO) satellite networks, communication on a global basis is becoming much less dependent on wire-line connections. Cell phones and personal palm units, which a decade ago were considered a novelty, are as commonplace today as a previous novelty—the pocket calculator. And these units are becoming increasingly capable of delivering much more than simply voice signals—images and data are now commonplace.

The results? An ability to acquire and deliver interactive media, including full-motion images in broadcast-quality resolution along with CD-quality sound, at any time of the day or night virtually anywhere on the globe—or in the air flying over it. This means to a cell phone screen or a small hand-held palm unit.

How will this type of environment affect corporate media producers? Again, we can only guess, but it would seem that interactivity will be one byword for the future. That likelihood means that producers should continue to develop skills involved in both designing and producing these types of programs.

DISTANCE LEARNING

Satellite technology will also make distance learning more prevalent, but instead of meeting in classrooms with TV monitors, cameras, and signaling devices, employees will surely be able to receive these programs in the comfort and privacy of their homes, sitting at their computers.

Modern PCs are coming equipped with signaling and interacting devices, as well as microphones, speakers, and miniature cameras. This will allow for personal teleconferencing and from an educational perspective, it will allow distant instructors to see their students, talk with them, and interact as if they were seated across from each other. As technology continues to shrink computer products and make them more affordable, who's to say that future employees might not keep their "complete instructional media packages" in briefcases and breast pockets!

This development should result in a continuing decrease in classroom training, reduced training costs, and thus expanded availability for training to more employees than at anytime in the past.

SALES AND INFORMATION PROGRAMMING ON THE NETS

As we know, corporate media programs encompass far more than training. Programs are produced to inform both employees and customers, and sales and marketing programs are used today by account executives in visits to customers and clients. If a software company has new products it hopes to sell to corporate clients, it is common to have an account executive visit the customer with a media presentation viewable in the customer's office.

In the days before digital technology, these presentations most often consisted of brochures, simple slide shows, and videotapes that could be placed in the customer's VCR and played as the client and sales executive discussed them.

These days, sales programs on CD-ROMs presented on laptop computers are commonplace. These in turn often launch to the Internet where full-motion sales and demonstration programs can stream directly to the customer's PC online. If the customer takes an interest in a particular product, he or she can then navigate further into that area and obtain price quotes, technical specifications, delivery times, and of course, ordering information.

A CHALLENGING TOMORROW

In short, the future prospects for corporate media and media in general appear exciting and challenging. The key words appear to be *interactivity, networks, wireless,* and *streaming media.* All of which is to say, if you are just beginning your media production career, it would certainly be wise to include these three critical words in your career goals and objectives.

Glossary

A/C (cable) A/C stands for *alternating current* and refers to the standard electricity required to power the lights, recorder, camera, and so on. When used in production, A/C also refers to the cables into which the lights and other equipment are plugged.

"Action" The director's cue to crew and actors that the scene should begin.

Alternate An alternate version, usually of a master scene, to provide the director with a different perspective on the action, dialogue, or both.

Ambience The background noise present at any location. Room ambience is also called room *tone*. Ambience on a street corner would include traffic sounds such as horns honking and perhaps pedestrian chatter.

American Federation of Television and Radio Artists (AFTRA) One of two primary unions to which many actors belong. AFTRA members work in television and radio, not the feature film industry. (See also *Screen Actors Guild–SAG*.)

Angle on A camera term noting that the angle should be on a person or thing but not specifying a focal length, such as medium close-up or close-up.

Apple box A multipurpose, hollow wooden cube. Used in production as stops, wedges, platforms, etc. Various sizes are called *full apple, half apple,* and *quarter apple*.

Assistant director (AD) Also called *associate director*. The initials are much more commonly used than the full name. This person is the director's closest assistant and helps him or her accomplish any and all details, which gives the director the freedom to work on his or her primary responsibilities.

Audio The sound portion of a script–narration, dialogue, sound effects, and music. In the column format, the sound or audio column is usually written on the right side of the page. In the screenplay format, it appears both in the scene descriptions and in the dialogue or narration column down the center of the page. The term *audio* also refers to the sound portion of a tape or film recording.

Audio sweetening The process by which the final audio enhancement and mix-down is done on a program. The sweetened audiotrack is laid back onto the edit master of the program as a final step in the postproduction process. Also known as *post audio*.

Audiovisual (AV) Any type of sound (audio) and picture (visual) presentation. AV is usually used to describe a slide or overhead presentation, rather than a film or videotape production.

Audition An actor's tryout for a part. Usually set up by the assistant director and attended by the director and producer and, in some cases, by the client as well.

b.g. A script abbreviation for *background*.

Backlight A light directed at an actor from behind, which highlights his or her head and shoulders and makes the actor stand out from the background. Also called *rim light*.

Barn doors The flat black metal flaps or cutters that are attached to the front of many production lights. Barn doors allow the light to be cut off from certain areas of a set or scene.

Bars and tone A video and audio reference used to assure that chroma (color), luminance (light intensity), and audio (sound) are kept consistent between pieces of production equipment and recorded segments of tape. Appears as a series of different colored vertical bars spanning the color range. Tone is a high-pitched, 1,000-cycle tone.

Big shot   A very wide, establishing shot.

Blocking   Actors' movements on the set in relation to the camera. Blocking should appear motivated to look natural.

Boom   An extendable pole on which a microphone is attached. The boomed microphone is held in close relation to actors during a shot. It wires back to the audio mixer and, ultimately, the videotape recorder. Also called a *fish pole*.

Breakdown (script)   An itemization of all script elements, which enables an assistant director or production assistant to begin lining up each of those elements for the production.

"Buy"   A director's term of acceptance for a shot. The *buy take* is the best of the takes recorded and most likely the one the editor will use in the show. It is noted in the master script with a circle around the take number. Also called the *circled take*.

CD-ROM (Compact Disk–Read Only Memory)   A plastic disk identical to an audio CD but containing sound, visuals, and text program information. Used as a delivery medium for corporate programs, videogames, and educational programs. Because CD-ROMs can hold large amounts of randomly accessible information (about 700 megabytes), they are often used as a medium for interactive programs and feature film rentals.

C stand   A versatile, three-legged metal stand used in production for a variety of purposes, but primarily to hold up flags, silks, and nets.

Chroma   An engineering term meaning *color*.

Chroma key   A process by which a picture element is combined with another picture. Chroma keying is usually accomplished by shooting one element, such as a person, in front of a blue background in a studio. A video switcher can then replace the color blue behind the person with a totally different picture source, such as a shot of a downtown city street. Also called a *key*.

Circled takes   The director's buys, which the assistant director or script supervisor circles in the master script notes. These notations later let the editor know which shots the director preferred.

Character acting   An acting discipline in which the actor bases the performance on the personality make-up of a character. The immediate and distant personal history of the character often comes into play. For instance, an actor playing a depressed executive might want to know about the character's childhood, education, job history, and parents to create role credibility.

Client   The person requesting, approving, and often paying for the program. As such, the client is one of the key individuals in the production process.

Close-up (CU)   A shot of an actor or item that fills the majority of the screen. In a close-up of a female character, for instance, we would see her entire face and the upper part of her shoulders. In a close-up of a glass, we would see the entire glass and a small area of the surrounding surface.

Code   A term referring to SMPTE time code, the digital signals that allow very precise editorial control. Code may also refer to computer software programming. (See also *Society of Motion Picture and Television Engineers*.)

Column format   A script format in which the sound and picture elements are separated into two columns on the page. Usually, the picture column is on the left and the sound column is on the right. Often used by television directors because of its ease of use in multicamera production.

Concept   The basic premise on which the script, or segments of it, will be based. Concepts link content and design with visualization, structure, and storyline. Concepts are often *thematic* or *analogous*.

Content expert   A person who is an authority or expert on the subject about which the director is shooting. Also called a *subject matter expert (SME)* or a *technical adviser*.

Controller   Although there are various types of controllers, the term is often used to mean the piece of equipment used in an edit bay to interface the two videotape machines. Allows the editor control over the record, playback, and shuttle functions. In some cases, also provides the automatic list management function.

Control track   A system of videotape editing in which continual pulses are recorded on the tape by the camera and later used to isolate specific segments for transfer. Control track offers less flexibility than SMPTE time code and is thus less desirable.

Corporate culture   The basic philosophy or standards system that a large company or corporation uses as a framework for its day-to-day business activities. For instance, a corporate culture may be conservative, in which case all management employees might be required to wear certain kinds of business attire.

Corporate politics Personal preferences and maneuvers that affect what should be strictly business decisions. For instance, a finance manager might not like a peer in the accounting department; therefore, he rejects a valid proposal, which could be production-related.

Corporate television Television productions produced for an in-house audience of company employees. The term "television" commonly refers to live broadcasts such direct broadcast satellite (DBS) programs.

Corporate video Video productions designed for an in-house audience of company employees. The term "video" commonly refers to programs recorded on videotape. Also called *industrials*.

Corporate media Any of several communication methods used to train, motivate, or inform employees. Can include video, film, CD-ROM, DVD, distance learning, and in some cases, print material such as brochures.

Coverage A term referring to the amount and type of footage shot to allow a scene to be properly edited. Standard coverage typically consists of a wide shot of all action, medium shots of most portions of the same action, close-ups of parts of the action that need emphasis, and extreme close-ups or inserts of detailed action, such as a number being dialed on a telephone or a specific key being struck on a computer.

Crab A sideways dolly movement, usually perpendicular to the original direction of travel.

Crane A platform on a large boom on which the camera, the cameraperson, and an assistant (or the director) can be seated. Used to get high-angle shots during which the camera is raised up or lowered down.

Cut An instantaneous picture change used as a transition between scenes. Also used within scenes to facilitate viewing the action from different angles.

DV Acronym used to connate *digital video* cameras and recording and editing formats.

DVD (digital video disk) A CD containing large amounts of space for audio and visual media. Virtually the same as CD-ROM, but with much greater storage capacity.

DVE See *digital video effects*.

Dialogue Conversation spoken between at least two actors in a role-play situation.

Digital video Video signals recorded or converted from analog or wave frequency state to bits of digital information characterized by ones and zeros. Once made digital, video signals become much easier to manipulate, utilize, and store.

Digital video effects (DVE) Video effects used in editing that are created by digital-effects generators. Effects include pictures that shrink away off the screen, are posterized to look like paintings, break up on the screen, and many others.

Director The person responsible to the producer to analyze and execute the written script into film, audio, digital, or video footage appropriate for editing into a completed program. "Director" may also refer to Macromedia Director interactive software.

Director of photography (DP) The person in charge of ensuring that all pictures recorded for the program are properly lit, exposed, and photographed. The director of photography assists the director in recording action to create the type of mood and pace required. In videotape production, also called the *lighting director* or *director of videography*.

Dissolve A transitional effect in which one picture fades out as another fades in. Most often used to suggest a passage of time or a major location change. Also used to "soften" jarring or abrupt cuts.

Dolly A forward or backward movement of the camera during a shot. This is opposed to a *truck*, which is a left or right sideways camera motion. The terms *truck* and *dolly* are, however, often used synonymously. Dolly also refers to the piece of equipment used to execute the traveling motion.

Dub Jargon term meaning a duplicate of a program, shot, scene, etc.

Dulling spray An aerosol spray that is applied to shiny items seen in a video picture. Cuts down on glare and thus reduces hot spots.

Dupe master In videotape, equivalent to an internegative in film—a high-quality source (copy of the program) from which distribution copies can be made.

Edit Can refer to the modification of a piece of writing, such as a script or treatment. In videotape, *cut* also refers to the points at which different shots are placed *(edited)* together to create a completed program. Also refers to the *type* of edit—a dissolve, a cut, a wipe, etc.

Edit master The final edited version of the program, which results from the online editing session. The edit master is created from the original footage and first-generation duplicates as much as possible for maximum sound and picture quality. Differs from a dupe master in that the audio tracks typically remain separated to allow for possible future editing.

Editor   The person responsible for assembling an offline or online copy of the program from the original footage or duplicates.

Edit decisions list (EDL)   A list of time code numbers that reflect the exact edit points chosen by the offline editor.

Engineer in charge (EIC)   The head engineer on a studio or location shoot. Typically, the EIC is responsible for the operation of all electronic equipment. Usually works closely with the director of photography to establish proper video levels. Also works with the sound engineer to assure proper audio levels or may double as the sound engineer or technical director.

Entrance   An actor's cue to move on stage or into the camera's frame.

Establishing shot   Usually the first wide shot seen of a particular environment. Sometimes written this way: WIDE SHOT–TO ESTABLISH.

Executive producer   Typically, the person providing or arranging for the financing needed to produce the program. In corporate media, usually the department head or manager for whom the producer works. Oversees the quality and cost-effectiveness of the producer's work and is directly accountable for all or part of the department's budget.

Exit   An actor's cue to leave the stage or camera's frame.

EXT.   Abbreviation for *exterior*. Used in scene headings.

Extreme close-up (ECU)   An extremely close camera focal length. In an extreme close-up of a face, we would see only a part of the entire face. The lips or eyes, for instance, might fill the entire screen.

FADE IN/FADE OUT   Editing terms used to begin and end a script or note a major transition. The word *fade* means that the picture fades in from black or some other color or fades out to that color.

False start   Term used in production when something goes wrong in a scene just after it has begun. When the director or assistant director calls out "false start," this indicates that a new slate and scene number are not needed. Some signal is usually made for the editor, however, such as the cameraperson waving his or her hand in front of the lens for a moment to indicate that a new start will follow.

f.g.   A script abbreviation for *foreground*.

Flag   A black-cloth, wire-rimmed, fanlike object used to shade light from an object or actor.

Flash   An interactive authoring program used to develop motion sequence for use on CD ROM, DVD, or Internet applications.

Flat fee   A payment arrangement in which the director is offered a preset amount of money for a project, regardless of the time required to prepare and shoot it.

Fill light   Refers to the use of, or need for, a fill light to dim or fill in the shadows created by the key light.

Focus puller   A camera assistant who changes focus on the fly as the camera moves during recording.

Freeze frame   A picture that is stopped at some key spot, often for dramatic effect, such as the freeze frame of an athlete crossing the finish line in a race. Also used to create a still image background panel for superimposed titles.

Gaffer   An electrician; first assistant to the videographer or director photography (DP).

Gaffer's tape   Very strong tape; usually three inches wide and gray in color. Used in production for a variety of purposes.

Gels   Thin pieces of colored film placed over light sources. Change the color of the light being emitted and, in some cases, correct it to a specific color temperature.

GIF Image   GIF stands for *graphic interchange format*. GIFs are the most common image format used on the Internet.

Grip   The person whose primary job is to load and unload or move equipment and cables. A grip usually works under the gaffer, helping to build and strike lighting and camera setups.

Handheld   Footage shot with the camera placed on the cameraperson's shoulder or in his or her hands instead of on a tripod or dolly. News crews often shoot handheld in the interest of time. Production crews shoot handheld for effect, to facilitate camera movement, or when shooting in tight quarters.

High angle   A camera angle shot from above, looking down on the action.

HMI   An acronym referring to a *halogen metal iodide* light, a production light that creates bluish light and is used to mix with or "create" sunlight or moonlight.

Host   An on-camera spokesperson; the host talks directly to the audience (camera).

Insert   Usually a close-up or extreme close-up of an object that is inserted into the main action. For example, a character may begin dialing the telephone in a wide shot. An insert of her fingers turning the dial is cut in so we are able to recognize the number she is calling. When the dialing is completed and the character begins to talk, we return to the wide shot or some other angle.

Instructional design A method of custom designing instructional material based on such criteria as audience factors, objectives, the problem to be solved, and program utilization. Design documents, such as a program needs analysis (PNA), are sometimes given to the director with the script at the outset of a project.

INT. Abbreviation for *interior.* Used in scene headings.

Interactive Any form of media that involves the viewer as an active participant. In its simplest form, this might be a workbook that must be read in conjunction with a videotape presentation. Videogames and simulators are examples of interactivity in its most complex form.

Internet A worldwide network of computer servers, which is accessed and "navigated" via telephone lines by individual computer users.

Jib Arm An arm on a fulcrum with counterweights on one end and the camera on the other. Jib arms allow the camera to be hoisted ten to fifteen feet into the air for spectacular shots. It can also be brought down in very smooth moves as the scene is being recorded.

JPEG JPEG stands for "Joint Photographic Experts Group." This is the name of the committee that wrote the standard. JPEG is designed for compressing either full-color or gray-scale images of natural scenes. It works very well on photographs and naturalistic art. JPEG handles only still images, but there is a another standard called MPEG for compressing motion pictures.

Key Short for *chromakey.* Used to denote the combining of pictures or a picture and title. For example: KEY IN LOGO OVER SHOT or KEY TITLES. Sometimes used synonymously with *super,* meaning *superimpose.*

Key light The main source of light used to illuminate a scene. Usually placed close to the camera and shines down on the actor(s) at approximately a 45-degree angle.

Lavalier Usually a small, condenser-type microphone often placed on a tie clip or easily camouflaged under a collar or lapel.

Limbo A seamless, usually featureless background, often of one color. Used as a generic set environment. A spokesperson or a vignette using role-play actors might be set in limbo. This is usually done for a dramatic effect or because it is cheaper than building a set.

"the Line" An imaginary line that runs through any person or object in motion on the screen. The line establishes screen direction, meaning the logical direction of motion or attention to which a viewer becomes oriented. If the line is crossed when shooting, the screen direction of the person or object changes, often disorienting the viewer. Also called *the stage line* or *the screen direction line.*

Location Any place other than in the studio where a film or videotape shoot is taking place.

Low angle A camera angle shot from below, looking up at the action.

Luminance An engineering term meaning light intensity.

Macromedia Director An authoring program used to develop interactive multimedia programs used on CR-ROM, DVD, or Internet applications.

Master script The script brought to the field on which the production notes are taken during the shoot. Later, it is used by the editor to locate the circled takes or "buys" of each shot. It is often filed and retained when the program is completed.

Master shot A complete segment of action shot uncut in one pass. Often, a master shot is a wide focal length containing all actors and showing all action.

Medium close up (MCU) A camera focal length that frames an individual's face, starting at the chest.

Medium shot (MS) A camera focal length in which the majority of a person's body can be seen. A medium shot is framed roughly from the thighs up. A *medium two shot* would include two people in about the same focal length.

Method acting A school of acting that relies on detailed sensory memories recalled from an actual past experience and applied to a scene being played in the present. For instance, an actor might recall the smells, temperature, touches, voices, sounds, and textures present in her dentist's office to accurately portray a character who is anxious about having a tooth pulled.

Mini DV A videotape recording format that has helped revolutionized the corporate, news and documentary production processes. A Mini-DV videocassette is similar in size to an audio cassette. Because the format is so small, it is considerably cheaper than formats such as Betacam SP and Digital Beta, but it still offers high quality sound and image reproduction. Mini DV cameras and associated equipment are also much less expensive than their Beta counterparts.

Mixer *Sound mixer* refers to the person responsible for the point of input of all sound sources. He or she *mixes* the sound to the proper levels as it is being recorded or *sweetened*. A *mixer* is also the piece of equipment used by the sound mixer—a point of termination for all sound sources, with controls to change the volume of individual sources as needed for a smooth mix.

Monitor A high-quality version of a television without the tuner for channel selection. A monitor has controls allowing for precise picture tuning and clarity from sources such as cameras. It also has video and audio inputs compatible with production cabling and hardware.

Montage A series of images, often fast paced and cut to music, used to suggest a compression of time. Also used for dramatic effect, many times in the openings of programs.

MPEG MPEG was developed by the "Moving Picture Experts Group". This committee also developed the standards known as MPEG-1 and MPEG-2. These are media compressions standards which made interactive video on CD-ROM, DVD, and Digital Television possible.

Multicamera A form of production in which multiple cameras are switched on the fly to edit the scene as it plays out. News shows and sports events are examples of live multicamera productions. Soap operas are also shot multicamera style, but they are recorded on videotape.

Multimedia Various forms of media, such as video, animation, and sounds used together in program presentation, usually incorporating the use of computers to display or manipulate.

MUSIC UP/MUSIC UNDER/MUSIC OUT Script notations. *Music up* denotes a music increase in volume; *music under*, a decrease to allow other sounds more prominence; and *music out*, a complete fade out.

Narration Words spoken by a narrator or host. Narration is spoken directly to the audience (camera).

Narrator An off-camera spokesperson. A host is an on-camera version of a narrator.

Net A wire-rimmed, fanlike object with material similar to nylon stockings stretched taut across it. Used to shade an actor or object.

OC or OS Abbreviations for *off camera* or *off scene*, meaning generally the same thing as voiceover (VO)—a voice is heard while the speaker is not seen. Usually used in the dialogue or narration heading.

Offline edit The first editing session, in which a director's work is assembled into a complete program. Also called the *rough cut*. Low-quality workprints of the original footage are used to allow decision making involving timing, pace, and the inclusion or deletion of certain shots. The director is usually involved in the offline edit, and the client and producer typically approve and have input on it before the final, online edit is performed.

Online edit The final edit, in which music, effects, titles, the final "tightening," and polish are applied. The online edit is based primarily on prior decisions made in the offline edit. Also called the *fine cut*.

Original footage The footage brought back from the field or studio. Original footage has the highest quality picture and sound. Quality begins to deteriorate with each generation of duplicates.

Over the shoulder (OTS) A camera angle looking over one person's shoulder at another. "OTS–Jill" would mean we are looking at Jill over someone else's shoulder.

Pan A horizontal rotation of the camera on its head. Short for *panorama*.

Ped up or ped down A rising or lowering of the camera on its head. Short for *pedestal*.

POV A script abbreviation for *point of view*.

"Prep" Jargon for *preparation* or *preproduction*—the period given to the director to prepare for the shoot. Also refers to the work that goes on during preproduction.

Producer The person responsible and accountable for all aspects of a film, video, digital, or audio production—from script development through shooting and editing.

Production assistant (PA) A person usually brought in by the assistant director or producer to handle duties such as phone calls, paperwork, or deliveries in preproduction or production.

Program needs analysis (PNA) A short analysis of certain basic information such as the client's needs, audience knowledge, and so on. The PNA is usually written by the producer and is used to determine whether a videotape is the proper tool for the job and, if so, what basic design the program should take.

Rack focus A drastic change of focus to create emphasis or change the viewer's perspective. For example, the camera might rack focus from a street sign in the foreground to a man walking in the distance.

Reflector A shiny reflective surface (usually hard and board-like) used to bounce sunlight onto a subject as a lighting source.

Registration An engineering term meaning that the red, blue, and green images produced by a video camera are in proper alignment—perfectly superimposed over each other.

Reveal A zoom, pan, or other camera move that reveals something in the frame the viewer had not previously been aware of. For example: ZOOM OUT TO REVEAL John entering the office.

Reverse angle A view that is 180 degrees from the preceding shot. For example, if we are looking over the shoulder of a driver moving down the street in a car, a reverse angle would be the view looking directly backward out the rear window.

Rewrite A major overhaul of an existing script.

Role play A scene designed to dramatize a situation. Can be serious or humorous.

"Roll tape" A director's cue to the technical director or camera operator. When a director says "roll tape," it signals the crew that he or she is satisfied that the scene is ready to be recorded.

Rough cut See *offline edit.*

Screen Actor's Guild (SAG) One of two primary unions to which many actors belong. SAG is the primary union for performers in the feature film industry. (See also *AFTRA.*)

Screenplay format A script format in which the scene descriptions are written across the entire page and the sound is written in a column down the center. The standard "Hollywood" format. Most often used for single-camera shooting.

Screen right/screen left The position of something in the scene as viewed from the camera's perspective. The direction is the opposite from anyone on the set who is looking back at the camera. An actor's right, when looking at the camera, is screen left.

Scrim A wire mesh insert, usually circular, that is placed into a lighting instrument to diffuse or lower its level of intensity. Scrims are numbered by density to produce a predictable effect on the camera's f-stop settings.

Script The framework for an audiovisual production. The script is a precisely written, visual description of all program elements that is used by the director and producer to create a program.

Setup The setup for a shot consists of camera placement, all lights, flags, and so on. Also used to mean camera setups only. The term *setup* also refers to the setup of certain pieces of production equipment, such as waveform monitors and vectorscopes, which ensure proper and consistent color and light intensity levels between different recorded or broadcasted segments.

Shooting schedule The itemized shot-by-shot schedule outlining the entire production. Includes all scene numbers, locations, time required to get each shot, and any important notes regarding a particular shot. Usually written by the director and approved by the producer.

Shooting script The final draft, with all changes made. A production crew takes the shooting script to the field.

Shotgun A long, slender microphone usually used on the end of a boom. Its pickup pattern allows it to record sounds in a conelike area directly in front of it, but it picks up very little sound behind it.

Shot list The list of all shots required to cover the material in the script. Written by the director.

Silk Sheet-like material that is stretched over a square or rectangular frame and mounted over a scene or actor. Used to diffuse harsh shadows, often from sunlight.

Single One person only seen in a medium close-up or medium shot.

Single camera A form of production in which a single camera is moved to different positions and the scene, or parts of it, is recorded several times from various perspectives. This "coverage" is then edited together later.

Slate A small board placed in front of the camera at the "head" of each scene. The slate gives that scene its own informational "signature." This allows the editor to later choose the proper scenes for inclusion in editing. The slate usually contains the name of the project, a project number, the date, the video or film reel, the scene number, the take number, and the director's and camera operator's names.

Society of Motion Picture and Television Engineers (SMPTE) The association that standardized SPMTE time code. (See also *code.*)

SOT Abbreviation for *sound on tape.* Used to indicate the fact that sound is coming from some prerecorded tape source, rather than live—as it might be spoken by an actor or narrator.

Sound effect Notation written into a script to call for a sound effect. Also called or written in as *SFX.*

"Speed" A verbal signal to the director from the technical director or camera operator to indicate that recording has begun and the "action" cue can be given.

Sting A short piece of music used to punctuate a transition or to heighten a dramatic moment.

Stock footage Footage pulled from a library or archive to be included in a program.

Story outline Another term for *treatment*. A scene-by-scene description of the story, written in simple narrative terms.

Streaming Media With the growing popularity of the Internet as a business and entertainment media distribution vehicle, digital engineers realized that a means of sending audio and video over the Internet was a logical advancement. Before streaming media, however, if one wanted to view a video presentation sourced from the Internet, he or she had to first download the entire presentation onto a hard drive. This was often a problem because motion picture information requires a very large amount of storage space. Using MPEG compression standards, streaming media allows the video and audio signals to stream *through* a media player (thus also be viewed) without being saved.

Strike Jargon term meaning to dismantle a setup or an entire set once production is complete at that location.

Subject matter expert (SME) Another term for *content expert*. Often acts as a technical advisor on the script or during production

Super Short for *superimposition*. Refers to something superimposed over a picture. For example: SUPER OPENING TITLES.

Switcher An electronic interface device capable of switching video sources instantaneously as cuts or with the use of various special effects such as wipes, dissolves, and fades. Used primarily in studio production and online editing.

Talent Jargon for *actors*.

Tape op Short for *videotape operator*. A tape op is normally used in editing and studio productions that require a remote videotape machine to be rolled at a specific time. This source is then taken by the technical director at the switcher and is thus routed to the production recorder or outgoing broadcast circuit.

Technical adviser A subject matter expert who is usually present on the set.

Technical director (TD) The technician responsible for the electronic aspects of a studio recording. The TD "switches" or operates the production switcher, which controls camera signals that are recorded or broadcast. The TD also controls video levels, sets up, and monitors all studio equipment associated with the shoot.

Teleprompter A device that is mounted on the front of a camera and projects the actor's lines on a translucent pane of glass positioned in front of the camera's lens. Allows the actor to look directly at the camera and read the lines.

Tilt up/tilt down A vertical rotation of the camera on its head.

Time base corrector (TBC) A device used to control and enhance the stability of a video picture.

Time code generator An electronic device that generates time code for recording on video and sometimes audiotape.

Treatment A scene-by-scene narrative describing the story and visual aspects of a script that often is yet to be written. Used as a prescript approval step to be sure clients and producers like the concept the writer has envisioned.

Truck A movement of the camera in a sideways motion—right or left. This is opposed to a *dolly*, which is a movement forward or backward. *Dolly* is often used interchangeably with truck.

Tungsten–halogen A production light that creates an orange-colored light used to mix with or "create" interior room light.

Two shot A shot of two actors, positioned close together, usually in conversation.

Upstage/downstage Terms referring to areas in relation to the camera. *Upstage* is the area in the background, farthest from the camera. *Downstage* is in the foreground, closest to the camera.

Vectorscope An electronic scope used to align precisely and ensure consistency and accuracy of the colors in a video picture.

Video The picture column in a two-column script format. Also refers to the video portions of recorded programs and is used loosely to refer to complete programs and the entire field.

Vignette See *role play*.

Voiceover (VO) Portions of narration or dialogue heard while the viewer is seeing something other than the person speaking. Means a voice heard "over" pictures.

Waveform monitor An electronic scope used to measure and adjust various elements of a video signal. In production, the waveform is used primarily to ensure consistency of the luminance (light intensity) of a video picture.

Wide shot (WS) A camera focal length encompassing the entire scene or a large part of it. Often used to establish a room or environment in which the scene is taking place.

Wipe A transitional effect in which one picture is wiped off the screen by another. Can take place horizontally, vertically, or in circular or rectangular patterns.

World Wide Web The commercialized name for the Internet. Characterized by personal and commercial "home pages" or "Web" pages. Pages are simply digital information media creations posted on computer servers worldwide. Most have hypertext links that allow "visitors" to "navigate" or move to different "virtual" locations.

Zoom in/zoom out A change of focal length by the camera. For example, from a wide shot, the script might call for a "ZOOM IN TO CU–JENNY."

Zoom lens A lens that allows changes of focal lengths either by sliding or rotating an external metal ring similar to a focus ring or with the use of a small electric motor that attaches to the lens.

Bibliography

Writing

Van Nostran, William. *The Media Writer's Guide Writing for Business and Educational Programming.* Burlington, MA: Focal Press, 1999.

Dancyger, Ken. *Alternative Scriptwriting Successfully Breaking the Rules.* 3rd ed., Burlington, MA: Focal Press, 2001.

Garrand, Timothy. *Writing for Multimedia and the Web.* 2nd ed., Burlington, MA: Focal Press, 2000.

Preproduction

Simon, Deke, and Wiese, Michael. *Film & Video Budgets.* 3rd ed., Burlington, MA: Focal Press, 2001.

Lutzker, Arnold. *Content Rights for Creative Professionals Copyrights & Trademarks in a Digital Age.* 2nd ed., Burlington, MA: Focal Press, 2002.

Production

Lyver, Des. *Basics of Video Lighting.* 2nd ed., Burlington, MA: Focal Press, 1999.

Musburger, Robert B. *Single-Camera Video Production.* 3rd ed., Burlington, MA: Focal Press, 2002.

Millerson, Gerald. *Video Production Handbook.* 3rd ed., Burlington, MA: Focal Press, 2001.

Brown, Blain. *Cinematography Image Making for Cinematographers, Directors, and Videographers.* Burlington, MA: Focal Press, 2002.

Ely, Mark. *DVD Production: A Practical Resource for DVD Publishers.* Burlington, MA: Focal Press, 2000.

Uva, Michael. *Uva's Guide To Cranes, Dollies, and Remote Heads.* Burlington, MA: Focal Press, 2001.

Postproduction

Ratcliff , J. *Timecode: A User's Guide.* 3rd ed., Burlington, MA: Focal Press, 1999.

Kauffmann, Sam. *Avid Editing: A Guide for Beginning and Intermediate Users.* Burlington, MA: Focal Press, 2000.

Dancyger, Ken. *The Technique of Film and Video Editing History, Theory, and Practice.* 3rd ed., Burlington, MA: Focal Press, 2002.

Young, Rick. *Easy Guide to Final Cut Pro 3 for New Users and Professionals.* Burlington, MA: Focal Press, 2002.

Browne, Steven. *Video Editing: A Postproduction Primer.* 4th ed., Burlington, MA: Focal Press, 2002.

Roberts, Charles. *Final Cut Pro 2 for FireWire DV Editing.* Burlington, MA: Focal Press, 2001.

Audio

Lyver, Des. *Basics of Video Sound.* 2nd ed., Burlington, MA: Focal Press, 1999.

Watkinson, John. *Introduction to Digital Audio.* 2nd ed, Burlington, MA: Focal Press, 2002.

Directing

Fairweather, Rod. *Basic Studio Directing.* Burlington, MA: Focal Press, 1998.

Kagan, Jeremy. *Directors Close Up: Interviews With Directors Nominated for Best Film By the Directors Guild of America.* Burlington, MA: Focal Press, 2000.

Comey, Jeremiah. *The Art of Film Acting: A Guide For Actors and Directors.* Burlington, MA: Focal Press, 2002.

Internet Resources

www.Videomaker.com

http://directory.google.com/Top/Arts/Video/Training/

www.TheWorkshops.com

www.AFI.com

www.Creativecow.net

Sony training Institute: (http:gsscsel.sony.com/professioal/training/index)

www.ITVA.org (International Television Association/mci-a)

www.BHUSA.com

www.Digitalmedianet.com

www.dmforums.com

http://www.dmnnewsletter.com/cgi-bin/sub_news_main.cgi

www.411publilshing.com

www.sag.com

www.aftra.com

Periodicals

AV/Video Multimedia Producer. White Plains, New York, Knowledge Industry Publications.

Emedia Professional. Wilton, CT, Online, Inc.

Inside Technology Training. Medford, MA, Ziff-Davis Professional Publishing Group.

Videography. New York, Miller Freeman PSN, Inc.

Videommaker. Chico, CA 95927

Index

A

A/B rolls, 223
Accessibility, director's need for, 201
Acting
   description of, 152
   simplification of, for employee talent, 206-207
   techniques of, 203
Actor. *see also* Talent
   ability to take direction of, 149
   appearance of, 148
   application of own makeup by, 180
   auditioning of, 147-150
   communication with, 202
   encouragement of, 204-205
   motivation of, 152
   performance by, 147
   performance capability of, 148-149
   personality of, 149
   recognition of, by director, 202
   rehearsal for, 105
   review of performance of, 149-150
   vulnerability of, 152
Adler, Stella, 203
Adobe After Effects, 123
AFTRA. *see* American Federation of Television and
      Radio Artists
AG Duxigo camera, 116
Agreements
   example of, 96f-97f
   preproduction and, 92
   rental, 97
Ambience, sound affected by, 177
American Federation of Television and Radio Artists, 94
Animation
   creation of, 104
   Flash program used for, 123-124
   nonlinear editing and, 229-230
   virtual production with, 122
Apple box, description of, 121
Apple Quick Time, streaming video and, 116

Artist, director as, 9
Artwork
   creation of, 104
   nonlinear editing and, 229-230
Assistant director, 22
   auditions coordinated by, 148
   continuity controlled by, 181
   cost of, 90
   description of, 22
   makeup responsibility of, 180
   master script package and, 216
   preproduction and, 90
   props acquired by, 179-180
   role of, 18
      after production, 127-128
      during production, 125-126
      in studio production, 131
Audience
   analysis of, 31-32
   attitudes of, 31
   demographics of, 31
   knowledge level of, 31-32
   multiple, 32
   sensitivity to, 209
Audio, digitization of, 225
Audio boom operator, description of, 23
Audio booth, description of, 134
Audio engineer
   description of, 25
   role of, in audio sweetening, 232
Audio production, 20, 134-137
Audio recording
   continuity of, 182
   on location, 136
   script for, 135-136
   studio, 134
Audio recordist, role of, during production, 126
Audio sweetening, 21, 232-235
   nonlinear, 234-235
   traditional, 232-234

Audiotape
  film recording and, 111
  recording on, 136
Audiovisual aesthetics, 156-178
Audition, 147-150
  as preproduction task, 18
  review of, 149-150
Authoring program, 123-124
Automatic list management function, offline editing and, 221
Avid Express, nonlinear editing with, 225, 228*f*

B
Back light, 125
Background
  abbreviation for, 65
  frame composition and, 171
Balance, in frame composition, 168-170
Bars and tone, lighting and, 126
Behavioral objectives, 30
Benefits, research, 40
Betacam SP VTR, 115*f*
  nonlinear editing with, 227
  recording with, 113
B.g. *see* Background
Blocking
  example of, 106*f*
  as preproduction task, 18
  during rehearsal, 150-151
Bookings, as preproduction task, 18
Brainstorming, 48
  example of, 55
Broadcast, corporate information distributed on, 4
Budget
  creation of, 91-92
  example of, 93*f*-94*f*
Budgeting, as preproduction task, 18
Bureaucracy, corporation as, 10
Buy, definition of, as production term, 19

C
C stand, lighting and, 121
Camcorder, video recording with, 113
Camera
  movement of, 161-162
    audiovisual aesthetics and, 157
  nonstandard movement of, 160-161
  nonstandard placement of, 160-161
  placement of, audiovisual aesthetics and, 157
  position of
    change in, 167
    continuity and, 183-192
    tone affected by, 193
  terminology used for, 63-65
  video, 115-116
Camera operator, description of, 23
Canon XL, description of, 115-116
Casting, 147
  preliminary, 102
CD-ROM. *see* Compact disc

CDP. *see* Client, design, producer review
Character, believable dialogue and, 70-71
Character acting, 203
Character development, script analysis and, 144
Character profile, script analysis and, 143-144
Clarity
  director's communication and, 202-203
  in script, 142-143
Client
  design, producer review, 48
  director as consultant to, 198
  preproduction and, 90
  profiles of, 12-13
  sensitivity to, 209-210
Close-up shot
  definition of, 64
  description of, 166
  example of, 166*f*
Coach, director as, 202-207
Colloquialism, use of, in dialogue, 71
Color temperature, definition of, 119
Communication
  with actors, 202
  director's need for, 201
Compact disc
  corporate information distributed on, 5
  digital files on, 4
Company standards, wardrobe and, 180
Composition system, description of, 123
Computer, nonlinear editing with, 224-230
Concept
  examples of, 49-51
  types of, 48
Concept development process, 49*f*
Concept thinking, 48
  documentation of, 52
Consultant, director as, 198
Content, focus on, in narration, 73
Content expert, scriptwriting and, 17
Content outline, 39-46
  description of, 17
  formal, 42-44
    example of, 44-46
  informal, 42
  organization of, 42-44
  preproduction and, 92
  research for, 39
Content quality, visual quality compared to, judgment about, 210-211
Continuity, 181-183
  performance, 182
  physical, 181-182
  of screen direction, 183-192
Contract
  deal memo as type of, 92
  non-union, 94-97
  preproduction and, 92
Contractions, use of, in dialogue, 71
Control booth, audio production and, 134
Control track, video editing with, 218

Conversational tone, narration and, 71-73
Copyright, ownership of, 92
Corporate culture, description of, 10
Corporate media
    background on formats of, 3-4
    changing role of, 3-6
    delivery systems for, 4-6
    on demand, 241
    distribution systems for, 4-6
    evaluation of, 236-240
    future of, 241-242
    key players in, 7-13
Corporate media production
    having fun in, 202
    rehearsal in, 150-152
    tone of, 194
Corporate politics, 10
    sensitivity to, 209
Corporation
    environment of, 10
    media groups in, 14-16
    media used in, 4
Cost/benefit impact, program needs analysis and, 36
Craft, knowledge of, respect for director and, 206
Crane, description of, 120
Creative concept, 47-51
    scriptwriting and, 17
    types of, 48
    types of presentation of, 47
    visual, 48
Crew
    cost of, 90
    deal memo for, 92
    hiring of, 103
    recognition of, by director, 202
Crew list, director planning and, 199
CU. *see* Close-up shot
Cut
    definition of, 62-63
    transition with, 196

D
DAT. *see* Digital audiotape
Day, as scene heading term, 65
Deal memo
    example of, 98*f*
    preproduction and, 92
Decision making, director and, 201
Delivery systems, media, networking and, 241
Design
    interactive, media program and, 33
    summary of, 34
Dialogue, 68-73
    character motivation in, 70-71
    continuity of, 183
    credibility of, 68-71
    definition of, 68
    example of, 68-70
    natural speech patterns in, 70

in script, 56
    stilted, 154
    test of, 71
Digital audiotape, recording on, 136
Digital era, corporate media in, 3-4
Digital video disc
    corporate information distributed on, 5
    digital files on, 4
Digital video effects, 21
    definition of, 63
    online editing and, 223
    transition with, 197
Digitization, nonlinear editing and, 227-228
Direct broadcast satellite, corporate information distributed
        through, 4
Director, 139-212
    as artist, 9
    assistant (*see* Assistant director)
    auditions handled by, 148-149
    as coach, 202-207
    as consultant, 198
    continuity controlled by, 181
    contract for, 92
    cost of, 90
    definition of, 8-9
    demand of excellence from, 205
    description of, 8-10
    judgment of, for visual *versus* content, 210-211
    judgment skills of, 208-212
    makeup responsibility of, 180
    as manager, 199-200
    nonlinear editing and, 228
    people skills needed by, 198-207
    performance continuity controlled by, 182
    physical continuity controlled by, 181
    preproduction and, 88
    props acquired by, 179-180
    role of, 141-146
        in preproduction meetings, 201
        during production, 125-126
        for small location shoot, 130
        in studio production, 131
    rough-cut screening and, 222
    script analysis by, 142, 145
    as supervisor, 201-202
    technical, description of, 23
Director, Macromedia, 123-124
Director of photography
    description of, 23
    role of, 18
        during production, 125-126
    visual elements of production and, 157
Dissolve
    definition of, 62
    online edit and, 223
    transition with, 196-197
Distance learning, 5, 242
Distractions, during production, 152-153
Distribution, as postproduction task, 21-22

Documentary, example of concept of, 50
Documentation, program evaluation and, 236, 237
Dolly
    definition of, 65
    description of, 120
Dolly grip, description of, 23
DP. *see* Director of photography
Duplication, 215-216
    as postproduction task, 21-22
    video formats and, 215
Duplication master
    nonlinear audio sweetening and, 234
    nonlinear editing and, 230
DV. *see* Recording, digital
DVD. *see* Digital video disc
DVE. *see* Digital video effects

E
ECU. *see* Extreme close-up shot
Edit
    offline, 219-223
    online, 219-223
Edit bay, 219, 220*f*
Edit decision list, 20, 99, 221, 223
Edit master
    nonlinear audio sweetening and, 234
    nonlinear editing and, 230
Editing
    client review of, 230
    controller for, 216
    cuts-only, 222
    director's role in, 9
    nonlinear, 21, 224-231
        future of, 230
        process of, 227-230
    offline, 219-223
        as postproduction task, 20
    online, 20-21, 219-223
    overview of, 215-218
    for pace, 195-196
    as postproduction task, 20
    process of, 220-221
    producer review of, 230
    rapid, pace affected by, 195
    terminology used in, 62-63
    time code and, 216
    types of shots and, 159-160
Editor
    nonlinear editing and, 228
    offline, description of, 24
    online, description of, 24-25
    role of, 219
    rough-cut screening and, 221-222
EDL. *see* Edit decision list
EIC. *see* Engineer in charge
Electronic news gathering, 130
Employee
    coaching of, 206-207
    production with, 154

ENG. *see* Electronic news gathering
Engineer, audio sweetening, 25
Engineer in charge, 118-119
    description of, 24
English, simple, in narration, 73
Equipment
    lists of, 103-104
    preparation of, for shoot, 105-107
    rental agreement for, 97
    rental of, 103-104
    video production, 115-121
Equipment list, director planning and, 199
Establishing shot, definition of, 63
Evaluation
    administration of, 238
    indices, 240
    program, 236-240
        example of, 239*f*
    types of, 237-238
Excellence, director's demand for, 205
Excitement, sense of, editing for, 195
Expenses
    logs for, 99
    receipts for, 99
Exterior, abbreviation for, 65
    in script, 65
Extra, release for, 99
Extreme close-up shot
    definition of, 64
    description of, 166

F
F-stop, frame composition and, 171
Fade, online edit and, 223
Fade in, definition of, 62
Fade out, definition of, 62
Feedback
    audience, 237
    client, program evaluation and, 236-237
F.g. *see* Foreground
Fill light, 125
    effects of, 175*f*
Film recording
    description of, 111-112
    formats for, 112-115
Final Cut Pro, nonlinear editing with, 227*f*
Flag, as lighting accessory, 120
Flash, animation with, 123-124
Flexibility, director communication and, 203-204
Floor manager, description of, 23
Focal length
    changing of, 167
    continuity of line and, 192
    description of, 162
    frame composition and, 171
    types of, 162
Focus of attention
    continuity and, 187*f*
    continuity of, 183

Foreground
  abbreviation for, 65
  frame composition and, 171
Frame composition
  balance in, 168-170
  depth and, 171-172
  description of, 168-176
  lighting and, 173-176
Frame for frame, duplication and, 215
Frame size, description of, 162
Freelancer
  corporate media reliance on, 16
  as producer, 7
  as scriptwriter, 11

G
Gaffer
  description of, 23
  role of, during production, 125-126
Gaffer's tape, description of, 121
Gels, description of, 119-120
General aesthetics, 193-197
  definition of, 193
  pace as part of, 194-196
  tone as part of, 193-194
  transitions as part of, 196-197
Gestures, continuity of, 183
Graphic art
  animated, virtual production with, 122
  creation of, 104
  nonlinear editing and, 229-230
  production and, 20
Graphic artist
  description of, 24
  interactive production and, 124
Grip
  description of, 23
  role of, during production, 125-126

H
High angle, definition of, 65
  as production term, 65
High definition recording format, 114-115
HMI. *see* Light, halogen-metal-iodide
Horizon, frame composition and, 170
Host role, description of, 143-144
Hot spot, lighting and, 126, 173
Human aesthetics, production and, 147-155

I
Improvement, producer's need for, program evaluation and, 236-237
Informational program, media used in, 4
Insert, as type of shot, 166
Interactive design, media program and, 33
Interactivity, media programs and, 241
Interior, abbreviation for, 65
  in script, 65
Internet
  media delivery through, 241

resources on, for nonlinear editing information, 231
  streaming video over, 116
Interview
  news-style, 155
  types of questions for, 154
Interviewing, techniques for, 40-42
Intranet
  corporate information distributed through, 6
  media delivery through, 241

J
Jib arm, description of, 120
Judgment, director, 208-212
  pressure of production and, 210
  for visual *versus* content, 210-211
Jump cut, description of, 166-167
JVC digital video camera, 116

K
Key light, 125
  effects of, 176*f*

L
LAN. *see* Local area network
Laptop computer, nonlinear editing with, 230
Layback
  audio sweetening and, 232-233
  as postproduction task, 21
Laydown
  audio sweetening and, 232-233
  as postproduction task, 21
LD. *see* Lighting director
Legal issues, documentation of, 92
Lens
  prime, 162-163
  zoom, 163
Liability, insurance for, 99
Light
  back, 125
  color of, 119
  description of, 119-120
  fill, 125
  halogen-metal-iodide, 119
  key, 125
  tungsten-halogen, 119
Lighting
  accessories for, 120
  creation of mood, tone, and texture with, 174-175
  flat, effects of, 176*f*
  frame composition and, 173-176
  for production, 126
  three-point, 175
  tone affected by, 193, 196
Lighting director, role of, 157
Limbo, frame composition and, 171
Line
  acceptable crossing of, 189-192
  changes in, continuity and, 186
  continuity of, 183-192

Listening, interviewing and, 41
Live-on-tape, production and, 131-132
Local area network
    corporate information distributed through, 6
    media delivery through, 241
Location
    arrangements for, as preproduction task, 18
    audio recording on, 136
    cut as transition for, 196
    production on, 125-133
    release for, 97-99
    scouting of, 102
    sensitivity to audience taste and, 209
    shooting on, 121
    small, production at, 130
Long shot, definition of, 63-64
Low angle, definition of, 65
    as production term, 65
Luminance
    lighting and, 173
    video recording and, 112

M
Macromedia Director, 123
Makeup, technical inaccuracies and, 180
Makeup artist
    description of, 24
    use of, 180
Manager, director as, 199-200
Master file, creation of, 92
Master File Checklist, 92
Master scene, definition of, 157
Master script
    example of, 128f-129f
    production and, 127
Master script package, 216
Master shot, definition of, 158
MCU. *see* Medium close-up shot
Media
    corporate (*see* Corporate media)
    print *versus* visual, 47
Media 100, nonlinear editing with, 225
Media group
    large in-house, 14
    small in-house, 15
    types of, 14-16
Media program, unneeded, 29
Medium close-up shot
    definition of, 64
    description of, 163
    example of, 165f, 172f
Medium shot
    definition of, 64
    description of, 158, 163
    example of, 164f
Method acting, 203
Microphone
    boom, 117, 177
    description of, 117-118
    handheld, 117

    lavalier, 117, 177
    shotgun, 117
    types of, 177
    wireless, 118
Mini DV format, for recording, 114
Misner, Sanford, 203
Mix, audio sweetening and, 232-233
Mixer
    audio, 118
    description of, 23
Mixing board, audio sweetening and, 232-233
Model, release for, 99
    example of, 100f-101f
Monitor
    video, 118-119
    waveform, 118-119
Mood, creation of, lighting and, 174-175
Motion picture, script for, 56
Motivation
    of actor, 152
    character, believable dialogue and, 70-71
    clarification of, 204
Motivational program, media used in, 4
Movement, continuity of, 183
MPEG, video streaming and, 114
MS. *see* Medium shot
Multicamera, use of, 19
Multimedia, definition of, 4
Music
    release for use of, 99
    selection of, in preproduction, 104-105
    terminology for, 66
Music library, buyout, 104
Music video, example of concept of, 50

N
Narration, 68-73
    content focus in, 73
    definition of, 71
    example of, 71-73
    in script, 56, 143
    simplicity in, 73
Needle drop fee, 104
Net, as lighting accessory, 120
Networks
    media delivery systems and, 241
    satellite
        distance learning and, 242
        media program delivery through, 241
    wireless, 242
Night, as scene heading term, 65
Nonlinear editing. *see* Editing, nonlinear

O
Objectives
    behavioral, 30
    instructional, 30
    motivational, 31
    program, 30
    statement of, 30

Offline edit, 219-223
Online edit, 219-223
Organization, director's need for, 199
OTS. *see* Over the shoulder
Over the shoulder, definition of, 64
Overdirecting, nonprofessional
    talent and, 154

P
PA. *see* Production assistant
Pace, 194-196
    editing for, 195-196
Pan, definition of, 65
    as production term, 65
Panasonic AG Duxigo camera, 116
Panasonic DVC PRO, video recording with, 114
People skills, 200-207
Performance
    continuity of, 182
    director coaching for, 202
    tone affected by, 196
Permit, location, 102
Plot, in script, 144-145
PNA. *see* Program needs analysis
Point of view, definition of, 64
Postproduction, 213-235
    overview of, 20-21, 215-218
    traditional *versus* nonlinear, 215
POV. *see* Point of view
Preproduction, 87-107
    budgeting in, 91-92
    crew hiring during, 103
    description of, 18-19
    detail in, 89
    key players in, 89-90
    master file created in, 92
    meetings in, 105, 201
    music selection in, 104-105
    planning meeting in, 199
    props acquired during, 179
    script blocking during, 105
    script review during, 99
    shooting schedule developed in, 102-103
    talent auditions in, 101
    tasks in, 91-107
    wardrobe acquired during, 180
Pressure, director judgment affected by, 210
Prime lens, 162-163
Producer
    client relationship with, 12-13
    description of, 7-8
    director as consultant to, 198
    editing process and, 221-222
    freelance, 7
    line, description of, 22
    nonlinear editing and, 228
    preproduction and, 90
    program evaluation by, 236
Production, 109-137
    audio (*see* Audio production)

checklist for, example of, 95*f*
corporate, rehearsal in, 150-152
distractions during, 152-153
equipment lists for, 103-104
execution of, 152-155
formats for, 111-124
human aesthetics in, 147-155
importance of sound in, 136
interactive, 124
lighting for, 119-120
on location, 19, 125-133
multicamera, 57, 122
narration in, 143
overview of, 17-21
roles of people in, 22-25
scheduling of, 19
single-camera, 58, 121
studio, 19-20, 125-133
    audio recording in, 134
styles of, 121-124
titles in, 143
types of, 19-20
virtual, 122-123
visual elements of, 157
Production assistant
    cost of, 90
    description of, 22
    preproduction and, 90
    role of, 18
Production company, outside, 15
Production log, preproduction and, 99
Production manager, description of, 22
Production plan, director planning with, 199
Program
    budget for, 91-92
    concepts for, 48
    design of, 29-30
    evaluation of, 236-240
        example of, 239*f*
    need for, 30
    rough cut of, 221
    structures of, 74-75
    treatment for description of, 53
    utilization of, 32-33
Program (computer), authoring, 123-124
Program needs analysis, 17, 29-38
    commentary on, 36-37
    concept thinking and, 48
    decision to produce program and, 37-38
    example of, 34-36
    program evaluation and, 237-238
Project manager, producer as, 7
Property owner, release from, 100
Props
    continuity in, 181
    preproduction and, 99-102
    technical inaccuracies and, 179-180
    tone affected by, 196
Prosumer, description of, 15-16
Public program, media used in, 4

Q
Questions, open-ended, 40-41
    nonprofessional talent and, 154
Quick Time, streaming video and, 116

R
Rack focus, definition of, 65
    as production term, 65
Reading
    actor, 148
    rehearsal and, 150
Real 1 Player, streaming video and, 116
Recognition
    actor's need for, 205
    crew's need for, 202, 205
Recording
    analog, 112
    digital, 112
        formats for, 114
    formats for, 112-115
    high definition, 114-115
Recording session, 134-135
Reel-to-reel, video recording with, 112
Rehearsal
    in corporate media production, 150-152
    preproduction and, 18-19, 105
    production and, 127
    on set, 151-152
    for studio production, 131
Release
    location, 97-99, 102
    music, 99
    types of, 97-99
Research
    benefits of, 40
    content, 39
    sources for, 40-42
    verification of, 40
Respect, director earning of, 206
Reverse angle, definition of, 65
    as production term, 65
Role
    dramatic, 144
    host, description of, 143-144
    humorous, 144
Role-play, dialogue and, 68
Roll tape, as production term, 127
Rough cut
    editing and, 221
    nonlinear editing and, 226
    as postproduction task, 20
Run 'n' gun shoot, 90-91, 130

S
Safety, wardrobe and, 180
SAG. see Screen Actors Guild
Satellite networks
    direct broadcast, corporate information distributed through, 4
    distance learning and, 242
    media program delivery through, 241

Satellite technology, corporate information distribution with, 4
Scene
    description of
        in script, 56
        in the treatment, 52
    detailed description of, 66-67
    master, 66-67
    terminology used for, 65-66
Scheduling, in preproduction, 102-103
Screen Actors Guild, 94
Screen direction, continuity of, 183-192
Screen direction line, continuity of, 183-192
Screening, rough cut, 221
    nonlinear editing and, 226
Screenplay, 78-84
    example of, 78-84
Scrim, as lighting accessory, 120
Script, 27-84
    aesthetics of, 141-146
    analysis of
        audiovisual aesthetics and, 156
        visualization and, 156
    audio, 135-136
    blocking of, during preproduction, 105
    breakdown of, director planning and, 199
    character profiles in, 143-144
    clarity of, 74
    dialogue in, 56, 68-73
    director's analysis of, 142
    discussion of, during rehearsal, 150
    dramatic elements in, 142
    example of, 57, 58
        terminology used in, 66
    formats of, 56-61
    informational clarity of, 142-143
    interactive, 58-59
    master
        in master file, 99
        production and, 127
    narration in, 56, 59-61, 68-73, 143
    pace of, 146
    plot in, 144-145
    resources for, 84
    review of, during preproduction, 99
    scene descriptions in, 56
    scene headings in, 56
    screenplay format for, 58, 78-84
    shooting, preproduction and, 92
    storyboard format for, 59
    structure of, 74-77, 145
    terminology used in, 62-67
    tone of, 146
    transitions in, 74-77, 145
    two-column format for, 57
Scriptwriter
    description of, 10-12
    freelance, 11-12
    staff, 11-12
Scriptwriting. see also Writing
    corporate, 10

entertainment, 10
  overview of, 17-18
  research for, 11
  resources for, 83
Sensitivity, director's need for, 208-209
Set
  arrangements for, as preproduction task, 18
  design of, in preproduction, 103
  rehearsal on, 151-152
  tone affected by, 196
Set designer, 103
SFX. *see* Sound effects
Shoot
  run 'n' gun, 90-91, 130
  small location, 130
  smaller production and, 132-133
Shooting schedule
  director planning and, 199
  preproduction and, 102-103
Shooting script, 18
Shot
  content of, pace and, 194-195
  description of, 163-166
  insert, 166
  length of, pace and, 195
  over-the-shoulder, example of, 165*f*, 173*f*
Shot list
  director planning and, 199
  offline edit and, 219
  preproduction and, 97
Shot report, example of, 217*f*
Silk, as lighting accessory, 120
Slate, use of, 127
SME. *see* Subject matter expert
SMPTE, time code with, 216
Society of Motion Picture and Television Engineers, time code for
      videotape editing from, 216
Soft cut, transition with, 197
Software, interactive, 33
Sony Betacam, 115*f*
  recording with, 113
Sony Betacam SP VTR, nonlinear editing with, 227
Sony DV Cam, video recording with, 114
Sound
  digitization of, 225
  importance of, in production, 136
  production aesthetics and, 177-178
  quality of, 177
    in nonlinear editing, 226
  sweetening of, 177
  terminology used for, 66
  types of, 177-178
Sound effects, 66
  postproduction and, 21
Sound recordist
  description of, 23
  role of, for small location shoot, 130
Special effects
  nonlinear editing and, 230
  online edit and, 223

Speech, natural patterns of, 70
Speed, sense of, editing for, 195
Spreader, description of, 120
Stage line, continuity of, 183-192
Stage manager, description of, 23
Standard coverage, description of, 157-159
Stanislavsky, Konstantin, 203
Stock footage, description of, 104
Storyboard
  creation of, during preproduction, 105
  description of, 59
  example of, 60*f*, 106*f*
  as preproduction task, 18
Storyline, structure compared to, 75
Strasberg, Lee, 203
Streaming media, corporate media production and, 242
Streaming video
  corporate information distributed on, 5
  description of, 116
Strike
  definition of, 127-128
    as production term, 19
  description of, 127-130
Structure, 74-77
  benefits bookends, 76-77
  contrasting actions, 77
  corporate, 75-77
  creative use of, 77
  dramatic, 74
  example of, 75-77
  storyline compared to, 75
  tell 'em, 75-76
Studio
  nondramatic production in, 132
  production in, 125-133, 130-132
  shooting in, 121-122
  smaller shoot in, 132-133
Subject matter expert, corporate media and, 5
Supervisor, director as, 201-202
Sweetening, audio, 21, 232-235
Sweetening room, 232

T
Take one, description of, 127
Take point, definition of, 57
Talent. *see also* Actor
  auditioning of, 102
  deal memo for, 92
  employee, coaching of, 206-207
  nonprofessional, 154-155
Talent booking sheet, director planning and, 199
Tape recorder, interviewing with, 40
TD. *see* Technical director
Technical aesthetics, 179-192
  inaccuracies in, 179-181
Technical director
  description of, 23
  role of, 20
Teleconferencing, distance learning and, 242
Teleprompter, description of, 24

Television, corporate information distributed through, 4
Tension, sense of, editing for, 195
Texture, creation of, lighting and, 174-175
Tilt, definition of, 65
  as production term, 65
Time code
  editing and, 216
  offline edit and, 219
  online editing and, 222
  SMPTE, 216
Time code generator, 216
Time frame, cut as transition for, 196
Timeline, program, nonlinear editing and, 228, 229
Title
  character-generated, creation of, 104
  nonlinear editing and, 229-230
  online editing and, 223
Tone, 193-194
  corporate, 194
  creation of, lighting and, 174-175
Training, media used in, 4
Training films, background on, 3
Transition, 74-77
  techniques for, 196-197
Treatment, 52-55
  definition of, 52-53
  example of, 53-54
  preproduction and, 92
  scriptwriting and, 17
  summary of, 53
  writing of, 52
Tripod, description of, 120
Truck, definition of, 65
Two shot, definition of, 64

U
U-matic, video recording with, 112-113

V
VC. see Video control engineer
Vehicles, rental of, 103-104
Verification, of research, 40
Video control engineer, description of, 24
Video recording
  camera for, 115-117
  continuity of, 181-182
  description of, 112
  digitization of, 225
  formats for, 112-115
  high definition, 114-115
  proper level and value for, 173-174
  quality of, in nonlinear editing, 226
Video streaming, description of, 116
Video switcher, online editing with, 21
Videocassette, corporate information distributed on, 4

Videographer
  description of, 23
  role of, 18
Videotape
  as corporate media, 3
  editing of
    control track for, 218
    time code and, 216-217
  formats of, duplication and, 215-216
  transfer of audio to, 136
Videotape recorder
  camera for, 115
  description of, 112, 116
Videotape recorder operator, description of, 24
Virtual developer, interactive production and, 124
Visual quality, content quality compared to, judgment about, 210-211
Visualization, of script, 156
VTR. see Videotape recorder

W
Wardrobe
  continuity in, 181
  preproduction and, 99-102
  sensitivity to audience taste and, 209
  technical inaccuracies and, 180-181
  tone affected by, 193
Waveform monitor, lighting and, 173
White balance, lighting and, 126
Wide shot
  definition of, 63
  description of, 163
  example of, 164f
Windows Media Player, streaming video and, 116
Wipe
  definition of, 63
  online edit and, 223
  transition with, 197
World Wide Web
  corporate information distributed through, 5-6
  digital files on, 4
  media delivery through, 241
  streaming video on, 5
Writer
  contract for, 92
  script aesthetics and, 141
Writing. see also Scriptwriting
  corporate media production and, 17-18
  print-oriented, 47
  visual, 47
WS. see Wide shot

Z
Zoom, camera movement by, 161
Zoom lens, 163

9 780240 805146